NORTHEAST BACKYARD HOMESTEAD 3-IN-1 FORAGER'S COLLECTION

YOUR NORTHEAST BACKYARD HOMESTEAD + NORTHEAST FORAGING + NORTHEAST MEDICINAL PLANTS - THE #1 BEGINNER'S NORTHEAST HOMESTEAD COLLECTION

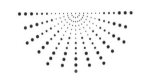

J. B. MAXWELL

For my son, may the world be your garden and may you grow whatever you choose to.

CONTENTS

Your Northeast Backyard Homestead - What to Plant, How to Plant, and When to Plant for Your Climate	25
Introduction	29
1. KNOW YOUR CLIMATE	33
Climate in the Northeast	35
2. THE LAY OF THE LAND	37
3. BUILDING YOUR BEDS	41
Strategies for Making the Most of Your Raised Beds	43
4. HOMESTEADING FOR THE WIN	47
Getting Settled	50
Raising Animals	53
Composting	59
Ideal Plant Environments	60
Maximizing Your Yield	65
5. ESSENTIAL SOIL	69
6. INCORPORATING PERMACULTURE	75
Ethics and Principles of Permaculture Design	76
Perennial and Annual Plants	81
7. SPRING	83
Spring Vegetables	84
Spring Fruits and Herbs	86
Spring Flowers	87
8. SUMMER	91
Summer Vegetables	91
Summer Fruits and Herbs	92
Summer Flowers	94
9. FALL	97
Fall Vegetables	98
Fall Fruits and Herbs	100
Fall Flowers	101

10. WINTER — 103
   Winter Trees and Shrubs — 104

11. TIPS AND TRICKS FOR ULTIMATE SUCCESS — 107
   Optimizing the Space on Your Property — 108
   Planting Success — 109
   Insect Management — 110

   Afterword — 115
   Northeast Foraging from Your Backyard Homestead - Native Herbalist's Guide to Identifying 101 Tasty Wild Edible Foods — 117
   Introduction — 123

12. FORAGING 101 — 127
13. IDENTIFYING YOUR PLANTS — 131
14. LIVING IN TUNE WITH NATURE'S CYCLES — 139
15. AMARANTH — 147
16. APPLES — 151
17. ASPARAGUS — 155
18. BASSWOOD — 157
19. BARBERRY — 159
20. BEACH PLUM — 163
21. BEE BALM/BERGAMOT — 165
22. BIRCH — 167
23. BLACK CHERRY — 171
24. BLACK LOCUST — 173
25. BLACK WALNUT — 175
26. BLUEBERRY — 179
27. BRAMBLES — 183
   Raspberries, Blackberries, and Blackraspberries — 183
28. BURDOCK AND RHUBARB — 187
29. BUTTERNUT — 191
30. CATTAIL — 195
31. CHICKWEED — 199
32. CHICORY — 203
33. CLEAVERS — 207
34. COMMON ELDERBERRY — 209
35. COMMON MALLOW — 211
36. COMMON MILKWEED — 213
37. COMMON STRAWBERRY — 215
38. CORNELIAN CHERRY DOGWOOD — 219

39. COW PARSNIP	223
40. CRANBERRY	227
41. CURLY DOCK	229
42. CURRANT	231
43. DANDELION	233
44. DAYLILY	237
45. EASTERN REDBUD	239
46. EASTERN WHITE PINE	241
47. ENCHANTER'S NIGHTSHADE	245
48. EPAZOTE	247
49. EVENING PRIMROSE	249
50. FALSE SOLOMON'S SEAL	251
51. FIELD GARLIC	253
52. FRAGRANT SUMAC	255
53. GARLIC MUSTARD	257
54. GINKGO	259
55. GLASSWORT	261
56. GOLDENROD	263
57. GOUTWEED	265
58. GRAPE	267
59. GREENBRIER	271
60. GROUND CHERRY	273
61. HAWTHORN	277
62. HENBIT	281
63. HICKORY	283
64. HIGHBUSH CRANBERRY	285
65. HONEWORT	287
66. HOPNISS, GROUNDNUT	289
67. JAPANESE KNOTWEED	293
68. JERUSALEM ARTICHOKE	295
69. JEWELWEED	297
70. JUNEBERRY	299
71. JUNIPER	301
72. LADY'S THUMB	305
73. LAMBS QUARTERS	307
74. LILAC	311
75. LOTUS	315
76. MAPLE	317
77. MAYAPPLE	319
78. MELILOT, SWEET CLOVER	321

79. MINT	323
80. MUGWORT	325
81. MULBERRY	327
82. MUSTARD	329
83. NASTURTIUM	331
84. NETTLES	333
85. OAK	335
86. OSTRICH FERN/ FIDDLEHEADS	337
87. DAISIES	339
88. PARSNIP	343
89. PAWPAW	345
90. PEACH	347
91. PEAR VS PRICKLY PEAR	351
92. PEPPERGRASS	355
93. PINEAPPLE WEED	357
94. PLANTAIN	359
95. POKEWEED	361
96. PURPLE DEAD NETTLE	365
97. QUICKWEED	367
98. RAMPS/WILD LEEK	371
99. RED CLOVER	373
100. ROSE	375
101. SASSAFRAS	379
102. SHEPHERD'S PURSE	383
103. SILVERBERRY AND AUTUMN OLIVE	385
104. SOLOMON'S SEAL	387
105. SOW THISTLE	389
106. STAGHORN SUMAC	391
107. THISTLE	393
108. VIOLET	395
109. WATERCRESS	397
110. WILD BEAN	399
111. WILD CARROT, QUEEN ANNE'S LACE	401
112. WILD GINGER	403
113. WILD LETTUCE	405
114. WOOD SORREL	407
115. YARROW	409
116. WILD POTATO VINE	411
Afterword	415

Northeast Medicinal Plants Foraging from Your Backyard Homestead Native Herbalist's Guide to Identifying Wild Herbs for Health and Wellness   417
Introduction   423

117. WILDCRAFTING BASICS   427
Why Wildcraft Medicine for Yourself and Your Family?   427
Ethical Foraging   429
Sustainable Foraging Tips   430
Tools   431
Safety   437
10 Benefits of Foraging with Herbal Medicine   439

118. PLANT IDENTIFICATION   443
Recognizing a Plant   443

119. AGRIMONY   451
Latin Name   451
Description   451
Habitat   452
Season to Gather the Plant   452
Parts of the Plant to Use as Medicine   452
Benefits and Properties   452
Medicine Preparation   453
Using the Herb   453
Side Effects and Warnings   453
Fun Tips and Facts   454
Author's Personal Story   454

120. ALDER   455
Latin Name   455
Description   455
Habitat   456
Season to Gather the Plant   456
Parts of the Plant to Use as Medicine   456
Benefits and Properties   457
Medicine Preparation   457
Using the Herb   457
Side Effects and Warnings   458
Fun Tips and Facts   458
Author's Personal Story   458

121. BEECH — 459
    Latin Name — 459
    Description — 459
    Habitat — 460
    Season to Gather the Plant — 460
    Parts of the Plant to Use as Medicine — 460
    Benefits and Properties — 460
    Medicine Preparation — 460
    Using the Herb — 461
    Side Effects and Warnings — 461
    Fun Tips and Facts — 461
    Author's Personal Story — 461

122. BIRCH — 463
    Latin Name — 463
    Description — 463
    Habitat — 464
    Season to Gather the Plant — 464
    Parts of the Plant to Use as Medicine — 464
    Benefits and Properties — 465
    Medicine Preparation — 465
    Using the Herb — 466
    Side Effects and Warnings — 466
    Fun Tips and Facts — 466
    Author's Personal Story — 467

123. BLACKBERRY — 469
    Latin Name — 469
    Description — 469
    Habitat — 470
    Season to Gather the Plant — 470
    Parts of the Plant to Use as Medicine — 470
    Benefits and Properties — 470
    Medicine Preparation — 471
    Using the Herb — 471
    Side Effects and Warnings — 472
    Fun Tips and Facts — 472
    Author's Personal Story — 472

124. BLACK CHERRY — 473
    Latin Name — 473
    Description — 473

Habitat	474
Season to Gather the Plant	474
Parts of the Plant to Use as Medicine	474
Benefits and Properties	474
Medicine Preparation	475
Using the Herb	475
Side Effects and Warnings	476
Fun Tips and Facts	476
Author's Personal Story	476
125. BLUE VERVAIN	**477**
Latin Name	477
Description	477
Habitat	478
Season to Gather the Plant	478
Parts of the Plant to Use as Medicine	478
Benefits and Properties	478
Medicine Preparation	478
Using the Herb	479
Side Effects and Warnings	479
Fun Tips and Facts	479
Author's Personal Story	479
126. BORAGE	**481**
Latin Name	481
Description	481
Habitat	482
Season to Gather the Plant	482
Parts of the Plant to Use as Medicine	482
Benefits and Properties	482
Medicine Preparation	483
Using the Herb	483
Side Effects and Warnings	483
Fun Tips and Facts	484
Author's Personal Story	484
127. BURDOCK	**485**
Latin Name	485
Description	485
Habitat	486
Season to Gather the Plant	486
Parts of the Plant to Use as Medicine	486

- Benefits and Properties — 486
- Medicine Preparation — 486
- Using the Herb — 487
- Side Effects and Warnings — 487
- Fun Tips and Facts — 487
- Author's Personal Story — 488

128. CATNIP — 489
   - Latin Name — 489
   - Description — 489
   - Habitat — 490
   - Season to Gather the Plant — 490
   - Parts of the Plant to Use as Medicine — 490
   - Benefits and Properties — 490
   - Medicine Preparation — 490
   - Using the Herb — 491
   - Side Effects and Warnings — 491
   - Fun Tips and Facts — 492
   - Author's Personal Story — 492

129. CHICKWEED — 493
   - Latin Name — 493
   - Description — 493
   - Habitat — 494
   - Season to Gather the Plant — 494
   - Parts of the Plant to Use as Medicine — 494
   - Benefits and Properties — 494
   - Medicine Preparation — 494
   - Using the Herb — 495
   - Side Effects and Warnings — 495
   - Fun Tips and Facts — 496
   - Author's Personal Story — 496

130. CHICORY — 497
   - Latin Name — 497
   - Description — 497
   - Habitat — 498
   - Season to Gather the Plant — 498
   - Parts of the Plant to Use as Medicine — 498
   - Benefits and Properties — 498
   - Medicine Preparation — 499
   - Using the Herb — 499

Side Effects and Warnings	500
Fun Tips and Facts	500
Author's Personal Story	500
131. CLEAVERS	**501**
Latin Name	501
Description	501
Habitat	502
Season to Gather the Plant	502
Parts of the Plant to Use as Medicine	502
Benefits and Properties	502
Medicine Preparation	503
Using the Herb	503
Side Effects and Warnings	503
Fun Tips and Facts	503
Author's Personal Story	503
132. COMFREY	**505**
Latin Name	505
Description	505
Habitat	506
Season to Gather the Plant	506
Parts of the Plant to Use as Medicine	506
Benefits and Properties	506
Medicine Preparation	507
Using the Herb	507
Side Effects and Warnings	507
Fun Tips and Facts	508
Author's Personal Story	508
133. COMMON MALLOW	**509**
Latin Name	509
Description	509
Habitat	510
Season to Gather the Plant	510
Parts of the Plant to Use as Medicine	510
Benefits and Properties	510
Medicine Preparation	511
Using the Herb	511
Side Effects and Warnings	511
Fun Tips and Facts	512
Author's Personal Story	512

134. CRAMP BARK ... 513
    Latin Name ... 513
    Description ... 513
    Habitat ... 514
    Season to Gather the Plant ... 514
    Parts of the Plant to Use as Medicine ... 514
    Benefits and Properties ... 514
    Medicine Preparation ... 515
    Using the Herb ... 515
    Side Effects and Warnings ... 515
    Fun Tips and Facts ... 516
    Author's Personal Story ... 516

135. CRANBERRY ... 517
    Latin Name ... 517
    Description ... 517
    Habitat ... 518
    Season to Gather the Plant ... 518
    Parts of the Plant to Use as Medicine ... 518
    Benefits and Properties ... 518
    Medicine Preparation ... 518
    Using the Herb ... 519
    Side Effects and Warnings ... 519
    Fun Tips and Facts ... 519
    Author's Personal Story ... 519

136. DANDELION ... 521
    Latin Name ... 521
    Description ... 521
    Habitat ... 522
    Season to Gather the Plant ... 522
    Parts of the Plant to Use as Medicine ... 522
    Benefits and Properties ... 522
    Medicine Preparation ... 523
    Using the Herb ... 523
    Side Effects and Warnings ... 524
    Fun Tips and Facts ... 524
    Author's Personal Story ... 524

137. ECHINACEA ... 525
    Latin Name ... 525
    Description ... 525

        Habitat   526
        Season to Gather the Plant   526
        Parts of the Plant to Use as Medicine   526
        Benefits and Properties   526
        Medicine Preparation   527
        Using the Herb   527
        Side Effects and Warnings   528
        Fun Tips and Facts   528
        Author's Personal Story   528

138. ELDER   529
        Latin Name   529
        Description   529
        Habitat   530
        Season to Gather the Plant   530
        Parts of the Plant to Use as Medicine   530
        Benefits and Properties   530
        Medicine Preparation   531
        Using the Herb   531
        Side Effects and Warnings   531
        Fun Tips and Facts   532
        Author's Personal Story   532

139. FEVERFEW   533
        Latin Name   533
        Description   533
        Habitat   534
        Season to Gather the Plant   534
        Parts of the Plant to Use as Medicine   534
        Benefits and Properties   534
        Medicine Preparation   535
        Using the Herb   535
        Side Effects and Warnings   535
        Fun Tips and Facts   536
        Author's Personal Story   536

140. FIELD GARLIC   537
        Latin Name   537
        Description   537
        Habitat   538
        Season to Gather the Plant   538
        Parts of the Plant to Use as Medicine   538

    Benefits and Properties   538
    Medicine Preparation   538
    Using the Herb   539
    Side Effects and Warnings   539
    Fun Tips and Facts   539
    Author's Personal Story   540

141. GARLIC MUSTARD   541
    Latin Name   541
    Description   541
    Habitat   542
    Season to Gather the Plant   542
    Parts of the Plant to Use as Medicine   542
    Benefits and Properties   542
    Medicine Preparation   543
    Using the Herb   543
    Side Effects and Warnings   543
    Fun Tips and Facts   543
    Author's Personal Story   544

142. GERMAN CHAMOMILE   545
    Latin Name   545
    Description   545
    Habitat   546
    Season to Gather the Plant   546
    Parts of the Plant to Use as Medicine   546
    Benefits and Properties   546
    Medicine Preparation   546
    Using the Herb   547
    Side Effects and Warnings   547
    Fun Tips and Facts   548
    Author's Personal Story   548

143. GOLDENROD   549
    Latin Name   549
    Description   549
    Habitat   549
    Season to Gather the Plant   550
    Parts of the Plant to Use as Medicine   550
    Benefits and Properties   550
    Medicine Preparation   550
    Using the Herb   550

- Side Effects and Warnings — 551
- Fun Tips and Facts — 551
- Author's Personal Story — 551

144. HORSETAIL — 553
- Latin Name — 553
- Description — 553
- Habitat — 553
- Season to Gather the Plant — 554
- Parts of the Plant to Use as Medicine — 554
- Benefits and Properties — 554
- Medicine Preparation — 554
- Using the Herb — 555
- Side Effects and Warnings — 555
- Fun Tips and Facts — 556
- Author's Personal Story — 556

145. JAPANESE HONEYSUCKLE — 557
- Latin Name — 557
- Description — 557
- Habitat — 558
- Season to Gather the Plant — 558
- Parts of the Plant to Use as Medicine — 558
- Benefits and Properties — 558
- Medicine Preparation — 558
- Using the Herb — 559
- Side Effects and Warnings — 559
- Fun Tips and Facts — 559
- Author's Personal Story — 559

146. LARCH — 561
- Latin Name — 561
- Description — 561
- Habitat — 562
- Season to Gather the Plant — 562
- Parts of the Plant to Use as Medicine — 562
- Benefits and Properties — 562
- Medicine Preparation — 562
- Using the Herb — 563
- Side Effects and Warnings — 563
- Fun Tips and Facts — 563
- Author's Personal Story — 563

147. LEMON BALM 565
    Latin Name 565
    Description 565
    Habitat 566
    Season to Gather the Plant 566
    Parts of the Plant to Use as Medicine 566
    Benefits and Properties 566
    Medicine Preparation 566
    Using the Herb 567
    Side Effects and Warnings 567
    Fun Tips and Facts 567
    Author's Personal Story 567

148. LINDEN 569
    Latin Name 569
    Description 569
    Habitat 570
    Season to Gather the Plant 570
    Parts of the Plant to Use as Medicine 570
    Benefits and Properties 570
    Medicine Preparation 570
    Using the Herb 571
    Side Effects and Warnings 571
    Fun Tips and Facts 571
    Author's Personal Story 571

149. MINT 573
    Latin Name 573
    Description 573
    Habitat 574
    Season to Gather the Plant 574
    Parts of the Plant to Use as Medicine 574
    Benefits and Properties 574
    Medicine Preparation 574
    Using the Herb 575
    Side Effects and Warnings 575
    Fun Tips and Facts 575
    Author's Personal Story 575

150. MUGWORT 577
    Latin Name 577
    Description 577

Habitat	578
Season to Gather the Plant	578
Parts of the Plant to Use as Medicine	578
Benefits and Properties	578
Medicine Preparation	578
Using the Herb	579
Side Effects and Warnings	579
Fun Tips and Facts	579
Author's Personal Story	579
151. MULBERRY	581
Latin Name	581
Description	581
Habitat	582
Season to Gather the Plant	582
Parts of the Plant to Use as Medicine	582
Benefits and Properties	582
Medicine Preparation	582
Using the Herb	583
Side Effects and Warnings	583
Fun Tips and Facts	583
Author's Personal Story	583
152. MULLEIN	585
Latin Name	585
Description	585
Habitat	586
Season to Gather the Plant	586
Parts of the Plant to Use as Medicine	586
Benefits and Properties	586
Medicine Preparation	586
Using the Herb	587
Side Effects and Warnings	587
Fun Tips and Facts	587
Author's Personal Story	587
153. OAK	589
Latin Name	589
Description	589
Habitat	590
Season to Gather the Plant	590
Parts of the Plant to Use as Medicine	590

    Benefits and Properties   590
    Medicine Preparation   591
    Using the Herb   591
    Side Effects and Warnings   591
    Fun Tips and Facts   591
    Author's Personal Story   592

154. PINE   593
    Latin Name   593
    Description   593
    Habitat   593
    Season to Gather the Plant   594
    Parts of the Plant to Use as Medicine   594
    Benefits and Properties   594
    Medicine Preparation   594
    Using the Herb   594
    Side Effects and Warnings   595
    Fun Tips and Facts   595
    Author's Personal Story   595

155. PLANTAIN   597
    Latin Name   597
    Description   597
    Habitat   597
    Season to Gather the Plant   598
    Parts of the Plant to Use as Medicine   598
    Benefits and Properties   598
    Medicine Preparation   598
    Using the Herb   598
    Side Effects and Warnings   599
    Fun Tips and Facts   599
    Author's Personal Story   599

156. RASPBERRY   601
    Latin Name   601
    Description   601
    Habitat   602
    Season to Gather the Plant   602
    Parts of the Plant to Use as Medicine   602
    Benefits and Properties   602
    Medicine Preparation   602
    Using the Herb   603

Side Effects and Warnings	603
Fun Tips and Facts	603
Author's Personal Story	603
157. RED CLOVER	**605**
Latin Name	605
Description	605
Habitat	605
Season to Gather the Plant	606
Parts of the Plant to Use as Medicine	606
Benefits and Properties	606
Medicine Preparation	606
Using the Herb	606
Side Effects and Warnings	606
Fun Tips and Facts	607
Author's Personal Story	607
158. SAINT JOHN'S WORT	**609**
Latin Name	609
Description	609
Habitat	610
Season to Gather the Plant	610
Parts of the Plant to Use as Medicine	610
Benefits and Properties	610
Medicine Preparation	610
Using the Herb	610
Side Effects and Warnings	611
Fun Tips and Facts	611
Author's Personal Story	611
159. SASSAFRAS	**613**
Latin Name	613
Description	613
Habitat	614
Season to Gather the Plant	614
Parts of the Plant to Use as Medicine	614
Benefits and Properties	614
Medicine Preparation	614
Using the Herb	615
Side Effects and Warnings	615
Fun Tips and Facts	615
Author's Personal Story	616

160. SHEPHERD'S PURSE ... 617
    Latin Name ... 617
    Description ... 617
    Habitat ... 618
    Season to Gather the Plant ... 618
    Parts of the Plant to Use as Medicine ... 618
    Benefits and Properties ... 618
    Medicine Preparation ... 618
    Using the Herb ... 619
    Side Effects and Warnings ... 619
    Fun Tips and Facts ... 619
    Author's Personal Story ... 619

161. SOLOMON'S SEAL ... 621
    Latin Name ... 621
    Description ... 621
    Habitat ... 622
    Season to Gather the Plant ... 622
    Parts of the Plant to Use as Medicine ... 622
    Benefits and Properties ... 622
    Medicine Preparation ... 622
    Using the Herb ... 622
    Side Effects and Warnings ... 623
    Fun Tips and Facts ... 623
    Author's Personal Story ... 623

162. STINGING NETTLE ... 625
    Latin Name ... 625
    Description ... 625
    Habitat ... 625
    Season to Gather the Plant ... 626
    Parts of the Plant to Use as Medicine ... 626
    Benefits and Properties ... 626
    Medicine Preparation ... 626
    Using the Herb ... 626
    Side Effects and Warnings ... 626
    Fun Tips and Facts ... 627
    Author's Personal Story ... 627

163. SUNFLOWER ... 629
    Latin Name ... 629
    Description ... 629

Habitat	630
Season to Gather the Plant	630
Parts of the Plant to Use as Medicine	630
Benefits and Properties	630
Medicine Preparation	630
Using the Herb	631
Side Effects and Warnings	631
Fun Tips and Facts	631
Author's Personal Story	631
164. TEASEL	**633**
Latin Name	633
Description	633
Habitat	634
Season to Gather the Plant	634
Parts of the Plant to Use as Medicine	634
Benefits and Properties	634
Medicine Preparation	634
Using the Herb	635
Side Effects and Warnings	635
Fun Tips and Facts	635
Author's Personal Story	635
165. VALERIAN	**637**
Latin Name	637
Description	637
Habitat	637
Season to Gather the Plant	638
Parts of the Plant to Use as Medicine	638
Benefits and Properties	638
Medicine Preparation	638
Using the Herb	638
Side Effects and Warnings	639
Fun Tips and Facts	639
Author's Personal Story	639
166. VIOLET	**641**
Latin Name	641
Description	641
Habitat	642
Season to Gather the Plant	642
Parts of the Plant to Use as Medicine	642

    Benefits and Properties   642
    Medicine Preparation   642
    Using the Herb   643
    Side Effects and Warnings   643
    Fun Tips and Facts   643
    Author's Personal Story   644

167. WILD SARSAPARILLA   645
    Latin Name   645
    Description   645
    Habitat   646
    Season to Gather the Plant   646
    Parts of the Plant to Use as Medicine   646
    Benefits and Properties   646
    Medicine Preparation   646
    Using the Herb   646
    Side Effects and Warnings   647
    Fun Tips and Facts   647
    Author's Personal Story   647

168. WILLOW   649
    Latin Name   649
    Description   649
    Habitat   649
    Season to Gather the Plant   650
    Parts of the Plant to Use as Medicine   650
    Benefits and Properties   650
    Medicine Preparation   650
    Using the Herb   650
    Side Effects and Warnings   650
    Fun Tips and Facts   651
    Author's Personal Story   651

169. WINTERGREEN   653
    Latin Name   653
    Description   653
    Habitat   653
    Season to Gather the Plant   654
    Parts of the Plant to Use as Medicine   654
    Benefits and Properties   654
    Medicine Preparation   654
    Using the Herb   654

Side Effects and Warnings	654
Fun Tips and Facts	655
Author's Personal Story	655
170. YARROW	657
Latin Name	657
Description	657
Habitat	657
Season to Gather the Plant	658
Parts of the Plant to Use as Medicine	658
Benefits and Properties	658
Medicine Preparation	658
Using the Herb	658
Side Effects and Warnings	659
Fun Tips and Facts	659
Author's Personal Story	659
Afterword	663
References	665
Bibliography	669
Bibliography	691

© **Copyright 2023 - All rights reserved.**

The content contained within this book may not be reproduced, duplicated or transmitted without direct written permission from the author or the publisher.

Under no circumstances will any blame or legal responsibility be held against the publisher, or author, for any damages, reparation, or monetary loss due to the information contained within this book, either directly or indirectly.

Legal Notice:

This book is copyright protected. It is only for personal use. You cannot amend, distribute, sell, use, quote or paraphrase any part, or the content within this book, without the consent of the author or publisher.

Disclaimer Notice:

Please note the information contained within this document is for educational and entertainment purposes only. All effort has been executed to present accurate, up to date, reliable, complete information. No warranties of any kind are declared or implied. Readers acknowledge that the author is not engaged in the rendering of legal, financial, medical or professional advice. The content within this book has been derived from various sources. Please consult a licensed professional before attempting any techniques outlined in this book.

By reading this document, the reader agrees that under no circumstances is the author responsible for any losses, direct or indirect, that are incurred as a result of the use of the information contained within this document, including, but not limited to, errors, omissions, or inaccuracies.

YOUR NORTHEAST BACKYARD HOMESTEAD - WHAT TO PLANT, HOW TO PLANT, AND WHEN TO PLANT FOR YOUR CLIMATE

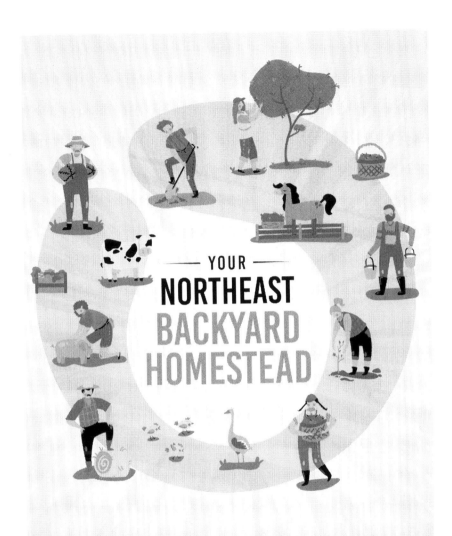

YOUR NORTHEAST BACKYARD HOMESTEAD

WHAT TO PLANT, HOW TO PLANT, AND
WHEN TO PLANT FOR YOUR CLIMATE

J. B. MAXWELL

INTRODUCTION

Let the beauty you love be what you do
— RUMI

It is possible that you are feeling run down and burned out from living in an urban environment. You could want to cut down on living expenses and get back in touch with nature, or you could be someone who is driven by self-sustainable practices. No matter the case, living off the grid or partially off the grid can help you find solutions to a lot of the stress and turmoil of everyday life. This book is a guide for how to start a new off-the-grid property in the Northeast and make the most of homesteading practices. I will go through the initial phases on your property, how to best plan your success, and the needs that your Northeast farm will have during each of the four seasons.

Living in the Northeast means that you will constantly be surrounded by beautiful landscapes and experience all that the four seasons have to offer. However, while the Northeast can be beautiful, starting a homestead in the Northeast can come with its own challenges, especially if you are looking to live off the grid. Northeast farmers face drastic temperature changes that they must account for when they are developing a garden, and a wide range of pests and insects that will be attracted to their gardens. The freezing temperatures that parts of the Northeast experience for large portions of the year also add to the challenges of starting a farm. Nevertheless, starting a homestead in the Northeast is an incredibly fulfilling process that requires time, attention to detail, and labor. By the end of your first or second year on your property you will have bountiful harvests and a gorgeous farm that will make all the effort of living in the Northeast worth it.

According to the Conservation Institute, over 1.7 billion people are living off the grid, meaning they do not rely on public utilities for electricity and water. In addition to that, over 250,000 people in the United States live off the grid and over 1.7 billion people around the globe live off the grid. In 2019, 79 million households used solar energy to fuel their off the grid homes (BigRentz, 2020). The benefits of living off the grid are clearly driving more and more people to cut the cord. Some of these benefits are self-sufficiency, a better connection with nature, improvements in conserving energy, and a generally more environmentally friendly life. Living off the grid can considerably cut down the costs of living in an average home. Most people in the United States spend over $2,000 a year on utility bills (BigRentz, 2020). In 2017, the energy consumption for a four family house in the United States was 10,399 kWh. While this may seem fine, reducing your energy intake can improve your carbon footprint. Right now, in the United States, renewable energy only accounts for 11% of energy consumption while the rest is used for fossil fuels (BigRentz, 2020). I don't expect that you are drilling for oil or that you are solely responsible for fossil fuel energy consumption, but to offset the impacts of climate change as a result of fossil fuels, improving your renewable energy consumption can help.

Living off the grid can also mean drastically reducing your costs of living. If you don't have rent and utilities to pay for, you will have more capital to invest toward your farm and property. The following figures for off-the-grid farming are subject to changes based on the location and time that you are looking to develop a homestead. Some of the initial costs to living off the grid include the cost of land, electricity, heating, water, waste management, and food. Finding the right land for your homestead is highly dependent on where in the world you want to be. In the United States and Canada, 5 acres of land typically costs about $3,000 per acre. You will want to save about $15,000 if you are considering buying a property with no existing structures on it.

There are many options when considering how you will power your house. A lot of off-the-grid homesteaders will opt for solar energy. Solar panels range in price and quality; the average cost per watt for solar panels is about $3. If you have a 2,500-square-foot home, you will need to save about $20,000 for solar panels. In addition, many states offer tax incentives and other benefits if you opt into sustainable energy for your property. The alternative options are wind power and hydro power to power your home, which also range in cost. You will want to consider what the most abundant source for renewable power is on your property. If you have a large pond or river, investing in a hydropower system may be more prudent.

Similar to power, heating your home can also have a lot of options. Geothermal heat pumps, solar heating, and biomass boiler systems are all possible considerations. Again, for a 2,500-square-foot home, you will want to save about $7,500 for a heating system. A water pump, well, or rainwater collection system are all options for considering how you will get clean water into your off-the-grid home. I highly recommend that if you are starting your first property, you buy a plot of land that already has a well on it. It can be very costly to dig a new well: depending on how deep you will need to dig for water, and the type of system you choose to have, you will want to save about $6,000 to $10,000 for a water system. Waste management is probably the most controversial area that you will need to consider for off-the-grid living. A septic tank or composting toilet are both options for waste management. Septic tanks require a lot of money upfront to have installed. I would estimate saving another $6,000 for a waste management system. These prices will vary a lot depending on if you are building structures yourself, updating existing structures, or paying a contractor to build these structures on your property.

Finding food for yourself and your family is where the homesteading aspect of living off the grid begins. There are many prudent methods for establishing your homestead so that you have access to high-quality foods that cost a fraction of the price that they would in a grocery store. Depending on the size of your property and the space that you want to allot to crops, gardening, and raising livestock, I would recommend saving about $30,000 to $35,000 for your off-the-grid farm. In total, starting such a homestead will run about $80,000 to $90,000 at the outset. The benefit of this initial investment is that beyond the maintenance that you will have to do on your property, additional costs will be incredibly low (BigRentz, 2020).

I have been homesteading for 10 years and during my time I have made many mistakes trying to figure out the best way to run my farm. Now, I want to offer you some sage advice about how you can thrive on your new property. Even if you haven't made the purchase yet, *Your Northeast Backyard Homestead* can help you put into perspective the benefits of living in nature and being self-sustaining.

1
KNOW YOUR CLIMATE

Homesteading is an incredibly beneficial process that you can engage with if you are someone who prioritizes working in nature, self-sustainability, and self-reliance. In the Northeast, homesteading can be slightly trickier because of the climate. In this geographical area there are drastic seasonal changes that require an extra level of preparedness when you are planning your property: cold winters, short and at times humid summers, early frost, just to name a few.

However, before I begin talking about the specifics that are required when you are starting a homestead in the Northeast, it is important to cover what exactly homesteading is. Homesteading is the practice of living a self-sufficient and -sustainable lifestyle. Many styles of homesteading call for off-the-grid living and self-reliance, but it is possible to create an urban or apartment homestead as well to begin practicing different methods before you even invest in this lifestyle. The Homestead Act of 1862 was the act that stated that any public land in the western regions of the United States could be granted to any citizen to farm on for 5 years. Similarly in Canada, there was an act in 1872 called the Dominion Lands Act that espoused a similar standard. Both of these acts were put in place to encourage more people to move out of urban areas and foster agricultural industries. In the continental United States, nearly 10% of all the land was allotted to homesteaders as a result of the act (Culver, 2021).

Homesteading today has taken on many different forms. There are options for both urban and rural families to practice different homesteading techniques to become more self-sustaining. If you are living in an urban or suburban area and you are interested in a more self-sustaining life, try starting small. Beginning with a small garden on your balcony, collecting rainwater, or cultivating yeast are great small steps to take when starting your journey with homesteading. Another great option is to get your family engaged. A backyard garden, small chicken coop, or a rabbit coop are great for smaller children to engage with. There are essential life lessons that children can glean from hard work and a sense of fulfillment when they see their first crop blossom. Needless to say, homesteading is a way to sustain yourself and find a greater sense of self-reliance. The cost of living, the bustle of urban life, and a dependency on your own work will all provide a mindset for homesteading that is pivotal to the process.

One of the benefits of starting a homestead in the Northeast is the weather changes and varied pursuits that you can start on your property. You can do anything, from building a greenhouse, planting a typical garden or crop field, to raising animals, and many other ventures. The region in the United States that is called the Northeast spans from the southernmost point of New Jersey and goes up through the northernmost points in Maine. If you are considering living in the Northeast in the United States, it is important to note that global temperatures are slightly rising and the Northeast has seen a lot of climate changes as a result. The average summer temperatures have risen by 2 °F over the last 100 years, and as a result there have been longer summer heat waves, an increase in rainfall, and slightly shorter winter seasons in the northern parts of this region (US EPA, 2016). Where I live in Pennsylvania, we see temperatures as high as 95 °F in the summer time to 10 °F in the winter. These temperature changes absolutely impact what and when I choose to plant in my gardens. I keep a calendar where I track the first and last frosts of the year to give me insight on when I should start planting outdoors and when I should start seeds in my greenhouse. While these dates change from year to year, I have found that keeping an eye on the forecast and planning accordingly has helped my garden thrive.

CLIMATE IN THE NORTHEAST

Approximately, 64 million people live in the Northeast of the United States. With more than 180,000 farms that annually net $17 billion, the Northeast is a great place to start your homesteading journey (National Climate Assessment, 2021). The landscape in the Northeast is largely made up of forests. There are some grasslands, beaches, and wetlands. There is also a large fishing industry. The region is characterized by a diverse climate that sees about 20 inches of rain per year, depending on the proximity to the coast and elevation. The area also sees floods, heat waves, hurricanes, and nor'easters (big snowstorms!). There is always a chance that living in the Northeast will mean that you will have to invest in a backup generator as a result of some of the weather patterns in the region. In 2016, we got nearly 20 inches of snow in January, which led to power outages across my state. On my property, I had a backup generator, survival storage, and a lot of candles stocked up in case we lost power. I knew that buying a property in the Northeast meant that power outages could be a possibility, and I was so happy that we had planned for the inevitability of one. We were living comfortably while the snow came down outside, or at least I was until it came time to start shoveling the snow.

The average temperatures in the Northeast during the year range from 26 °F to 85 °F, and in some areas the winter temperatures can fall below 14 °F and the summers can see temperatures above 93 °F. According to WeatherSpark, the Northeast is one of the most extreme regions in the United States that sees humidity variation throughout the year. The humid season in the Northeast lasts from the end of May until the end of September. The most humid month of the year is July, with an average of 19 days that will reach 66% humidity. The clearest months in the Northeast are from the end of June until the first weeks of November. The clearest month in the Northeast is September. The cloudiest parts of the year in the Northeast last from November until the middle of June. The cloudiest month during the year in the Northeast is January, with 52% of the sky covered in clouds throughout the month (WeatherSpark, 2020). The rain season in the Northeast lasts from the beginning of April until the end of August; the rainiest month of the year is July, with an average of 11 rain days per month. The inverse of the rainy season is the drier season of the year, with January being the month that sees the least amount of precipitation. Precipitation in the Northeast accounts for both the rain and snow seasons.

2
THE LAY OF THE LAND

When you are thinking about the size of your property and what will be the best amount of land to fit your needs, I would recommend considering your budget. There are so many options for property sizes, depending on where in the Northeast you are looking to settle down. I remember when I bought my first plot of land. It was 1 acre, and yet I felt out of my element when it came to filling up the space and utilizing it in the best way possible. When you are starting this journey, consider what you will want to spend your time doing and the space that can accommodate those activities. I personally love having a small garden near my kitchen, raising some small furry friends, and leaving space for my family to enjoy nature.

A great first step is to consider the goals that you have for your property. Consider your answers to the following questions:

- How much time do you expect (or want) to spend maintaining your property?
- How much time do you want to spend outdoors enjoying nature, not working?
- How much land do you have available to dedicate to gardening or raising animals?
- What are the local ordinances in your area?
- Do you want to turn homesteading into your full-time job?

- How involved will your family be in your homesteading journey?

These questions may be tricky to answer at first if you are still narrowing down your property options. Once you have your sights set on a piece of land, consider your answers to these questions and remember, it is perfectly acceptable if the answers change over time. The next step that I encourage all beginners to take is to create a list of your homesteading goals, the amount of land that you will need to dedicate to those goals, and the materials that you will need on hand to build and maintain that area. For example, if you want to keep a small kitchen garden outside of your backdoor, you will probably want to allot about 0.1 acre to that area. For livestock, you will want to have 1 to 3 acres of space, depending on the animals. Keep in mind that smaller animals need less room than larger livestock. Each goal that you list for your property will require certain tools to build the structures and maintain the systems you put in place. When I started my first homestead, I was convinced that I wanted to raise some rabbits. I built a handful of hutches for them, but during certain seasons it was difficult to get my hands on the right hay for their enclosures. I didn't make a list of the resources that I would need to maintain the area, so I came up against an avoidable hurdle. You don't have to be like me in the beginning! My goal is that you can learn some of the strategies that I have developed so that you can avoid those mishaps.

After you have established your goals, I recommend that you spend some time thinking about how self-sustaining you want to be. If your goal is to go totally off the grid, you will probably require more land than someone who is staying on the grid and still buying food from the grocery store. I am by no means saying that one method is more legitimate than the other, but if you are going for the off-the-grid method, it is always better to consider getting a larger piece of land. However, with strategic planning and consideration of your goals, you don't actually need that much space to start a homestead. A lot of processes can be rotated out of areas on your property so that you are making the most of the land!

There are endless creative options to pursue when you are starting your first homestead. In the Northeast, there is a lot of available land, but if you need to ask yourself: What is the smallest amount of land that I could have to start a traditional farm? The minimum amount of land that you can have for a homestead is about an acre. Keep in mind that with an acre of land, you will probably only be able to have a garden. For animals or a forest to harvest wood, you will need 2 to 10 acres. This is not to say that this is the only way to start a farm. There are a lot of urban homesteading options where people have developed creative solutions to limited space. I have a friend who lives in Boston who works on a cooperative farming operation out of shipping containers. They utilize vertical farming and aquaponic farming to achieve the same results that someone would achieve on a large rural farm. When you center self-sustainability in your practice of farming, the options for how to make accommodations for your space are endless. However, this book will focus on the starter farm that will range from 1 acre to about 5 acres.

Now that you have an understanding of the space required to farm, your goals for your property, and the mindset that is essential when you are starting this journey, it is time to consider the nuances of your property. For a small garden the essential components of laying out your area are the accessibility, light, safety, and plant health. When you are considering the accessibility of your property, it is crucial to think about how far away aspects of your farm are. It is a great practice to consider permaculture zones to inform the layout of your farm. The general rule is that you want to keep things closer to the house on your property that will need daily attention. I will discuss more of the details of permaculture design in Chapter 6.

Once you have decided where you will place your garden and the first structures on your property, consider the light and safety that your plants will need. Access to sunlight, shade, and a lack of wind will be pivotal to a successful garden. In the Northeast, there are many months in the year where your plants will get direct sunlight. Depending on the crops that you want to grow, they will need different access to sunlight. Consider a space on your property that gets both direct sunlight and shade so that your plants can thrive. Keep in mind that if the garden is too close to your house, the garden will be shaded considerably by the shadow cast by the house. Be careful in the planning phase to think about the direction of the sun throughout the entire day and at different times of the year. The general rule is to keep your garden at least 10 feet away from any walls of your house. You will also want to see how much wind your area gets. In the Northeast, there are seasons that are windier than others. This step can be completed before you move onto your property. Regional maps of your area can indicate the average wind speeds that your farm will experience. Consider if the wind speeds on the property will be too rough during some months of the year and how that can damage your crops. Typically, crops don't love an excess of wind: their leaves can be damaged or the entire plant could be uprooted, leading to a headache and a mess. While this may seem like a minor setback, if you are staking your meals and income on the success of your plants, be sure that you research and observe your farm so that you can have a thriving garden.

With the age of technology, finding all of the information about a plot of land you are interested in purchasing before you buy has become incredibly accessible. I regularly hop on Google and look for properties that I find interesting. As an exercise, I will plot out the best farming layout for the property to see if I can catch every contingency that needs to be thought through. Google Maps is a great resource in this process because you can get a fairly detailed look at the property from an aerial view. When it comes time to actually choose a property, there are some other calls that you can make to get even more information about the area. Contacting the local utility companies is a great practice because there may be wiring or pipes under your property and it would be a mess if you accidentally dug into one. All of the Northeast states have Dig Safe laws that require you to notify the county if you are going to be excavating on your property in order to go about the process safely. Failing to adhere to the Dig Safe laws in your area can result in hefty fines. Calling utility companies or contacting your county to learn about your property and what might be hiding underneath your property can give you great insights on where to plan different aspects of your farm. It may be the case that you have a city water pipe under your property that prohibits you from farming over it. This is a great way to narrow down the options you have for where to place your gardens.

3
BUILDING YOUR BEDS

When you are planning the best ways to grow crops in your garden, raised beds are a great option that maximize harvests and protect your plants. Raised beds are garden beds that are built above the ground instead of into the ground. There are many different methods for how to achieve a raised garden bed. Often you will see wood panels or larger steel drums that enclose the raised bed. Raised beds are also sometimes referred to as 'garden boxes.' The purpose of gardening above the ground instead of directly into the soil is that you can better control the pH of the soil, the depth of the roots, and protect your crops from pests that may damage your plants.

In addition, some benefits of using raised beds on your farm are improved soil quality, improved soil drainage, ease of gardening, longer growing seasons, and cultivating an aesthetic form. Not tilling the soil is better for your plants. When you are setting up your raised beds or maintaining them between seasons, you will be able to add fertilizer, soil, and compost to the top of the bed without the added work of tilling the ground. This creates a faster process, where you have more control over the nutrients and soil quality that your plants are getting. Raised beds also keep pests out of your garden more effectively than planting directly into the ground. Many of the garden pests that you will want to protect your plants from cannot climb up the sides of the raised bed and will be discouraged from trying to eat your crops. Similarly, in the Northeast, there is a large deer population that will definitely be attracted to your crops. With a raised bed, it is easier to add deer fencing above the crops so that the deers cannot access the leafy green vegetables that they love. When I set up my first raised bed, I wanted to plant some strawberries, borage, and mint into my raised beds. The borage and mint are deer favorites and I knew that spending a little extra time to secure my raised beds would mean that I got a great harvest at the end of the season that was not littered with deer bites. I also opted to plant some shrubs on the edges of my property so that the deers could have a snack that I was less invested in if they happened to stop by.

Raised beds also offer better soil drainage. One of the trickiest pieces of setting up a homestead is your water supply and drainage. It takes a lot of careful consideration to set up the water system on your farm so that you are not overwatering your crops or underutilizing the water at your disposal. With raised beds, because of their height, the soil is able to drain quicker and keep your plants healthier longer. The standard raised bed is between 11 and 12 inches high. This is the perfect height that plants need for drainage. If you are living in an area that is prone to flooding, which is common in some areas of the Northeast, raised beds may be your only option for high-quality farming. Otherwise you will run the risk of your plants drowning or being overwatered. Similarly, if you are in an area that gets a lot of rain, the 12-inch raised beds will allow the soil to drain at a consistent rate without risking the health of your crops. An additional benefit to raised beds is that they can elevate some of the back-breaking work that gardening calls for. With the beds being raised off the ground, you can avoid spending hours hunched over tending to your garden. The beds also make weeding much easier.

Good soil drainage in your raised beds is great if you are using raised beds to feed your family or community. The crops will be fresh and delicious, as well as abundant. Keep in mind, this largely works because of soil quality and density. You will want to ensure that your soil is the correct pH and you are adding the proper nutrients so that your plants can thrive. The last benefit of raised beds is that they are really pretty. Your garden will look neat and contained. You can easily plant crops in a single raised bed that compliment one another. Your garden will undoubtedly look lush and vibrant if you utilize raised beds on your farm.

STRATEGIES FOR MAKING THE MOST OF YOUR RAISED BEDS

So how do you actually go about building raised beds? There are many different methods for building them and the materials that you use can vary. The general rule to building raised beds with wooden sides is that you avoid using pressure-treated wood. Plywood and other chemically treated woods can leach chemicals into your soil and compromise your plants' health. If you have never built a raised bed before but you are interested in having some on your farm, Home Depot offers raised garden bed plans and kits that will make your life easier as you start your farming journey. If you have a little more experience with building and want to cut down on cost, a great method for building a raised bed is to buy cedar planks the length, width, and height of your raised bed, as well as 2 × 2 or 4 × 4 pieces of wood for the corners of your raised bed. The cedar planks can be any size that works for your farm as long as you get four planks to surround the area that you are building your raised bed in. I highly suggest that the height of your raised beds be 12 inches so that you get the best soil drainage as possible. The corner pieces should be taller than the height of your raised bed so that you can secure netting or other protective measures over the top of the bed.

Another strategy that a lot of raised bed gardeners use is called 'lasagna gardening.' This is the process of layering multiple layers of mulch, compost, and other organic materials into your raised bed to improve the soil quality and nutrients that your plants receive. There is no standard for how to lasagna garden, but in my experience, I have had the most success when I have layered branches and rough mulch over the ground, then grass clippings, wet newspaper, compost, and straw mulch. Be sure that you water each layer as you place them into your garden. This is also a great way to cut down on cost as you will be able to find most of the materials for lasagna gardening on your farm already. Of course, you can always add the soil of your choice for specific crops if you want to ensure that they get the exact pH or nutrients that are required for them to grow.

Some alternative raised garden bed methods are fabric raised planters, elevated raised gardens that usually require adding legs to your garden box, tiered raised beds, galvanized metal raised beds, trough raised beds, and many others. The benefit of raised beds is that you can be endlessly creative in the materials used to contain the small gardens. I have even seen people make their raised beds in old tires! The possibilities are endless and you can utilize the materials that you have available to you on your farm or you can invest in store-bought materials to create the gardens.

Now that you know why people use raised beds, the benefits of the small gardens, and some additional design ideas for how to build the beds, there are some things that you will need to prepare before you start building. You will first want to identify the space on your farm that is ideal for the garden. Remember, you want to have your gardens relatively close to your house so that you can monitor them regularly, but not so close that the gardens are prone to shadow for too many hours a day. Another consideration to make is if you want to remove the grass from below the raised beds. Some farmers will take the time to cut out the grass patches below so that they can plant deeper into the raised beds. This isn't an entirely necessary process if you aren't planting deep-rooting crops. However, if you decide to remove the grass from under your raised beds, a great strategy that will cut down on time is to place the raised beds on your farm at the end of the fall season: place a layer of cardboard or newspaper over the ground and let the grass decay over the winter. At the start of the spring, you will have a grassless area.

Irrigation is another consideration that you will need to make before you finish the construction of your garden. Raised beds that are made out of galvanized steel or trough call for irrigation systems that are a little more intense and require a water hookup for them to be successful. For the traditional raised bed, you can add a pipe that runs through the bottom third, with holes in it. The pipe can be connected to a rain collection bin or a water pump and you can automate the watering process. Otherwise, it is perfectly acceptable to add 'watering your crops' to your list of daily farm chores!

Here are some additional tips and tricks to consider when you are starting your garden of raised beds:

- The first crops that you start planting in your raised garden beds should be the herbs and vegetables that you will want to eat. Herbs are very forgiving crops that can withstand a little neglect. Developing your own systems to tend to the crops that

you will most enjoy will make the gardening experience all the more fulfilling.
- If you have any areas where you raised beds are more shaded, plant leafy greens. Most crops will benefit from 6 to 8 hours of sunlight per day, but leafy greens can handle a little less sunlight and still thrive. Plant spinach, borage, and lettuce in the more shaded areas of your garden.
- Keep a ledger of the crops that you plant from year to year. Having a way to track the crops that were planted in a specific raised bed will inform you on what to plant the following year and the accommodations that you will need to make to the soil, compost, and mulch that is still in the raised bed.
- Along with keeping a ledger of your crops, when you go to plant your seedlings, be sure that you are planting them in rows. This will ensure that the weeding and tending processes are faster and easier. Also, planting your crops in rows will mean that you don't accidentally pull up one of your crops because you mistakenly thought it was a weed (and believe me, weeds are masters at impersonation).
- Consider companion planting when you are planning your raised beds. I will dig deeper into the benefits of companion planting in Chapter 4, but when you are considering what to plant, some crops get along nicely with others and can be planted in the same bed. Companion planting will also maximize your harvests as the crops have a symbiotic relationship with each other.
- Plant annual cover crops like ryegrass or clover. These cover crops can be seeded into your raised beds at the start of spring and will provide necessary nitrogen and other nutrients to your raised beds between growing seasons. Plus, a bunch of clover peeking out from your raised beds during the non-growing seasons is really adorable.

4
HOMESTEADING FOR THE WIN

There are a couple more steps to cover before you actually get on to your new property. When you first start this process, it is not only important to plan systems for your success but also to ensure that you have a mindset that will lend itself to a prosperous adventure. One of the most key aspects to tackling a new property or a brand new journey is to push yourself to continue to learn. There are thousands of resources available to you on your homesteading journey that can inform your practices and projects on your farm. It is vital that you find creative solutions to different systems on your property and continue to innovate. While there are a lot of steps to the planning phase of your journey, once you start implementing systems it is important to continue to learn about those systems. You may have a well on your property that you are using to water your gardens and provide water to your home, but what happens in the winter if the water in the well freezes? Finding creative solutions and learning more about systems like water distribution will be prudent to making a homestead last. The mentality to continue to learn is essential to setting up your property for longevity and success.

Now that you are driven to continue to learn, it is important to be able to think critically about how the information that you have gathered fits your situation. While I encourage everyone to dig into the resources at your disposal, they will not be useful to you if you can't apply them to your situation. I remember reading about keeping bees on my homestead and I was really excited to start a beekeeping project on my farm. However, when I got to the property, I realized that I would have to do a lot of work upfront to prepare for the bees. I needed to clear some space, plant pollinating flowers near where I wanted to place the beehives, and get the equipment necessary to keep bees. While the information that I got was vital, it would have been useless if I didn't apply my own situation to the information. Applying the information that you are getting from other resources to your situation can help you avoid unnecessary time loss while you are navigating how the project will work for you.

In addition, it may be tempting to get all of the information about different projects for your homestead from online resources, but I want to encourage you to get help and information from other sources as well. There are vibrant communities both online and in person that you can participate in when you are discovering new information or when you come up against a hurdle. Asking for help when you need it from trusted sources is another mindset shift that every new property owner needs in order to be successful. I will talk at more length about the benefits of cultivating relationships with your neighbors in a later part of this chapter, but for now, the importance of joining or cultivating relationships with trusted people is paramount. If you find that you are in a bind and need help, the internet may provide you with information that is general but it won't fit directly to your situation. If you have the ability to explain your exact situation to a trusted friend or neighbor, or even the owner of the local gardening nursery or hardware store, you will receive much more sage advice on how to proceed.

The next mindset that every farmer should have is to be aware of how much you can take on. Be honest with yourself while you are planning the projects that you want to have on your farm. How much can you reasonably do in a day and how much effort do you want to put into different projects? Maybe you want to only spend your time gardening. How many hours of the day can you do that? What if you only want to raise rabbits and maintain a small kitchen garden on the side? Discover exactly how much time and effort you want to put into different projects and then budget at least half the amount of time to unexpected situations. In the Northeast, there are bound to be weather events or storms that will throw your perfect systems into disarray. You can have some animals on your farm that get sick and you will need to spend extra time caring for them. Or you may not have protected your coops enough and your animals get targeted by predators. There are always going to be unexpected twists and turns, the goal is to accurately determine how much time you can spend doing the things that make you happy while budgeting time for those unexpected events. This will also ensure that you are not constantly exhausted from having to run around your farm all day because you planned to accomplish too many different tasks. I personally love to take a day off every week so that I can read and relax. When I first started my farm, I knew that I had to set up systems so that at least one day a week, I could take some time off for myself and my family.

Once you have established some ideas for what you want on your farm and how much time and energy you can devote to those things, it is time to consider your finances. Making smart financial decisions that won't ultimately be detrimental to your success is a tricky process, but it is one that every farmer needs to master. There are going to be financial investments that you will need to make into building materials, seeds, and animals, but all of those investments come with added costs. You may want to raise chickens and they will need a coop, pen, and feed. The profit that you make from selling the eggs or meat may not cover the initial costs that it took to raise them. It is important to consider all of the expenses for the projects that you want to start and the type of return on your investments that you can expect. In addition, you will want to consider the market that you are selling into. With the age of technology, there are many money-making practices that you can capitalize on while you are homesteading. However, if you take a more traditional route and sell your produce or animals locally, there may already be sellers in your area and the market for your goods might not be available.

Making these considerations before you get onto your property will ensure that you don't waste money on the initial investments to set up a project without turning a profit down the line. It's the same as writing a business plan for a new venture. I suggest setting up a list of the projects you want to accomplish, the cost of every aspect of those projects, and what types of profit you may be able to reap from those projects. For example, if you want to raise chickens, consider all of the costs involved in raising the chickens and the types of profit that you can make from them depending on your area. It is also especially important to consider the weather in addition to finances. What costs are associated with keeping your chickens warm during the winter or ensuring that their water bowls don't freeze? How will it impact your finances if a predator gets into the coop and wipes out the flock?

There are also areas that you can invest in that will yield higher profits than others. Your garden is a great example of this. The cost of seeds is very low and setting up your garden doesn't have to be a particularly costly venture. Selling your produce will net you a lot more than your initial investment. The goal is to find the right market to sell to. Regardless of the type of profits that you are expecting to reap from your farm, I want to warn you that the return on your money will probably be slower than you are expecting. For your first homestead, there are a lot of other considerations that need to be made and systems to put in place before turning a profit becomes a viable option. The last and arguably most important mindset that every new farmer needs to have is that homesteading is a long-term investment: you may invest years into a project before that project pays off the initial investment. The homesteading lifestyle transcends the money-making ventures that you could make and there are many benefits to being outside in nature and living a less fast-paced life. Keep in mind that while it will feel fulfilling to make money from your hard work, the real goal of homesteading is to spend time on your farm doing things that make you happy.

GETTING SETTLED

So what do you do when you have your property? The best piece of advice that I can give you is to start slowly. It could be argued that this is another mindset shift that you will need to engage with before you start your farm, but starting slow and ensuring that you are comfortable on your property before you start tackling larger projects will be key to your success in the first year on your property. When you get the keys to your property, don't do everything right away. It is important to feel settled before you can begin to tackle the different projects you want to start. I have heard a lot of stories of people getting to their homestead and immediately starting a garden, while all of their clothes and furniture were still in boxes. Feeling settled on your property will provide you more space and time to dedicate to fleshing out the projects that you want to accomplish and to do them in a well-thought out manner. There are also a lot of benefits to planning out the space in your home. Once you start tackling different tasks on your farm, you will need to set up systems inside your house that will promote those projects. You may be growing a lot of food, but how will you store the food? Do you want to can or pickle your harvests so that you can preserve them? You will need to have some extra cabinet or refrigerator space to keep your preserves fresh. Unpack your things and set up systems inside your house for success before you begin tackling bigger projects on your farm.

Another great first step to take once you get onto your property is to meet your neighbors. This is going to be especially crucial if you are living in a rural place. You may have less access to resources and developing solid relationships with your neighbors can lead to fostering a community where you help one another. In rural areas, it will take a lot more time to get certain resources and you will be responsible for the general maintenance of structures around you. It may be the case that you are sharing roads or fences with your neighbors and if they need repairs; it will be far easier to get those jobs done if you enjoy being around each other and are clear as to who owns what and who is responsible for those areas. Working cooperatively with the people in your community can be a saving grace on your first homestead. In addition to meeting your neighbors, it is important to understand the access issues that you may encounter on your property. Living in more rural places will require that you know everything about the land around you. If you are living in the Northeast, there is a large possibility that you will get snowed into your house. Knowing where the access roads are, having access to a snowplow, and relying on your neighbors will be crucial. It is also important to know where power lines and water pipes are. This will give you more insight into the area. You can get this information from your neighbors as well as the county.

Living in a state of preparedness will also be essential once you move into your new property. Storage and survival storage are really important systems to have set up early on when you move into your new home. Buy the food that you need in bulk and preserve it in areas that you've set up in your home. There may be busy days or emergencies that will require you to have extra food on hand: for example, if you have a day where cooking seems like too much effort because you're dealing with an emergency or you get snowed in. Another aspect of preparedness that is essential to consider is your access to water. It is very likely that your house will already have running water unless you are building your house on your own. I highly recommend buying a property that already has a well on it so that you can start gardening projects when you are ready. Otherwise, you will need to devise creative irrigation systems around your farm. Inside your house, be sure that you keep an extra tank of water on hand if you are in a relatively rural place so that there is no chance that you will run out of water if there is a power outage or some sort of weather intervention that would prevent you from accessing water.

Along the same lines as storing excess water, be sure that you also store excess power and fuel. Living in the Northeast comes with extreme weather events that may make getting electricity or fuel more difficult. Ensure that you have extra fuel containers to power your car or a backup generator. The way that you choose to power your house will also come into play as you first move in. For off-the-grid homes, there are many types of renewable energy sources that require initial investments to install. Regardless of your power source, it is always a great practice to keep a backup generator on hand in case of a storm. The last thing that you should have on hand in case of emergencies or distances from a hospital, are medical supplies. Be sure that you have first-aid kits and any extra medical supplies that you or your family will need on your property. Taking these necessary precautions and prioritizing preparedness when you start on your first homestead will make it so that you are ready for any situation.

Another step to take once you get the keys to your new property is to observe your land. I will discuss later the key aspects to permaculture design, which will provide you with insights on how to best lay out your farm projects. However, when you first get onto your property, observe how the existing structures on your farm will influence the layout of your property. Observe how different organic structures on your farm will impact the day-to-day experience on your farm. You may have a little dip in the land that floods when it rains. It would be hard to preemptively know that this would happen and you would hate to place a raised bed in that area, only for it to get destroyed or compromised when it rains. There are many other observations that you will make in the first couple of weeks on the homestead. These observations will inform how you begin planning the layout of your farm without accidentally placing a structure in an inopportune spot. After a couple of weeks of unpacking and observing your property, it is time to plan all of the zones on your farm before you start your projects. The general rules for permaculture design are that you want the areas that are closest to your home to be the areas that you visit and maintain regularly. The farther away you get from your home, the less those areas require maintenance. Observing your property first is imperative to discovering the best way to do this.

At this point you should have a general idea of how you are going to plan out your farm and what projects you will want to start building. The next step is to *continue* planning, as there are going to be many different areas on your property that will require some detailed thought and preparation before you can start building or developing processes. Plan before you start gardening, plan before you start coppicing trees, and plan before you buy animals. How are you going to maintain your animals and where can they graze? Be sure that they have an area to roam outside of their enclosures. Think about the feed that they will need. Also consider how you are going to store all of the resources for your animals and how that storage process will be affected in the winter. Be sure that you secure a local veterinarian. This is also a moment where neighbors become great resources. If you have a neighbor who is also raising animals, they may know a local veterinarian who makes house calls or they may know how to identify or treat issues that your animals may be having, so you don't need to call the veterinarian every time (as vet bills can add up!). All of this is to say that planning and taking things slowly when you first get onto your property will be crucial in creating and maintaining systems that will stand the test of time.

RAISING ANIMALS

Planning and considering everything that you will need to make your homestead run smoothly is great, but what happens when you want to buy your first animals? Animals can be a tricky investment and I highly recommend that you spend a lot of time researching the proper care for any animals that you want to buy. In the Northeast, three of the best animals to start with on your homestead are chickens, goats, and bees. These animals will thrive in the Northeast climate and can handle the colder winters.

Raising Chickens

The very first step before you buy chicks is to make sure that your city or town allows backyard chickens. Some areas do not permit you to raise chickens. Be sure to check that you have the green light to raise chickens before you purchase any. Don't buy eggs to incubate! Incubating eggs for your first round of chickens is an incredibly delicate process. For inexperienced chicken parents, this process can be needlessly stressful. I recommend buying baby chicks and raising them from when they are young.

Deciding which breed of chickens you want to raise depends on what you want the chickens for. If you want to only have chickens that lay eggs you will want to go with Brahams, Cochins, Orpingtons, or Wyandottes. If you are looking to get eggs and meat from your chickens, you will want to get a dual-purpose breed, such as Barred Rock, Rhode Island Red, Sussex, or White Leghorn chickens. If you are only looking to raise chickens for their meat, I would suggest purchasing Cornish Cross or Red Ranger chicks. Once you have decided on the breed of chicks and purchased them, it is important to keep them extremely warm for the first couple of weeks of their life. Chicks are usually supposed to be with a broody hen that will keep them warm through body heat, and without that they will need a constantly warm environment. Keep the chicks in your home during this period, as a heat lamp in an outdoor coop will not be warm enough. During the first couple of weeks, you will want to line the chick enclosure with pine shavings or a rubber mat so that they aren't slipping around. The chicks will also need chicken feed specifically for chicks, and water.

Usually, once the chicks are 8 weeks old, they are ready to be moved to their coop. Be sure to ready to coop with all of the necessary aspects, but leave out any feed or water bowls. Leaving food inside the coop will attract predators and rodents, which you do not want in your coops. Some general precautions to take when you are setting up the chicken coop is to ensure that it remains dry inside the coop to avoid mold, have sturdy latches for all of the doors, and be sure that there is good ventilation throughout the coop. Chickens require some daily chores but other than that, the chores that you will need to complete for your chickens are manageable and can happen on a weekly or monthly basis. Daily, you will want to feed your chickens, make sure they have fresh clean water, and sweep out any droppings that were left overnight. Weekly, you will want to fully clean out the coop and replace the hay. Monthly chores will consist of scrubbing the entire coop, feeds, and water bowls.

The benefits of raising chickens are that you have access to free fertilizer and pest control, organic eggs, and an additional stream of revenue. Collecting the droppings from your chickens is a great way to get organic fertilizer for your gardens. Chickens love to eat bugs and can be used as a great form of pest control for your gardens. However, be careful to note that allowing your chickens unfettered access to your gardens will mean that you will lose some crops, as they are equal-opportunity omnivores. You are also bound to get organic eggs from your chickens if you raise hens. Organic eggs are healthier than store-bought eggs and remove the risk of insecticides and other harmful chemicals. When you collect chicken eggs from your hens, they also don't need to be refrigerated because they were not processed. This can save you a lot of refrigerator space and provides extra time for you to use or sell the eggs. Chicken eggs and meat can be a great source of income for your farm. Depending on the breed of chickens that you raise, you may have access to relatively large organic eggs that other people would love to buy.

Raising Goats

Goats are another easy and manageable animal to raise on your Northeast farm. If you are interested in raising animals for their milk, fiber, or just general companionship, then you may want to invest in some goats. Goats are incredibly personable animals that are easy to care for and will leave a smile on your face every time you are with them. If you are interested in buying goats for their milk, there are five breeds of goats that are perfect for this purpose: Alpines, Nigerian Dwarfs, Nubians, La Manchas, and Saanens.

Alpine goats are great if you are living in an area that gets cold winters, as they do great in cold temperatures. This breed of goat is a medium size and often has really lovely markings. Milking these goats is great for dairy as well as cheese making. Nigerian Dwarfs are small goats that only grow to about 20 inches tall. These goats are great if you don't have excess amounts of land but you want to raise some tiny friends. Nubians are another medium-sized goat breed. They are adorable, kind, and very vocal. If you are starting a homestead with children, Nubians are a great addition to the family. La Manchas are another great option if you are living in the northernmost part of the Northeast as they are relatively cold-hardy animals. The last of the goat breeds to consider for your homestead are Saanens. These goats tend to be large, with calm personalities that are easy for first-time goat owners. However, you will want to have plenty of space on your property for these goats to roam.

Once you have decided what type of goat you'd like to raise, there are some other essentials that your goats will need before they arrive. The goats will need a home, access to clean water, food, and fencing. I recommend that if you are going to raise goats, you either have a property with a barn on it already or build a barn on your farm. In the Northeast specifically, the goats will need a warm place to stay during the winter months. The top priorities for a goat barn are that it is well-ventilated, draft-free, and dry. You will want to keep the barn dry for the same reasons that you will want to keep a chicken coop dry.

Goats, similar to chickens or any animal that you raise on your farm, need constant access to clean drinking water. This is a relatively inexpensive system to set up but it is important that you consider how you will keep the water from freezing during the winter. There are some heated water bowls that you can use for chickens, but for goats that need a larger water source, a creative option is worth considering. Goats like to browse instead of graze. A goat will hop from food source to food source so that they have variety in their diets. Allowing your goats access to different types of food will leave your goal with a healthier and more well-rounded diet. You can also add hay to their barn for extra food when needed. Woven wire fencing or electric fencing that is tall are the best options if you are raising goats. Goats are smart and inquisitive animals and they will find a way to test your fences if they can. Goats can also jump and climb with ease, so ensure that your fencing is tall if you want to keep your goats inside their enclosure and predators outside of it.

Beekeeping

Raising bees is not only a fulfilling process that will leave you with delicious wild honey, but it is also an act of sustainability. There is a shortage of bees across the United States and without bees the ecological systems in the country will suffer tremendously. If you are considering raising bees, do as much research as you can about keeping bees before you buy a colony. There is a lot of information on bee health and safety that you will need before you can safely start an apiary. It would be heartbreaking if you bought a colony, the colony suffered for some reason that you were unprepared for, and the colony died as a result. Buying colonies can be pretty expensive and if you don't have all the information that you need before you get them, you will waste your money.

The next step, after you have researched keeping bees, is to get the equipment that you will need. At the most basic level, you will need a beekeeping veil and jacket, gloves, pillars, hive tools, a smoker, and a bee brush. All of these tools are humane to use on the bees and to keep yourself safe while you are handling them. The initial investment in the tools required for beekeeping and one hive will cost a little more than $700 (Melanie, 2020). The best time to order a bee colony is in the winter. Many bee distributors sell out pretty fast, so once you've settled on the bees that you want to keep, be sure to order quickly. Picking a spot to keep your bees is also a crucial step in the process. Bees like to be in spots that are partially shaded and with close access to flowers and other crops that flower for pollination. If the bee hive is kept too far from pollinating flowers, the bees will fly too far and potentially die on the way back to the hive. A weak hive will be targeted by other bees and eventually die as a result.

Once your bees arrive, check the health of your queen bee before you place the bees into the hive. Sadly, without a healthy queen bee, the hive will fail. Place the hive in your desired location and insert the colony at the beginning of spring. A great tip for the first few weeks of having an active colony is to place some small dishes of sugar water out for the bees. If they are feeding on the sugar water, they are still trying to locate the best flowers. Once they stop feeding from it, they have found flowers and have begun feeding themselves. During the growing season, your beehive won't need too much maintenance. Check the hive once every 2 weeks. Also learn to spot bee eggs. If the queen bee is laying eggs then the hive is thriving! I think that bees are an excellent investment for your first homestead, but similar to many other farming methods and projects, it is critically important that you do as much research on beekeeping as you can. Bees are fragile and need to be cared for by a farmer that knows how to do it.

COMPOSTING

Along the same view of living a self-sustainable life with a focus on healthy practices, composting is another great option for your homestead. Composting is the act of recycling kitchen scraps and other organic materials into a bin. The composting bin should be placed outside of your house and away from direct sunlight. The contents of the bin can be left to mulch over the course of a couple weeks, at which point you can use the mulch as fertilizer for your crops.

Composting has a variety of benefits: not only can you use the composted materials as organic fertilizer for your farm, but you also significantly cut down your own waste production that add to landfills. The fertilizer that you can get from composting is often rich in nutrients that your crops will crave, and you can create luscious gardens out of the composted materials.

In order to begin composting, you will need a shaded area that is away from your home. On a larger property, you want to put your compost in an accessible place that isn't so far from your home that it is a chore to get to. To build a compost bin from scratch, there are many different design options that you can choose from. You can make a compost bin out of a large plastic bin, safe pallet wood, or pieces of wood that have gathered around your farm from other projects. Regardless of the design, it is important that your compost bin has ventilation and a solid latch to avoid any scavengers looking for food. It should also be accessible enough to you that you can add content to the compost bin without hassle. Before you can start regularly adding to your compost bin, you will want to *cold compost*, which is the process of adding leaves, small branches and twigs, newspaper, and kitchen scraps to your compost pile. Be sure to never add any meat or animal products to your compost as that can compromise the integrity and health of your compost pile. Allow all of these materials to break down over the course of a couple of weeks before you begin regularly adding to your compost pile. Cold composting sets the groundwork for a healthy compost bin.

Another aspect to consider when you start composting are the types of materials that you are adding to the bin. There are *brown* materials and *green* materials that will create catalysts for different chemical reactions to occur. Brown materials are leaves, newspaper, or dead grass. The brown materials will supply carbon to your compost bin. Meanwhile, green materials are kitchen scraps, coffee, or fresh grass. The green materials will add nitrogen to your compost bin. Both nitrogen and carbon are essential for a healthy compost bin and generally you will want to add more carbon suppliers or brown material to the compost bin over nitrogen suppliers. The benefits of consciously considering what you are putting in your compost bin will pay off down the line as you are able to create carbon- and nitrogen-rich fertilizer to add to your gardens.

IDEAL PLANT ENVIRONMENTS

Greenhouses

Greenhouses are undoubtedly one of the best environments for your plants to thrive if you are interested in early propagation or growing plants that aren't native to your area. When you are considering building and maintaining a greenhouse on your property, it is important that your greenhouse has adjustable heat, plenty of sunlight, humidity and ventilation control, and as much automation as possible.

There are many different styles of greenhouses that can be built to accommodate exactly what you hope to grow on your farm. There are five aspects to building and maintaining a greenhouse that are essential for your plants' health. The first is the temperature of the greenhouse. As plants are left in a closed space, they will take in CO_2 and release oxygen, which can create a warmer environment if left unattended. There are many ways to control the temperature in your greenhouse through technology, and living in the Northeast, this is definitely an option worth thinking about. If you want to grow crops that would typically struggle to grow in Northeast temperatures, a greenhouse is a perfect solution. Plants like tomatoes, cucumbers, hot peppers, and sweet peas all need a little extra warmth to thrive. As a general rule, you will want the greenhouse on your farm to run north to south so that it gets the most sun that it can during the day. The shelves and crops on the east side of the greenhouse should be lower to the ground and the shelves on the west side should be higher up. This allows the plants to constantly have access to the warmth that they need from the sun.

When considering how much sun your plants want, it may be the case that you have plants in your greenhouse that don't require direct sun for long periods of the day. Place these plants either closer to the ground so that there is more chance that they will  be shaded or utilize shade covers. I also recommend that if you are building your own greenhouse, you invest in UV-filtering polyethylene plastic. This plastic will filter out any harmful rays and ensure healthier plants all around. As a result of the sunlight and photosynthesis that is occurring in the greenhouse, your greenhouse will become very humid. Humid greenhouses are the ideal environment for many crops that thrive in warm or tropical climates. However, if your greenhouse remains too humid for too long there is a chance that harmful mold or pests can grow. It is important to balance the humidity of the greenhouse with proper ventilation so that you reduce the risk of mold growth. Many of the new construction designs for greenhouses will call for vents to be built directly inside of the greenhouse so that there is constantly proper ventilation. Having solid ventilation is key to fostering the ideal environment for your plants. In the Northeast, there is a chance that the summer months will mean more humidity and it may be worth investing in fans or vents. However, if you are on a budget, adding a couple of hatches into your greenhouse to promote natural ventilation from the wind outside can also be a great option.

The last aspect to building a greenhouse on your property is automation. With the advancement in farming technologies surrounding greenhouses, there are many ways to automate the climate controls, light, and ventilation. To purchase a more automated greenhouse can be quite expensive, but if you are new to farming and have room in your budget for one, I suggest that you go for it. The automations available to you can ensure that you create a thriving environment for your plants to grow with little risk that they won't make it to harvest.

Water and Sunshine

If you are growing in a traditional garden or making use of a greenhouse, it is important to plan out how your plants will be watered. Plants need water in order to grow and for the vast majority of plants, they will take up water through their roots systems. Each plant that you grow will have its own preferences for how often it is watered and the watering cycle will also be affected by the climate. Luckily, in the Northeast, there aren't long periods of drought that you will have to worry about. There will be periods in the summer months when there are heat waves that could jeopardize your plants' health, but with a little extra water and some shade they will make it. When it comes to the daily chore of watering, you can either choose to water by hand using a watering can or hose, which is great for a smaller garden, or you can choose to water your gardens with an irrigation system. For traditional gardens there are underground irrigation systems or sprinkler systems that will work great to automate the watering process. For underground irrigation systems, you will need to invest in some pipes and have a water source that is elevated from where your gardens are. A great practice when you have a water source that is at a higher elevation than your gardens is to allow gravity to do the work for you and feed water through an underground pipe system that will water your crops. For sprinklers, the main hurdle is setting up the technology for them. Supplying water to the sprinklers can come from established water sources on your property, a well, or the county water source that you use to get water in your home. Whichever case works best for you, be sure to plan how you will water your crops and make sure that you are prioritizing that chore when you start on your farm.

Another way to ensure that you create the ideal environments for your plants is to understand the amount of sunlight that they will need. Virtually every plant will need sun in order to grow. During the observation phase, be sure to get a sense of where the sunniest areas are on your property, as well as the ones that get some shade. Each crop will have a preference for how much sunlight that it gets during the day. For traditional gardens in raised beds, find areas that get slightly shaded during the day for the crops that need less than 6 hours of sunlight per day. Similarly, find areas that have access to a lot of sun for the crops that need more than 6 hours of sunlight. In addition to the sunlight that your crops will need, consider your greenhouse as well. If you have a greenhouse on your property, it is important there will be no structures that cause shade on the greenhouse. You can absolutely grow crops in the greenhouse that don't require more than 6 hours of sunlight, but you will need to invest in shade protection if you are looking to do this. When I first built my gardens and greenhouse, I bought a couple of mess shades from Home Depot that were easy to move around my farm. This was a cheap investment that made all of the difference on my property. I was able to move around the shade when I did my daily walks around the farm and as a result, during my first year of growing, I saw incredible results.

Companion Planting

Companion planting is the process of planting different crops near each other because they provide symbiotic relationships to one another. This can be through the way that one crop shades another or how the growing cycles can prevent pests from moving from one crop to the other. In either case, companion planting is a great option when you are first starting your gardens because it provides more access to different crops as well as a healthier garden.

There are endless benefits to companion planting. Some of the benefits include that you save space in your garden, add additional shelter to fragile plants, attract beneficial insects, help maintain nutrient-rich soil, reduce the risks of plant diseases and pest intervention, and cut down on the amount of time you spend weeding.

One of the largest benefits of companion planting is the way that it saves space in your gardens. If you are using the raised-beds technique, you will want to maximize the space that you have in your gardens at all costs. By companion planting you can utilize all of the space in your garden and your crops will thrive as a result. Based on the types of plants that you want to grow using the companion planting method, the plants can provide protection and shade to others. For example, taller plants like tomatoes and beans can provide protection to shorter plants like cabbage and lettuce. Corn stalks can act as a trellis for viney plants. Thus, these companion planting methods can also help you to avoid having to add extra structures into your garden to support smaller crops.

Companion planting can provide great insect control in your gardens. By utilizing specific companion planting methods, you can repel harmful insects and attract beneficial ones. For flying pests that eat at your plants, they will get easily confused by the smell of garlic and onion growing in the garden. Meanwhile, planting Cosmos, black-eyed Susans, and other native flowers can attract ladybugs and other helpful insects that will prey on the harmful insects. Similarly, if you plant diverse native flowers that have varied blooming periods, you will attract bees and butterflies, which are essential pollinators for your garden. For more advanced farmers, you can utilize the trap cropping method, where you plant a perimeter of crops around your garden that attract harmful insects. They will fall for the trap that you have set and not touch the crops that you want to see thrive. Planting collards and Chinese mustard around the perimeter of your yard will attract moths and beetles, while protecting cabbage, spinach, and chard growing in your garden.

Companion planting with nitrogen-efficient crops is a great way to improve your soil quality and allow the plants to share their nutrients. I mentioned earlier that a great way to increase the quality of the soil in your raised beds is to plant cover crops, like ryegrass and clover. This is also a beneficial practice when companion planting because these nitrogen-efficient crops will share their nitrogen with the surrounding crops. There are few crops that can process nitrogen from the air, but by adding a few of these crops into your garden, the soil and other plants will be healthier. Some nitrogen-efficient crops to add to your garden are peas, beans, and any other plant from the legume family. In addition to nutrient sharing, it is also important to rotate your crops between growing seasons. By rotating the nitrogen-rich crops, you can ensure that all of the soil in your garden is nitrogen rich. You can even plant legumes at the end of the season and till them into your soil at the beginning of the spring season for an added nitrogen boost and green compost.

When you are utilizing companion-planting methods, you will be avoiding monocultures, which are gardens that only grow one type or variety of a plant. These types of gardens are incredibly susceptible to disease and harmful insects. Most gardeners will tell you to avoid monocultures as much as possible. It would be such a headache to buy a ton of seeds for one specific crop that you want to grow, only to see them all be ravaged by insects or fall victim to a disease. By utilizing companion planting, most diseases don't have the ability to fester because of the variety of crops in one area. In addition, weeds will grow in your garden if there is too much space between your crops. For the first growing season, an easy way to avoid excessive weeds is to plant your companion crops close together. You can also try intercropping or sequential cropping. Intercropping calls for planting two crops close together at the same time. This will allow the companion crops to grow at a relatively well-paced rate and avoid competition from weeds. Sequential cropping calls for planting crops sequentially so that there is never a time where there isn't a crop being established. Again, this will cut down on the competition from weeds and decrease the time that you will spend removing weeds from your garden.

There is a resource on *The Old Farmer's Almanac* website that allows you to plot your gardens using the companion-planting method before you even get started on your property. I highly recommend utilizing this tool to make planting easier down the line. Some examples of companion plants that you may want to incorporate into your garden are:

- Plant marigolds, cosmos, garlic, and onions throughout your gardens to encourage helpful insects to find homes in your garden. Note to keep the garlic and onions away from any beans.
- Basil and tomatoes can be planted together.
- Borage can be planted near tomatoes, strawberries, and squash.
- Basil is a great companion crop for almost every other crop that you can grow in the Northeast.

Some general tips when you start companion planting are to plant short, shade-loving plants beneath taller plants. Be sure to keep tall sun-loving plants on the north end of your garden and short shade-loving plants on the south end. Planting herbs throughout your garden can decrease the number of harmful insects that are attracted to your crops. Plant mint and basil throughout the garden, but beware that mint grows aggressively and will need to be monitored.

Consider the ideal conditions for every crop. Just because two crops are companions doesn't mean that they need the exact same care. Consider the sun, water, and wind conditions that the individual plants need in order to thrive. Some of these aspects will be negated as a result of companion planting, but you will still need to regularly tend to your garden in order to make the most of a companion-planting method. Also think about the maturation rates for each crop so that you can maximize on space. Planting your crops sequentially based on how long they take to mature can improve the space in your garden and ensure that you have consistent harvests.

MAXIMIZING YOUR YIELD

Before you start working on the farm, there are some steps that you can take to prepare for the season that will maximize your yields. Before the season starts, establish dedicated beds, collect rainwater, plan your beds and choose your crops, and extend the growing season. During the growing season, you will want to nourish the soil, feed your plants what they crave, provide shade to your crops, and take preventative pest-control measures. While these steps may sound like a lot of things to consider, they will start to naturally flow as you get a feel for the growing season.

Establishing dedicated beds for your gardens can be accomplished by setting up your raised beds. I am a personal fan of raised beds because they are versatile and can work on almost any property, so long as you have a sunny spot on which to garden. To take it a step further, you can maximize your yields by automating your raised bed watering systems. There are many raised bed designs that call for irrigation systems and proper drainage that can save you a lot of time that you would otherwise spend watering. Before the growing season starts, you will also want to spend some time collecting rainwater. Rainwater is an incredibly healthy option for your plants, as it will always have the right pH for your crops and is softer than treated water. Rain collection bins are a relatively inexpensive investment that will aid in the growing season. During the off season, set up your rain collection bins so that you have plenty of water stored before the start of the growing season.

Planning your garden beds before the start of the season will also help to maximize your yields. If you have a dedicated plan and you know exactly what you are going to plant where, you will be ultimately more successful during the growing season. I suggest doing as much research as you can about the crops that you want to plant and their preferred conditions, so that you are ready for any obstacle. Use the strategies that I laid out in the companion planting section to do this more efficiently. In Chapters 7, 8, 9, and 10 I will describe the best crops to grow during the three growing seasons in the Northeast, but as a general rule you will want to prioritize growing crops that are native and thrive in your area. Growing crops that are not native to your area will mean that they will have a harder time reaching harvest. For crops that prefer more tropical climates than you are in, use a greenhouse rather than an outdoor garden bed.

Another step to take to maximize your yields before the growing season is to discover when the first and last frost of the year will be. You can plan to extend the growing season each year by putting in plant protections so that you get more harvests during the season. One strategy is to propagate your crops in your greenhouse a couple of weeks before the last frost of the season. Doing this will mean that your crops are ready to be transported outdoors right at the start of the season. You can also invest in cold frames, cloches, and row covers to protect your crops if you are transporting them into your garden when it is still a little chilly outside.

Once the growing season has started you will want to consider your soil and plant nourishment in order to maximize your yield. In the following chapter I will take a deeper dive into maintaining your soil so that you have healthy plants. The general rules for nitrogen-rich soil on your farm will be to use the lasagna compost layering method in your raised beds. Finding every way to ensure that your soil is nitrogen-rich will lead to maximized yields and plenty of harvests. In addition, you can add fertilizer concentrates and natural teas to your crops during the growing season to boost their growing cycles. A great practice, and one that I have utilized in the past, is to grow comfrey near your compost bin. Comfrey is a flowering plant from the borage family that is great to use in fertilizing teas for your crops. The comfrey clippings can also be added to your compost to speed up decomposition, which is great if you are looking to add compost to your gardening beds between seasons.

The last two steps in maximizing your yields are to add shade protection to your gardens and take preventative measures to avoid pests. There are many plants that will thrive in shaded areas and utilizing the shaded areas on your farm can increase the harvests that you reap. Leafy greens and cold-hardy berries will thrive in shaded areas on your farm. I have previously discussed some pest-prevention strategies in your garden. In addition to the strategies, another great tactic to take when trying to prevent pests is to keep the area around your garden clutter-free. Pests will make homes in overturned pots or other small containers and feed on your crops. Maximizing your yields requires an attention to detail for the conditions that your crops will thrive in, and making preemptive efforts will ensure that you are using your space well and providing your garden with adequate support. Following these simple steps will lead to a bountiful garden each and every season.

5
ESSENTIAL SOIL

The soil in your garden will be the backbone of the development and health of your plants. It is incredibly important that you understand the soil in your yard and ways to improve the quality of the soil. The four functions of the soil in your garden are to provide a habitat for organisms, provide the foundation for the projects on your farm, recycle raw materials, and be the catalyst for plant growth.

Soil provides water, oxygen, anchorage, temperature modification, and nutrients to your plants. The water added to your soil hydrates the root systems of nearby plants and can cool the plants as the water evaporates from the leaves. This is particularly important if you are growing seasonal crops that require warmer temperatures than are available in the Northeast. Water also carries essential nutrients from the soil into the plants. The oxygen in your soil allows the roots to break down sugars and release energy as part of the photosynthesis cycle. Soil also allows your plants to anchor themselves to the earth. Without soil, the roots system would have nothing to hold on to to support the plant's growth. Soil can also modify the temperature of the roots. The soil can both insulate during cold seasons and provide cooling during the warmer seasons. When you add green compost and other natural fertilizers to your soil, the soil acts as a conductor for those nutrients into the plant's root system. Needless to say, having healthy soil that promotes your plant's growth is crucial to a sustainable garden.

Now that you know why soil is so important, how do you go about finding if your soil is viable and healthy? For the most part, the soil on your property will probably require some intervention when you first get there. Soil that is excessively compacted from foot traffic or vehicles often loses its gardening viability and will need some help. To perform the initial test on your soil, you are going to want to consider the texture, structure, pore space, organic matter, and horticultural capacity. That may seem like a lot but the best way to start a successful garden is with healthy soil

The texture of your soil relates to the amount of sand, silt, and clay in the soil. As a general rule, you want your soil to be 40% sand, 40% silt, and 20% clay. This is hard to determine with the naked eye, but by feeling the soil on your property, you can get a sense of the texture and where to add to your soil to improve it. Next, you want to consider the structure of your soil. It is easy to spot sand in the soil because of its color, but spotting clay and silt is a little tricker. As a general rule, clay and silt stick together to form aggregates. The amount of aggregates in your soil determines the structure of your soil. Higher quality topsoil or loam (the preferred mixture of sand, silt, and clay) is typically granular with few aggregates. If you have good soil structure the soil will have more pore space and promote healthy root penetration. Pore space is the amount of space between the aggregates and other soil components that would allow roots to take hold. As water enters the soil, it creates small pathways that then evaporate as temperatures elevate. These pathways are the perfect homes for roots. Good soil has a combination of large and small porches that provide a balance between the air and water that plants will need during the growing cycle.

The next aspect to consider when you are surveying your soil is the organic matter. Organic matter are the living and organic organisms that you can find in your soil. These could be anything from worms to the leaves that decompose on top of your soil. Having good organic matter can promote water retention and add clay or silt into your soil if it is missing. The horticultural capacity of your soil measures the viability that the soil has to promote healthy plant growth. Good horticultural soil contains 50% soil material, with 5% of that being organic matter and 50% pore space (Berg Stack, 2017). A great way to improve the horticultural capacity of your soil is to irrigate the soil and allow it to drain. If the soil is dry the day after irrigation, it is likely that your soil is dominated by sand. If the soil is wet, there is too much clay in your soil and you need to introduce more organic material to your soil. The best soil ratio for growing vegetables on your farm is a 50:50 ratio between compost and topsoil or loam. The best soil for flowers depends on how you are planting your flowers and the type of flowers you are growing. Flower bulbs thrive in sandy loam soil, and soil mixtures of compost, peat, and topsoil are great for flower gardens from seeds.

The chemical properties of your soil will also come into play when you are observing the viability of the soil on your property. Nitrogen and pH levels are incredibly important to consider when you first start farming. Nitrogen-rich soil allows your plants to thrive as they absorb the nitrogen, which improves their growth cycles. You can add nitrogen to your soil through compost and mulching. The pH levels of your soil are also vitally important because each crop that you plant will have different pH preferences in order to thrive. The pH levels in your soil indicate how acidic or alkaline the soil is. Some plants prefer acidic soil, some prefer alkaline soil, and others prefer base soils. Testing your soil is a great way to get a gauge on how viable your soil will be during the growing season. This process should happen right when you get to your property and before you begin planting. You can test your soil with a pH test that can be purchased at hardware stores or you can mail a sample of your soil to a soil-testing lab. The pH soil testing kits are valuable because they can tell you the pH levels in the soil and there are ways to adjust them. Sending your soil to a soil-testing lab is a great way to get comprehensive information about the pH, texture, nutrients, and other factors in your soil, as well as recommendations for how to treat your soil. The University of Minnesota has a highly esteemed soil testing lab that tests samples from across the country, and their testing prices that start at $17.

Some natural ways that you can improve your soil, maybe while you are waiting for your soil test results, are to till, mulch, and manage the organic matter levels in the soil. You can also naturally alter the pH levels of your soil. Tilling your soil will loosen the soil and add aeration and pores. This is great because it allows more root systems to become established and provides space for you to add other soil components. Mulching your soil is the process of adding organic composted materials, which introduces more nitrogen and organic matter. Mulch also helps to retain warmer temperatures and moisture. If you add mulch to your soil you can also decrease weed growth and harmful insect presence. Introducing and managing the organic matter levels can additionally improve the soil quality. Adding leaves so that they can decompose will introduce new organic matter into the soil. Alternatively, you could start a worm farm so that there are plenty of earthworms paving new root pathways in your soil. The more you manage the organic matter, the more fertile and long-lasting your soil viability will be.

Improving your soil pH through natural means will look very similar to the previously listed ideas for how to improve your soil. Adding organic matter, maximizing the drainage and air exposure that your soil gets, keeping the soil covered, avoiding chemical interventions, and rotating crops will all lead to more sustainable pH levels. Adding organic matter will improve the pH because of the chemical interactions that organic matter introduces. Worms can be a great way to change the pH levels of your soil as they add new matter that will alter the pH to be more basic. Worms and other organic matter can also create more air and water exposure and improve the drainage that your soil has. This is great if you are looking to get more alkaline pH levels. Keeping your soil covered with leaves and mulch can also improve the pH because the natural erosion that soil will encounter when left exposed to the elements will alter the pH. Covering the soil will give you more control over the soil pH and introduce nitrogen-richness.

I don't know about you, but when I started the self-sustaining homestead journey, I was determined to find natural solutions to farming projects. Adding chemical pesticides and other soil treatments seemed to go against this goal. Not only do I have no idea what the chemical interactions will do to my soil, but I was also nervous that all of the hard work that I was doing to improve the soil pH would be undone. Stay away from chemical pesticides and other treatments because they can in fact alter the soil pH and damage your plants. There are different remedies to intercept harmful insects that don't require chemicals. You also don't want to indiscriminately remove all insects from your garden. There are many helpful insects that can promote healthy plant growth in your garden and fertilize different areas.

The last way to improve your soil pH is by rotating your crops between growing seasons. If you have perennial crops planted in one area, it is fine to let them stay in that area, but for the crops that you transported inside, find a new home for them the following spring.

Rotating your crops from garden bed to garden bed will introduce new soil conditions and lead to an overall healthier soil across your garden.

The role of fertilizer and adding your compost to your soil is another way that you can improve the soil. Composting can increase your self-reliance and establish a system on your farm that can be beneficial to your crops. However, I would be remiss if I didn't outline the difference between *mineral* and *organic* fertilizers. So far, I have been promoting the idea of organic fertilizers. Organic fertilizers consist of composted materials that you collect on your farm. The benefits of composting are that the compost can add much needed nutrients to your soil and promote self-sustainable practices. However, composting takes a while to decompose and you need to be very conscious of what you are putting in the compost. The goal of composting to add to your soil is that you are providing the soil with the correct balance of nutrients that it needs. There are 17 different nutrients that plants need to thrive in a garden; if you are not considering what you are putting in your compost, it is possible that you will miss some of those key nutrients.

On the other hand, you can consider mineral fertilizers. Typically, farmers utilize mineral fertilizers when they have extensive farms that they simply can't supply with compost. Mineral fertilizers add all of the necessary nutrients that plants need and can be purchased. The benefits of mineral fertilizers is their convenience and balance. You won't have to consider the nutrients in mineral fertilizers because they are all there. Whichever you choose is a matter of preference. For smaller gardens, conscious composting is definitely the way to go and it will save you money. For larger homesteading operations, it may be worth taking a look at getting some mineral fertilizers.

Regardless of the fertilizing method that you choose, it is also important to note that whatever you put in your fertilizer will come back to you through consumption. If you go the natural fertilizer route, keep in mind what types of things you are adding to your compost pile. Those nutrients will be present in the crops that you harvest. If you go the mineral fertilizer route, be sure to research the type of mineral fertilizer and the minerals that you are putting into your soil. These minerals and the nutrients that they provide will also show up in your food.

6
INCORPORATING PERMACULTURE

*P*ermaculture stands for permanent culture or permanent agriculture. The permaculture design method is one that prioritizes how your farm will work as one cohesive unit with permanent structures that support your agriculture. One of the founders of the permaculture design strategy said that permaculture is the integrated design system that's modeled on nature (April, 2016). A perfect permaculture design would mean that the systems you've set up around your property perfectly manage the other systems with limited interference from things that exist outside of nature. At its core, permaculture is a system that promotes self-reliance and sustainability.

Incorporating permaculture into your gardens calls for four types of gardening: companion planting, raised beds or vertical gardening, edible gardening, and keyhole gardening. Companion planting and raised beds, as already discussed, are my personal preference and systems that have worked exceptionally well for myself and others. In addition to those two types of gardening, there is also an option to vertical garden. Vertical gardening is typically used in smaller spaces to conserve the amount of square feet needed to build and maintain a garden. Permaculture gardening also calls for edible gardening. Edible gardens are often called 'kitchen gardens' or 'survival gardens.' This is the practice of gardening for self-sustainability. You eat and serve what you harvest from your gardens in an effort to be reliable and sustainable. Keyhole gardening, much like raised beds or vertical gardening, is a different style of gardening that calls for horseshoe-shaped gardens. This style of gardening promotes companion planting and helps to cultivate both perennial and annual plants. All of these gardening techniques can be combined on your property or you can modify the techniques so that they adjust to the space that you have available on your farm.

ETHICS AND PRINCIPLES OF PERMACULTURE DESIGN

When you are implementing permaculture design into your farm, there are three ethics that permaculture design is based on. Upholding these three ethics will inevitably lead you toward a more productive farm and a cultivated community to enjoy it. The first ethic is care for the Earth. Caring for the Earth calls for the careful consideration of the land that you are interacting with, as well as care for all living and nonliving things that inhabit the Earth. It can also be called conscious consumerism. Permaculture design calls for taking care of the Earth so that it will thrive under natural circumstances and consuming foods and products that are also made with the care of the Earth in mind. The second ethic is caring for people. Caring for people calls for the maintenance of all of the basic needs that people have to be met. Food, shelter, water, education, employment, and socialization are all aspects of caring for people that should simply be given without the promotion of status or wealth. While this may seem like a far-fetched idea that is rooted in idealism, the importance of caring for people when you are living on a farm can start small. Ensuring that all of the basic needs for you and your family are met is adhering to the caring for people ethic of permaculture design. Hopefully, once you have established the ethic for yourself and your family, you can broaden your scope to other people in your community. The third and final ethic of permaculture design is fair shares. This ethic combines the ideologies of the first two. It is pointless to engage in caring for the Earth and caring for people if there is not an expectation that everyone is entitled to the same level of care. Fair shares call for everyone having access to their basic needs and giving back to the Earth in a sustainable way.

Beyond the three ethics that underpin the ideas of permaculture design, the founders of the design system also create the 12 principles of permaculture design. The first principle of permaculture design is to observe and interact with the Earth and others. The more we observe the world around us, the more we will be able to consciously interact with it. This is also a great way to learn from your environment about its needs. You may be sitting out in your garden and observing the slope in your lawn. You can see how the organic shapes of the land inform the best way to grow crops in those areas.

The second principle is to catch and store energy. Ultimately, permaculture design is geared toward off-the-grid living. This doesn't necessarily mean living in isolation, but rather living as self-reliantly as possible. Collecting energy from the wind or sun is a great way to begin this process. You can also collect other renewable resources to generate energy on your property, like rainwater or the energy from a rushing river.

The third principle is to obtain a yield. Planting and cultivating crops in an effort to be self-sustainable is one of the central tenets to permaculture design. However, this principle has a hidden agenda. The more time that you spend outside, the happier and at peace you will feel with your environment.

The fourth principle is to apply self-regulation and feedback on your homestead. In a world that is facing drastic consequences as a result of climate change, it is important to center sustainable changes into your permaculture design. The goal of the fourth principle is to reduce your negative impacts on the Earth and note where you can do better.

The fifth principle is to use and value renewable resources. Again, this principle is calling for a more sustainable lifestyle. Switch away from non-renewable resources and prioritize renewable options. We already have all of the skills to use renewable resources in our day-to-day lives but because of convenience, we have overlooked more sustainable options. It is time to go back to the renewable options if we want to prolong the life of the planet.

The sixth principle is to produce no waste. I mentioned earlier that permaculture design foundationally calls for using everything on your farm for multiple purposes. Composting and recycling materials that you collect on your farm will make it so that you can adhere to the sixth principle with ease.

The seventh principle of permaculture design is to design from patterns to details. I am a very detail-oriented person and when I first discovered homesteading, I was determined to create multiple options and ways of designing a farm. I spent weeks thinking about all of the materials I would need to buy, ways that I could use the land around me to support different projects, and the impacts that those projects would have on the Earth. I soon learned that actually being on the farm made all the difference. Some days are harder than others and that can lead to convenience being more tempting than sustainability. However, I learned that prioritizing designing from the broad ideas down to little details made the process much easier. It is easier to plan for all of the little things when you take your time and know exactly what you are working on and how it will impact the land.

The eighth principle is to integrate and avoid segregation. The best example of segregation in your garden is planting a monoculture. To adhere to permaculture design, you want to be enriching the earth and giving back. A monoculture limits your ability to do this and comes with a high failure rate. Instead of planting a monoculture, plant a polyculture: a garden that has many different crops growing that support one another and the ecosystem around them. This can be applied to many other areas of homesteading as well. Get invested with the community around you and don't rely on isolation.

The ninth principle is to practice small and slow solutions. By going slow and working on pieces of different projects on your farm, you will be able to remedy issues in a way that doesn't disrupt the ecosystem that you are cultivating. Going fast and large with your projects can mean causing undue chaos on areas of your farm and potentially risk the integrity of the other systems you have created. This principle also applies to starting new projects. Diving head first into new projects can leave space for mistakes that may cause you or your farm harm. Take it slow and ask a lot of questions!

The tenth principle is to use and value diversity. I have said this before, but growing a monoculture garden is bound to lead to issues. With a polyculture garden, the diversity of produce as well as the overall impact on your ecosystem is far more beneficial. The nature on your farm is bound to thrive if you value the diversity of your area and make all of the aspects of your farm work in tandem.

The second to last principle is to use edges and value the marginal. Thinking creatively and problem solving on your farm to fit your specific needs will demonstrate much higher yields for your farm than taking routes that are well established. Of course there are well-established means for developing a farm, but you will need to fit them to your situation. Discover the marginal ways that you can problem solve or integrate new systems into your farm that may be less well established, or take a creative spin on an established farming technique.

The last principle for permaculture design is to creatively use and respond to change. This principle ties together a lot of the ideas that permaculture design espouses. Taking a holistic approach to your farm will allow you to observe and intervene in different areas at the right time instead of forcefully implementing new systems. You want to be creatively working with the organic ecosystem around you.

Permaculture Zones

Within permaculture design, when you are ready to start planning the layout of your farm, there are five zones to consider. The permaculture zones are general guidelines for the layout of your farm so that each zone is accessible and functional within your ecosystem. Zone 0 is your house. This zone is all of the systems that you set up inside of your house to benefit your experience on the farm. Whatever you want to have in your home to make you comfortable and lead to a more sustainable life will be part of zone 0. The next is zone 1. Everything in zone 1 is immediately outside of your house. The elements in zone 1 are things that need daily attention. Your zone 1 could include a kitchen garden, an area to enjoy lunch outside, or a small kitchen coop. The goal of zone 1 is for it to be immediately accessible to you once you step out of our house. The systems in zone 1 should be those that require regular attention and maintenance. You wouldn't want to put your chicken coop 10 minutes away from your front door if you have to go there every day.

Zone 2 is the farming zone. This zone will also require daily attention but there should be an emphasis on a well-integrated system. Your larger gardens and crops should be growing in zone 2, with an irrigation system and access to fertilizer and compost. Zone 2 can also be an area where animals are housed. Chickens, rabbits, ducks, and other animals are great to place in zone 2, as you will regularly visit them and set up systems for them that can be maintained a couple times a week.

Zone 3 is reserved for larger animals and seasonal crops. Larger animals will do great in zone 3 because there is more space for them to selectively graze and fertilize seasonal crops with their droppings. Having a large annual crop garden in zone 3 is also a great option because they don't need consistent care. You will need to have an integrated system for irrigation and maintenance as you may not be visiting it regularly.

Zone 4 is the home orchard, forest, and foraging zone. If you are looking to start an orchard, zone 4 is a great place to put it. Orchards do not require daily maintenance and can provide some snacks for your grazing animals. Zone 4 is also great as a forest for collecting wood or setting up a coppicing operation.

The last zone is zone 5, your wildlife zone. This zone should remain relatively untouched. This is a great place to observe nature and see how the ecosystem around your farm interacts.

The zones are a guideline to create a well-integrated farm that works on a feedback loop. You will want everything on your farm to serve multiple purposes, and by following the permaculture zones, you can accomplish this much more easily. It is important to note that many properties are not large enough to reach zones 4 and 5. That is perfectly acceptable. You don't have to have every zone on your farm for it to be successful. The goal is to use what you have and work with the nature around you.

Benefits and Drawbacks

One of the benefits to permaculture gardening is that nothing is wasted. Everything has multiple purposes and can be used to cultivate your garden. If I get an early frost on my Northeast farm and some of my plants are shocked and can no longer be harvested, I place the plants into my compost bin. Once the plants have decomposed, I use that compost as additional nutrients in the soil for the following growing season. In addition to the benefits of not wasting anything on your farm, permaculture farming also improves that quality of your gardens. I have discussed some of the methods for collecting water and promoting healthy insect intervention in your gardens. These principles all stem from permaculture design. You want to create a small ecosystem in your garden that is self-sustaining. By recycling rain water and planting flowers that will attract helpful insects, your garden will thrive under conditions that it would if it were growing in the wild.

Inversely, one of the drawbacks to permaculture design is working with what you have. If you buy a property that isn't conducive to a specific type of energy storage or farming technique, you need to roll with the punches. Finding creative solutions can be an exhaustive process where you spend days or weeks racking your brain for the right way to work with the nature around you. Creative solutions can also mean that you are developing new systems on your farm a lot slower than people who opt out of permaculture design. However, the ecological benefits from following permaculture design methods will mean that your systems will ultimately be healthier for yourself and the planet, with long-lasting results. People who opt out of permaculture often find themselves fighting against nature rather than working with it.

PERENNIAL AND ANNUAL PLANTS

Now that you understand the basics of permaculture design, it is time to consider the best plants to grow in your garden. There are two categories of plants that you can grow: perennial and annual. Perennial plants are those that are seeded in the spring and will regrow each year without much intervention. Annual plants are plants that are seeded in the spring but die at the end of the growing season. Annual plants need to be replanted each year. As a bonus, there are also biennial plants, which are seeded at the beginning of spring and will seed again the following spring, but they won't be ready to harvest until the end of the second growing season. Most biennials will drop seeds at the end of their growing cycle and in another two growing seasons, they will be ready for harvest again.

In general, it is common for most gardeners to use a combination of both perennial and annual plants in their gardens. In the Northeast, depending on how cold it gets in the winter, you can grow almost any annual plant in your garden or greenhouse with the added benefit that you don't have to worry about it surviving the winter. Perennial plants in the Northeast must be cold-hardy so that they can survive the winter months and regrow the following spring. The combination of perennial and annual plants that you chose to grow is a matter of preference. In the following chapters, I will discuss the best perennial and annual crops to grow in each season on a Northeast homestead.

7
SPRING

In the Northeast, there are specific steps that you will need to take on your farm to prepare and thrive during each season. From February to May, as the frost clears, it is time to take those initial steps to set up your farm for a productive year. The first step is to inspect your farm. If this is your first year on the farm, take note of any cold or ice damage that has been left on the farm from the winter. Be sure that all of your raised beds are clean and remove any frost that may be covering them. Next, take a look at the exterior of the existing structures on your farm. Do any walls or windows have cold damage, chips, or leaks? Be sure that all of your existing structures are repaired before you dive into preparing for the growing season. Once your farmhouse, barns, and other structures are patched up, move on to spring cleaning. Rake out any dead foliage and be sure that the area for your raised beds is cleared.

Having a clean farm to start the season will mean less chaos later in the season. On my first farm, I didn't patch up some of the walls on my house that bordered my kitchen garden. Before I knew it, I had some vines growing up and into my house. While I thought it was pretty, it became more of a nuisance than anything else. I patched up the holes in the summer and learned from the experience. You can avoid my mistake by taking stock of your property before the start of the growing season. The next couple of steps are to set you up best to start growing. Test your soil, adjust as needed, and prune any trees or shrubs that have overgrown. The importance of testing and adjusting your soil cannot be understated. As discussed in Chapter 5, starting the growing season with nitrogen-rich soil will maximize your yield and lead to less plant death throughout the year. You can also add the clippings from your trees and shrubs to your compost for nitrogen-rich compost that you can add to your raised beds in a later season.

Before you begin planting your seedlings into your raised beds, be sure to divide your perennial and annual seeds so that you can maximize your yield and not accidentally unearth a perennial plant. Now you can lay out your raised beds and place any stakes or trellises necessary for the specific plants that you are growing. Be sure to grab some extra protective resources for your outdoor garden in case of any cold nights, to avoid plant death at the start of the season if there's a late frost. The listed vegetables that you can grow in the spring are relatively cool-hardy crops that will wither on hot days or nights. To avoid having them suffer through hotter temperatures, plant these vegetables in the early spring so that you can harvest them before the summer. These same crops can also be planted in late summer and fall due to the cooler temperatures.

SPRING VEGETABLES

The ideal vegetables to grow on your farm during the first half of spring are peas, onions, radishes, spinach, lettuce, and turnips. Each of these crops has specific conditions that need to be met so that they can thrive. These vegetables can generally be planted in some Northeast farm regions during the week of Valentine's Day in February. However, for more northern regions in the Northeast, the first couple of weeks in February is when you want to start your seeds indoors. Of these vegetables, peas, radishes, spinach, lettuce, and turnips are annual and onions are perennial. When you are ready to get started in the spring, follow these steps to get the best yield from your vegetable garden.

All of the following plants can be directly planted outside in February in any Northeast region not still under snow. Plant peas 1 inch into the soil at least 2 inches from other crops. Peas will take at least 60 days to reach their first harvest. Water your peas once to twice a week. Peas are companion plants with green beans, cucumbers, lettuce, squash, and corn. Onions should be planted ½ inch into the soil at least 4 inches from surrounding crops. They will take anywhere from 60 to 90 days for their first harvest, depending on the variety. Water your onions once a week.

Onions are companion plants with radishes, carrots, and tomatoes. Plant radish seeds ¼ inch into the soil at least 3 inches from surrounding crops. Radishes will reach their first harvest in 35 days. They need to be watered once to twice a week. Companion plants to keep near radishes are green beans, cucumbers, lettuce, and squash.

Spinach seeds should be planted a ½ inch into the soil. Be sure that the spinach seeds are at least 4 inches from other crops. They will take 35 days to reach their first harvest and will need to be watered once to twice a week. Plant your spinach near radishes, peppers, and tomatoes. Plant lettuce ¼ inch into the soil at least a ½ foot from other crops. Lettuce will take 45 days to reach its first harvest. Water your lettuce once to twice a week. Companion plants to keep near lettuce are tomatoes, cucumbers, onions, garlic, and radishes. The last crop to plant in this round is turnips. Plant turnips ¼ inch into the soil with at least 6 inches away from other crops. Turnips will be ready to harvest 35 days after they are planted and only need to be watered once a week. Turnips are companion plants to broccoli, Brussels sprout, and cabbage.

Along with the previously listed plants, the following can also be planted in February but they should be started indoors. Of these plants, broccoli, cauliflower, and cabbage are annual and Brussels sprout are biennial plants. Plant broccoli and Brussels sprout ¼ inch into the soil at least a foot or two from other crops. They take around 50 days to reach their first harvest. Water your broccoli and Brussels sprout once to twice a week. Plant your broccoli and Brussels sprout near green beans and lettuce. Cabbage and cauliflower should also be planted ¼ inch into the soil and you can expect your first harvest at least 60 days after they are planted. Both crops need to be watered at least once a week. You can plant your broccoli, Brussels sprout, cauliflower, and cabbage seeds indoors from March 27th through April 10th, or you can plant the seedlings outdoors in the following 2 weeks. As a general rule, the leafy green crops can be in more shaded areas of your garden, while the other vegetables want more access to the sun.

The second round of spring vegetables consist of beets, carrots, Swiss chard, potatoes, and parsnips. These plants can generally be planted in the last 2 weeks of May or early April. All of the second-round crops only need to be watered once a week. Beet seeds should be planted ½ inch into the soil with at least 4 inches between them and surrounding crops. Beets will have their first harvest 45 days after planting. Carrots and parsnips should be planted ¼ inch into the soil with 3 inches between seeds.

Carrots will harvest 60 to 70 days after planting and parsnips will take at least 105 days to reach their first harvest. Plant your Swiss chard seeds ½ inch into the soil with at least 4 inches between the seeds and surrounding crops. Swiss chard will take at least 50 days to reach its first harvest. You can get a headstart with your Swiss chard seeds by propagating the seeds indoors between April 10th and 24th. The seedlings should be ready to be moved outdoors during the first week of May. Potatoes need to be planted 6 inches into the soil with at least a foot of space between the seeds and surrounding crops. Potatoes will take at least 70 days to reach their first harvest.

SPRING FRUITS AND HERBS

Due to the frosts in the Northeast, fruits and herbs are a little difficult to grow early in the season. Mint, nettles, thyme, oregano, and strawberries are all great options to plant later in the spring season. These plants will suffer if exposed to frost. Mint plants only need partial-sun exposure, so they are great for the more shaded areas of your garden. Mint should be planted toward the end of the spring season or the beginning of summer. Be sure to leave at least a foot of space between mint and other crops, as it is an aggressive grower. Water your mint plants at least once a week for the best results. Nettles, like many of the spring vegetables, should be started indoors about 6 weeks before the last frost. Nettle seeds should be planted ¼ inch into the soil and need to be watered at least once a week. Your first harvest will come 80 days after you transplant the nettles outdoors. Wear gloves when you are harvesting nettles as they have tiny hairs that can get embedded under your skin and cause allergic reactions.

Plant thyme at least 4 weeks into the spring season, as they cannot withstand any frosty nights. Thyme plants need to be planted at least a foot from other crops and they want to be in full-sun areas of your garden. Water your thyme plants at least once a week. Oregano can be planted alongside thyme with similar harvest times. Oregano is an aggressive grower, so be sure to prune the leaves after the first harvest to avoid it taking over areas of your garden. Strawberries are a great spring fruit to put into your raised beds. Strawberries need to have at least 18 inches between surrounding crops when planted. Water your strawberries every week for the best results. The best time to harvest your strawberries is early in the morning and place them directly in your refrigerator to preserve their freshness.

SPRING FLOWERS

There are many different flowers that you can grow in the Northeast, as many of them require planting bulbs at the end of fall that will blossom in the spring. Flowers are a great option for your gardens because they attract helpful insects and can bring a vibrancy that will leave you feeling serene each time you tend to your garden. Daffodils, grape hyacinth, and pansies are three great options when you are considering flowers for your Northeast homestead garden.

Daffodils are full-sun flowers that need access to plenty of sun and water during the growing season. If you are growing daffodil bulbs, you can plant the bulbs 2 to 4 weeks before the ground freezes in the fall. Daffodils won't spread too far in your garden and you can harvest daughter bulbs from your initial bulbs when you harvest the daffodils. As a general rule, if you are planting bulbs, they want to be planted two times deeper in the soil than they are tall. Daffodils need to be watered regularly or they may wither and die. You can only plant grape hyacinths as bulbs at the end of fall. These beautiful flowers are sure to bring vibrant life to your garden. Grape hyacinths are aggressive growers and should be kept at a decent distance from other crops so that they don't take over an area. Don't be scared if you see grape hyacinth leaves breach the soil during the fall; they are cold-hardy bulbs that will blossom in the spring. Once the hyacinths blossom, they don't need excessive watering and often do just fine from rainwater. Pansies are full-sun flowers that will grow all year if treated well. However, unlike daffodils and grape hyacinths, pansies are annual flowers that will need to be replanted each spring. I recommend for your first growing season to buy established pansies instead of trying to start from seeds, as they are very delicate and can easily die during propagation. When you plant your pansies, be sure to leave about 12 inches of space between the flowers and other crops. Pansies need to be regularly watered and maintained as they are susceptible to many harmful insects and mold. With a little extra care, your garden will be full of a rainbow of pansies.

Some other flowers to consider adding to your garden are English daisies, nemesia, twinspur, Icelandic poppies, monkey flower, fritillaries, snowdrops, and violets. All of these flowers fare well in the Northeast. English daisies are a great addition to your spring gardens because they bring added vibrancy to your raised beds and they will blossom at the start of spring. It is important to note that these daisies are aggressive growers and should be contained in a raised bed so that they are more manageable. They are also partial-sun biennial flowers that will not blossom the first year that you plant them but will come into full bloom the second year that they are in your raised beds. Place your English daisies in the shadier spots on your farm that need a little extra color. Nemesia is an annual flower that you can add to your garden that is very low maintenance. For beginners, buy your nemesia plants or bulbs from a nursery if you'd like to add them to your garden, as they usually don't do well if transported into a garden as seedlings. Plant your nemesia bulbs before the first frost in the fall and wait for them to bloom in late spring. They do well in cooler temperatures, so if your farm gets too hot in the summer, it is best to keep these flowers in a slightly shaded spot.

If you are looking to add flowers to your garden that will attract helpful insects that will pollinate your garden, consider planting twinspur. Twinspur are tall flowering plants that can act as a companion plant to those that are low to the ground and require more coverage. They will thrive in full-sun spots in your garden and need to be watered at least once a week. Twinspur can be planted directly into the soil of your raised beds at the end of spring, once temperatures have risen and there is no more risk of frost. Another flower to add to your gardens that will attract helpful insects are Icelandic poppies. These poppies thrive best in later spring and early summer. Icelandic poppies need to be planted in late fall in order to blossom in the spring. Be sure to keep these poppies in full-sun areas and water occasionally; rainwater will most likely do the trick. Try your best not to transplant these flowers to other areas in your garden once they begin to germinate, as they don't fare well during transport.

If you enjoy planting bulbs in the late fall to see a blossoming garden in the spring, add fritillaria flowers to your garden. Depending on the variety of fritillaria flowers that you plant, they can either thrive in shaded raised beds or full-sun raised beds with good soil drainage. The bulbs should be planted in fall, around September or October, for the best results. Fritillaria may attract unwanted beetles, slugs, and snails to your garden and it is best to remove the insects by hand if you encounter them to discourage their presence in your garden beds.

Many Northeast properties will have natural water structures running through the farm or areas that get damp after rainfall. If you have an area like that on your property, consider planting monkey flowers there. Monkey flowers are great Northeast flowers as they are cold-hardy and will attract native butterflies to your garden. These flowers want to be started indoors during the last few weeks of winter and the first weeks of spring. They can be planted at the start of spring and still thrive if there is frost. Once temperatures rise, they will begin to blossom if they are planted in partial-sun raised beds on your farm. A similar flower that will thrive in colder temperatures are snowdrops. Snowdrops are sold as bulbs and should be planted in the fall. These flowers will blossom very quickly and add life to your garden during the winter months. They are also pest-resistant. If you are creating a perimeter garden to ward off unwanted insects and critters, plant snowdrops to keep them away. Be sure to keep your snowdrops in well-draining soil in shaded areas. Snowdrops will become dormant in the spring but they will blossom again in the fall.

Finally, if you are looking for a low maintenance flower that can add color to your garden, violets are the way to go. Wild violets have a tendency to grow aggressively and spread quickly across your farm so be sure to place them in a raised bed to control their growth. Violets are very self-sustainable and will seed the ground without any intervention. They can be planted in virtually any condition and only need rainwater to thrive.

8
SUMMER

The spring season is always going to be one of the busiest seasons of the year because you will be preparing for a whole year of growing. In the summer months, from June to August in the Northeast, you have time to refine your gardens and add new crops into place as your spring plants come to harvest. After your first harvests from your spring crops, it is time to do some light maintenance of your farm. Go into your raised beds and remove any weeds or dead leaves. Add a new layer of mulch to the garden beds and put in new supports to any plants that may need the helping hand. Treat any harmful pest problems or diseases that may have arisen during the spring. Once you have taken care of the summer cleaning, you can move on to sequentially planning new summer crops.

If you haven't done so already, at the start of the summer is a great time to place aeration tubes in your raised beds. Aeration tubes will bring water directly into the root system. These are a great stop measure to ward against any droughts or heat waves during the summer months.

SUMMER VEGETABLES

At this point in the year you will start to see great yields from the spring growing season and you will feel driven to continue planting. Many of the spring vegetables can be replanted or you can continue to plant them into the summer. The best summer vegetables to add to your Northeast garden are cucumbers, peppers, pumpkins, summer and winter squash, tomatoes, and corn. These vegetables can be started indoors or after the last frost on your property. All of the summer vegetables are annual and will require replanting each season. Cucumbers need to be planted ½ inch into the soil and about 6 inches from other crops. Your first cucumber harvest will come at least 45 days after they are first planted. Cucumbers need to be watered every week. Peppers do best when they are planted ¼ inch into the soil and at least a foot from other crops. Peppers will come to harvest after 65 days from when they are first planted. Peppers don't require weekly watering and will do fine with rainwater and bi-weekly watering.

Pumpkin seeds can be planted in shallow ditches in your raised beds, about ¾ of an inch into the soil. Pumpkins need a lot of space and should have 3 to 4 feet between their seeds. After you plant your pumpkins, you can expect harvests after 85 days of growing. Pumpkins, like peppers, don't require constant watering. Summer and winter squash should be planted in the same way that pumpkins are. Winter squash require 4 feet between surrounding crops. Summer squash will be ready to harvest 45 days after planting and winter squash will be ready after 85 days. Both squashes require semi-regularly watering: once a week to every other week. Tomatoes also want to be planted ¼ inch into the soil with at least 2 feet between the tomato seeds and other crops. Tomatoes will be ready to harvest after 65 days if they are watered once a week. Corn is very susceptible to frost and will not grow if temperatures drop too low. In the summer, try sowing the corn every 2 weeks for 6 weeks to get the best yields. Be sure to keep the corn crops about 10 inches from one another. Plant your corn 1 inch deep in moist summer soil. Be careful with the corn roots as they are very fragile during the growing phase. Also take care of any weeds in the area as they can also disrupt the corn roots.

SUMMER FRUITS AND HERBS

The summer is a great time to get all of the delicious fruits and herbs into your raised beds and orchard. The best fruit to plant in the summer are apples, blueberries, cherries, melons, peaches, raspberries, cantaloupe, nectarines, pears, plums, and watermelon. You can also replant any herbs from the spring that were struggling or that you want more of in your kitchen, in addition to basil.

In general, fruit trees need a lot of sun and a lot of space. Plant your fruit tree saplings in the earliest weeks of the summer so they have plenty of time to root during the growing season. Be sure to leave a well around the base of the fruit tree so that the roots get well watered when you irrigate them. Stake your trees when they are still small to support their growth. Be sure to mulch your fruit trees often when they are growing. Trees soak up a lot of nutrients from the soil, as well as water, and will need a lot of attention during the early phases of growth. Great fruit trees to grow on a Northeast farm are apples, cherries, nectarines, peaches, pears, and plums. Each of these trees follows the previously mentioned guidelines, with some exceptions. Be sure to research the right fruit trees for your area, as prioritizing native fruit trees will ensure their success.

Berry bushes also want to be planted in the early part of the summer for the highest yield. Blueberries and raspberries are a great option for virtually every Northeast homestead. Be sure to test your soil pH before planting a berry bush, as they are very susceptible to the pH levels in the soil. If the pH isn't right, you might want to plant your berry bushes in raised beds so that you can have more control over the soil. Raspberry bushes will particularly thrive if they are planted near garlic and onions.

Melons, cantaloupe, and watermelons are also summer fruits that can be grown during the first few weeks of summer. Melons can actually be planted toward the end of spring but will fare just fine when planted in the summer. Be sure to give your melons plenty of space to spread out during their growing cycle. Melons, cantaloupes, and watermelons are full-sun plants that love moist, well-draining soil. Cantaloupe is not very cold-sensitive but watermelons and honeydew can wither if they are exposed to frosts. Be sure to plant your melons, cantaloupes, and watermelons at least 2 feet apart in raised beds that are at least 6 feet away from other beds. Wherever you choose to plant your melons, it is important to regularly add nutrients to their soil as the leaves of the melon plants will add extra sugars into the soil. To balance out this interaction, regularly add compost, mulch, and other organic fertilizers to the raised beds that are housing the melons. To ensure that your melons are getting the proper water that they need, add a soaker hose or drip system to your melons. They need constant moisture in order to thrive; however, stop watering the crops once they begin to ripen as the excess water will make the melons taste bitter. All three melon types mature at different rates but they will assuredly yield great harvests when treated well. As a general rule, your melons will be ready to harvest when the rind becomes soft and the melons produce a sweet smell in your garden. If you knock on the melon rind and hear a hollow sound, they are ready to be harvested.

SUMMER FLOWERS

The summer is also a great time to add more color to your garden. Zinnias, four o'clocks, marigolds, nasturtiums, cosmos, and sunflowers will be perfect additions to your raised beds. All of the summer flowers are annual and will not rebloom in the spring. Zinnias will attract butterflies to your garden, which are helpful insects to have around, especially if you are growing in raised beds. Butterflies will help pollinate the surrounding flowers and even the vegetables that have a flowering stage. There are three types of zinnias to choose from for your garden, all of which will attract butterflies: single-flowered, double-flowered, and semi double-flowered zinnias. The difference between the three types is purely aesthetic and indicates the amount of petal rows that will be visible at the center of the zinnia. Plant your zinnia seeds directly into your garden beds in a permanent location as they suffer if transported. Zinnias are full-sun flowers that should be grown during the warmest parts of the summer. Be sure to water your zinnias at least once a week. For some added beauty, consider growing four o'clocks, as they bloom at night and will add a gorgeous ambiance to your gardens. Four o'clocks can be planted as early as the last frost or later into the growing season. Be sure to plant them in a permanent location and water about once a week. Four o'clocks don't experience a lot of harmful pest intervention and can encourage helpful pollinators to reside in your garden. Another flower that will attract helpful insects are cosmos flowers. Cosmos seeds should be planted directly into the soil of your raised beds at the start of summer and after there is any chance of frost. It is a great practice to sow the cosmos seeds at least a foot apart, as they rapidly expand in an enclosed area. Cosmos flowers don't need special soil requirements and can be watered semi-occasionally for the best results.

Marigolds are a particularly easy flower to grow as they don't require a lot of maintenance. Rainwater is a perfectly acceptable source of water for marigolds and you can skip watering them during your farm chores. Marigold seeds should be planted directly into your raised beds at the end of spring and early summer. They require full-sun in order to thrive.

Marigolds can also act as companion plants to your vegetables because they can dissuade harmful insects from targeting your vegetables. There are three types of marigold seeds that you can buy from your local nursery: tagetes erecta, tagetes patula, and tagetes tenuifolia. Each type of marigold relates to their height and flower head size. Depending on how you want to utilize the marigolds in your garden, consider their size and structure so that you can make the most of the flower. Sunflowers are another great companion plant for vegetables. They can help beans and other vining crops that need extra vertical support. Sow the sunflower seeds directly into the soil of your raised beds. Sunflowers thrive in full-sun areas with well-draining soil that has lots of nutrients. Sunflower roots can run incredibly deep into the soil and will soak up as much as they can, so be sure to regularly add compost, mulch, and other organic fertilizers to your raised beds that have sunflowers in them. They will require semi-regular watering as they are developing.

If you enjoy foraging and creating a fully edible garden, nasturtium flowers can act as a great addition. The nasturtium flower heads are fully edible and the flowers will naturally cascade. Use nasturtium flowers in raised beds for extra decorative vining flowers or in window boxes. Nasturtium flowers thrive off of rainwater alone and need very little attention to begin blossoming. The best practice for nasturtiums is to plant the seeds in their permanent location and allow them to do their thing. You can check on them occasionally if you would like, but they largely thrive when left to their own devices.

Something to keep in mind if you are planting flowers in your raised beds is that they attract slugs. A great way to get rid of slugs is to space out your flowers or add a layer of flowers at the perimeter of your garden so that they don't venture inward. You can get rid of slugs by heading out just before dawn and picking them off of your crops. *The Old Farmer's Almanac* suggests putting out a dish of beer near your garden, as this will also attract slugs and you can pick them off of the plate each morning.

9
FALL

September, October, and November are the best times of the year to replant and maintain any perennial crops in your garden and start preparing for the winter. In September, remember to clean up fallen leaves. They make great additions to your compost pile but if you leave the leaves alone, they can kill your grass by smothering it and become a safety hazard because they get slimy. Be sure to collect all the leaves on your property before it rains because they become more difficult to move when they are soggy. Leaves can also be great mulch for your fruit trees. Also in September, if you have any areas on your property where you maintain a lawn, this is the best time to reseed and repair the lawn before it starts snowing. For your garden, remember to continue weeding, especially if you have perennial crops. Weeds can continue to grow throughout the fall and damage your crops.

In October, start planting spring-flowering bulbs halfway through the month and into November. You can protect your bulbs from rodents by encasing them in chicken wire. Your fruit trees and shrubs will begin their dormancy periods for the winter, be sure to avoid pruning the trees because you don't want to stimulate new growth during the winter. You can continue to plant new trees and shrubs through October so long as the ground has not frozen yet.

November is the final time that you have to prepare for the winter. There are a couple of other steps to take that I have listed at the start of the Winter section that can begin in November. As a reminder, you want to get as much done outdoors before it starts to snow. Depending on where you are in the Northeast, you may want to start these processes in October as the first snow will come early in November, or even earlier.

FALL VEGETABLES

Most of the vegetables that you have been planting so far can continue to grow through the fall. If you want to maintain some perennial crops in your garden, the fall is the best time to replant them. Some other crops to consider planting in the fall are asparagus, arugula, zucchini, shelling beans, and fennel. To start planting asparagus, dig 6 inch holes in the soil and place in the asparagus crowns. Asparagus are partial-sun plants and can be kept in shaded areas of your garden. Asparagus are perennial and can survive through the winter. In your first year, the yield of asparagus plants won't be super high but if you continue to regularly water and add compost to your asparagus, they will thrive in the following years. Arugula is a fast-growing plant that will yield harvests within a month of planting. Plant your arugula seeds consistently throughout the growing season, as they grow quickly and will begin to flower if left unattended. Once the arugula plants flower, it is time to remove them and plant new seeds. Arugula requires full sun and can be planted 3 inches apart from surrounding seeds.

Zucchini are another easy crop to grow during your first growing season. Zucchini seeds can be planted directly into your raised bed or they can be started indoors. If you are running out of space in your raised beds and you want to practice sequential farming, start your zucchinis inside so that they are ready for transport when space opens up. Zucchinis need a spot in your garden that gets full sun and they need to be watered every week. Zucchini are very vulnerable to harmful insects, so starting them indoors will mean that you have more robust crops that can withstand a possible insect invasion. You should be ready to harvest your zucchinis when they are 6 to 8 inches long. However, if you want an extra-large zucchini, let them grow a little longer for a bigger yield.

There are two types of shelling beans that you can plant in the fall: pole beans and bush beans. Pole beans will require stakes or trellises for support. You can also utilize companion planting and plant pole beans near sunflowers or corn so that they can use the strong and tall plants for support. You can expect the first harvest of your beans 6 weeks after planting them. Bush beans are shorter plants that make a great addition to raised beds because they don't need a lot of space to grow. You can expect your first harvest of bush beans 3 to 4 weeks after they are planted. Both types of beans can be directly planted into the soil of your garden and don't need to be started indoors. Shelling beans are full-sun crops that require minimal water and can thrive on rainwater alone. Be sure to harvest all of your beans quickly to maximize your yields during the fall.

There are two types of fennel that you can grow in your fall garden: Florence fennel and sweet fennel. Florence fennel is an annual crop that will need to be replanted each year. Sweet fennel is perennial and can survive relatively mild winters outdoors, or you can transport them into your greenhouse at the end of the season to preserve them for the following year. Both types of fennel are full-sun crops that require weekly watering. Fennel will attract both helpful and harmful insects to your garden. If you are seeing small green caterpillars attracted to your fennel, consider planting Queen Anne's lace nearby and transporting the caterpillars to the flower. Carrot rust flies are also attracted to fennel and they can damage the crop. Consider covering your outdoor fennel with a mesh fabric to keep the flies away.

FALL FRUITS AND HERBS

Again, you can continue to plant new fruit trees and berry bushes through the fall months but be sure not to prune them as they are getting ready for the winter. You can add grapes, cranberries, and chicory to the list of fruits and herbs that are growing in your garden. Any herbs that you have in your garden that you want to continue enjoying throughout the winter need to be repotted and moved indoors or into your greenhouse during the fall. Grapes can be started in May or June once the last frost has cleared your area. However, many fruit trees and shrubs are best planted in the fall so that they have time to develop a deep root system. There are many different varieties of grapevines that you can choose from when you are starting grapes on your farm. The difference in variety indicates what you will do with them. If you are growing grapes to make wine, consider growing Frontenac, La Crescent, Marquette, Swenson white, or St. Croix grapes. If you are growing grapes to eat or to make into jelly, consider growing Bluebell, Edelweiss, or Swenson red grapes. The seedless grape varieties that you can grow in the northeast are Mars, Petite Jewel, and Somerset Seedless. To plant your grapevines, soak the vines in water for a couple of hours before you plant them. Grapevines don't need to be planted too deep into the soil but will require initial supports from stakes or trellises. Watering your grapevines can mostly be accomplished from rainwater in the early weeks of growth.

If you are going through a heat wave or drought, be sure to water your grapes at least once a week.

There are two types of cranberries that you can grow on your Northeast farm: North American cranberries and North American low-bush cranberries. The North American cranberries are the classic Thanksgiving cranberries that are tart and best eaten with sugar. The North American low-bush cranberries act just like other fruit shrubs and can be eaten directly off the vine. While most classic cranberries are grown in bogs, this is not necessary for growing great cranberries on your farm. Both types of cranberries require moist soil. When you are planting your cranberries, dig an area that is 10 inches deep into the soil and plant your cranberries 2 feet apart. Fill the 10-inch hole with peat moss and fertilizer for the best results. Cranberries are a long-term investment and you won't actually see any fruit until they are 3 years old. However, both types of cranberries are delicious and can add a lot of value to your farm. They may require some protection during the winter but don't worry, they are cold-hardy and will survive the Northeast winters.

Chicory seeds are started indoors typically 5 weeks before they are transplanted outdoors. Chicory will grow best if transported in the early weeks of September. Sow the seeds 6 inches into the soil and 2 feet apart from surrounding crops. Chicory will thrive if temperatures remain below 75 °F, which makes them perfect fall crops. Be sure to water your chicory at least once a week and transport the plant back indoors or to your greenhouse before the winter.

FALL FLOWERS

The work that you will be doing with the flowers in your garden during the fall is mostly going to consist of prep for the winter and following spring. Many of the bulb flowers that you have in your garden at this point will have made daughter bulbs that you can dig up and replant. Additionally, you can add wildflowers and Persian buttercups to your fall gardens for the last bits of color for the year. Wildflowers are a great project to get started in the fall, as they require very minimal maintenance and can attract helpful insects to your gardens. Wildflowers are native to different areas in the Northeast; be sure to get a mix of wildflower seeds that are native to your area so as not to introduce invasive species to your garden. Planting wildflowers in the fall will mean that they will remain dormant during the winter and blossom in the spring. Wildflower seeds are a great option for the perimeter of your raised beds or to add color to an area of your property that is lacking it. When you till the soil for your wildflower seeds, be sure the seeds are planted 1 to 2 inches into the soil. For the first few weeks after planting your wildflowers, be sure to water the area at least once a week so that the seeds can properly germinate. Once the flowers are 1 to 2 inches tall, you can stop watering and let the rainwater handle your wildflowers. If you are finding that your wildflowers are looking dull, you can mow the area with a tall mower or weed whacker. Persian buttercups are annual flowers in the Northeast that can be planted in either the spring or fall. When you are planting your Persian buttercups in the fall, be sure to transport them back indoors for the winter. When planting the buttercup tubers, you will need to plant them 2 inches deep into the soil and 6 inches apart. They are full-sun flowers that require bi-weekly watering.

10
WINTER

There are a couple more seasonal chores that need to be completed at the start of the winter season on your farm. Depending on where you are in the Northeast, these chores may need to be started in late October and can run through the beginning of December. First, ensure that any outdoor water sources are drained and stored for the winter months. Be sure to shut off any water valves that are exposed to the elements so that they do not freeze, which can cause burst pipes. Cover the faucets for winter with protective coverings so that they don't leak or freeze. Next, take another walk through your property and note any damage that you need to repair for the winter. Cracks, scratches, and holes in your existing structures can lead to intense drafts in the winter that will suck away all your warm air. Last, shelter your raised beds. In December or earlier (definitely before the first snow), be sure to cover your perennial crops with mulch and turn the soil. If you have perennial crops growing in your raised beds, be sure to cover them with their preferred coverings. If you are transporting crops back indoors or to your greenhouse, now is the time to do so.

December is also a great time to get hardwood cuttings from your trees and shrubs. These hardwood cuttings can be sprinkled over your raised beds to protect them from the frost and decompose for a more robust soil in the spring. Some of the trees and shrubs that you may plant in December could have bagworms; be sure to remove these by hand. This is also your last chance to inspect the fencing around your property for holes or tears before the snow comes in full force. As an additional deterrent to any deer or other wild animals, hang a bar of soap in cheese cloth from a tree near the perimeter of your property. Animals don't like the smell as it reminds them of humans and they will stay away.

The winter season on your Northeast farm doesn't have to just be a barren expanse of land. Winter can bring color, vibrancy, and new opportunities, just like any other season. While you may not be able to tend to your garden as much as you may have grown accustomed to, you can spend your time observing your farm and looking at new areas for improvement. During the winter, after all of the leaves have fallen, you have the opportunity to see where you have gaps on your property. It may be that you have a lot of space that was once covered by tree branches, to add a new structure or expand your garden. Take the winter to plan out and research new ideas for your homestead and practice the permaculture principle of observation.

Winter is also a great time to consider your view. When the trees no longer have their leaves, you can see much more clearly across your farm. It may be the case that your neighbors now have direct sight onto your property. Consider where you'd like to plant new trees and shrubs in the following seasons. You can also spend the time manicuring your property, provided that the temperature doesn't deter you from going outside. If you get that itch to be active in nature, you can do some needed clean up on your property. I am sure at this point in the year you have overgrown trees or bushes that are merely part of the landscape. Take the time to trim them down and create a more cohesive looking farm.

WINTER TREES AND SHRUBS

While these are some ideas for how to spend your winter, there are certainly more options for gardening to consider this season. You don't have to spend your winter staring at a blank gray and white scene. Instead, consider planting cold-hardy winter trees and shrubs. The winter trees that thrive in the Northeast are juniper trees, evergreens, euonymus, and nandina trees. Red twig dogwood, cherry laurels, and winterberry holly shrubs can also add a pop of color to your farm.

There are many different varieties of juniper trees and bushes and you can choose from many different winter-hardy varieties for your farm. When you are planting juniper trees, be sure to find a spot that gets at least 6 hours of sun per day. Dig a small trench around the base of your juniper trees so that the soil can drain from snow or rain. Other than that, junipers are very easy to grow and will add vibrancy to your winter farm. If you are thinking about adding evergreen trees to your property, consider purchasing saplings rather than trying to propagate the trees on your own. Propagation of trees is a tricky process that may require additional research to do correctly for your area. Planting evergreen saplings is a great place to start and can add a bit of holiday cheer to your property. Most evergreen trees want access to the sun, so find a spot on your farm that gets direct sun for a lot of the day. When you find the right spot, dig up a hole for the base of the tree to rest in. You want the soil to be looser than the surrounding area so that the evergreen tree roots can take hold. Water the soil and roots considerably when you first plant the tree so that the roots are well hydrated. If you are planting your trees at the end of fall or beginning of winter, be sure to add a trench around the base of the tree so that any precipitation can drain through the soil.

Euonymus plants can be another addition to your winter farm. They tolerate any type of sun or shade condition and are incredibly resilient. There are six types of euonymus plants that you can add to your farm: wintercreeper, evergreen, America, winged, spindle, and spreading euonymus. Be sure to plant euonymus before the first snow because they do well when planted in dry conditions. Nandinas are another great option for your winter farm that will speckle your landscape with a gorgeous red color in the winter. They are not picky about the amount of sun that they get, so add them wherever you want on your farm. Nandina do require good soil drainage in the early weeks of their growing cycle. Be sure to add a trench around the plant to support better drainage. You will want to buy nandina saplings from a nursery and gently loosen their roots before planting.

Red twig dogwood is a great shrub to add to your winter landscape that is not picky and very resilient. Like the nandina, you can plant the red twig dogwood in full sun or full shade and it will thrive. This shrub is a fast grower and will require some light pruning during the winter, but the added pop of red to your farm is definitely worth it. Winterberry holly can also add some seasonal color to your winter farm and produce adorable berries in the summer, but don't eat them; they are merely there for aesthetic purposes. The holly bushes do best in full sun or partial shade. Be sure to fully saturate the soil before planting the holly bushes because they do best in moist soil. There are eight varieties of winterberry holly that you can choose from that are native to the Northeast: Aurantiaca, Berry Poppins, Cacapon, La Have, Oosterwijk, Red Sprite, Winter Red, and Winter Gold.

The best time to plant cherry laurels is in the late fall and early winter. They are cold-hardy plants that will blossom in the spring. They too need a sunny area with well-draining soil in order to thrive. Water the cherry laurel for the first few weeks and then allow the roots to take hold during the winter. In the spring, add fresh fertilizer and compost to the soil around the cherry laurel for the best results.

11
TIPS AND TRICKS FOR ULTIMATE SUCCESS

Figuring out your homestead design is an essential step when you are starting on a new property. In Chapter 6, I covered permaculture design principles and the ways to incorporate those principles on to your farm. Now I want to discuss some more tips and tricks to keep in mind when you are beginning a new farm. The first tip is to discover your short-term and long-term goals. This is a great way to inform the design of your farm. If you have a short-term goal or raising ducks, then you need to decide how and where to build a duck coop, a water source for them, and ways to automate their feeding times. If you have a long-term goal of setting up a home orchard, then you might section off a piece of land and reserve the area for your orchard when you are ready to tackle the project.

Next, make a list of the large-scale projects that you may want to accomplish. I discussed this briefly in an earlier section. I can't stress the importance of designing from the idea down to the small details. When you are deciding which large-scale projects you want to accomplish on your farm you need to do a lot of research to develop how you are going to tackle the projects. If you are building a greenhouse, how are you going to build it, what materials will you need, and will you require contract work to accomplish the project? Ask yourself these questions and then detail the exact expenses for every aspect. This practice has the added benefit of giving you an eye for details. Once you get in the habit of detailing every minute detail of a project, you will start doing this on your farm and in your home. Considering the small details and ensuring that everything is working with a purpose is crucial to a self-sustaining lifestyle. It will also mean that you aren't spending frivolous money on projects that could have been accomplished if more details were fleshed out.

While I have written at length about the importance of planning and observing your property before you start building or farming, you need to also consult your city or county. Every region has specific zoning laws that need to be adhered to. You may also be in an area with a Homeowners Association that has regulations about what you can and cannot do on your property. Be sure to consult the regulations and laws for your area so that you don't invest time and resources into a project just to find out that you can't have it. When I knew that I wanted to start homesteading, I started a small garden in my backyard and put up some trellises to practice some farming techniques. I found out after a few weeks that the location of my garden violated the Homeowners Association's regulations for my area. I had to completely dismantle the garden and relocate all of my crops. I ended up losing a lot of my plants in the process. Don't be like me: do the research first so that you don't have to tear down a project that you worked hard on.

Something that I think a lot of people overlook on their first property is fencing. Fences, whether man-made or organic, should be some of the first expenses for your property. Fencing can help, especially in the Northeast, to keep deer and other larger animals off of your property. It also has the added benefit of keeping any small critters or children safely *on* your property. Raised beds also count as fencing against smaller rodents that may have found their way onto your land. These initial investments are critical to the long-term success of your farm.

OPTIMIZING THE SPACE ON YOUR PROPERTY

An area of your home that I cannot stress the importance of enough is storage. Whether you invest in a survival storage system or just an everyday storage system, storage will be key to keeping your house chaos-free and streamlining some of your processes. You want to have access to quality storage on your farm so that you can preserve your produce and ensure that your family always has food. In the Northeast, you are bound to get long and cold winters, where your capacity for gardening will be limited. Ensuring that you have a substantial storage system to keep all of your goods fresh will make the winters seem like a breeze. My biggest tip for storage is to set this up before you start working outside on your property. You are going to want to have plenty of shelving, a couple of refrigerators, and some freezers to preserve the harvest from your garden.

PLANTING SUCCESS

Planting for successful growing seasons requires a lot of attention to detail and a plan for how you are going to create environments for your diverse garden to thrive. I suggest starting your own planting calendar. *The Old Farmer's Almanac* has a general planting calendar on their website that lists the best times to start plants indoors and outdoors throughout the growing season. In the Northeast, due to the varied temperatures, I suggest creating your own. A planting calendar will be able to tell you what dates you should start seeds, depending on the first and last frosts of the year. This style of planning will maximize your yields. Starting plants indoors will mean that they will be ready to harvest quicker once you transport them outdoors. A planting calendar can also account for rain. If you create your own planting calendar you can add a tracking system for rain days. Knowing when it has rained will also influence how often you need to water specific plants, as well as the best time to plant new crops. Another benefit of planting calendars is that they are uniquely useful if you are using a sequential farming method. Sequentially farming different crops using a planting calendar can help you map out when to rotate out a crop after it has been harvested so that you have a bountiful garden all year long.

In addition to a planting calendar, I also want to encourage you to learn how to propagate new plants from clippings. Propagation is a money-saving farming technique that allows you to start new crops from the clippings of existing plants in your garden. This is also great if you love a particular crop and want to continue growing it in your greenhouse over the winter months. Propagation is safe for plants and can save you a lot of money in the first couple of years on your farm. Why spend extra money on plants at the nursery if you can take a clipping from your garden and grow an entirely new plant?

Water sources are another consideration that will be crucial in the beginning phases of planning your property. Collect rainwater in bins for your gardens. Rainwater is gentle and incredibly rich in nutrients. There are other irrigation systems that you can implement once you expand your gardening operation. However, in the beginning, invest in some rainwater collection bins and reroute that water to your gardens. Another DIY-friendly watering method is to collect your wine and other glass bottles to use as drip irrigators. Placing water in a wine bottle and sticking the nose of the wine bottle into the soil will allow the water to slowly drain in the soil. If you have followed the previously mentioned steps about how to have quality soil with good drainage, drip irrigators are a great option. The water will slowly drain through the soil and the root system of nearby crops will absorb the water. You can even use recycled soda bottles as drip irrigators and there is more flexibility with the style and breadth of irrigation with plastic bottles.

The last water management tip that I want to tell you about is a *greywater* system. Greywater systems have become incredibly popular as more people are moving in tiny homes and vans. Greywater is the water that you have used in your kitchen, shower, or sinks. You can collect this water and reuse it for other purposes around your farm. Utilizing the greywater on your farm is a sustainable practice that is healthy and eco-friendly. Greywater systems are also energy efficient because instead of pumping water into the sewer or septic tank, you can reroute the water to your garden.

INSECT MANAGEMENT

I have briefly mentioned the benefits of helpful insects in your garden and ways to avoid harmful insects. However, there are some more concrete ways to improve your garden by decreasing the harmful insect population and increasing the helpful population. The first and most important step is to ensure that you have clean and quality soil. If you start with soil that is uninhabitable to your crops, you will attract harmful insects and diseases to your garden. Clean soil is soil that is rich in helpful organic matter and has been layered and tilled with compost and mulch. Refer back to Chapter 5 for a more in-depth look at how to treat your soil.

Once you have established clean soil, you will want to water your crops in the morning, control weeds and regularly clean out your gardens, and aggressively thin out your plants. Watering your plants in the morning allows your plants to perform photosynthesis during the day and dry off by the time night falls. It is also more efficient as the heat of the sun often evaporates water before it reaches the plants if you water during the day. If your plants are damp during the colder parts of the day, they can become overridden with mold and attract harmful insects. If you are not an early riser, drip irrigators and soakers are a great investment to make so that your plants are watered in the morning while you are still sleeping.

Controlling the weeds in your garden will also decrease harmful pest intervention and allow your plants to thrive. Weeds compete with your plants for space and nutrients and are notoriously aggressive growers. Using the permaculture methods and companion planting in your raised beds will eliminate a lot of the space that weeds could take up. It is a generally great practice to weed your garden every week or every other week as you continue to work on your farm. This goes hand in hand with ensuring that your garden is clean. Remove fallen leaves and twigs from your garden as they can introduce new harmful insects. You can also improve the rate of decomposition in your compost by regularly adding the debris that you find in your garden to the compost pile. Accomplish two tasks at once by keeping your garden clean: aggressively thinning plants is a way to avoid weaker plants that are prone to diseases from spreading those diseases to other plants; and thinning plants can also remove harmful insect larvae and eggs from your garden. Prune dead leaves, shoots, and branches from your garden so that you can restore airflow to struggling plants.

You will also want to promote helpful insect populations in your garden. A great way to do this is to add some pollinating flowers to your garden to attract bees and butterflies. If you are raising chickens, you can also allow your chickens to roam through your garden for controlled periods of time, as they will eat a lot of the harmful insects that are hiding among the plants. Similarly, ladybugs, praying mantises, and wasps are other beneficial garden insects that you can entice to your garden with their preferred flowers. If you are buying helpful insects to introduce to your garden, avoid any chemical insecticides. Chemicals in your garden will kill any insects that reside there, regardless of their usefulness to your garden. The last way to promote a healthy garden with helpful insects is to rotate your crops. I wrote briefly about this in Chapter 6, but rotating your crops can reduce the risk of plant disease and will mean that harmful insects have a harder time locating specific crops on which to feed.

Leave a 1-Click Review!

Customer reviews

 5 out of 5

3 global ratings

5 star	██████████	100%
4 star		0%
3 star		0%
2 star		0%
1 star		0%

˅ How are ratings calculated?

Review this product

Share your thoughts with other customers

Write a customer review

AFTERWORD

Starting a homestead in the Northeast is an excellent opportunity to cultivate a farm that experiences all four seasons, engage in a sustainable lifestyle, and bring an overall happiness to your life that you might be missing. The essential tools that you will need when you are starting your Northeast farm are to take your time and do as much research as you can. This is your journey and finding the best ways to do things doesn't need to be a rushed process. Consider the permaculture design principles when you start designing your homestead. Remember to center the projects that you want to accomplish on your farm with an adherence to the natural flow of the ecological systems around you. Homesteading and permaculture protocols and principles will not only help save the planet, they will also streamline everything for you in a very productive fashion.

In the Northeast, the seasonal changes demand a lot of attention. The benefits of these changes are that you can get a wider range of plants in your garden and you can learn more about horticultural principles for each plant. Becoming a master at your craft will take time and on a Northeast farm: you have so much more access to different plants and methods than in other areas. Take your time while you are engaging with these practices. For the most success on your farm, don't do anything major during the first year on your property. Take some time to just observe the land and establish ideas for projects that you may want to implement.

Overall, the homesteading journey is one that will span many years. Many people who start homestead farms call their properties their 'forever homes.' Finding your forever home means that you have plenty of time to spare. Not only will living in tandem with nature fuel your happiness, but it will make you a healthier person at the same time. Sustainability means working with what you have and if you have a vegetable garden on your farm, then you will definitely be eating more greens and less processed foods.

When you put down this book, I want you to consider all of the projects that you have bubbling up in your mind. Write down as many as you can and keep them around. Then, once you get onto your property, really observe what is around you. Learn to roll with the changes that you will face as a result of learning how to live on your property. The worst thing you can do is try and force a project into place when the ecology around you is fighting the project. Creating the tangible first steps for your homestead is a great way to begin because you are engaging your mind and thinking critically about the nature around you.

At the end of the day, this is your journey and the pace that you set for your journey is completely your own. Remember to stay focused on the overarching goal that homesteading is a long-term project and investment. There will be setbacks and obstacles to overcome, but mastering your craft and learning new lessons will make them a more pleasurable experience. If you are considering the homesteading lifestyle and you want to be part of a community of people who are doing the same, join our Facebook group: Northeast Homestead Gardeners and Foragers. In this group we discuss more detailed tips and tricks about starting your Northeast farm. There are also community members who will be willing to give you direct feedback about your farm that is tailored to your experience. If you found this book helpful for your homesteading journey, consider leaving a review to help other people learn skills for their first farm. I wish you all the luck in the world as you start your journey into farming in the Northeast!

NORTHEAST FORAGING FROM YOUR BACKYARD HOMESTEAD - NATIVE HERBALIST'S GUIDE TO IDENTIFYING 101 TASTY WILD EDIBLE FOODS

NORTHEAST FORAGING
FROM YOUR
BACKYARD HOMESTEAD

NATIVE HERBALIST'S GUIDE TO IDENTIFYING
101 TASTY WILD EDIBLE FOODS

J. B. MAXWELL

"The person who takes medicine must recover twice, once from the disease and once from the medicine."
—William Osler

INTRODUCTION

We need plants. Plants are around us all of the time, but often we are not fully aware or appreciative of this. There is a term for this called "plant blindness." The basic definition of "plant blindness" is a term describing our tendency to be oblivious to the plants around us. Take, for example, wood. Think about how much wood we use in our surroundings, but it goes farther than that. All around the world people are connecting to plants by studying them, eating them, or finding beauty in them.

Plants keep us alive. The problem is that the world is getting harder and harder to live in—for both us and the plants. There is a lot of stress about the state of the world and what we can do as individuals, not only to help but also to find peace and purpose among this chaos. Everyday people are thrown statistics like this:

- The World Wildlife Fund (WWF) found that humans are using 1.6 times the amount of resources we have on earth.
- According to the University of Michigan (MIT) between 1990-2020, 75% of all agricultural crop biodiversity was lost.

The loss of species is not only in the animal kingdom, and the stress of the climate crisis can feel overwhelming to the point of doom for many. Foraging is a two fold solution in this case. Foragers are typically people who have formed a connection to the land, are conscious of the amount they take, and how to give back to it. Foraging for food, at least as a supplement to store bought, is a hobby that positively affects the environment and your personal footprint because it does not require clear cutting large acres of diverse land.

Among the stresses of the larger issues of the world, people are so busy with their lives that they don't get a chance to utilize the wilderness. People have been segregated from the outdoors and it's unnatural. Foraging is mentally stimulating in the research stage and it creates a deeper connection to nature. This common feeling of dissociating or living in a stimulation can be in part blamed on the disconnect that people have with the outside world. Humans are not meant to be blind consumers. They have always been part of the food chain and removing this natural habit and purpose is unfulfilling. While this sounds complicated and scary, we should just think of ourselves as way more simple. Like pets, sometimes people need mental stimulation that mimics what we are innately built for.

Not only are there mental reasons for adding foraging for food as a habit or hobby, there are physical reasons as well. Being out in nature is an excuse to increase exercise. For those who find it difficult to get the recommended amount of exercise, it feels different when there's a purpose that means more to them. Foraging is a passive exercise, but it is more in tune with the natural habits of humans and can counteract those immobilized by work. Foraging for food increases the diversity on your plate. According to the CDC (2022), only 6% of Americans eat enough fruit and vegetables. By starting a more intentional relationship with food, you will begin to see it in a more dynamic way. Once again, instead of this segregated exercise and diet culture, it is something that becomes integrated into your life naturally. It surpasses commercialized dieting and health; it opens up eating a more balanced diet that puts plants on the forefront.

As an average person trying to survive with food anxiety, money, lack of agency, and even feeling lost in the sea of information, many think that the solution has to be complex. The benefit of adding foraging into your tool belt is that you are able to feel like you're taking action, and you can feel less lost in the natural world around you. Being able to take control of food insecurity ensures that you feel comfort in knowing you can fend for yourself.

This book is set up as a dictionary about 100 plants you will be able to find in the Northeast. As you learn more about herbs and plants, you can eventually become self-sufficient, be more intentional with your health, and save money. As you slowly become more comfortable being in the world and interacting with the background, you will begin to see your tangible opportunities grow. Eventually you will feel comfortable using these plants like you would anything you pick up in the grocery store, and you might even start using them for natural healing. This book starts with the basics of foraging, then each chapter looks at one plant, specifically how to identify it, what it is used for, how to prepare it, and how to cook with it.

I grew up in a small farm town with no red lights in Maryland. I currently live in Pennsylvania with my wife and son. I am very family oriented, and they are a part of my life outdoors: hiking, nature, and gardening. Being outdoors brings peace to a world that is unpredictable. I have always loved the idea of fostering my own healthy, clean, organic food and producing enough food for the whole family and neighbors without having to rely 100% on the grocery store. I think teaching other people this knowledge about herbs and foraging wild herbs and plants is the first step.

There's something about producing your own food that gives it a taste unrivaled to anything anyone could ever buy. I absolutely love taking control of my own food and being more hands-on when it comes to providing for my family. I have been practicing homesteading principles on two different properties (one 0.75 acres, the other 1 acre) for a little over 8 years now. I have learned a lot throughout my life this way—from studying within the sphere of Western Medicine to traveling through the East and learning about Chinese Eastern Medicine and Ayurvedic practices. I have found great comfort and gratitude in having such knowledge about ancient wisdom. Because of all of the kindness of the spread of knowledge, I now live off-grid and wish to simply ensure that everyone else doing the same or similar feels safe and empowered as they do so.

I have acquired this knowledge by studying, listening, and doing hands-on experience like exploring the forest and mountains. I know that I am safe and protected no matter what happens, precisely because of studying wilderness survival and living it firsthand for over 10 years. This has led to a long and continued journey of knowledge expansion. Helping others achieve a healthier lifestyle and being able to be self-sufficient is my absolute passion because I know that it leads to so much freedom, joy, and better health. I want to be able to help others improve their relationship with Mother Nature.

If you're a food lover, you can expand beyond what is handed to you in the store and find what grows in the same cycles you live in as well. If you want to improve your health with foods and connect to the natural world, do it naturally. Herbs and plants have healing properties, and by eating a few of them daily, you are treating your body and your mind. It is only difficult at the start, and once you start putting plant names to their faces, the rest will be history.

12
FORAGING 101

Foraging is the activity of collecting food from natural and wild sources. Picking berries off of a bush for a mid-afternoon snack when you are a child is a great example of foraging. Becoming a forager means adhering to the ethics of foraging and maintaining a relationship with the natural environment around you. The goal of sustainable and ethical foraging is to gather food from wild sources in a way that promotes the ecology of a given area. Foraging helps foragers to learn about the natural environment around them and how to work with those environments in ethical ways. Foragers understand that there is a give and take relationship within the natural world.

The ethics of foraging are incredibly important because they help you remain safe, promote ecological harmony, and practice legal foraging. In every region there are foragable plants that are in season and at risk. If you are outside of the Northeast, be sure to research both types of foragable plants when you start your foraging journey. The USDA plant map is a great online tool to help you discover what is available in your area.

This guide will help you through your foraging journey, but it is important to gather as much material as you can to learn how to identify all of the foragables in your area. Being able to accurately identify the foragables that you find can mean the difference between life and death. There are many dangerous and unsafe foragables that you are bound to find and without the proper knowledge, you could inadvertently harm yourself. Learning to identify plants will mean understanding what they look like, their leaf shapes, the fruits that they make, the general locations that they prefer, fragrance, and life cycle. Learn everything you can about what you may find so that you keep yourself safe.

When you are foraging, be sure to leave a majority of what you find behind. Depending on the abundance of a given foragable, it is important to only take up to a third of what you have found. This allows the natural life cycles and ecosystem to continue thriving without human interference. In addition to only taking a fraction of what you find of a particular foragable plant, be sure to leave the area that you are foraging in a good or even better condition than before you got there. Avoid drastically changing the landscape or disrupting the ecosystem to the best of your ability. This also means picking up any garbage you may have with you or cleaning up any that you find along your way.

In order to be the most ethical forager, it is important to know the laws surrounding foraging in your area. In the Northeast, state parks have specific requirements and restrictions around foraging. There are also laws in most Northeast states that prohibit foraging on private property. Be sure to look up the laws for where you want to forage and the zoning in the area you are in.

Making a Plan

When you go out for a day of foraging, be sure to have a plan that includes the following things:

- Know what you are looking for.
- Where you can find it.
- Take a picture of your new findings and consult a field guide to determine if it is safe to go back and forage for that plant. It is easy to get distracted and find something new to forage. Sticking to your foraging plan and minimizing distractions can mean avoiding potential danger by misidentifying a plant.
- In a foraging sense, clean areas are areas that are pollution and litter free. It's best to avoid foraging in urban and industrialized areas in order to ensure that you are finding safe plants to harvest and snack on.

You will also want to invest in foraging equipment to make the most of your excursions. The essential items that you will need when you head out on a foraging adventure are

- either a basket or a lightweight cross-body bag for collecting foragables
- a field guide
- zip-lock bags
- a hand lens for closer identification
- sturdy gardening or hiking boots
- gardening gloves
- a long sleeve shirt and pants

Some additional tools that you may consider bringing along, depending on your foraging plan for the day, are

- pruning shears or saws
- weeding or gardening knives
- a compact (pocket) knife
- a shovel
- a hoe
- scissors

Something to keep in mind as a forager is that you might not have interacted with these plants before. Even if you are someone who doesn't commonly have allergic reactions to things, allergies are the body's reaction to foreign bodies in the system. Whenever you are trying a new food, it's best not to feast on something you or your family has never interacted with before. Plants can contain things like latex that you might not even consider before you try. Even if it's not necessarily an allergic reaction, taking the time to see how your body reacts to these new foods means you stay safe and are able to decide whether you will be looking to forage for more in the future.

Foraging should not happen blindly. When you are out in nature, it is not a vacuum of the plant you want to forage and you. Each area comes with its specific situation, and it is up to the forager to know their skill level. This starts with their expertise level in being in nature in general. Those who have not spent time outdoors in wild spaces might find themselves greatly overwhelmed with the huge diversity of plants, as well as the exertion of being in nature—whether that be hiking, being in swampy areas, or even getting through thick brush. Beyond this, foraging isn't a task tackled in a day. Be sure to build up your skill level. Have respect for the wild, and solidify the respect you have for yourself in the wild.

WASHING YOUR FOOD

Everyone should wash their food, either when they bring them home or are about to cook with them. This includes produce, rice, and even cans before you open them. You don't know what has touched anything before you did. Even though most people clean their food when they cook, oftentimes no one has taught them how to clean your food effectively.

1. In a clean bin or bucket, add warm water. I do not recommend using your sink. Even if your sink is clean, it is still a place that usually holds bacteria, harsh chemicals, and more. A designated cleaning bin is more sanitary.
2. In this bin, add cold to hot water, depending on what you are cleaning. Leafy or delicate food should be done in cold water so it does not wilt. Anything more tough like roots or nuts should be cleaned in hot water.
3. Add about a cup of white or apple cider vinegar to the water. This won't make your food taste like vinegar since it will be rinsed, but it is a safe product to disinfect and clean your food.
4. Let it soak for 15 minutes.
5. Agitate the water and food, making sure any debris is loose. With hardier foods, you might even scrub.
6. Remove food from the bin. If there is visible dirt or the water is very dirty, rinse the bin and fill with water again. Submerge your food and give it a deep rinse, agitating and letting the remainder of the dirt rinse off.
7. Remove the food from the bin. Give it a rinse under cool water and place it on a dish towel.
8. Make sure your food is dry before storing or cooking with it.

13
IDENTIFYING YOUR PLANTS

There are a few ways to approach the identification process of a plant. It is really important that foragers become knowledgeable about the plants in their area before they go out in the field. Foragers who want to have success and confidence in foraging need to take the task seriously. While in many cases "inedible" does not necessarily mean "deadly," there are a plethora of unpleasant side effects to eating things that don't belong in the human body. Careless mistakes like this could really deter those from continuing down this path, but that does not need to be the case. There are lots of plants out there that you never knew were edible, so let's stick to those and figure out how they work.

If you have some background knowledge on plant names, it's important to know that there are often multiple nicknames or common names for a plant. This might cause confusion if you only know one variant of the name, so it's important to get familiar with its scientific name which is always more reliable. Another thing to remember when it comes to species and genus, there is often a species of a genus called the 'common' version, for example "common daisy" or Bellis perennis. It is common for plants that have the title 'common' dropped, which can be confusing when it comes to other variants in the genus. Before you forage something based on a broad name, you should identify its specific species for edibility. There are many flowers that look like daisies and are part of the daisy family, and they all range from what they are used for in food to how upset they could make your stomach.

In the last chapter we talked about the idea of a plan and why it's important to know what you are going for before you go out. In your research, you need to know what plants you are going for, where those plants can be found, and what time of year those plants are found before you need to worry about specifics on the plant itself. If you have a specific location that you want to check out for foragables, you can note the climate and create a list of plants you might hope to see. With this list, also familiarize yourself with plants you should avoid as well. This book tries to take note of some dangerous look-alikes to some specific plants, but that doesn't necessarily take into consideration location specific issues or plants like poison ivy or poison oak that can harm you and contaminate those plants around it with its oil.

As we start looking at the identification of plants, we need to gain an understanding of the vocabulary that is used. In this book there will be a mixture of common and scientific phrases. We want identification to be accurate, since scientific terms in some cases flag more specific characteristics, but gaining knowledge in this field does not require heavy research or even excessive page flipping. There is a learning process in understanding these specific characteristics that needs to go farther than 'leaf', but foragers should not feel like this book, or foraging in general, is not accessible to them. In each description, a reader is able to start with the general idea of a plant, then have a closer look at each of these details in a way that will allow them to apply their knowledge in the field.

When foragers are starting the identification process, the first thing they will typically notice is the form of the plant, then slowly work their way through the subcategories until they reach their answer. While there are some plants that can be more tricky, specifically when moving from small shrub and vine or bush herbaceous plants to large shrubs and small trees, subcategorizing them is the easiest and quickest way to narrow down plants. Below is a chart that represents how to move through the identification process.

Note: this book does not go through any mushroom identification.

Identification Flow Chart

When identifying plants, there are multiple branching categories, the most used are family, genus, and species, which are the last three on the tree. When reading the scientific name, the first word is the genus, spelt with a capital, and the second word is the specifying species, spelt with a lower case; for example, the giant sunflower is called *Helianthus giganteus*.

Form

Tree: Some plants can take the form of a tree or shrub. Single stem is woody—called a trunk, typically very hard or thick (large branches can look like multiple trunks). Typically over 10 feet is considered a tree.

Shrub (bush/ground cover/woody vines): Shrub is about 10 feet at its full height (this definition can vary) and has several woody or semi-woody stems. They can look dense like hedgewalls or sparse. *Some herbaceous plants can look "bushy" but are not actual "bushes."*

Bush: Bushes are shrubs on a scientific level. They are woody but tend to be shorter with branches that are not as densely packed.

Woody vines: Scientifically called *liana*, or sometimes called brambles. These can form shapes that look like shrubs but are *not* shrubs.

Ground cover: Any plant that covers the ground including grass. Short shrubs can be ground cover.

Thicket: An area of densely packed plants, including trees, shrubs, and woody plants. Sometimes called a brier.

Herbaceous: refers to plants that are not woody, but herbaceous plants can have very hardy stems, including some types of bamboo, tomatoes, etc.

Flower: Scientifically flowering herbaceous plants are categorized as **forbs**. Flowers are usually referred to as **annuals** (life cycle within the year and reseeds) and **perennials** (lasting though years).

Grass: Grasses are considered **graminoids**, a simple definition is blade like leaves and no flowers. Grasses do flower, but often they are non distinct.

Fern: Ferns reproduce by spores, not flowers or seeds. They produce a uncurling stem that expands into fronds (divided leaf)

Moss vs Lichen: Moss and lichen look very similar, but moss is a plant and lichen is both a plant and a fungus. Moss will have very small stems and leaves, and a lichen will appear more like a crusty layer of peeling paint, sometimes like little tufts of branches.

↓

Narrowing Characteristics (At least down to genus)

Tree: Coniferous (typically needles leaves) or Deciduous (typically herbaceous leaves) → Size (height, thickness of trunk, and branches → Characteristics of leaves/needles (length, color, shape, how many, stem, pattern) → Fruit (size, hardness, color, texture, time of year) and Flower (size, color, shape, single or clustered, time of year)→ Seeds or nuts (size, hardness, color, texture, time of year) → bark (color, texture)

Shrub: Size (height, thickness of trunk, and branches) → Characteristics of leaves/needles (length, color, shape, how many, stem, pattern) → Fruit (size, hardness, color, texture, time of year) and Flower (size, color, shape, single or clustered, time of year)→ Seeds or nuts (size, hardness, color, texture, time of year) → bark (color, texture)

Flower and grass: Flower (size, color, shape, single or clustered, time of year) → Size (height and width) and Leaves (length, color, shape, how many, stem, pattern) and Stem (color, shape, how many, branching, texture) → Fruit (size, hardness, color, texture, time of year) → Seeds or nuts (size, hardness, color, texture, time of year)

Fern, Moss, Lichen: : Size (height and width) → Leaves (length, color, shape, how many, stem, pattern) →Stem (color, shape, how many, branching, texture)
↓

Forgeability and specifying species

Age of plant: The age of the plant from tree to flower can affect these characteristics.

Gender: Some plants have genders, this is especially notable in trees. This means that not all trees produce fruit. This is especially frustrating in urban environments where female trees, the ones with fruit, are not planted because they are more messy.

Time of year: Time of year affects when plants are producing foragable parts, but it can also help determine look-alikes from each other. Often plants that look similar are not flowering or producing at the same time, even from the same genus.

Climate/habitat: For plants you are actively seeking out, you already know where they like to grow, but for identifying a plant you have stumbled upon, checking the growing habits can eliminate many options, including plants of the same genus. This can include larger **geography** of the world, local **ecosystems and surroundings**, or **growing conditions** such as soil and sun.

Flower and leaves: Flowers and leaves can help narrow down to a family or genus, but a closer look at their biology can give a closer look at the subtle differences between similar flowers. See next part.

Leaf Biology
Start with the most obvious characteristics of the leaves

- Color: summer and fall
- Size: length and width
- Texture: stiff, limp, hairy, waxy, thick, wrinkled, or folded
- Shape: silhouette, lobed, and edges

Each leaf will have

- **Base:** The base of the leaf is the bottom edge.
- **Margins:** The margins are the distance between the veins and the edge of the leaf.
- **Tip:** The tip is the point of the leaf, there may be multiple tips.
- **Veins:** The veins are the small structures that run along the leaves to provide water and nutrients to the plant.
- **Midrib:** The midrib is the center vein on the leaf.
- Some leaves have **petioles** as well, which is the **stem** that connects the leaf to the bush, tree, or flower it is a part of.

Identify the shape of the leaf arrangements.

- If the leaf is a single structure, it is a **simple leaf**.
- If there are multiple smaller leaves that stem from the same place, you are looking at a **compound leaf.**
- The most common leaf arrangements that you will find while foraging are parallel, dichotomous, palmate, and pinnate leaves.
- **Parallel** leaves can be both simple and compound structures, where all of the veins are parallel to each other.
- **Dichotomous** leaves form a Y shape and are often part of a group of leaves.
- **Palmate** leaves resemble an open hand. Maple leaves in the Northeast are a perfect example of a palmate leaf arrangement. Palmate leaves have veins and a midrib that starts from a common point and extends outward through the leaf.
- **Pinnate** leaves are smaller leaves that extend from one central stalk or axis.

Identifying a plant's **branching patterns** can also help you to quickly identify the foragable that you are looking for.

- Plants that have **opposite branching** are those whose leaves grow on opposite sides of the stalk or axis. Mint is a great example of an opposite branching plant.
- **Alternate branching** plants have alternating leaf patterns, where the leaves connect to the axis on alternating sides one at a time. These two types of branching patterns are the most common in the Northeast.

Flower Biology

You may also be foraging for **flowers** or blooming foragables. First, you will probably notice these characteristics of a flower

- Color: single or multiple
- Size: unnoticeable (grass), small (babies breath), medium (daisy), big (rose), or large (sunflower)

The next thing you will probably notice is the **Inflorescence**. This is a cluster of flowers. This can get complicated and specific, but in this book it will usually refer to the clusters in descriptive words, like 'floret', for ease. The shapes of the inflorescence/floretes are categorized as spike, catkin, racemose, umbel, head, and more.

- **Shape:** Flower shape, or petal arrangement, can often best be described in reference to common or well known flowers.
- Many flowers are simple, 5 petal flowers that fan out flat from the edge of the center and are described as **star-shaped**.
- **Trumpet or funnel** flowers usually have petals that fan out at the ends or cup, but tapper down in the center like a funnel; for example, petunias.
- **Cup** shaped flowers have petals that don't spread out flat. Instead, they create a cup or bowl shape, like tulips or buttercups.
- **Global** flowers, like dandelions, have a ball shape.
- **Bell shaped** flowers typically are shaped like bells **and** hang from their plant.

- **Tube** flowers can be single petals or multiple that form a narrow tube.
- **Rosette** flowers that have petals that create a dense overlapping, usually in a circular pattern.
- **Flat, fanned rosette** flowers are like daisies that are flat, like a star shaped flower, but have more petals.
- **Non-symmetrical** flowers are flowers that might have a petal like a tongue or hood.

Like a solitary flower or a floret, the individual flowers can then be observed by

- Number of flower petals
- Shape of the petals
- Brackets (joint of flower and stem)
- Center (stigma, stamen, pistols, ovary, etc.)
- Sepals (sometimes leaf like, sometimes petal like, this is the outside of the flower as its blooming)

14
LIVING IN TUNE WITH NATURE'S CYCLES

Spring Foraging

Spring is a time for growth, renewal, and creativity. Living cyclically with nature during the spring can leave you feeling full of energy and confidence. You will want to learn more and explore after the winter season. This might be the first time for many to get back out in nature. Take action, plant, and forage during the spring to capitalize on these feelings.

When it comes to spring foraging, the flavors are fresh and crisp with all the new growth. A lot of your foraging options are early shoots and leaves. If you are a new forager, this can be difficult because shoots often do not have the most distinguishing characteristics of the plant yet. It can help if you know where you have seen these plants grow in previous years or have spent time observing them in different stages.

Foraging in spring is often a little time sensitive. Flowers can bloom for short periods of time, and young shoots are only edible when they are tender. It is a good idea to preserve what you can because, in many cases, they won't be there for the rest of the year.

Plants found in spring

- Asparagus (Shoots)
- Amaranth (leaves)
- Basswood (flowers)

- Birch (twigs, sap)
- Burdock (stems)
- Cattails (shoots)
- Chickweed (greens)
- Chicory (leaves)
- Cleavers (stems)
- Cow Parsnip (stems, leaves, and flowers)
- Curly dock (leaves)
- Dandelion (all)
- Daisy (leaves and flowers)
- Eastern Redbud (flowers and buds)
- Epazote (leaves)
- Evening Primrose (root and leaves)
- False Solomon's Seal (shoots)
- Fiddleheads (stems)
- Field Garlic (leaves)
- Garlic mustard (leaves and stems)
- Ginkgo (leaf)
- Glass weed (stems)
- Goutweed (leaves)
- Groundnut (root)
- Henbit (flowers, leaves, and stems)
- Honewort (leaves)
- Japanese Knotweed (leaves, stem)
- Lady's thumb (leaves)
- Lambs quarters (leaves)
- Leeks (root and leaf)
- Maple (spring)
- Milkweed (shoots)
- Mint (leaves)
- Mugwort (leaves)
- Mulberry (fruit)
- Nettles (leaves)
- Plantain (leaf)
- Pokeweed (leaves)
- Purple Dead Nettles (leaves)
- Quickweed (leaves, flowers, and stems)
- Red cover (leaves and flowers)
- Sassafras (leaves and twigs)

- Sweet clover (leaves)
- Violet (flowers)
- Watercress (leaves)
- Wild lettuce (leaves)

Summer Foraging

Spring comes quickly, and before you know it the world is just buzzing with life again. I find one week the trees are bare, and suddenly overnight, they are lush and green again. This is a time of energy and prosperity. The summer is a time that overlaps with harvest after harvest. For those learning to forage, it is a great time to get to know plants at their fullest. The plants you might already be familiar with are great learning blocks to observe closer. Take note of things that you may not have thought about. Expanding your knowledge of what is already familiar can be easier than introducing yourself to completely foreign plants without being able to reference the characteristics to something you know. Foraging in the summer has a plethora of options. It can be overwhelming too. Make a plan to go out and observe without foraging and get used to your local plants. You don't need to know everything, but getting a foot in the door can help.

Even though it's a lot at once, this is the time to think ahead too. Try to notice where winter, or even spring, foraging can happen? Plants are the most recognizable now, so take notes or map out where these plants can be found. Since the time is prosperous, divide your time between foraging for fresh food and foraging for preservable plants. Build your inventory of dried, jam or jelly, frozen, pickled, and canned foods.

Plants found in summer

- Amaranth (leaves, seeds)
- Black cherry (fruit)
- Beech Plum (fruit)
- Beebalm (leaves)
- Birch (twigs)
- Black cherry (fruit)
- Blueberry (fruit)
- Brambles (fruit)
- Cattails (flower and pollen)
- Chicory (root)
- Common Elderberry (berry)

- Strawberry (fruit)
- Cherry Dogwood (fruit)
- Curly dock (leaves)
- Current (fruit)
- Dandelion (all)
- Daylily (flowers and root)
- Enchanter's nightshade (fruit)
- Epazote (leaves)
- Field Garlic (leaves and flower)
- Garlic mustard (leaves and stems)
- Ginkgo (leaf)
- Glass weed (stems)
- Goldenrod (leaves and flower)
- Goutweed (leaves)
- Ground Cherry (fruit)
- Grape (fruit)
- Juneberry (fruit)
- Lilac (flower)
- Mint (leaves)
- Mugwort (leaves)
- Mulberry (fruit)
- Mustard (leaves and flowers)
- Nasturtium (leaves and flower)
- Daisy (leaves and flowers)
- Quickweed (leaves and stems)
- Pepperweed (leaves)
- Plantain (leaf)
- Red cover (leaves and flowers)
- Rose (flower)
- Quickweed (leaves, flowers, and stems)
- Queen Anne's Lace (fruit and flowers)
- Wild bean (seed)
- wild ginger (root)
- Watercress (leaves)
- Wild lettuce (sap)

Fall Foraging

The fall is a time characterized by slowing down. There is something in the air as fall comes close that feels like the ending. This is a time of closure, wrapping things up, and bringing comfort. There is a sort of before and after in the fall that comes with the first frost. Most herbaceous plants die at this point, most fruit goes bad, and those should be a priority in foraging before any heartier plants. While the fall is the time of closing, it is also a time to harvest for many crops. Those who have their own garden and grow squash and more are finally seeing the fruits of their labor.

Because winter is coming, the forager should take advantage of any fresh food that they can get while they still can. Stocking up on preservatives, especially the late summer into fall fruit, is a good idea. If you have a garden or backyard plants, they might need to be protected over the winter.

- Ameranth (leaves and seeds)
- Apples (fruit)
- Barberry (fruit)
- Beebalm (leaves)
- Birch (twigs)
- Black cherry (fruit)
- Black walnut (nut)
- Butternut (nut)
- Cattails (roots)
- Common Mallow (root)
- Cranberry (fruit)
- Curly dock (leaves and seeds)
- Dandelion (all)
- Evening Primrose (root and leaves)
- Epazote (leaves)
- False Solomon's Seal (berries)
- Field Garlic (leaves)
- Fragrant sumac (berries)
- Ginkgo (leaf and nut)
- Glass weed (stems)
- Goldenrod (leaves and flower)
- Goutweed (leaves)
- Ground Cherry (fruit)
- Grape (fruit)
- Hawthorn (fruit)
- Highbush cranberry (fruit)

- Hickory (nut)
- Honewort (root)
- Groundnut (root)
- Jerusalem artichoke (root)
- Juniper (berry)
- Lambs quarters (seeds)
- Lotus (root and seed)
- Mayapple (fruit)
- Mint (leaves)
- Mustard (leaves, flowers, and seeds)
- Oak (nuts)
- Parsnip (root)
- Pawpaw (fruit)
- Peach (fruit)
- Pear (fruit)
- Pepperweed (seeds)
- Pineapple weed (fruit)
- Plantain (leaf)
- Rose (fruit)
- Sassafras (root)
- Thistle (root)
- Autumn Olive (berry)
- Queen Anne's Lace (root)
- Watercress (leaves)
- Wild Potato (root)

Winter Foraging

Winter is a time of rest, peace, and often family. For those who get snow, winter can be a very isolating time, especially if you find an escape in the outside world. On the nicer days it's a good idea to try to get outside and enjoy the sun as much as you can. Luckily, you can forage in the winter.

Foraging in the winter is obviously the most complicated, even more so in places with snow. For some, this might be a welcome challenge. Most foraging in the winter is done by finding any nuts or fruit that wasn't harvested in the fall. If the ground is not frozen, roots are a great option, as well as some cold resistant greens.

Here are some plants to forage during the winter:

- Common Mallow (roots)
- Curly Dock (leaves)
- Dandelion (all, but mostly root)
- Evening Primrose (root and leaves)
- Fragrant sumac (berries)
- Highbush cranberry (fruit)

15
AMARANTH

*A*maranth is a name for a genus of plants under the scientific name *Amaranthus*, also known as 'Pigweed.' The most commonly foraged species of amaranth is *A. retroflexus* and *A. hybridus*, but many of the genus can be eaten. This plant should be used with caution as it pulls high amounts of nitrogen from the ground.

IDENTIFICATION OF THE PLANT

The two species noted above get as tall as 7 feet with a single erect stem, but other plants in the genus range from 3-10 feet tall. The plants are usually an average green and may have a red hue.

The characteristics of the leaves are as follows: simple, ovate alternating leaves with a slight waved edge on some species, some with more prominent points, and some that are completely smooth. *A. retroflexus* leaves reach up to 4 inches long and 3 inches wide. *A. hybridus* can be up to 6 inches long and 2 inches wide.

The flower is very small and densely packed into a spike. *A. retroflexus* has a more weedy look, with a green flower that takes a spike shape at the top of the plant that reaches up to eight inches, is fairly narrow, and typically seen late summer to fall. This plant is more ornamental and goes bright red like some garden varieties. The spike might have slightly longer offshoots, making it look like a bunch of caterpillars. However, it has less of a droop than some of the other more decorative species.

Where to gather it

Amaranth is a common weed. As such, it likes most places, including areas that are overgrown, meaning places where the ground has been disturbed at some point. It can be found in spring, summer, and fall. It thrives in temperate climates, which makes it perfect for the Northeast.

How to gather it

In the spring, gather the greens. Once it is established, it will become woody. Seeds can be harvested from the flower spike, but be sure to time this right because the seeds have to develop before they drop to the ground. You might place a sort of mat on the ground to collect the seeds by shaking the plant or by gently cutting the spike off completely.

How to cook with it

Edible: the seeds of the plant are packed with protein. They can be eaten raw or you can roast them, use them as a porridge, popcorn, ground into flour, etc.

The leaves can be eaten raw like regular leafy greens or you can boil them, similar to spinach, or dry them and use them as a herb. They have a hearty flavor to them mixed with a hint of sweetness.

Amaranth Porridge

Time: 25 minutes
Serving Size: 4 servings
Ingredients:

- 1 cup of Amaranth seeds
- 2 cups water
- 1 tsp honey for taste
- 1 pinch salt for taste
- optional: other warming spices like nutmeg and cinnamon

Instructions:

1. Bring water and salt to a boil.
2. Add Amaranth seeds and reduce heat to a simmer.
3. Cover the pot and let simmer for about 20 minutes so the seeds absorb the water.

4. Take the hot cereal off of the heat.
5. Add honey and spices of your choice (optional).

Author: Pigweed is desirable because it provides vitamin A and C as well as a balance of other minerals and daily nutrient needs. It has been used in medicine for soothing common symptoms of ailments. It is also used as a natural yellow and green dye.

16
APPLES

There are many kinds of apples, all genetically selected and bred based on people's specific preferences. This identification should help you determine that the tree belongs to the genus *Malus*, but apple trees are particularly hard to identify down to the specific species. This is because the seeds of an apple are unpredictable, using genetic code completely different from the apple that it came from. This occurred as a result of settlers using apples for drinks, not typically for food, and not caring to grow apples from grafting, which is the only way to ensure the kind and quality of apples. Finding an apple in the wild is luck of the draw when it comes to quality. The difference between an apple and a **crabapple** is the size of the fruit. An apple that is four inches across or smaller is considered a crabapple.

IDENTIFICATION OF THE PLANT

The trees can grow up to 40 feet by a huge range, the smallest being more shrub-like than a tree at 10 feet tall. They typically have a solo trunk and a mushroom-like top. The trunk is light gray to brown that cracks and peels from a smooth surface as it matures. The leaves are up to four inches long. They are a simple shape, slightly thick in texture, smooth to the touch, and lighter green.

The flower of the apple tree has five petals, which are typically white but can be pink or even red. These grow on long stamens, but can be bunched together on the tree, giving the blooming tree a dense look.

The fruit of an apple ranges quite a bit in between species. Crabapples are typically smaller. Crop apples can get as large as five inches wide. They are round and range in color from red, to yellow, green and more. When cut in half, the apple will have a star-like pattern at the core that contains the seeds.

Where to gather it

Apples bloom in the spring and are ready to pick in the fall. They like areas that have a lot of sun and slightly shelter, possibly from surrounding trees. They like well-drained soil with just enough moisture.

How to gather it

Apple blossoms are edible, but too much can be poisonous. Forage at your own discretion as picking blossoms can mean not letting an apple grow in its place. They would be plucked off the tree in the spring. Apples are ready to eat in the fall. The stem will be brown, making it easy to twist off the tree. You can also taste test if you know the species to see if the apple has reached its desired flavor.

How to cook with it

Edible: Yes.

Apples in nature are the same as apples from the store. Depending on the flavor of the apples, you should determine the best way to use them—whether raw or in pies, drinks, or sauces. Apple blossoms can be used as a floral in spring salads.

APPLE CRISP RECIPE

Time: 1 hour
Serving Size: 6 servings
Ingredients:

- 2 cups peeled and chopped apples
- 1 cup flour
- 1 cup white sugar
- 1/2 cup softened butter
- 1 tsp lemon juice
- ¾ cup rolled oats
- a pinch of salt
- warming spices like nutmeg and cinnamon

Instructions:

1. Preheat the oven to 350 °F.
2. In a bowl, mix the apples, spices, lemon juice, and sugar.
3. In a separate bowl, add the oats, flour, salt, and butter.
4. Cut the butter into the dry ingredients until the pieces are the size of a pea.
5. In a buttered baking sheet, add the apple mixture.
6. On top of the apples, layer the dry mixture evenly.
7. Bake for about 45 minutes.

Author: Apples have a fairly good shelf life, even as a raw fruit. It's possible to pick more than a day's worth and not waste anything. Eating a freshly picked apple from a tree and enjoying the crunch of it on a sunny autumn day is one of the most amazing feelings.

The leaves and tender twigs are an agreeable food to many domestic animals, like cows, horses, sheep, and goats; the fruit is sought after by the first, as well as by the hog. Thus, there appears to have existed a natural alliance between these animals and this tree. The fruit of the Crab in the forests of France is said to be a great resource for the wild-boar.

17
ASPARAGUS

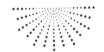

If you've never seen an asparagus—scientific name *Asparagus officinalis*—growing from the ground, you might be caught off guard to see one naturally. Young asparagus shoots come out of the ground, and it looks like someone just stuck a piece of asparagus in the ground.

Identification of the plant

Wild asparagus looks as described above in the spring: a stalk up to 12 inches long, erect, with a scaly pointed top. As it matures, it gets up to six feet tall and very thin and spindly. It looks like an herbaceous tree by the fall if it hasn't been harvested, with lots of thin branches and thin, dill-like needles.

The flower is a pale yellow that hangs off the stem in opposite pairs with about a 2 inch stem. The flower has 6 sepals that create a long bell shape and a small golden pistils (interior/center).

The fruit of the asparagus is a bright red, blueberry sized berry that hangs off the stem in opposite pairs with about a 2 inch stem. It contains round black seeds that are toxic.

Where to gather it

You can find asparagus in well drained areas that have been disturbed. If you are able to spot the larger, mature plant out of season, take note and come back in the spring. You might be able to notice last year's remains to help identify their spot.

How to gather it

Carefully take a sharp pair of scissors or a knife and cut the young shot an inch or so from the ground. You might be able to come back and find more shoots as well.

How to cook with it

Edible: Cook young shoots for about 15 minutes in whatever recipe you choose. They can be boiled, steamed, or roasted. Do not eat mature plants as they can be poisonous.

Roasted Asparagus

Time: 20 minutes
Serving Size: 4 servings
Ingredients:

- 10-15 Asparagus spears
- 5 tbsps Olive oil
- garlic, adjust to preference
- 1 pinch salt and pepper for taste
- 1 pinch sesame seeds

Instructions:

1. Preheat the oven to 425 °F.
2. Lay the asparagus spears on a tray flat.
3. In a bowl, mix everything else, then drizzle over the asparagus, but make sure they are covered.
4. Cook for up to 15 minutes.

Author: Asparagus is high in fiber and antioxidants and are commonly used for detoxing. White asparagus is found in places where the young shoots are covered to keep them away from sunlight for better flavor; however, it has less nutrients. The seeds and roots of asparagus have been used in medicine, but there has been no scientific evidence for it. I prefer to boil them freshly picked and eat them with salt, lemon, and hollandaise sauce on the side.

18
BASSWOOD

merican basswood can also be called Liden or *Tilia americana*.

Identification of the plant

This plant is a tree with leaves that grow up to 120 feet tall and 5 feet wide, making it rather huge when it has reached maturity. As long as the tree is under 100 years old, it will probably seed. The bark is gray to brown and smooth. The newer growth on the wigs are green with a reddish hue.

The leaves are heart-shaped with a saw-like edge, and more of a darker green with a slight gloss to it. The leaves have a pain vein down the center with parallel straight veins that spread out of it. The young buds of the flower have got a red hue to it.

The flowers hang from long stems that branch off to more flowers. They are small and yellow, and they start round and open to long, fanned stamens. The fruit is small, round, and hard. It starts light green, then turns brown.

Where to gather it

The buds are some of the most desirable parts of the tree, which come out in very early spring. The flowers bloom in late spring and into early summer.

How to gather it

If you can find a tree with branches that are low hanging enough in the spring, you can pick or cut off the buds. The leaves are always edible, but taste better when they are younger. Similarly with the flowers, they can be plucked off of low hanging branches when they are in bloom.

How to cook with it

Edible: Yes, all parts of the tree can be safely eaten, but the buds and the flowers are the only parts typically eaten for enjoyment.

The buds are eaten raw or dressed up in salad. The leaves are edible all year, but are best as buds. If you like the mature leaves, they can be used up until the fall when they fall from the tree. The flowers can be dried for tea. The tree can also be tapped to make a syrup.

LINDEN TEA

Time: 2-20 minutes
Serving Size: 1 serving
Ingredients:

- a few tsps dry linden flower
- 1 cup water
- honey for taste

Instructions:

1. Put water on the heat and remove just before boiling.
2. Add leaves to your tea pot or cup.
3. Let steep for 2-20 minutes.
4. Remove tea leaves by removing the bag or strain.
5. Serve hot.

Author: This tree is a favorite because not many people can eat the leaves off of a tree. While the leaves are preferred when they are younger, it can be a funny party trick to start eating a leaf right off a tree.

The first time I ever had it was in my grandma's house when I was a kid. She prepared this delicious salad, and instead of lettuce, she used basswood leaves. It was so tasty and quickly became one of my favorite dishes at her house.

19
BARBERRY

Barberry is a name for a genus of plants scientifically named *Berberis*. The berries from the barberry plant can be picked from many of the species, but there is a strong preference for specific species, and there is more evidence about safety with these common species. The barberry is invasive, and in some places in the United States is actually illegal to plant. If you are foraging in your backyard, it is a good idea to keep your bush from spreading and taking over other plants.

Other things to remember when foraging the barberry shrub is that they can be a home to ticks, thorns, and rust. Rust is an orange colored mold that can infect other plants. Ticks are bugs that can carry lyme disease. They are no joke, unlike other bugs that are annoying, these bugs are not harmless and can cause long term health issues. Be safe. When you are foraging, make sure to wear thick, long pants and high boots, some even duct tape the seam of their boot and their pants to make sure that the ticks have no way in. Wear gloves and check yourself and any pets you brought along with you for ticks if you come in contact with one.

The species of barberry that this chapter will cover is *B. Vulgaris*.

IDENTIFICATION OF THE PLANT

The bush can grow up to 10 feet, but it is common to see them smaller. The shrub is not necessarily dense, but the long, spindly branches can create quite a cover. They are thin and reddish yellow when they are young, turning gray as they mature. The branches are covered in long thorns. The leaves are alternate, but they seem to come out of the branches crowded in rows of about 5, creating a circular fan look. The leaves are about 2 inches long and have an oval shape that is rounded on the ends. They have a prominent margin and slightly fold into it. It is also slightly toothed on the bottom. The color can range from a yellow green with a very faint red rim around the edge to a dark, attractive red in the fall.

The flowers bloom in the spring and droop in triangle florets, which is the shape and size of a regular grape cluster. The individual flowers are yellow and form a round cup look, opening wide to a round flat, pale green disk on a stigma. The fruit droops in clusters of about 10. They are a bright red, although more orange than purple. The individual fruit is about half an inch long and oblong like a stretched out grape. Similar in appearance to the cranberry.

Where to gather it

The shrub is invasive, which means that it is typically fairly adaptable, although it prefers more open areas. Any disturbed or typically weedy area is a good place to start. The berries are ready to pick in the fall. The red color of the berries is a good indicator they are ripe.

How to gather it

As noted above, it's important to follow more serious safety precautions when harvesting from the barberry. When the berries are in season, you can pick the berries off of the bush. If the area is infested with barberry, you might have a harder time getting through the thicket.

How to cook with it

Edible: Yes, the ripe berries can be eaten, but nothing else.

The berries can be used in jams and other preservatives, but also has a place in savory dishes. It's especially popular in Persian cooking.

BARBERRY RICE

Time: 40 minutes
Serving Size: 4 servings
Ingredients:

- 1 cup rice (basmati recommended)

- 1 tbsp unflavored greek yogurt
- 1 pinch saffron
- ⅓ cup barberry
- 1 tsp sugar or honey
- 1 pinch salt and pepper, onion, garlic (other spices optional)
- 1 tbsp oil

Instructions:

1. Clean and wash the rice and berries.
2. Put the barberries in a heat safe container and cover with 1 tbsp of boiling water.
3. Repeat in a separate bowl with saffron.
4. Wash the rice and add it to a pot with water and salt.
5. Bring it to a boil on high heat.
6. Once the rice has hit a boil, add the barberries.
7. Cover, turn down to simmer.
8. About 15 minutes later, when the rice is ready, take off the heat, keep the lid on, and let it sit for 5 minutes.
9. Fluff after 5 minutes, add pepper, saffron, and saffron water, but don't overmix.
10. Serve with greek yogurt, add in spices based on your own preference.

Author: The barberry plant is poisonous since it contains a chemical called berberine. This chemical, while poisonous as a food, is used as a medicine against infection, especially orally. Unless you have the proper research on how to use this plant as a medicine, you should stick to a professional provider's advice, but if you are getting into the multiple uses of a plant, this is something to consider.

20
BEACH PLUM

There are a few varieties of the beach plum, but this species is called *Prunus maritime*.

IDENTIFICATION OF THE PLANT

This plant grows up to 10 feet tall but is considered a shrub. The branches are slightly hairy when young and produce alternating leaves that are three inches long and simple with a slightly jagged edge.

When the plant flowers, it has a few flowers per cluster, they are only about half an inch wide and are white in a star shape. The fruit, which is round and rather small (i.e., slightly larger than a cherry), is the most important part of the plant. The color of the fruit varies, just like normal plums, from dark red, blue, or yellow.

Where to gather it

Beach plums live up to their name because they like to grow in sandy areas. The fruit is ripe in late summer.

How to gather it

A beach plum can be enjoyed by plucking it from the tree. You can taste test it to see if the ripeness of the fruit is to your liking.

How to cook with it

Edible: Yes, you can eat the fruit.

It is recommended to use these plums in jams or the like, desserts, or turn them into prunes.

Beach Plum Jelly

This recipe makes about 8 jars of jelly.
Time: about 30 minutes
Ingredients:

- 8 cups beach plums
- 1 cup of water
- 6 cups sugar
- 3 oz liquid pectin
- optional: warming spices like nutmeg and cinnamon

Instructions:

1. In a large pot, bring the beach plums and water to a boil.
2. Cook until the fruit is soft.
3. Strain juice from any flesh or pits.
4. Pour 4 cups of this juice back into a clean pot with sugar.
5. Sugar should dissolve and come to a boil.
6. Add pectin and bring to a boil again.
7. Remove from heat, start adding it to jam jars that have been sterilized.
8. Don't wait until cool because it will turn solid and be harder to jar.
9. Seal the jar and store for up to a year, make sure to label.

Note: Once the jars are sealed, it's recommended to take the ring off of the jar. This ring is only used to keep the top on when initially sealing. If it is kept on the jar and if the seal breaks, the ring can reseal the lid, making the jar contaminated and rotten without you knowing.

Author: The pit is rather large for this fruit and some might find this recipe too much work because of that. The pit should not be ingested because it contains chemicals poisonous to humans.

The first time I tried this plum straight from the tree it was so acidic that my entire face flexed. I told my friends that this was the best plums they'd ever have and so they'd bite into them and feel the same sensation. I loved playing this game as a kid with my friends, sister, and family.

21
BEE BALM/BERGAMOT

*B*ee balms and Bergamot are part of the genus *Monarda*. Specifically, wild bergamont is called *M. fisulosa*. This plant is actually part of the mint family.

IDENTIFICATION OF THE PLANT

The plant is small and creeps across the ground, but can grow up to three feet tall. The flowers bloom on the top of stems, but they typically grow in clusters. The color of this species of flower is a light purple. They are not cultivated for their ornamental use, unlike others from this genus. The flowers are less flashy, opening with thin 10-14 petals and fanned stamen.

The leaves are opposite and ovulate. The color varies a bit from light to dark green.

Where to gather it

This plant grows in rich soil but likes well drained areas. They like sunlight with protection, and, as such, they are found near openings of trees. This plant blooms in the summer and into the fall.

How to gather it

You can harvest the leaves and flowers off the main plant or cut the whole thing and garble it inside.

How to cook with it

Edible: The leaves are edible raw or cooked. They can be used in salad or boiled in cooked greens. The flowers are used in teas for floral taste and can be dried.

Bee Balm Bread

This recipe makes two small loaves.
Time: 2 hours
Ingredients:

- 1 cup 1/2 warm water
- 1 pack yeast
- 4 cups flour
- 1 cup bee balm petals
- 1 egg
- 1 tbsp softened honey
- 3 tbsps butter

Instructions:

1. Activate yeast in a bowl with ½ cup warm water, let sit until it creates a bit of a foam (around 30 minutes in a warm room).
2. After the yeast has activated, add the rest of the water, butter, and honey, then mix.
3. Add flour and bee balm. Stir together well.
4. Form into a ball and cover. Let it rise for 1 hour.
5. Take a ball of risen dough and knead for 10 minutes.
6. Bread should be stretchy, so that it does not rip right away.
7. Preheat the oven to 400 °F.
8. Let sit for 20-30 minutes, while preheating in a baking pan or split into 2 pans.
9. Egg wash a beaten egg gently onto the top of the dough.
10. Bake for 30-40 minutes or until bread looks golden on the top.

Author: This plant is used and noted for a multitude of reasons, starting with attracting hummingbirds, due to its pleasant smell. It is also used in herbal medicine for relieving common cold symptoms and more.

22
BIRCH

*B*lack or sweet birch, also known as *Betula lenta*.

IDENTIFICATION OF THE PLANT

The tree typically only grows to about 30 feet but has the possibility of growing up to 100 feet in the right habitat. The bark is similar in texture to the typical peeling, like the thin bark that is associated with birch trees, but it is a dark gray. If scratched, the young branches emit a minty smell. As the tree matures, it leaves the thin bark behind and becomes thick and cracked. The leaves alternate; they grow up to six inches long. They are an elongated, simple shape, with a main vein down the center and parallel veins moving out and upward straight from it. The edges are very finely jagged. The color is green to yellow in the fall.

The flowers are drooping two inch catkins. They are thin, small, ball-like flowers. They are yellowish green to a burnt yellow.

Where to gather it

The trees can be found commonly in forests, they prefer well drained soil. It can be harvested any time of year, which is especially useful and tasty in winter. The sap is best harvested in the early spring when the sugars are flowing.

How to gather it

It is best to avoid eating the inner bark of a tree because it can cause a lot of damage to the tree. Young twigs can be cut off the tree. If there are any roots that are at ground level, they can be sawed and harvested.

How to cook with it

Edible: Yes, twigs, inner bark, root bark, and sap.

The inner bark is only used in emergency situations. It can be dried or boiled. When dried, it can be grinded and made into a flour. Tea can be made from steeping twigs and inner bark. Sap needs to be boiled into a syrup. All parts need to be cooked first.

Birch Twig Tea

Time: 45 minutes
Serving Size: 4 servings
Ingredients:

- 1 cup Birch twigs

Instructions:

1. The birch twigs should be fairly young and small. Cut them into small pieces, about an inch long.
2. Heat the oven to about 325 °F.
3. On a tray lay the pieces out flat and evenly.
4. Roast twigs for about half an hour.
5. Let rest until cool.
6. In a mortar and pestle or other grinding device, gently grind the twigs. Do not over grind, this is a tea, not a coffee. If it is over ground it will be harder to strain leaves after steeping.
7. Store dry tea in a dry and cool area.
8. Use one spoon of tea leaf for 1 cup of hot water to make tea.
9. Because of the roasting and grinding process, you only need to steep for up to 5 minutes, unlike other wood or root teas that need to be boiled or steeped longer.

Author: This is not a plant that needs to be at the top of the foragers list. Preferably, it should be used by those who may want to try some more advanced methods and plants for foraging.

It was in Norway. This tall bearded man with long blond hair took me into the woods. He brought a bottle, a string, and a metal straw and told me that I'd be about to drink the best water of my life. He stopped at a Birch tree and dug a little hole to put the metal straw inside, attached the bottle, and told me to prepare myself mentally for this elixir. We kept walking. After 1 hour we went back to the same tree. The 1-liter bottle was filled with this birch water, called birch sap. I took a sip of it and felt my body healing. It's something magical that everybody needs to try at least once in their lives. Don't forget to be respectful towards nature. Don't drain the tree because, ultimately, this sap is the tree's blood.

23
BLACK CHERRY

*T*he black cherry is scientifically named *Prunus serotina*.

IDENTIFICATION OF THE PLANT

The tree grows up to 70 feet. The bark of this tree is fairly dark bark that is smooth, but cracked. The leaves are a glossy darker green and thick in texture. They are ovate in shape and slightly toothed along the bottom margins. They might turn yellow, orange, or red in the fall. The flowers are very small and white with 5 petals in a star shape. These flowers grow in six inch racemen.

The fruit is the same as the cherry-round, coming off of long stems, and red, dark red, or even appearing black.

Where to gather it

You might find the tree in any forest as it is fairly adaptable. In the late summer to early fall, you might be able to pluck the fruit from the tree.

How to gather it

Alternatively, you might have to wait for the fruit to fall from the tree, in which you can lay down a tarp or similar. It is best not to let them fall directly on the ground because the fruits will start rotting right away.

How to cook with it

Edible: The fruit can be used as its equivalent from the store. They can be eaten raw, put in desserts, or preserved as jams.

WILD CHERRY PIE FILLING

This recipe makes one pie.
Time: About 20 minutes
Ingredients:

- 5 cups pitted cherries
- 1/2 cup water
- 2 tbsps lemon juice
- ¾ cup sugar (Adjust if needed. This recipe is for wild berries which tend to be more sour)
- 4 tbsps cornstarch
- optional: ¼ tsp almond extract

Instructions:

1. In a pot, combine all ingredients **except** the almond extract.
2. Bring to a boil while stirring.
3. Cook for 10 minutes.
4. Add extract.
5. Take off heat.
6. Store in the freezer or add to pie crust right away.

Author: Just like the regular cherry, you should be cautious of the pit of the cherry because it can contain cyanide. I love to treat my wife by preparing her a chocolate cherry cheesecake with fresh cherries. She goes crazy for it!

24
BLACK LOCUST

*T*he black locust is scientifically named *Robinia pseudoacacia*.

IDENTIFICATION OF THE PLANT

The tree reaches up to 30 feet on average, but in some cases it can grow past 150 feet. It is typically very erect. The bark is very rough in texture and gray with a red undertone. The leaves are dark green compound leaves, which are 1-2 inches in length and oval shaped, noticeably more round than most leaves at the point.

The white flowers hang down in short drooping stems. The flowers are about an inch wide and are spread out across the stem alternatingly. The flowers are trumpet shaped and asymmetrical. The short individual stems are 1-2 inches and red. There is a reddish cupped bracket that holds the flowers onto the stem. There are quite a few of these drooping branches on the tree, giving it a beautiful show when it is in bloom.

Where to gather it

The tree likes lots of sun and drier areas. The bloom period is about two weeks in late spring: around May to June.

How to gather it

You can gather the flowers by snipping off the drooping flower branches. They are fairly large, so you will need to have scissors as well as a large enough basket. If the tree is not located somewhere you naturally see every day in the spring, make sure to check on the tree regularly at this time of year so that you don't miss the short bloom period.

How to cook with it

Edible: The flowers can be eaten raw, battered, or fried. All parts of the flower can be eaten, the reddish cup bracket being the sweetest part. They can be made into syrup.

FRIED BLACK LOCUST FLOWER

Time: About 30 minutes
Serving Size: 4 servings
Ingredients:

- 12 bunches of Locust flower
- 1 cup flower
- ⅔ cup water
- 1 pinch baking soda
- 1 pinch salt for taste
- 1 tbsp honey
- oil for frying (best if it's fresh)
- 1 tsp sugar

Instructions:

1. Wash the flowers in cold water and remove any inedible pieces.
2. Dry them off well.
3. Mix together flour, baking soda, salt, water, and flour to make a batter and let rest for a few minutes to a half hour.
4. Heat a pan with oil. Make sure it isn't too hot, but hot enough that it won't over cook the petals.
5. The batter should be a beautiful crunchy golden color.
6. Sprinkle it with sugar and serve.

Author: It can be a little inconvenient to time getting this plant right, but it is a beautiful and delicious plate to create. So, if you have the time and the tree, it's worthwhile to try and forage for some black locust flowers.

25
BLACK WALNUT

*T*he black walnut is also scientifically known as *Juglans nigra*.

IDENTIFICATION OF THE PLANT

The black walnut tree can grow up to 130 feet tall. The bark on the tree is very dark, thick, and rough textured with cracks. On younger growth, the color might appear lighter. Leaves are compound and alternating on a 1-2 foot stem with about an inch between each leaf. The leaves are more triangular in shape but elongated to four inches and narrow. Slight teeth on the margin. There are flowers in the shape of catkins in the spring but they are unremarkable.

The fruit is green to brown, round, and about three inches in diameter at their largest. Inside is the nut, which is the same as a store bought walnut nut appearance, resembling a brain with lobes and deep wrinkled texture.

Where to gather it

The black walnut tree likes low land areas with the combination of well drained soil. The nuts are ready to harvest in the fall.

How to gather it

Unlike fruit, you can pick the nuts off the ground that have fallen from the tree. When they fall on the ground, they are fully aged. The harder part of this process is to husk the outside of the black walnut. This process may take a while and may involve heavy duty steel brushes and other tools to ensure its clean.

How to cook with it
Edible: Yes.

Once you have cleaned the husk of the nut, it needs to go through a drying process that might take a few days to completely dry. After this, the shell still needs to be broken. This can be a dangerous process if you don't have the right tools and aren't careful. Once you have broken the shell open, you need to boil all the material for about 30 minutes. This can help separate the nut and the shell, but it can also release the oil that can be used in cooking. This leaves the nut left to be used like any other nut in cooking.

BLACK WALNUT COOKIES

Time: 20 Minutes
Serving Size: 1 batch
Ingredients:

- 1 cup black walnuts
- 3 cups all purpose flour
- 1 cup white sugar, 1 cup brown sugar
- 1 cup butter
- 1 pinch each of salt and baking soda
- 2 eggs
- optional: warming spices like nutmeg and cinnamon

Instructions:

1. In a large mixing bowl, add cream, butter, and sugar, then beat in the eggs.
2. In a separate bowl, mix flour, baking soda, and salt.
3. Mix the dry ingredients into the wet ingredients.
4. Once mixed, add in the walnuts.
5. Refrigerate until firm.
6. Preheat the oven to 350 °F.
7. Roll dough into small balls and flatten. Don't play with them too much because it'll warm them up.

8. Bake for 1o minutes.

Author: The husk of the walnut is used for homemade dyes. My parents would make the 'nocino' liqueur and put it in the dark cellar to soak for months until it was done. I loved sneaking into the cellar and grabbing a little glass, filling it with this delicious alcoholic drink, adding some sugar to it, and having some sips of it. It was a great replacement for a sweet treat when my mum wouldn't get me the candy I wanted.

26
BLUEBERRY

There are two kinds of blueberries that you might run into: the first being *Vaccinum corymbosum* or the swamp blueberry, and the second *Vaccinium angustifolium* or the lowbush blueberry.

IDENTIFICATION OF THE PLANT

Both species of blueberries grow in shrubs, but there is an obvious height difference, with the swamp blueberry growing up to 12 feet and the lowbush growing up to 1 foot.

On both blueberries, the leaves on the plant alternate and are simple —up to three inches on the swamp berry and half that on the lowbush berry. The small flowers cluster and hang from short stems into off-white, thick petaled bells.

The fruit on the lowbush berry tends to be slightly more blue, whereas the swamp blueberry tends to be a little darker, both with a dusty-like coat. The berries are small and round with a little jagged crown on one side.

Where to gather it

As the name swamp blueberry implies, this variation of blueberry is more common in wetlands. Alternatively, the lowbush berry likes higher elevations and rocky, dry land. They fruit in the summer.

How to gather it

Unlike the other berries that are foraged in bramble bushes, the blueberry tends to be a **little** bit easier since it grows in a more manageable shrub. You can pluck the fruit right off of the plant when it is ready and taste test to see if they are right.

How to cook with it
Edible: Yes, the fruit.

Blueberries can be treated like any blueberry you find in the store. This means they can be eaten raw, preserved, dried, or cooked into dishes of your preference.

BLUEBERRY MUFFINS

This recipe makes 10 regular sized muffins.
Time: 30 minutes
Ingredients:

- 1 ½ cups all purpose flour
- 3/4 cup white sugar
- 2 tsps baking powder
- 1/3 cup oil (canola or vegetable)
- 1 large egg
- 1/2 cup milk of choice
- 1 ½ tsp vanilla extract
- 1 cup fresh or frozen blueberries
- a pinch of salt

Instructions:

1. Preheat the oven to 400 °F.
2. Butter the muffin tin or use cupcake liners.
3. In a bowl, mix together liquids. In another, combine the dry ingredients.
4. Combine the two, mix only as much as necessary. The trick to fluffy muffins is to avoid over mixing. Add more milk if necessary. The batter should be fairly liquidy, unlike cookie recipes.
5. Add in blueberries, then fold the batter over lightly.
6. Pour or scoop batter into muffin tin.

7. Bake for 15 minutes, do a toothpick test. Then bake for another 5 minutes and try again.

Author: While blueberries are obviously blueberries when you are careful, always take some extra caution when it comes to eating strange berries. A lot of wild berries are the same shape and, without care, might be misidentified.

Also, wild blueberries aren't comparable to the ones you find in the supermarket. Make sure to sit down next to blueberry bushes and enjoy the sweetness of these delicious berries.

27
BRAMBLES

RASPBERRIES, BLACKBERRIES, AND BLACKRASPBERRIES

Brambles are an umbrella term for plants that are able to be more shrub-like in some environments and, in others, might climb like a vine or just be a thick brush. It is easier to group them together in these cases because the plants themselves look similar, and it's a matter of identifying which berry you have in front of you. In this chapter, when we are talking about brambles, it's specific to the rubus genus.

Identification of the Plant

Brambles: The shape of each of these plants are brambles: long thin stems that are semi-erect, sometimes creating an arch shape once the vine becomes long enough and droops.

Raspberries are a small red berry that looks like a hollow stack of small balls. It has little hairs that come out of the fruit. Similarly black raspberries also share a resemblance to raspberries but are different in color.

Blackberries are solid, not hollow, and have a glossy look to them. Black berries, while similar to raspberries, are also slightly bigger and sometimes longer than a raspberry. While they are both edible, it's important to know the distinction. When blackberries are not ripe, they are red and can look like a raspberry, but it is not recommended to eat blackberries until they reach maturity.

Where to gather it

Brambles like a lot of sunlight and some shelter from other harsh elements. This means you might find brambles in openings or on the edge of woods. Keep in mind they also do not like to sit in any water, so look for higher grounds.

How to gather it

Pick as fruit ripens. It is important to take some caution when dealing with vines or shrubs because they can be prickly. Since bramble plants do climb and spread, you might not be able to reach the entire plant for harvesting. If you are growing the plants yourself, you might have more luck training the plant for ease of access.

How to cook with it

Edible: The variety of berries that come from brambles is the same as the berries that you get in the store. They can be eaten raw or used in a number of dishes, mostly desserts. They can also be preserved in jam.

Mix Berry Jam

Time: 40 minutes
Serving Size: 6-10 jars
Ingredients:

- 6 cups of fresh berries of your choice
- 5 cups white sugar (adjust to your sweetness preference, but remember that sugar is what helps preserves, so don't undercut too much)
- 1 tbsp lemon juice

Instructions:

1. Put a small plate in the freezer.
2. In a large pot, add the berries and the lemon juice.
3. On medium heat the berries will slowly come to a boil and then soften.
4. Bring to a boil and reduce heat to a simmer for 15 minutes.

5. Add sugar off on low heat and stir until dissolved. Then bring back to a boil.
6. Boil for about 5 minutes.
7. Take out the plate in the freezer, put a small drop of jam to cool it quickly and test for jam consistency.
8. Once done, skim the top with a ladle for impurities and foam.
9. Add to sterilize jam jars.
10. Seal the jars and label.

Note: Once the jars are sealed, take the ring off of the jar.

Author: While thickets that are full of brambles can be less than fun to walk through, it is a great natural wall in your own gardens as well.

At my grandparent's table in the summer, they'd always have a bowl filled with these delicious berries in their fridge. I was always excited to drive to my grandparents, open the fridge, and put them on top of my favorite banana yogurt.

28
BURDOCK AND RHUBARB

Burdock is the common name for the genus *Arctium*. Both common burdock, scientific name *A. minus*, and greater burdock, scientific name *A. lappa*, are the most used when it comes to eating. Both are common in North America.

While Burdock and rhubarb are not part of the same family, rhubarb belongs to the *Rheum* genus, it makes sense to put them together because of how similar they look. Young burdock and rhubarb are almost identical, especially to those who do not know the difference, and the mistake is not one that can be overlooked. Rhubarb leaves are not edible and can make you pretty sick. Also, if you are trying to forage rhubarb stalks for a pie and end up with the celery-like burdock, you will find yourself with a less than pleasant dessert.

IDENTIFICATION OF THE PLANT

A. minus can grow up to 6 feet and *A. lappa* to 9 feet.

Very large leaves, spanning up to 20 inches long and 12 inches wide, in a heart shape. Its leaves have a wavy edge with thick, fleshy, and veined stems. The leaves are slightly textured by veining. *A. lappa* has solid stems, *A. minus* has hollow stems. When mature, they get a woody stem that gives them height and may have a reddish tone to it.

The difference in rhubarb and burdock at this stage is subtle. The leaves on a rhubarb curl or wrinkle up on the edges, while the Burdock's leaves have a slight hair on the underside. The stalks of a rhubarb are solid stems. Rhubarb's stems are also noticeably red or pink—but this should not be your only indication, as burdock can have a (typically not as bright) red hue.

These plants are known for their burrs, which contain their tiny purple/pink flowers at the top with long, white stamen. The burrs are green and brown when dried. They are covered in what looks like one inch thorns but have a small hook on the end for clinging on to a passerby.

One of the easiest ways to tell the difference between the two is that *A. minus*'s burs are usually singular, whereas *A. lappa* grows them in clustered florets. The other differentiator is that *A. lappa*'s leaves will be rounder, whereas *A. minus* will have slightly elongated leaves.

Where to gather it

Burdock is typically considered a weed, and finds itself in common weedy areas such as disturbed, grown over places. Best to harvest in the spring because the plant can get woody. Rhubarb is typically harvested mid spring and not preferred past July. Rhubarb likes full sun and well draining, fertile soil.

How to gather it

The young burdock plant can harvest the roots in the first year as well as the base of the leaf stems. In the second year, you can harvest the flower stalk. Use a sharp pair of scissors to sever thick vessels. Rhubarb can be broken off or cut at the base, removing the leaf. The stalk does not get completely red, so do not use that as an indicator. They are the best when they are about .5 to 1 foot long.

Dig the roots in the summer. They can be deep and hard to get out, so be prepared with the right equipment if you are planning to harvest.

How to cook with it

Edible: Yes, Burdock roots, leaves, and stalks. Rhubarb stalks, but NOT the leaves.

Burdock: For the roots, peel and slice like a potato. Boil for 20 minutes, change water and boil until tender. The flavor is described as crunchy, earthy, and nutty. Flower and leaf stalks similar to celery should be peeled, then used raw or boiled until tender.

Rhubarb: The stalks can be frozen. They are mostly used in pies or made into syrups.

. . .

Roasted Burdock Root

Time: 30 minutes
Serving Size: 4 servings
Ingredients:

- 1 pound Burdock root
- 3 tbsps Olive Oil
- 1 pinch salt, pepper, and other spices for taste
- optional: foraged field garlic, garlic mustard, wild leeks, or wild onion for taste.

Instructions:

1. Preheat the oven to 400 °F.
2. Prepare the root by washing, peeling, and cutting it up into slices about 1 inch wide.
3. Spread the root out on a tray and evenly coat them with oil and spices.
4. Cook for 10-15 minutes, flip, and cook for another 10 minutes.
5. Recommended: a splash of soy sauce.

Author: Burdock has a long history with herbal medicine, mostly being used as a blood purifier, among other things. The root is high in antioxidants. The burs of the burdock evolved to catch on passerby to spread their seed farther.

This makes the most delicious addition to a pumpkin soup. I like to sprinkle the roasted roots on top to bring out a very delicious zesty flavor! Just had this for lunch exactly as it's written in the recipe and you can't beat it.

29
BUTTERNUT

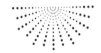

The scientific name for the butternut tree or white walnut is *Juglans cinerea*. It is illegal to gather or have in your possession in the state of Minnesota, but legal in every other state.

IDENTIFICATION OF THE PLANT

The butternut tree can grow up to 120 feet but mostly keeps to half that height. The bark is light gray, very deeply grooved, and thick. The leaves are alternate and pinnate, the main stalk being about 2 feet, and the leaves being up to 4 inches long with 19-21 leaves on the stalk. It will have a leaf at the end of the leaflet, meaning there should be an odd number of leaves. The shape of them is very simple, with a main vein down the middle and straight veins coming out of it parallel. The flowers of male and female trees are both rather unremarkable.

The fruit is oval and smaller than a lime, with green skin around the nut.

Where to gather it

The tree likes lowland forests. You can forage immature nuts in the summer for pickling or mature nuts in the fall when they fall from the trees.

How to gather it

If you are harvesting the young seed, pluck it off the tree in the summer. If you are going for the mature nut, pick them off the ground. They need to go through the same process as the walnut, being cleaned of the outer husk, dried completely, and then, after about a week, need to be removed from the shell before cooking.

How to cook with it

Edible: Yes, the nut.

Once you crack the nut, boil all parts, sift the oil off the top, and remove the nut from the shell. Use the oil for cooking and the nut for whatever nut recipe you choose. The younger nuts picked in the summer can be pickled after they are cleaned from the fuzz and boiled until the water runs clean.

White Walnut and Cleavers Pesto

This recipe makes 1 ½ cups of pesto.

Time: 20 minutes

Ingredients:

- ½ cup white walnuts/butternuts
- 2 cups cleavers
- ¾ cup parmesan
- ½ cup olive oil
- 2 cloves garlic, adjust for your preference
- pinch of salt and pepper
- 4 tbsps lemon juice

Instructions:

1. Wash cleavers and dry.
2. Add everything into a blender or food processor.
3. Blend until it's a thick liquid, but it doesn't need to be completely smooth.
4. Taste and adjust for your preference if needed.
5. Add to food like pasta or sandwiches.

Author: It is a good idea to expand your foraging from fruits and greens to nuts because they are able to have a longer shelf life and add a more diverse nutritional aspect to your plate. In foraging, it can be hard to find good sources of protein. While you should eat everything in moderation, if you are trying to supplement more of your diet from found food, nuts are a really good choice.

30
CATTAIL

Cattails or bulrushes are a common name for the genus *Typha*. The common foraging types of cattails are *T. latifolia* and *T. angustifolia*. Like the Amaranth, it filters the ground and water, so be cautious of where you are harvesting from.

IDENTIFICATION OF THE PLANT

Cattails are fairly easy to identify because they have a fairly unique look and their swampy home. Standing up to nine feet in some cases, cattails have their iconic brown catkins. The catkins are up to 1.5 feet long and fairly narrow at the top of a long stem, often being referred to as corn dogs or cigars. The catkins are soft and velvety on the outside, and when broken open is a very densely packed cottony seed that can burst with pressure. The catkin is the flower of this plant. The catkins on *T. latifolia* are longer and wider than the *T. angustifolia*.

The leaves alternate and are very long, growing up to eight feet, but are also narrow and only about one inch wide. Another way to tell the difference between the two species is that *T. angustifolia*, the narrow leaf cattail, has narrower leaves. The leaves are sheathing at the base. The leaves have parallel veining that give the thick leaves a coarse texture. They have smooth edges and come to a point.

Be cautious of water irises, as they look very similar to the cattail in foliage. To identify, you can notice the catkin on a plant that has matured. If you are identifying at a different time in the year, the cattails will have a round stem with the leaves wrapping around, versus the water iris, which is flat and fanning.

Where to gather it

Typically found in shallow water like ditches and ponds. You can harvest the root any time of the year but you can get the best results in fall and winter. Shoots and catkins for eating have to be harvested in spring before they mature. The flowers will bloom between June-August. Starting in July, the pollen can be collected after flowering.

How to gather it

Make sure to have waterproof boots and gloves. If there are little to no shoots to pull the ribosome out, the roots can be harvested by digging. The ground might be soft due to the swampy conditions that they grow in, but you should still bring a shovel along. Once the ground is loosened, simply pull up.

When gathering the shoots in the spring, you can snap or cut them off from the ground or the root. It is better to get the younger shoots because the older the plant is, the less preferable edible shoots there are. You can cut off the leaves and roots if you are not using them.

The catkins can be harvested, but timing it is difficult. In the spring, you can find green female catkins hidden amongst the leaves.

The pollen can be harvested by shaking the flower into a bag or other catcher. This might be done by keeping the plant intact, or carefully cutting it (so as not to shake out the pollen), and shaking it into a catcher to have more control over the movement.

How to cook with it

Edible: Yes.

The root needs to be cleaned, although only the main ribosome should be used and not the branching root growth, but you can use the sprouts of greenery. You can cook the root by boiling or roasting it. The root can be turned into a flower by being dried, cleaned, and grounded into powder.

The green catkins can be eaten like corn on the cob. The pollen can be used as flour. Young shoots can be eaten like asparagus. Unwrap the thicker pieces along the outside and cut off where the leaves turn green and flat. What is left is about a foot of narrow, white stalk. They can be eaten raw but are preferred cooked and roasted.

. . .

Fried Cattail Shoots

Time: 10 minutes
Serving Size: 2 servings
Ingredients:

- 1 cup Cattail shoots
- 5 tbsps vegetable oil
- garlic (adjust to preference)
- 1 pinch salt and pepper for taste
- 1 pinch sesame seeds

Instructions:

1. In a pan, warm up the oil and spices.
2. Cut and wash the cattail shoots.
3. Turn the heat up to high and add the shoots.
4. Fry for 5 minutes, stirring occasionally.
5. Add this to rice or other stir fry mixes.

Author: Cattails are a great plant for the forager to remember because the whole plant can be useful; it's multi-purposeful and is beneficial for different qualities all year long. If you are a forager for other purposes besides food, the cottony seeds are useful for stuffing and, when cleaned, can be used for a cotton ball replacement. The leaves have also been used in weaving. The gel found between leaves is used similar to aloe vera.

31
CHICKWEED

Common chickweed, also known as Stellaria media, is a great plant to have in your foraging arsenal because it is available all year long. *S. jamesiana* (James chickweed), common in the west, *S. holostera* (Greater stitchwort), and *S. graminea* (Lesser Stitchwort) are also part of the *Stellaria* genus and can be used in foraging. Also mistaken for the chickweed is the *Cerastium* genus because they have much more noticeable hair along the stem. Some warn against *Euphorbia maculata* as well, which will ooze a white cap when cut at the stem.

IDENTIFICATION OF THE PLANT

The common chickweed is more of a ground cover and doesn't get more than a few inches off of the ground. All four species can be identifiable by their white flowers that are a little less than half an inch wide. There are five petals that do not touch, but are divided about halfway down, giving it the look of two petals fused together or even the look of two completely different petals.

The leaves on the common chickweed are green, can be more dense, and might be almost succulent-like. They are smooth and oval and sometimes look more round with a slight wave. The closer to the ground, the longer the leaf stalk; if you look at the top of the plant, there is almost none. They come out of the stem in an opposite pattern. The bracts of the flower have noticeable hairs that can be slightly seen on the leaves and a single row down the stem. This is also noticeable on unopened flowers. The stem can be green or have a tinge of red.

Both Stitchworts reach about 1 foot, have a very delicate, hairless stem, and branches angularly. The leaves are opposite, about an inch long, narrow, triangular, and smooth edged.

Where to gather it

Common chickweed is considered a weed and is more likely to pop up in places that have been disturbed and well watered. Common chickweed is available all year. The stichworts are available in spring for the greater stitchwort, and spring through summer for the lesser stitchwort. Stitchworts prefer more medowie areas or woodlands. Since they winter well, by the spring they are already established.

How to gather it

For all species of this plant, cut off the younger, non flowering parts of the plant with scissors. Look for the tender leaves. It's best to harvest right after it rains to get a fresh and perky harvest. If you are looking for it in the winter, it might be hard if your area has a lot of snow. It helps that it likes shaded areas, which might mean less snow cover. If you know where you can find some, you might be able to harvest these greens all year.

How to cook with it

Edible: Yes.

The stitchworts and chickweed are both used as greeny in salad, or on its own. The leaves and the flowers are used, but you can also boil the green shoots. Boil for a few minutes as it is delicate.

Sauteed Chickweed

Sauteed Chickweed can be eaten as a side or as a topper for rice or chicken.

Time: 10 minutes

Ingredients:

- 2-3 cups Chickweed
- 1-2 tbsps butter (adjust as necessary)
- add spices like salt, pepper, garlic, onion, etc.

Instructions:

1. In a pan on medium high heat, soften onion and garlic.
2. Add any other spices you like.
3. Wash chickweed and remove wilted pieces.
4. Add chickweed in a pan for about 1 minute and not much longer.

Author: Chickweed is used for treating itchy skin but also contains saponin, which can cause some people in excess doses to be sick. It's a favorite amongst foragers, not only because it has a great nutritional value, but also because it has a great taste and is similar to spinach.

32
CHICORY

Chicory, also known as *Cichorium intybus*, is a well known coffee substitute. As a forager looking to source as much as you can locally and naturally, this plant might be your solution to having your morning pick-me up.

IDENTIFICATION OF THE PLANT

Chicory is most identifiable by its blue, pink, or white flowers in the summer. The flowers are about 2 inches wide. The flower is flat like a daisy, with petals that come to a flat end with a jagged edge. The plant itself can grow up to five feet tall, but its stem is sparsely covered with leaves and is thin and spindly. It might have a few branches. The leaves at the base are very similar to a dandelion, with a long stalk tinged with red jagged edges, and it starts narrow and gets wider towards the end of the leaf with a roundish tip, reaching up to 12 inches. The leaves up the stem alternate and are significantly smaller (maybe four inches long), narrow triangle shaped, and smooth edged. Chicory has a milky sap that can be seen when the plant is damaged.

Where to gather it

Chicory is a weed that likes disturbed areas, meaning it is commonly found on the side of the road. It's best not to harvest from near roads but think of similar areas. Gather roots fall through spring, and harvest leaves in early spring.

How to gather it

In fall through the spring, you can harvest the roots. Locate the plant and bring a shovel. You will have to dig to get to the root. For leaves, the earlier in the season the better, since older leaves become more bitter. You can simply pluck the leaves off the plant. The leaves at the base of the plant that look like dandelions are the preferable leaves.

How to cook with it

Edible: Yes.

Boil or chop and eat raw crown base leaves, comparable to other leafy greens. For the root, clean, roast, and grind up like coffee grounds.

Chicory Coffee

Time: up to an hour
Serving Size: 1 cup
Ingredients:

- 1 cup chicory
- 1 cup water
- optional: milk, sweetener, and cinnamon for taste
- optional: coffee grounds

Instructions:

1. Wash your chicory root well.
2. Cut your chicory root into 1 inch pieces. Optional: you can mince them to make the grinding part later easier.
3. Heat the oven to 350 °F.
4. Lay out the roots evenly on a tray.
5. Put in the oven to roast. The timing depends on the thickness of your chicory pieces and your oven. It will be approximately an hour and a half. A good indicator is when you are able to smell the aroma.
6. Take the roasted roots out and let them cool.
7. Grind the roots. Like coffee, the finer the grounds, the stronger the coffee. Don't ground too much, it should not be powder thin.

8. If you want, you can use this on its own or mix it with 1:1 with your usual coffee grounds.
9. Add to a coffee maker, french press, or however you make coffee.
10. Add milk and sweetener to your preference.

Author: Chicory also has a reputation for treating worms/parasites.

33
CLEAVERS

*T*he scientific name for cleavers is *Galium aparine*.

IDENTIFICATION OF THE PLANT

This plant is herbaceous and only semi-erect. The leaves come out in 8 out of the plant in rows fanning straight out. There will then be an empty stalk for a few inches, and then another fan of leaves. These leaves are narrow with slight fuzz. The flowers bloom in threes and are small and white. The fruits are two ¾ circles fused together with hooked hair.

Where to gather it

The best place to find clevers is in moist areas, like lakes and fields with rich soil. While I recommend harvesting this plant in the spring, you can also harvest the fruits in the summer.

How to gather it

It is best to pick the stalks when the plant is younger and tender. Once identified, you can cut and collect what you need.

How to cook with it

Edible: Yes, the young stalks can be steamed or boiled. The fruits can be dried, ground, and used as a coffee bean substitute.

. . .

Author: Cleavers have a lot of look-alikes, including goosegrass and more, but they all fall into this same category.

34
COMMON ELDERBERRY

The common elderberry is scientifically known as *Sambucus canadensis*.

IDENTIFICATION OF THE PLANT

The common elderberry is a shrub that grows to about nine feet tall. The leaves grow in an opposite pattern with up to nine leaves on leaflets. The leaves are long and narrow to a point, standing at about four inches long. They can look like they have been folded down the middle.

Its flower is a round, flat top floret with small white flowers, about up to 10 inches across. The individual flowers are star shaped with noticeable stigma. The fruit is a round berry but is smaller than a blueberry. It is round, smooth, and black.

Where to gather it

It likes sunny locations and is fairly adaptable. The berries are ripe in the late summer.

How to gather it

When the berries are fully dark purple or black, you can pick the berries off of the bush.

How to cook with it

Edible: Yes, the berries can be eaten. However, they should not be eaten raw because they are poisonous. The rest of the plant is also poisonous.

ELDERBERRY SYRUP

Time: 40 minutes
Ingredients:

- 2 cups water
- 1/2 cup elderberries
- ½ cup honey
- optional: spices, ginger, cinnamon, and cloves

Instructions:

1. Clean the berries.
2. In a pot, add everything but the honey.
3. Bring everything in the pot to a boil.
4. Once it hits a boil, bring to a simmer for 20-30 minutes. This should reduce the water by about half.
5. Take off heat and strain out any elderberry flesh and skin.
6. Let cool and add honey.
7. Store for 2 weeks in the fridge.
8. The consistency is not thick, but adding sugar instead of honey as it boils would create a more syrupy texture. This also extends its shelf life.

Author: Elderberries are packed with antioxidants and can boost your immune system. Even though it's a lot of work to prepare the berry, its ability to heal your body against colds is worth it.

COMMON MALLOW

Common mallow, also known as dwarf mallow, is scientifically called *Malva neglecta*. There are other plants in this genus that have more decorative flowers that you might see more often in gardens. Some species are used like lettuce. Europeans call *M. Sylvestris* common mallow, but this shouldn't be an issue foraging in the North East, as it is local to the middle east.

Identification of the plant

Common mallow is more weedy looking than the others of its genus that have more flashy foliage and flowers. This plant stays closer to the ground but can grow up to two feet. The flowers have five petals and can come in a variety of colors. Some flowers of this genus take on a more star shaped look, with more narrow petals, while some have bowel shapes with round, overlapping petals. The common mallow has a star-shaped flower that is white and can be tinged with pink.

The leaves alternate and are palmately lobed. They are rounded with 7 lobes and are slightly ruffled in texture, with jagged edges. The leaves come off longer herbaceous stalks.

Where to gather it

Common mallow is a common weed that likes areas with more moisture and full sun. It can be found in the summer, fall, and winter.

How to gather it

When you have identified the plant, you can clip off the leaves, or you can dig up the root and harvest the whole plant. It flowers in the summer, but roots later in the season.

How to cook with it

Edible: All of this plant is used. The seeds can be raw or cooked like rice. The leaves and flowers can be used in salads, but it's best not to eat it alone. When cooked, they turn into a mucus-like texture that is used for thickening. The root is boiled to create a mucus as well as a meringue, egg white substitute.

Mallow Meringue

This can be used on pie, meringue cookies, etc.

Time: About 30 minutes

Ingredients:

- ⅓ cup Mallow root or seeds
- 1 cup water
- ¼ tsp cream of tartar
- 1 egg white
- ¾ cup sugar
- 1 tsp vanilla extract

Instructions:

1. Wash and chop mallow root or peel the seeds.
2. Add dried root to water in a pot and bring to a boil.
3. Reduce water by half (you may or may not see the thickening).
4. Remove from heat and strain.
5. In a mixing bowl, beat the eggwhite until white.
6. Add cream of tartar, take ½ cup mallow thickener slowly add to mixing bowl, beating the mixture as you go.
7. Once mallow is all mixed in, repeat the process by slowly adding in the sugar and finally the extract (optional).
8. Beat until foam is fairly firm and fluffy.

Author: The plant is undesirable to livestock owners as it is toxic to graziers. The leaves have been used for sore throats and digestion.

36
COMMON MILKWEED

Milkweed is also known as the butterfly or silk flower, but it's scientifically known as *Asclepias syriaca*. The reason it is called the butterfly flower is because of the Monarch butterfly. The larvae or the butterfly *only* eat milkweed. Because of this and their decreasing population, be conscious of how much milkweed you take and whether it is necessary to take that much. Other species of milkweed and young dogweed can look like this plant. Dogbane has branches and no hairs, and other milkweeds have a more narrow leaf.

IDENTIFICATION OF THE PLANT

The plant grows up to six feet tall and mostly erect. The leaves are simple, smooth, and elongated. They grow up to 11 inches, have a prominent main vein, and a soft almost hairy underneath. The leaves are thicker, allowing them to be more erect. When damaged, the plant has a latex white sap.

The flowers are usually pink in florret clusters that are round, 1-5 clusters on each plant. The flowers are on short stems that originated from one center. The individual flowers are star shaped with prominent staples that open wide below the tiger shaped flower.

Where to gather it

The plant likes well dried soils with lots of sun. This plant is found in places that look more weedy, like ditches and meadows. The plant can only be eaten when it's young, so it's harvested in the spring.

How to gather it

Harvest shoots by cutting the young, tender plant before it matures.

How to cook with it

Edible: Yes, the young shoots, leaves, buds, flowers, and fruit are edible. The mature plant and fruit is toxic.

MILKWEED SHOOTS

Time: 25 minutes
Serving Size: 4 servings
Prep Time: 5 minutes
Cook Time: 20 minutes
Ingredients:

- 15 young shoots
- 2 cups water
- 2 tsps butter
- pinch of salt and other spices of your preference

Instructions:

1. Bring a large pot of water and salt to a boil.
2. Add shoots.
3. Boil for about 10 minutes, don't recuse water.
4. In a pan, warm up butter, garlic, onion, etc.
5. Add boiled shoots to a pan for a few minutes until you see a nice crisp forming.

Author: Milkweed is a favorite among many bugs because it's a good pollinator. Its flowers are very sweet and that is why it's their favorite snack.

37
COMMON STRAWBERRY

Also known for its latin name *Fragaria virginiana*, strawberries are a great example of how fruits can exist in the wild without being genetically bred. They do have a look-alike that might be called the mock strawberry or Potentilla indica. The plants are very similar, and although the claims that they are poisonous are wrong, they are still not edible, in the sense that it is hard and tastes undesirable. The flower is yellow, the fruit is more round, and the seeds stick out like spikes instead of fitting nicely in the side like the wild strawberry.

IDENTIFICATION OF THE PLANT

Of course the most identifiable part of the strawberry plant is the fruit. Like the strawberry that you find in the store, it is red. In the wild, however, they are much smaller, about the size of a raspberry. The flowers, at about .5 inches wide, are white and star-shaped, with five petals and a yellow round center. The plant is more of a ground crawler and doesn't have a main stem, but it does reach out with tentacles that spread the plant. The leaves cluster in threes, are oval shaped with very jagged edges and a deep folding texture with a slight fuzz underneath.

Where and how to gather it

The strawberry can be found in the woods and in more open areas too like meadows. They are available in the spring and well into the summer.

They are small, so keep your eye on the ground. The red fruit can be easier to spot. The fruit can be plucked right from the stem, and the leaves can also be harvested any time of year.

How to cook with it

Edible: Strawberries can be used in the same ways that store bought strawberries can be used, meaning that they are very versatile in use: pies, jams, or eaten raw. The leaves can be dried and used for tea.

STRAWBERRY AND RHUBARB PIE

Time: 45 minutes
Serving Size: 8 servings
Prep Time: 5 minutes
Cook Time: 40 minutes
Ingredients:

- 3 ½ cups chopped rhubarb
- 2 cups strawberries
- 1 cup sugar
- ½ cup flour
- 1 pie crust
- 1 tbsp butter

Instructions:

1. Preheat the oven to 400 °F.
2. In a bowl, mix flour and sugar.
3. Add cleaned and chopped rhubarb and strawberries.
4. Add mixture into pie crust, cover top with crust.
5. Add holes to the crust top, add little pieces of butter, and sprinkle with sugar.
6. Cook for 40 minutes.

Author: Strawberries can be a really great food to forage for because they can also be preserved fairly well in jams. While fresh strawberries can be enjoyed in the spring and summer, they can also be enjoyed all year round. They are high in vitamin C and a great pick-me-up in general.

38
CORNELIAN CHERRY DOGWOOD

Cornelian Cherry Dogwood is known scientifically as *Cornus mas*. The fruit is similar to cranberries and cherries. It is considered invasive. This tree looks similar to Forsythia; it has similar yellow flowers but does not grow bright red fruit.

Identification of the Plant

The small tree or shrub is actually quite attractive looking. The silhouette of the tree is similar to that of a large bonsai tree. The branches at the top spread out wide, but aren't as tall. The older growth of the bark is a dark brown, while the new growth is a green. The leaves are long ovals that reach up to four inches long at a point. They are slightly glossy and curl in towards the center from the sides.

The tree puts on a show in the late winter/early spring when it blooms. It becomes covered in clusters of little yellow flowers. There are no leaves at this point so it's just the yellow flowers. The individual flowers have 4 petals each and cluster in round florets on opposite branches.

The fruit is oval and olive-like with red or yellow berries. The fruit hangs in very short stems in clusters of 1-5.

Where to gather it

The plant can be found in woodland areas and public areas with dry soil because it's ornamental. The fruit is ready in the late summer.

How to gather it

Harvest the berries when they are bright red by plucking them off the tree.

How to cook with it

Edible: Yes, the cooked fruit is edible.

Mostly made into jams and mizde with other sour fruit; it can also be dried.

Cornelian Cherry Marmalade

Time: 22 minutes
Prep Time: 2 minutes
Cook Time: 20 minutes
Ingredients:

- 2 cups Cornelian cherries
- 2 cups water
- 1 cup sugar
- a pinch of ground cardamom
- 2 tsps lemon
- 1 tbsp orange zest

Instructions:

1. Bring water and fruit to a boil.
2. Cook for 10 minutes.
3. Strain with a large hole strainer and squeeze as much juice and flesh as possible out of pits and other impurities. Unlike jam, juice, and jelly, marmalade wants some of the flesh.
4. Add sugar, lemon, cardamom, and orange to the juice in a clean pot.
5. Bring to a light boil, reduce heat slightly and keep a steady light boil for about 10 minutes.
6. Add marmalade to jars, seal lids, and label.

Author: I always recommend taking note of plants that are attractive and grown for ornamental purposes. People are more likely to plant these attractive plants in public places like roads, parks, parking lots, etc. These are plants you can forage for in more accessible areas without needing to head into the forest.

39
COW PARSNIP

Cow Parsnip is known as *Heracleum maximum*. **Be careful** when handling this herb. The sap can react to the skin and cause a rash. For some the rash can be severe. Use gloves and tools when handing. This plant can be confused for giant hogweed, which is scientifically known as *Heracleum mantegazzianum*. Luckily hogweed is larger and the stem has a purple hue. If you have severe reactions, avoid consuming.

Identification of the plant

The plant grows up to seven feet tall and looks more like a small bush, almost comical. The stem is hollow and covered in hairs. The leaves are very big, being up to a foot and a half long. The leaves are deeply lobed and jagged on the edge.

The flowers branch off in very large florets that are round and flat. These large florets are made up of branches that jut straight out of a centralized spot. They are composed of individual white flowers. The florets can be eight inches wide. The white flowers have four deeply lobed petals.

The seeds are half an inch long.

Where to gather it

Harvest the plant when it is young. Young shoots in the early spring. Mid-spring harvest stalks and leaves. It thrives in high moisture areas with shade, but it is also adaptable. It likes well drained soil like sand, and blooms late spring.

How to gather it

The plant can be harvested by choosing the youngest plants that are tender and green. The flower and blossoms can be cut off the plant but avoid touching the sap from the stem. The seeds can be harvested by gently shaking the seeded plant.

How to cook with it

Edible: Yes, young plants, seeds, and flowers.

Shoots, stalks and leaves can be cooked like other leafy greens or celery. Flowers and flower blossoms can be fried or eaten raw. The seeds can be harvested, frozen, and even used as spice.

The plant is best used as a herb.

FRIED COW PARSNIP BUDS

Time: 15 minutes
Serving Size: 4 servings
Prep Time: 10 minutes
Cook Time: 5 minutes
Ingredients:

- 1-3 cups Cow parsnip buds
- 1 cup flour
- 1 egg
- 1 pinch salt and pepper for taste
- ¾ carbonated water
- 1 cup vegetable oil

Instructions:

1. Wash the parsnip buds thoroughly, then dry them.
2. In a bowl, combine wet ingredients and in another the dry ingredients.
3. Heat the pan with oil on medium high heat.
4. Coat the buds in the wet mixture, then dry. For extra crisp, wet the dried coating and put it back into the dry coating again.
5. Add buds to the pan, but don't overcrowd the pan.
6. Cook until gold and crispy.

7. Serve with soy sauce or the like.

Author: Plants like cow parsnip have a lot of look-alikes. The flower that comes from the plant, although it has a lot of its own distinctions, can be easily misidentified. It's important to be aware of the fact that this type of flower is common and can be found with some friendly and some not so friendly plants.

40
CRANBERRY

The cranberry is a genus of fruit bearing plants, the name of this genus is called *Vaccinium*. There are multiple cranberry varieties that are used to harvest the edible fruit. The cranberry is related to blueberries and huckleberries. The highbush cranberry is actually not part of the same genus, being scientifically named *Viburnum trilobum*. See the highbush cranberry on <u>chapter 56</u>.

IDENTIFICATION OF THE PLANT
The cranberry plant can vary a bit, ranging from a shrub to a ground creeping vine. The branches then to be thin in these plants with leaves that are simple that alternate. The plant is evergreen with dark glossy leaves. The leaves are thicker. Some of the leaves are rounded oval, or more elongated.

The flowers on *Vaccinium macrocarpon* have a long bracket that sticks out from the back of the flower, as it drops from pink stems. They are a darker pink or red. The flowers have 4 petals white/pink that curl back to the bracket A long dark center spike protrudes out an inch. The flowers on *V. vitis-idaea* are small and bell shaped.

The fruit is the common denominator, round red berries about .4 to 1 inch in diameter.

Where to gather it

The plant can be found in and near swamps, lakes, flood lands and the like. They are ready in the late summer and into the winter. They like acid soils and water.

How to gather it

The plant is scooped with a cranberry scoop. The bush is typically ground cover. If you pick an accessible place to forage them, you can just kneel down and pick the cranberries off the bush.

How to cook with it

Edible: Yes, the ripe berries can be eaten.

Cranberries are commonly consumed in cranberry sauce or juice.

CRANBERRY JUICE

Time: 20 minutes
Serving Size: 9 servings
Prep Time: 5 minutes
Cook Time: 15 minutes
Ingredients:

- 1 cup sugar
- 1 cup water
- 4 cups cranberries

Instructions:

1. Wash cranberries well.
2. In a large pot, boil water and sugar.
3. Boil until sugar is dissolved.
4. Add cranberries.
5. Bring to boil, then turn down to simmer.
6. When the cranberries are done, they will pop open.
7. Add any extras for your preference.
8. Add to jars, seal, label, and let cool.

Author: If you are a new forager, making cranberry jam for Thanksgiving or other holidays in the fall can be a great project to take on. The recipe is fairly easy since cranberries are in season, and it can be a special touch for the meal, without too much stress.

41
CURLY DOCK

Curly dock is also called curled or yellow dock. Its scientific name is *Rumex crispus*. Others in this family are edible, but curly dock is the most preferable.

IDENTIFICATION OF THE PLANT

Curly dock looks weedy and grows up to five feet tall. The leaves grow from a center point in the ground like dandelions. The leaves are much longer than dandelions, as they grow up to 10 inches, and are not lobed or scalloped. The leaves have a wave to them, and the edges look scalloped but are just curling back and forth, hence the name. The leaves have a prominent main margin.

The flower comes up in separate stems. They create a flower spike in a densely packed, green to burnt orange color. Branching into long, narrow smaller florets. The individual flower is rather indistinguishable.

The fruit is .2 inches wide; it is the burnt color that encloses three seeds.

Where to gather it

The plant is a common weed, so it grows in roadsides and overgrown areas. Leaves can be harvested from spring to winter. Seeds can be harvested in the fall.

How to gather it

Harvest the best looking leaves, preferably the youngest, whenever needed. In winter, they might be yellowed but are still fine. The seeds can be cut or cleaned off of the plant when they are ready.

How to cook with it

Edible: The leaves are cooked, similar to beets. The older the leaves, the more cooking it needs. Seeds are edible when made into a flour, but the effort is typically not worth it.

Use in other leafy green recipes.

Author: Yellowdock can be difficult to identify at the beginning of the spring, and since there are so many leafy greens that are available at this time, I like to stick to yellow dock in the winter, especially since it can be so much harder to access leafy food during this season.

42
CURRANT

Currant is a common name for a genus of plants that are scientifically called *Ribes*. A common look-alike is the gooseberry. An easy way to tell the difference between the two is that the gooseberry has thorns. It was illegal to grow currants in the US because they carry diseases that can be a danger to other plants like the pine.

The blackcurrant *R. nigrum* is a popular currant in the Northeast; there are also red and white versions.

IDENTIFICATION OF THE PLANT

The black currant is a shrub that grows up to five feet tall. It also grows about the same width, making it a rounder shape. The stem is narrow, smooth, and a light brown color. The leaves have three points; the larger leaf in the center is tall and the two on the side slightly jut out. The edges are jagged and the texture is slightly wrinkled. They grow on stems 1-2 inches long in an alternating pattern.

The flower is about a foot long or about the size of a smaller drooping spike. The flowers are sparsely spaced and a pale greenish yellow. The flowers are star shaped, with the petals curling back. The center is prominent and raised like a small cup. The berries are similar to a grape, growing in triangular clusters that droop. The blackcurrent berries tend to be less densely packed together though. The berries are a bit smaller and round, not oval, similar to a black blueberry.

Where to gather it

The plant can be damp areas with fertile soil. It flowers in the spring and fruits in the summer.

How to gather it

Pick the berries off the bush when they are dark purple or black. They stain, so wear protection and old clothes.

How to cook with it

Edible: While the berries can be eaten raw, they are usually processed. They are usually made into some jam like preservatives or wine. See brambles for berry jam recipe.

Author: My grandmother used to treat urinary bladder infections and used black currant, like many do, to treat it. It is high in vitamin C.

43
DANDELION

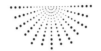

*D*andelions are scientifically known as *Taraxacum officinale*. They are a common weed in lawns, but dandelions are a powerhouse when it comes to foraging.

IDENTIFICATION OF THE PLANT

While most people know what a dandelion looks like, since they are not always in bloom, knowing the whole plant in all seasons is a good idea for foragers. The yellow bloom is iconix, being a half globe with sting like petals that are a dark yellow. This eventually turns into a cottony seed globe that people blow in the wind. The leaves come from a center point at the base of the flower's stem. These leaves are long, up to five inches, and narrow with irregular reverse scalloped pattern, jagged edge. The stem on the flower is circular and hollow. The plant might produce a white sap.

Where to gather it

Dandelions are really common, but they shouldn't be harvested from just anywhere. Because they are considered weeds, it is likely that people are using chemicals to kill them, so make sure that you only harvest from trusted areas. Dandelions like most places but are commonly found in places that are weedy and have been disturbed. You can find them in the summer, but they can be foraged in the spring, fall, and winter.

How to gather it

You can dig up the roots in the spring with the leaves or the fall and winter. This will probably need to be done with a shovel. You can pick the leaves during the spring as it's the best time for a fresher taste. The flower heads can also be harvested at this time.

How to cook with it

Edible: The yellow leaves are edible and can provide vitamin A and K. They are best eaten when they are young because they can quickly turn bitter. They can be used like most greens in salads and even boiled. The flowers are used in salads and for tea. Older plants and roots should be boiled before consumption. Roots can be peeled, boiled, and eaten or roasted and used for a coffee supplement.

DANDELION FLOWER COOKIE

Time: 17-22 minutes
Serving Size: 9 servings
Prep Time: 7 minutes
Cook Time: 10-15 minutes
Ingredients:

- 1/2 cup Dandelion flower tops
- 1 cup flower
- 1 cup oatmeal
- ½ cup vegetable oil
- 2 eggs
- 1 tsp vanilla extract
- ½ cup honey

Instructions:

1. Preheat the oven to 375 °F.
2. Clean dandelion heads.
3. In separate bowls, mix the liquid and dry ingredients.
4. Combine the dry ingredients and the dandelion heads into the wet ingredients.
5. Scoop the batter with a spoon onto an oiled tray.
6. Bake for 10-15 minutes.

Author: Dandelions are another flower that people use for its health purposes. They are full of antioxidants, they can help with blood sugar, cholesterol, as well as a diuretic. Because of their health benefits, you should double check to see if it can interfere with any medications you are taking.

My mum used to prepare dandelion salads every day for every meal in spring because, as she liked to say, they detoxed our liver and blood and made us restart fresh into the year's cycle.

44
DAYLILY

*D*ay lilies are actually not part of the lily family, and the most preferred, when it comes to flavor, is the orange daylily or *Hemerocallis fulva*. While a lily has small leaves that grow horizontally up the stem, a day lily has long leaves that stand the length of the plant. They can also resemble the iris whose leaves are thicker and erect.

IDENTIFICATION OF THE PLANT

There are multiple kinds of daylilies but we will look at the previously mentioned *Hemerocallis fulva*. The plant typically grows up to four feet tall. It has a stem that branches 1-5 flowers. The flowers are about 6 inches wide and 6 inches deep in the shape of a funnel. It branches into 6 petal-looking points. The color is a range of orange shades. A day lily bloom only lasts one day. The leaves, as described by looking at it from above, come from a center point at the ground and are semi-erect. They are four feet and droop around the main flower stem. They are green and narrow, at only about 1-2 inches. The amount can vary, with some looking more or less lush.

Where to gather it

This plant most likely won't be found in the wild, but once planted they can last a long time in gardens and abandoned areas. They like lots of sun. They bloom in the summer but can be harvested in the fall and spring.

How to gather it

Harvest root tubers with a shovel. Harvest only the frim part and replant what you aren't using. You can harvest bubs or blooming flowers by plucking or cutting them off the stem.

How to cook with it

Edible: You can eat the root raw or boiled, similar to potatoes. Cook buds (like green beans) and flowers, either by boiling or frying them, but don't eat it raw. You can also dry flowers and buds and use them as a herb later on. Don't eat the stamen inside.

DAYLILY ROOT

Time: 15-30 minutes
Serving Size: 4 servings
Prep Time: 5 minutes
Cook Time: 10-25 minutes
Ingredients:

- 4 cups daylily root
- 2 tbsps butter
- 1 pinch salt and pepper

Instructions:

1. Clean and chop the roots.
2. Bring water and salt to a boil.
3. Add the daylily roots.
4. Boil for 10-25 minutes until tender, and then strain.
5. Add butter, salt, pepper, or dress like your typical potato.

Author: This plant is poisonous to cats and should be used with caution. Some people can be allergic, and it can act like a laxative to some.

45
EASTERN REDBUD

The Eastern Redbud is also known as *Cercis canadensis*.

IDENTIFICATION OF THE PLANT

This is a short tree, usually only up to 30 feet tall. It is ornamental and has a bonsai looking silhouette. With it being flatter on the top, its branches grow wider. Their branches are more organic flowing but not dense. The bark is dark gray and smooth when young, and texturizes as it matures. The leaves are round, heart-shaped, smooth edged, and a medium green color. The leaves are also slightly glossy and alternate patterns. The seed pods look like green beans.

This plant is most identifiable with its show of pink flowers. It flowers mid-spring before the leaves come out. They grow in small clusters out of the branch on 1-2 inch pink stems. There is a round pink bracket at the base of the flower. The petals are pink as well, but more purple toned than the stem. There are 2 petals on one side that sit side by side. On the other side, two petals splay out like wings and, between them, a fifth, slightly darker petal that juts outward like a tongue.

Where to gather it

The plant is often planted for ornamental use but thrives in areas that are moist and sunny like a hill. It blooms mid-spring. Harvest the flower buds before they bloom, and keep an eye on the tree starting early spring.

How to gather it

The tree is short so it is easy to pick the flowers or buds off of the tree when they are in bloom. Since the flower grows in clusters right off the branch, it might be more time consuming than the plants that can be collected off of generalized stems. The seed pods are ready when they are green.

How to cook with it

Edible: The flower is eaten fresh like in a salad but can be fried or made into jams. The buds can be dried and used as a spice, eaten fresh, or cooked. The seeds can be roasted, although it's not very common, or eaten raw like peas.

46
EASTERN WHITE PINE

*T*he eastern white pine, often just called a white pine, is scientifically known as *Pinus strobus*. If you are a beginning forager, you might not know much about trees and how diverse the category of pine tree is. For example, the red pine has lighter peeling gray to red bark and sparse branches and needles. In general, that makes it not a very appealing tree to look at. For the most part, needled trees are not the first thought for a lot of foragers because they don't produce the same flashy fruit as most deciduous trees. As such, conifer trees can be a blind spot for many foragers. Once they are distinguishable, however, they have the potential to brighten up your kitchen.

IDENTIFICATION OF THE PLANT

The eastern white pine can be a beautiful tree, standing up to 230 feet tall. Its bark is thick and an ashy, medium brown color. It is deeply grooved and textured. While they do typically lose some of the lower branches, they still remain semi-lush. The lower branches can be fairly thick. The needles on this tree are about three inches long, thin, and dark green. This gives the tree a soft look and feel, they are not prickly like other needles. The new growth tends to be a lighter green and the older needles turn orange and fall off.

The pine cones are long, about half a foot, narrow, and taper slightly to the end. The cone opens, and the fold juts out; they are thick, like certain types of paper, but are also noticeably less dense or woody than other pine cones. The pollen cones stick out like soft white miniature-looking cones that shed an onion-like skin.

Where to gather it

The tree is common and can be found in most wooded areas. They like acidic, well draining soil. Pine nuts are ready late summer. The needles can be harvested any time.

How to gather it

Find a tree that has branches that are low enough to reach. The pine nuts have to be harvested from the pine cone before it opens. You'll know if the pine cone has opened if the flaps are pointed down. If they haven't opened, they will be flimsy.

How to cook with it

Edible: The pine nuts are a common food, often used in pestos. The needles are almost exclusively used to make tea. The bark is used as an emergency food, although it is typically not used anymore. The pine contains chemicals that can be poisonous with excessive use.

Eastern White Pine Cones

Time: 3-4 weeks
Serving Size: 9 servings
Ingredients:

- 1 bag of pine cones

Instructions:

1. Once you have collected the cones, they need to be dried. They are harvested before they are ripe, so they need to be kept in a bag with airflow like a fabric bag.
2. Place the bag in a sunny area and let them dry for about 3 weeks.
3. Once they are dry, you can hit the bag against a tree a few times to loosen the cones up and separate the pine nut from the cone.
4. Open the bag, checking that each pine cone has been smashed.
5. At the bottom of the bag will be the pine cone flaps mixed in with the pine nuts. Those can be sorted.

6. Most people prefer to toast the nuts. They can be eaten alone or added in recipes for flavor.

Author: Although the pine nuts are edible, the pine tree is usually seen as a very last ditch effort when it comes to foraging for food. This being said, it is a really common tree. For those worried about worst case scenarios, this tree is a comfort to them all. The bark on this tree can be eaten, although it's usually the inner bark that is dried and/or ground into a powder to use as flour.

47
ENCHANTER'S NIGHTSHADE

The enchanter's nightshade is scientifically known as *Circaea lutetiana*.

IDENTIFICATION OF THE PLANT

The Enchanter's nightshade grows up to about two feet tall. The thin stalks are covered in thin hair, and the bottom of the leaves are slightly toothed. The plant has opposite, simple leaves. The leaves are elongated and oval-to-point in shape. They get smaller the higher they are on the stem.

The flowers are white and bloom in the summer. They have 4 petals in pairs on either side of the center, 3 long stamen, and brackets that are pink in color and also covered in hair that are placed sparsely on the stem. This creates a small bur for a fruit.

Where to gather it

The plant can be found in woodland areas, especially near banks. It blooms in early summer.

How to gather it

Pick berries in mid-summer.

How to cook with it

Edible: No, it is used for medicinal tea.

The tea is made from berries but mostly used as a topical ointment on wounds.

48
EPAZOTE

*E*pazote, also known as Mexican tea, is scientifically known as *Dysphania ambrosioides*. It is poisonous in large quantities.

IDENTIFICATION OF THE PLANT
This plant grows up to four feet tall. The stem is red. The leaves are long and narrow, ending in a point, and the edges are lined with wide, dull points. The flowers are small, green, and unremarkable. There aren't many irregular branches and the plant looks rather weedy.

Where to gather it
The plant likes sunny areas with well draining soil. However, it also likes lots of water. It can be harvested whenever leaves come out in spring to fall.

How to gather it
Harvest the young leaves frequently to encourage more growth throughout the whole season. If you are not using it right away, dry it for later use.

How to cook with it
Edible: The leaves and young stems can be used fresh or dried to add flavor. However, it should be added to food at the end of cooking so as not to cook off the flavor. It's wonderful to make tea with it.

. . .

Epazote Tea

Time: 2-3 minutes
Serving Size: 1 serving
Prep Time: 1 minute
Cook Time: 1-2 minutes
Ingredients:

- 1 tbsp dried tea leaves
- 1 cup water
- lemon and sugar for taste

Instructions:

1. Bring water to a boil.
2. Add the tea leaves and boil for 1-2 minutes.
3. Remove from heat.
4. Steep 1-5 minutes.
5. Prepare as desired.

Author: One should not ingest too much of this plant because it has a plethora of medicinal qualities, most involving aids of the digestive tract, respiratory, and menstrual issues.

49
EVENING PRIMROSE

*A*lso known as *Oenothera biennis*, the flowers of the primrose open at night, hence the name "evening primrose." The evening primrose might be a name that rings a bell for you as it is a common supplement females take to help their premenstrual cycle symptoms. Since this plant is used for medicinal purposes, it is best to not over consume it if possible. There are some primrose that are poisonous and will cause skin irritation if touched, more specifically the german primrose.

Identification of the Plant

The plant can grow up to five feet tall with an erect stem. The leaves angle upward up the stem. They get smaller as they go up, giving it a triangular shape. They are long and thin, reach up to 10 inches, with smooth edges and a red hue on the stem.

It flowers in the second year, at which point leaves will alternate on the stem. The flowers are 1-2 inches wide, a bright yellow, and shaped like a cup. The floret has a small cluster at the top of the flower that has about 3-5 flowers blooming at once.

Where to gather it

The plant likes more open areas, especially places that are weedy. They can be harvested in the spring, fall, and winter.

How to gather it

It is best to harvest this plant's roots in its first year after it has gone dormant in the fall or winter. The leaves can be harvested in the early spring.

How to cook with it

Edible: Yes, roots and leaves.

Peel and boil the roots and use in a recipe. For the leaves, you can eat them raw or boil them to eat like any other greens.

Evening Primrose Root Condiment

Time: 2-3 weeks
Prep Time: 2-3 weeks
Cook Time: 0 minutes
Ingredients:

- 1 cup chopped root, 1 inch in diameter
- garlic cloves, adjust to your taste
- 1 cup white or apple cider vinegar
- 1 tsp rosemary
- optional: 2 tsps sugar

Instructions:

1. Clean and chop the roots.
2. In a jar, combine all of the ingredients and seal with a lid.
3. Let infuse for a few weeks in the fridge.
4. Use roots, garlic, and vinegar as addition to stir fry, sandwiches, salad, and salad dressing.

50
FALSE SOLOMON'S SEAL

False Solomon's seal is also called "feathery false lily of the valley" (note: there is another plant called "false lily of the valley," which is also known as the Canadian mayflower). Its scientific name is *Maianthemum racemosum*. The real Solomon's seal is listed in chapter 93. Lily of the valley is poisonous, so it's really important to identify them correctly. The real lily of the valley is much smaller, being only a few inches tall. The 2 or 3 leaves it has grows from the stem and forms around the center stem with flowers. The flowers—small, white, scalloped edged, and bell shaped—latch on a drooping stem. They dangle from small stems towards the ground.

IDENTIFICATION OF THE PLANT

False Solomon's Seal/False lily of the valley is about two feet tall and does not stand erect. The stem is woody. The leaves are long and narrow, at about seven inches long. It has about three parallel main veins running the length of the leaf. The leaves alternate in two rows on either side of the branch. The edges are smooth and the end comes to a point.

It stands on a branching floret, with many small white flowers in small balls. The fruit are small, white or red berries. They are round and smooth, and the skin is slightly transparent. They can range from dense clusters to only a few.

Where to gather it

The plant can be found in woodland areas, especially near banks with well drained soil. Gather shoots in the spring. Berries are ripe very late in the season, even into the later parts of fall.

How to gather it

Harvest shoots by cutting the young, tender plant before it matures. Pick the berries when they go completely red.

How to cook with it

Edible: Yes, all of it can be eaten.

Young leaves can be eaten, although they aren't preferred by very many foragers. They should only be consumed in moderation as they can have a laxative effect. Young shoots in the spring cook like asparagus. Roots can be boiled and eaten.

See Asparagus for recipe.

Author: Since the berries can aid in digestion, although they might not be the best snack, they can be helpful to have around when in need. This plant should be considered once a forager has a little bit more experience and is confident when it comes to identifying a plant early in the season, especially ones with many look-alikes.

51
FIELD GARLIC

*A*lso known as wild garlic or *Allium vineale*.

IDENTIFICATION OF THE PLANT

The field garlic grows up to a foot tall. It is centralized and looks like a tall patch of grass. The leaves are round, hollow tubes that end in a point. The leaves might be straight but often have a wave to them. The flower comes up in a separate stem, has a bracket and a cluster of small flowers in a floret called an inflorescence. The flowers are typically light purple, small but erect, and look almost spiked with a round silhouette.

The plant has a strong garlic smell.

Where to gather it

Field garlic is a fairly common plant that can be found in areas that are open from an undense wood to a field. You can find it in the spring through the fall, ready to harvest.

How to gather it

You can harvest the whole plant in the spring or fall, including the bulb under the ground. You can harvest the green leaves throughout the whole season. Collect flowers when they appear in early summer.

If you are harvesting the bulbs, they can be hung and dried to preserve them.

How to cook with it

Edible: Field garlic can be used as garlic in any dish. Every part of the plant can be used for this flavor. All of it can be thrown on dishes raw or cooked, but the more it is cooked the less strength it has. Since leaves are already more mild, they are typically used raw. The flowers are also typically used raw or as an ornamental look in foods like salads.

Use as a spice.

Author: Adding plants like field garlic, and other strong flavors, can be a great way for new foragers to start building dishes out of foraged material. A lot of other plants can be used as spices too, but having a reliable staple like this can bring so much more potential to substantial, enjoyable, foraged dishes.

52
FRAGRANT SUMAC

Fragrant sumac or lemon sumac is scientifically known as *Rhus aromatica*, not meant to be confused with staghorn sumac or poisonous sumac. It can resemble poison ivy; so, when in doubt, don't risk it.

Identification of the Plant

It grows into a spindly bush about five feet tall or stays close to the ground like a vine. The leaves are deeply lobed into three, giving it the look of individual triangle shape as it is narrow at the base and widens at the end. The ends are reversed. They are dark green, thick, and glossy. In the fall, they turn bright red.

The flowers are not very noticeable, growing in clusters at the end of the branches. They are pale yellow, small, and cup shaped. The berries grow in clusters that can be short, slightly pointed, but not as large as the staghorn. They are red, with sparse, fine, white hairs.

Has a lemon scent.

Where to gather it

They are fairly versatile, being able to grow in sun or shade. It is used to rehabilitate areas by giving ground cover. Sumac can be harvested in the summer to early fall.

How to gather it

The berries can be picked off the plant when they are ready in the summer.

How to cook with it

Edible: Yes, the berries are used to make a sour drink that is similar to lemonade.

See Staghorn Sumac for recipe.

53
GARLIC MUSTARD

arlic mustard's scientific name is *Alliaria petiolata*.

IDENTIFICATION OF THE PLANT

The plant grows in its second year up to three feet. Oftentimes because it's an invasive weed, it will be in clusters or patches. The plant is herbaceous, with heart shaped leaves that have large serrations on the edge. It has a small cluster of 5-10 small, white, star-shaped flowers at the top of the stem, and it leaves a garlicky smell.

Where to gather it

Garlic mustard is invasive, but it does best in areas that are slightly shaded. It can be harvested from spring through early summer.

How to gather it

You can harvest the younger plant leaves, flowers, and seeds. In many areas, it's encouraged to pull the whole plant out of the ground because of its invasiveness.

How to cook with it

Edible: Yes, it can be used raw in salads or boiled like spinach. Has a garlic flavor and can be used to add taste to dishes.

. . .

Foraged Cooked Mixed Greens

Time: 7 minutes
Serving Size: 4 side servings
Prep Time: 2 minutes
Cook Time: 5 minutes
Ingredients:

- 3 cups garlic mustard
- 3 cups chickweed
- 3 cups lambs quarters
- 1 cup dandelion leaves
- field garlic and onion for taste
- 2 tbsps butter
- 2 tbsps water

Instructions:

1. In a wide pan, warm the butter, garlic, and onion.
2. Add a handful of greens one at a time, then add water to the stem.
3. Cook for 5 minutes until tender.

Author: Garlic mustard is really strong when raw but mild when cooked. When the plant is raw, it is better used as a herb. When cooked, it's better used as a leafy green.

54
GINKGO

*G*inkgo is a tree, also known as *Ginkgo biloba*. This tree can cause an allergic reaction similar to that of the poison ivy family. Wear gloves, and if you have severe reactions to this family, do not eat it, even if cooked.

IDENTIFICATION OF THE PLANT

Ginkgo trees tend to be fairly large, reaching up to 120 feet. The branches are a little more organic in their shape, sometimes twisting. The bark is thick, light ashy brown, with deep grooves and texture. The flower is not distinct, being drooping, sparse florets, which are indistinguishable flowers. The fruit smells like vomit; they are round, yellow green to light orange, growing in clusters. The fruit is a thin layer of flesh around the nut, which is about an inch long and similar to an almond in appearance.

The easiest way, in my opinion, to identify this tree is the leaves. The leaves are distinct because they have this 1-2 inch green stem and then fan out, like a paper fan at the end. The sides of the fan are flat and the end is rounded out and slightly lobed. The leaves are also thin, watery, and a yellowish green that goes golden yellow in the fall. They grow alternately and sometimes out of clusters.

Where to gather it

The tree likes full sun. They are typically found in parks and other public spaces. They produce fruit in the fall. The leaves can be harvested from spring to fall.

How to gather it

The leaves can be cut or plucked from lower hanging branches. When the fruit is ripe it will fall off the tree. Using gloves you can pick them up. It is recommended you have a very good seal on whatever you are using to transport the fruit due to the smell.

How to cook with it

Edible: Yes, the fruit, the nuts, and the leaves.

Eating too many nuts can be poisonous. As such, try to eat less than five cooked pieces a day. The flavor is sweet to bitter with a hint of cheese. While the fruit can be eaten, most people prefer not to because of the vomit smell.

The leaves are mostly used to make tea.

Prepare Ginkgo Nut

The nut can be eaten alone in small amounts or used in cooking for its taste. **Ingredients:**

- 1 cup Ginkgo fruit

Instructions:

1. Outside, you can remove the thin layer of fruit from the nut, this can be done by hand or by soaking for a few hours in warm water. Be sure to use gloves the whole time.
2. Break the shell with brute force or soften the shell by boiling or roasting them.
3. The shell will crack, similar to a pistachio.
4. You will know the seed is cooked if it turns green or amber, glossy, and chewy.

Author: The leaves of the tree are used medicinally to improve cognitive function of all sorts.

55
GLASSWORT

lasswort is a name for the genus *Salicornia*.

IDENTIFICATION OF THE PLANT

The look of glaworts are fairly unique looking, although fairly area specific. They are small, only reaching a little over a foot in height. They have a shrubby look to them from a distance with its many branches. The branches are stiff and straight. The plant is actually succulent and does not have leaves, just the green branches. The branches have a texture to them that is scale-like, like asparagus. The flowers appear late in the season and are tiny and white out the side of the branches.

Where to gather it

Glasswort grows in salt areas, such as coastlines, salt lakes, and the like. You can harvest from spring to fall.

How to gather it

Pick the most tender tips from the plant's branches.

How to cook with it

Edible: Yes, you can eat the tender tips raw (you'll love how crispy they are). They can also be added to other dishes as a crisp and salty addition. They can also be pickled.

56
GOLDENROD

*G*oldenrod is a genus of yellow flowered plants under the scientific name *Solidago*. All varieties of goldenrod can be edible, but there is a preference for *S. virgaurea*.

IDENTIFICATION OF THE PLANT

On average, the plant gets to about 3-4 feet tall. The plant stands erect and has a hardy stem with slight toothing and a red hue. The leaves tend to be fairly long and narrow in an oval shape with a prominent tip. The leaves are also covered with slight toothing. The edges are uniform and slightly serrated.

The flower spike is on the top of the stem. It is formed by having multiple 1-2 inch stems that protrude from the main stem, creating a triangle shaped spike. Each stem is lined with multiple, very small, yellow flowers.

Where to gather it

Goldenrod blooms in the late summer and into the fall. Goldenrod is a common weed and can be found in typical weedy places such as ditches and other open places, especially ones that have been disturbed but aren't excessively damp.

How to gather it

There is fine toothing on the plant so be cautious. Harvest flowers when in season. Harvest the leaves right before the plant flowers. If you are planning on harvesting the flowers to dry, make sure the plant is still young enough that it won't go to seed.

How to cook with it

Edible: The flowers can be eaten raw or dried for teas. The leaves can be eaten raw and dried for teas as well, but it also functions as a leafy green and can be treated like spinach.

Author: Goldenrod has a bad reputation for causing the pollen for seasonal allergies, but it's actually ragweed that is responsible for hayfever. This being said, people who have seasonal allergies should be careful consuming anything that has pollen.

57
GOUTWEED

Goutweed is known by many names such as Ground elder, bishop's weed, and more, but it's all under the scientific name *Aegopodium podagraria*.

IDENTIFICATION OF THE PLANT

The plant is not very tall. It grows typically in small clusters from 1-3 feet tall. The leaves give the plant a fair amount of foliage. The stems stand straight and are hollow with a texture of grooves. The leaves are elongated oval shaped with jagged edges packed in groups of 5.

Goutweed looks very similar to wild carrot because its flower blooms in the spring and summer. The flower is a cluttered floret umbel that fans out flat in a roundish shape that's 4-6 inches wide. It consists of small white flowers.

Where to gather it

This plant is considered an invasive plant, meaning that it can go pretty much anywhere. Like most weeds though, they like places that have been disturbed or abandoned. It grows from the spring to the fall.

How to gather it

Gather only the young parts of the plant and cut back the rest. This plant is hearty and when it's cut back, it will grow more young leaves for further foraging.

How to cook with it

Edible: The young leaves can be used in the same way as spinach: in salad or cooked. It has a peppery taste.

NETTLE AND GOUTWEET SOUP

Time: 15-20 minutes
Serving Size: 4 servings
Prep Time: 5 minutes
Cook Time: 10-15 minutes
Ingredients:

- ½ cup Goutweed
- ½ cup Nettle
- ¼ cup dandelion
- 1 liter soup broth of choice
- ½ cup cream
- 1 onion
- 1 clove garlic
- 3 tbsps butter or other oil
- 1 tbsp flour
- for taste: parley, salt, and pepper

Instructions:

1. Clean all of your produce.
2. Chop everything finely.
3. In a pot, add the oil over medium heat to cook the garlic and onion.
4. Add in flour and stir.
5. Add broth, dandelion, nettle, and goutweed.
6. Bring to a boil, then remove from the heat.
7. In a blender, pour the soup and puree into a smooth texture.
8. Add in cream and spices and puree for a few seconds.

Author: The flower is used as a laxative, so be careful to only use the young parts of the plant. Similar plants are a young elder tree (hence the name) and Dog mercy, which has hair on the stem and leaves.

58
GRAPE

The grape is a fruit that grows from a grape vine. The genus of the grape is called *Vitis* and there are many species apart of this genus, but the ones that are popular to this area are *V. labrusca* (fox grape), *V. aestivalis* (summer grape), *V. vulpina* (frost grape), and *V. vinifera* (common grape).

Identification of the Plant

The grape vine is firstly identified by the form of its vine. Like most vines, this can mean that if it has somewhere to climb, it can climb up trees or across fences, but it can also crawl across the forest floor if it needs to. The older stem of the vine becomes woody, and, depending on the variety, it can become a few inches thick and create a thin, peeling bark. The younger parts of the plant are red or green, and while still hardy, it's got a smooth texture.

The leaves of the grape vine alternate, and while they vary, they do have similar looks, each being round with three or five main lobes with a main vein that branches to each and larger jagged edges.

The fruit of the grape can vary between the species. Just looking at the differences from the four species listed above, the fox grape is typically red and dusty, larger, and round. The summer grape is smaller and solid green to a solid purple color. The frost grape can range in size but is more of a bluish tone, and the common grape tends to have a more dense, larger cluster of berries.

Where to gather it

Grape vines like places with water and places to climb. This typically means that you can find them near wooded lakes and the like. The leaves are harvested in the spring and the fruit is harvested throughout the late summer and into the fall. The frost grape specifically should be harvested after the frost, to which it gets its name, for the sweet flavor.

How to gather it

The leaves should be young but fully grown, and they can be cut or plucked from the plant. The fruit can be cut off in its triangular clusters when ready to eat. You can taste test to see if the grape is desirable. If you are looking for grapes that are sweet enough to eat on their own, this is especially recommended since many wild grapes are tart.

How to cook with it

Edible: The fruits can be eaten and used like any other store bought grape. Typically since it's not as desirable in flavor, they are typically used in everything from deserts to preserves or raisins. The leaves can be boiled and eaten like other leafy greens.

WILD GRAPE JUICE

This recipe makes 3 cups of concentrate for 1 gallon of water or 3 tbsps for 1 cup.

Time: 30 minutes
Serving Size: 4 servings
Prep Time: 5 minutes
Cook Time: 25 minutes
Ingredients:

- 1-2 galleons grapes
- 3 cups sugar
- 2 cups water

Instructions:

1. Clean and remove grapes from stems.
2. Start pressing the grapes, squeezing the liquid from the flesh.

3. Once this is done, strain with cloth, squeezing as much juice out as possible.
4. Let sit in refrigeration overnight to let material settle.
5. The next day, gently pour off clean juice, throwing out the bottom impurities. Yield of juice 3-5 cups.
6. In a large pot, mix water and sugar over medium to high heat to create a syrup.
7. Add in grape juice.
8. Taste test and add in sugar if needed.
9. Bring to almost a boil, remove from heat.
10. Pour into sterilized jars, seal, and label OR Freeze (not in glass).

Author: Grapes, like other wild fruit, should be picked with caution. There are a lot of wild berries you can eat but also many you cannot. The grape's most similar look alike is the moonseed (*Menispermum canadense*).

GREENBRIER

*G*reenbrier usually refers to a genus, but in this chapter we are going to focus on common greenbrier. This species' scientific name is *Smilax rotundifolia*.

IDENTIFICATION OF THE PLANT

This plant is a vine, meaning that you might find it climbing something taller or you might find it creeping across the ground as it extends about 20 feet. It has thorns and creeps with tendrils. The older growth can become woody, so its stems can range from a herbaceous green to hard and brown. The leaves are a dark glossy color and the bottom of them is a paler green.

The flower usually branches out in clusters off of a stem. They start as a small green oval and bloom into small, star-shaped, white flowers. The berries are very similar to a blueberry but form a densely packed, round cluster.

Where to gather it

The plant can be harvested in the summer but it's typically sought out in the spring. It can be found in places with openings like ditches, open woods, banks, and the like.

How to gather it

The plant is easy to harvest since it is herbaceous and within arms reach, meaning you will only need some scissors. The trick is to harvest the part of the plant that is still young, or at least fresh. Include the tendrils, leaves, and new growth. Be careful because of the thorns.

How to cook with it

Edible: Yes, the younger parts of veins and leaves can be eaten raw, by itself, or part of a salad. Its shoots can also be cooked like asparagus, while the rest can be treated like other leafy greens. The roots have a gel that can be used for thickening.

See Asparagus for recipe.

Author: There is not much information on the edibility of the fruit; some sources say they are edible through the winter, but not substantial.

60
GROUND CHERRY

The ground cherry is known scientifically as the *Physalis* genus. This plant is mistaken for gooseberries and even called the cape gooseberry on occasion. Gooseberries do not have a lantern and look more grape-like than tomato-like.

IDENTIFICATION OF THE PLANT

The plant is native to the Americas, and therefore it's important to recognize the variety of the genus. The species can range from a few inches tall to a few feet tall. It is typically erect if the plant is of the taller variety.

The stem and branches can have a purple tone to it. The plant greatly resembles the tomato plant in its silhouette and can almost appear like its vining. The vining look is especially noticeable in the shorter species that grow out like ground cover instead of up. The leaves are also similar, being alternate, simple, and oval to a point, with some varieties having lobed or scalloped edges. The branches, stem, and leaves are covered in a soft fuzz. The flower is quite different from tomatoes, although it's a shallow trumpet shape with a dark brownish on the lower or inside portion of the petals and a very pale yellow outer edge. The center of the flower is a solid point, no prominent stigma.

Unlike many fruit bearing plants, you can't identify a ground cherry from its fruit because of its lantern-like husk. The fruit on the inside is very similar to a cherry tomato, and typically a yellow to orange color. The husk on the outside is thin like a membrane and green to light brown. It is round in shape around the base and comes to a point at the bottom of the fruit. It has seams from the top to the bottom point of the lantern, giving it panels.

Where to gather it

They like full sun and are not fond of the cold. They like places like a less dense wood because of the ability for it to be open and also slightly sheltered. The fruit is ready around late summer and should be harvested before the cold weather hits.

How to gather it

The fruit of the groundcherry can be a little more difficult for some foragers because it requires some strategy. The fruit of the plant typically falls before it is ready to be eaten, so it needs to be harvested beforehand. Once harvested, the fruit needs to be stored to allow it to ripen for up to a few weeks to get the sweet flavor. Unripe fruit can be poisonous. Store in a dry place.

How to cook with it

Edible: Yes, this plant can be eaten raw, used in deserts, or preserved. The fruit must be ripe and removed from its papery husk before eating or cooking. A good indicator of when the plant has ripened is when the husk is looking dried out instead of green. The flavor of ground cherries can be sweet and used like dessert, or more like its family member the tomato.

Ground Cherry Salsa

This recipe makes 1 large jar of salsa. This is not a preserved recipe.
Time: 24-48 hours
Prep Time: 24-48 hours
Cook Time: 0 minutes
Ingredients:

- 1 cup ground cherries
- ½ cup onion
- 6 tbsps chopped tomatoes
- 2 tbsps lemon or lime juice
- 1 clove garlic

- 1 tbsp Olive oil
- optional: ¼ cup jalapenos for heat
- optional: cilantro and other spices for your taste

Instructions:

1. Clean your produce.
2. Remove ground cherries from husks.
3. Chop all of the ingredients into fine chunks. If you prefer a chunkier salsa, chop the pieces slightly bigger.
4. In a bowel, add all of the ingredients together.
5. At this point you can let it rest for a day to absorb the flavors.
6. OR If you like very smooth salsa, you can add to a blender with a few tbsps of vinegar. This will keep the salsa preserved for longer in the fridge.

Author: Ground cherries are a part of the nightshade family. Nightshade is typically referred to when speaking of the poisonous varieties of the genus, but the genus *Solanum* is the umbrella for tomatoes as well. Plants like 'bittersweet', or *Solanum dulcamara*, grow in the Northeast and are part of the same family. This should not be an issue as long as the forager identifies the plant before foraging.

61
HAWTHORN

Hawthorn is the common name for a genus of plants that can take the shape of a small tree or shrub. The scientific name for this genus is *Crataegus*. There is another plant that goes by the common name hawthorn or Indian hawthorn with the scientific name of *rhaphiolepis*. This genus is common in Asia and is used for ornamental use, even being used for bonsai and sometimes bear fruit. The fruit is blue and the leaves are smooth edged, so there shouldn't be confusion beyond the name. The species *C. monogyna* is the most used for food, but all hawthorn berries are edible.

A common look-alike to the hawthorn is the blackthorn (*Prunus spinosa*), but once again the fruit is a dark blue, resembling a blueberry, and blooms later than the hawthorn.

PHYSICAL IDENTIFICATION OF THE PLANT

Typically a small tree, growing up to 40 feet for some species but can be as small as five feet for a fully grown shrub. The leaves alternate and are simple with variations of different points and usually with some level of jaggedness on the edge. They are deciduous, but some variations might be more hardy and therefore slightly evergreen, but not completely. This means that some leaves are more watery and yellow-green and some are darker and glossy.

The bark is gray and smooth when young. As it ages, it gets more texture for most species. Many of the variations have very stiff, straight branches.

The lucky thing about plants with foragable fruit, the fruit tends to be the easiest thing to identify, unlike plants that need to be harvested before their identifiable attributes are on display. Similarly, the fruit of most hawthorn varieties tend to be very similar. The fruit is similar to a cherry in size, but it is typically slightly more elongated like an oval than completely round and it also has a pit in the center. The color is a very bright red, and it hangs from a 1-2 inch stem. The bottom of the fruit has a small crown similar to a blueberry. In some cases, the fruit on some varieties can range from black to light yellow, but this is species specific.

Where to gather it

The fruit of the hawthorn genus is ready to pick in the fall, but the wide variety of hawthorns can be found in different environments. The fruit is not quick to rot though and may be reliable for weeks to even months. You might find hawthorn varieties near bodies of water, some small banks, some prefer the coast, or even on slopes like hills and mountains. Since they are all edible, finding the hawthorn that grows best in your area is the best bet.

How to gather it

The plant only grows into a small tree. So that when you find a hawthorn tree or shrub, you should be able to reach the fruit without a problem. You should be able to pick the fruit easily, but it may be in your best interest to taste test the fruit first to make sure it is to your liking and at the best ripeness. Since the fruit can stay on the plant for a while there is no rush. Be careful of thorns.

How to cook with it

Edible: This plant can be eaten as a fresh fruit, put in pies, or preserves. The fruit can also be used to make tea. It is likened to rosehips and can range from sweeter to very tart.

Hawthorn Ketchup

The ketchup is good for 1 year.
Time: 45-50 minutes
Prep Time: 35 minutes
Cook Time: 10-15 minutes
Ingredients:

- 2 cups berries
- 1 ¼ cup apple cider vinegar
- 1 ¼ cup water
- ½ sugar
- pinch of salt and pepper

Instructions:

1. Clean the berries and remove any stems.
2. Add to a pot with water and vinegar for an half an hour until skins come off.
3. Use a strainer to remove pits and other impurities.
4. In a clean pan, add sugar.
5. Put on low heat, wait until sugar is dissolved.
6. Bring to a boil, simmer until it starts to thicken (up to 10 minutes).
7. Add your spices
8. Put in a sterilized jar(s), seal lid, and label.

Note: Once the jars are sealed, it's recommended to take the ring off of the jar.

Author: Besides being a genus that is conveniently all edible, the hawthorn also has a long history in myth and lore. While this changes from culture to culture, it's comforting to know that many of our ancestors had a relationship with this plant. It has also been used as an herbal aid for heart health and digestion. Because of these effects, it's recommended to not overindulge.

62
HENBIT

Henbit is a deadnettle also known as *Lamium amplexicaule*, also very similar to *L. purpureum*. Nettles are a large group of flowers, some more or less friendly. See chapter 73 for more on nettles. The term deadnettle can sound ominous, but it actually is in reference to nettles that sting and create a rash or irritation. Dead nettle refers to the fact that the nettles are dead, meaning that they don't sting. They can look similar so be careful.

Identification of the plant

Henbit is a small herbaceous plant that reaches a little over a foot tall and is erect and square. The stem has fine hair and the leaves are heart shaped, at about 1.5 inches long. They come off the stem in an uniform opposite pattern, but in pairs on either side like a ladder. The leaves have a wrinkle-like texture. The edges are loved and have large serrations like points.

The flowers are a magenta pink. They grow right out of the stem. They are long and tubular and open at the end to a non-symmetrical formation. Two petals open out, away from the plant, and one petal on the other side is pointed up and over like a hood.

Where to gather it

Can be found in common weedy areas. It likes more open areas like fields. Young shoots are harvested in the spring. Flowers very early in the spring.

How to gather it

Harvest shoots by cutting the young, tender plant before it matures. Be aware of how early the plant flowers need to be harvested very early in the year.

How to cook with it

Edible: Yes, young leaves, shoots, stems, and flowers.

The edible parts can be eaten raw or cooked, used in the same way as other leafy greens like spinach. The plant is like a celery flavor with a slightly peppery taste.

Author: Deadnettles are also used for medicinal purposes, particularly aiding in digestion as a laxative.

63
HICKORY

*H*ickory refers to a group of trees under the genus *Carya*. Not all hickory nuts are edible. Mockernut hickory is one of the edible types that is native to the Northeast. It is scientifically named *C. tomentosa*.

IDENTIFICATION OF THE PLANT

The tree grows to about 60 feet tall. The bark is dark gray with groves that give narrow overlapping stripes. Leaves are compound opposite. It's leaflets have a pointed end that is oval in shape and narrows towards the base with parallel veining.

Flowers hang in three inch narrow catkin clusters. The fruit is a hard nut the size of a gold ball with a green outer layer. The nut inside is a little larger than an almond and oval.

Where to gather it

Likes areas that have sloped ground like hills and the like. Nuts are ready to pick in the fall.

How to gather it

Harvest the nuts by letting them fall. You will know they are ready and falling because the leaves will start to fall at the same time. Pick the ones off the ground or, if possible, place a tarp to catch them.

How to cook with it

Edible: Yes, the nut.

Choose nuts that are intact with no bug holes. The shells are thick, so you'll need to use a hammer to crack them open. Be sure to pick a location that can handle the process. Once you've cracked the nuts and loosened the flesh, add them to a pot of boiling water. The flesh will float to the top.

64
HIGHBUSH CRANBERRY

The highbush cranberry is actually not a cranberry, it is just the common name for *Viburnum trilobum*. It is more closely related to the guelder-rose. This being said, the berry that comes with the plant looks and tastes very similar and is even ready at the similar time of year. This is one of those similar plants that are genuinely similar; however, this is often not the case. It is still important to accurately identify before you forage and eat. There are plenty of other berries that look similar and are not edible. You should never get too comfortable eating strange berries.

IDENTIFICATION OF THE PLANT

The shrub gets up to 20 feet tall in some places. It can grow into a more sparse looking, strangely bush, or remain dense and round looking. The branches have a reddish-yellow color when young and end up gray, but still smooth, as it ages. The leaves are green and have three main points, with a main margin for each and some wider serration on the edges as well. It also has slight hair underneath.

The flower is a round, flat top floret with many white flowers. The flowers have five petals and are in a star shape, but unlike other flowers that share similarities, they are slightly bigger and the petals are rounder and wider. The floret doesn't typically bloom all at the same time, having a few flowers in each cluster at once. The florets are only about a few inches wide, but the plant usually produces many of them.

The berries droop in flat, wide clusters, ranging from a few to many, at about half an inch long. They are bright red and oval. Unlike the cranberry, they are more translucent instead of a solid color. They have a flat pit inside.

Where to gather it

The plant likes moist areas, lowlands, banks, and the like. The fruit is on the plant in the summer but is ready to harvest in the autumn or throughout the winter.

How to gather it

The berries can be picked off of the bush. Unlike the cranberry, the bush is tall and you won't be kneeling to collect. Since they like wet areas, make sure you wear waterproof boots and are safe near water. Taste test the berry; if it is not sweet in fall and winter, it might be the guelder-rose, not the highbush berry.

How to cook with it

Edible: The ripe berry tastes similar to the cranberry. It can be eaten raw, but it can be very sour, so it is typically made into jam. See Cranberry for recipe.

65
HONEWORT

*H*onewort, scientifically known as *Cryptotaenia canadensis*, has some very close look-alikes, many of which are not edible, since it is part of the carrot family. This plant, like the milkweed, is home to a butterfly, the black Swallowtail.

IDENTIFICATION OF THE PLANT

The plant stands up to three feet but is usually shorter. The stem is thin, green, and smooth. The leaves are compound in groups of three and each individual leaf has three lobes with edges that are slightly jagged. The texture is slightly wrinkled and four inches long, getting smaller up the stem.

The flower is a sparse looking floret with very small flowers off of thin branching stems. Individual flowers are not much bigger than the stem itself. They are white with five curling petals.

Where to gather it

The honewort likes moist conditions, as such it is typically found in woodlands. Blooms early summer.

How to gather it

Harvest shoots by cutting the young, tender plant before it matures.

How to cook with it

Edible: Yes, young plant and root.

The stems and leaves can be boiled like spinach or raw for a desired flavor that is mild, bitter, and earthy. Roots can be cooked like any starchy root.

66
HOPNISS, GROUNDNUT

The Groundnut goes by many names—like the potato bean, hopniss, etc.—but is scientifically known as *Apios americana*. There is another plant that goes by the name groundnut. While it's a family of flowering plants, the hopniss plant is a vine. The plant hosts the larva of a butterfly called the silver skipper.

IDENTIFICATION OF THE PLANT

The groundnut is a crawling vine that can grow about 20 feet long. It has a thin green stem and compound leaves. The six leaves are leaflets in opposite pairs with the seventh leaf at the point. They are typically longer and thin but can be more round like a basic leaf. The point is prominent.

The flowers are clusters in a short, dense, almost round, triangular shape about five inches long. The dark pink flowers themselves look sort of unusual with two round petals that open like cupped hands. From the side they look like oysters. The center is like a sideways disk that sticks out like a tongue between them. The root is round like a potato, although much smaller. The fruit is a pod about five inches long that looks like dark brown/green beans.

Where to gather it

The plant is a vine, so you might notice it crawling on the ground or climbing up other plants and such. They like damp ground and are found near the banks and edges of water. Recommended harvest is late fall or early spring, but they can be picked all year.

How to gather it

Since the plant is around banks and such, the ground might be easier to work with; however, still take a shovel, or better yet a garden fork, to dig and sift for the roots.

How to cook with it

Edible: Yes, the seeds and roots are eaten.

While it isn't actually a root, for all intents and purposes as it's a tuber underground, its root is not only edible but delicious. They are cooked like potatoes and eaten as starch. The fruit (bean pods) are also cooked and eaten. The seeds, once removed from the inside of the pod, can be eaten as a legume or bean. The flowers and stems are also edible but not a common snack.

CARAMELIZED GROUNDNUT

Time: 30 minutes
Serving Size: 4 servings
Prep Time: 5 minutes
Cook Time: 25 minutes
Ingredients:

- 2 cups groundnut root
- 2 cups broth
- pinch of salt
- 1 tbsp butter
- 1 tbsp honey

Instructions:

1. Clean, peel, and chop the root.
2. In a pan, add the root, broth, and salt, and bring to a boil.
3. Turn down to a simmer and cook until the root is tender as you would a potato. This should take about 10-15 minutes. The broth should greatly reduce.
4. Turn heat back up, add butter and honey until a sauce is formed.
5. Add seasonings of choice.

Author: A great thing to note about the root is that they are able to store like potatoes. If they are kept in a cool, humid place like a cellar, they can last for quite a while. This is great for winter preparations. While many jams and such can be used for the winter, having a starch like this can be a game changer for those who choose or need to live off of the land.

A really good friend of mine always invites me to eat hopniss. I feel so wild. I think of the Dakota tribe eating them like potatoes. Our meal is like a ritual—we eat on the ground, with our hands, and somehow we always end up with spiritual talks. Such a great time!

JAPANESE KNOTWEED

*J*apanese knotweed is scientifically known as *Reynoutria japonica* or *Polygonum cuspidatum*. It is not recommended to have this plant near buildings because it will grow through them and cause damage.

IDENTIFICATION OF THE PLANT

The plant can get fairly tall, up to 10 feet and erect. The stem is hollow, smooth, branching, and sometimes has a red hue. The leaves are alternating and heart shaped to basic oval-pointed. They are up to five inches long. The flowers are on about five inch long stems that create an erect spike. The veining tapers the leaf slightly. The spike is narrow and the individual flowers are very small and sparse. There are many spikes that line the branches and are thick in texture. Fruit is a small, papery disk with a seed inside.

Shoots look like asparagus with leaves, not scales, on top and bamboo-like seams.

Where to gather it

The plant can be found in weedy areas, like places that have been abandoned. It is considered a weed. Harvest young shoots in mid-spring.

How to gather it

Harvest shoots by cutting the young, tender plant before it matures. It can help to find the dead plant from the year previous to both spot and identify the plant. It's best eaten if the shoots are under a foot tall.

How to cook with it

Edible: Yes, the young shoots can be eaten raw or cooked. It tastes sour or tart. Can be used in sweet dishes like rhubarb or in savory dishes like asparagus.

Japanese Knotweed Relish

Time: 45 minutes
Prep Time: 5 minutes
Cook Time: 40 minutes
Ingredients:

- 5 cups Knotweed shoots
- 5 cups onion
- 3 cups cider or white vinegar
- 3 cups brown sugar
- 1 tsp each of your choice: cinnamon, black pepper, cloves, ginger, and garlic

Instructions:

1. Clean and chop knotweed shoots.
2. In a pot on medium heat, add the onions (garlic and ginger if using) and soften a bit.
3. Add sugar and vinegar.
4. Turn up heat.
5. Add ¾ knotweed and other spices.
6. Bring to a simmer, lower heat, and cook uncovered for 30 minutes.
7. When thick, add the rest of the knotweed, cook for 10 minutes, then remove from heat.
8. Seal in sterilized jars and label.

Author: Japanese knotweed is used in herbal medicine for many treatments. The whole plant is used to treat respiratory, skin, and oral issues.

JERUSALEM ARTICHOKE

Jerusalem artichoke has many names, you might know it as sunchoke or wild sunflower among others, but it is scientifically known as *Helianthus tuberosus*. While this plant is useful and has a lovely flower, it can become invasive. If you are considering planting it, keep an eye out to ensure that it does not overtake your garden. It is a part of the sunflower family but does not produce the seeds like many of them do.

IDENTIFICATION OF THE PLANT

The plant can get really tall, like many of the sunflower family, at up to about 10 feet. The leaves are opposite at the bottom and alternate up the stem. The leaves also get smaller up the plant, they are up to 12 inches long, with a rough hair. They are long and narrow in shape to a point with smooth edges.

The flower is shaped like a daisy but has a smaller center and longer, slightly wide petals. The flowers can grow up to eight inches wide. They are a bright golden yellow. The flowers can seem like they are solitary because of their shape and size, but technically they are part of a floret that branches up to about ten flowers at the end of the stem. The rubbers are tear-drop shaped and pointed down.

Where to gather it

Likes places with high moisture in the ground. Found in weedy areas like abandoned places or thickets. Harvest in the fall.

How to gather it

In the fall after the first frost, they can be dug up throughout the winter as long as the ground is not frozen. However, locating them might be hard without identifying tall stems or flowers.

How to cook with it

Edible: Yes, the root.

The tubers can be eaten raw or cooked like other root vegetables. They are sometimes pickled.

Author: I go crazy for it! It tastes so sweet and it has the texture of a potato but the taste of an artichoke. When topped with fresh parsley, it is honestly a journey for your taste buds!

JEWELWEED

Jewelweed is also known as spotted touch-me-not, orange jewelweed, and more, but is scientifically known as *Impatiens capensis*. The stems and leaves can be boiled to help relieve poison ivy rash.

This plant is called a touch-me-not because the seed pods can burst, shooting out seeds when touched.

Identification of the plant

The jewelweed grows up to five feet tall and is herbaceous. The stems are branched and smooth with high water content. The leaves alternate and grow up to five inches long. The leaves are narrow at the base and widen at the top, while the end is a rounded point. They are smooth and have a long stem. The plant is not overly dense or sparse.

It can bloom from spring to fall. The flowers are orange, sometimes with spots of darker orange. They dangle from a stem but open horizontally. The flowers are unique in shape; they are trumpet shaped but with a long narrow tube. The flower is not symmetrical, having one or two large darker petals on the bottom and a smaller, lighter petal hooding the top.

Where to gather it

The plant can be found in wet solids near bodies of waters like ponds or lakes.

How to gather it

Harvest shoots by cutting the young, tender plant before it matures.

How to cook with it

Edible: Yes, although the young shoots, flowers, and seeds should be eaten in moderation. Boil the leaves twice in new water before eating.

The plant is more commonly used as a medicinal herb to be used on the skin raw or made into other remedies.

70
JUNEBERRY

*J*uneberry refers to a genus of plant that can be trees or shrubs, scientifically called *Amelanchier*. They might also be called shadbush or wood, sugar plums, serviceberry, and more. Many, if not all, of the genus is edible, but the downy or saskatoon berry are some of the most common. They go by *A. arborea* and *A. alnifolia* respectively. Downy berries are more common in the East.

IDENTIFICATION OF THE PLANT

The plant can be a shrub or small tree, meaning it can be up to 40 feet tall. The bark is smooth, but the trunk can be twisted or furrowed, although it is typically more narrow. It is a gray color. The leaves are a basic pointed oval shape and a yellow green, growing up to four inches long. A muted red in the fall. They are in an alternate pattern.

The white flowers grow in clusters that cover the tree in the spring. The flowers are star shaped but the petals are long and narrow to prevent it from touching the hole at the center. Prominent stamen comes out of it. The berries are a mix of bright to dark red. They are almost identical to a blueberry, but the crown is red as well. They cluster off 1-2 inch stems in a spaced out group of 10 or so at the bottom few inches of the branches.

Where to gather it

Because of the variety in the genus, there is a variation on where they grow, although they typically grow in areas that have high moisture and a sloping ground. This can range from mountain-like areas to swamps. Berries are ripe in midsummer.

How to gather it

Harvest the berries by picking them off of the bush when they are ripe. You may need a step ladder.

How to cook with it

Edible: The berries can be eaten raw or cooked. They can also be made into jams, used similarly to bramble fruit.

71
JUNIPER

*J*uniper is a genus scientifically named *Juniperus*. They can take the shape of a shrub or tree. Only a few of the junipers are considered edible. They are not native to the Northeast. One of the most popular junipers is the california juniper and it, like the others, typically grows in the west. This being said, there are junipers in the Northeast, but they are not as favorable.

J. communis, or the common juniper, is used in cooking, but usually more for flavor. This will be the juniper talked about in this chapter. Be cautious eating other species unless you have identified it as an edible species.

Juniper berries are often confused for capers. Capers are similar looking to juniper berries but come off of the caper bush. Juniper berries can be pickled in a similar manner though.

Pregnant women should not eat this plant.

IDENTIFICATION OF THE PLANT

The common juniper is typically a low shrub. Junipers can be dense and used for hedges, but when natural the leaves and branches can spread out into clumps. Without maintenance they can become less appealing because of the rather bare inside branches. They can spread outwards instead of up, creating a flat, disk-like silhouette. This is a coniferous plant, meaning it has needles. The needles are short and prickly. The younger needles might be more green, but the older needles often have a bluish look to them, but not quite as dusty blue as the blue spruce. Some juniper needles appeared to be scaled. The bark is a reddish brown and slightly grooved.

The berries look like blueberries but smaller. They grow in small clusters off of the branches. The cones are very similar looking but not edible. They are more densely packed but slightly scaled and a dusty pale green. Before they mature, the cones are small and pale yellow.

Junipers are sometimes avoided in planting because of their smell, which smells distinctly like cat urine.

Where to gather it

The plant can be found in areas with well draining soil, preferably sandy. Berries are ready in the fall. It doesn't fruit the first year.

How to gather it

Harvest berries by picking them off the shrub when they are blue.

How to cook with it

Edible: The berries are not usually eaten raw because they are bitter. Instead, they are dried and used to season food, mostly meat and alcohol like beer and gin. **Do not eat the cones or leaves.**

Pickled Juniper Berries

This recipe is focused on pickled juniper berries that can be added to other food as a seasoning. If you are creating a pickling mix, do not use more than a tablespoon of the berries.

Time: 25 minutes
Serving Size: 4 servings
Prep Time: 5 minutes
Cook Time: 20 minutes
Ingredients:

- 1/4 cup juniper berries
- 1 cup pickling vinegar
- 1 tbsp salt
- 1 cup water
- 1 tbsp sugar
- spices of choice: garlic, mustard, onion, or pepper

- (if creating picked mix instead, beets and onions are recommended)

Instructions:

1. Wash juniper berries and other produce.
2. In a pot, bring water, vinegar, salt and sugar to a boil until the sugar is dissolved.
3. While the brine is heating, in sterilized jars (heat proof) add a mixture of spices and the berries. Leave room at top, and the berries should be fully submerged.
4. Pour hot brine over berries in the jars.
5. With heat protecting gloves on, tap or shift jars to make sure the brine reaches all the berries and there are no air bubbles.
6. Put on the lid and add to the fridge.

Note: these are not sealed. You can seal them if you want to for longer preservation. If not, they'll last at least three months in the fridge.

Author: The juniper is used in medicinal medicine to treat arthritis, diabetes, and infection. Juniper alcohol is sometimes used, but theriit bark is also used.

Junipers are sometimes the evil look-alike. Cedar trees are often more desirable. The false cedar is actually a juniper, which makes it all the more confusing. The Red Eastern Cedar leaves, berries, and wood are used in herbal medicine.

72
LADY'S THUMB

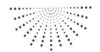

*L*ady's thumb is also called redshank or *Persicaria maculosa*.

IDENTIFICATION OF THE PLANT

Lady's thumb is a common weed, it even looks weedy. It grows up to three feet tall, standing erect. Prominent joints at the branch hinge, stem is green, and hued with red. Leaves are alternate. They are best identified by the dark marks on the leaves. They are patches that look like the plant has been damaged. It gets its name from this, claiming that it looks like a lady's fingerprint. The leaves are simple and elongated with a prominent point. They are light green with a main margin and parallel veining.

The flower is a narrow inflorescence on a stem. The floret is a straight spike like the shape of a hotdog. The individual flowers appear to be closed in an oval shape.

Where to gather it

Flowers in summer. Since it is a weed, it adapts to wet and dry areas. It is best found in disturbed, overgrown areas. Blooms through the summer.

How to gather it

The young leaves and shoots can be harvested in spring. The flowers can be picked when in bloom.

How to cook with it

Edible: The young greens can be eaten raw or cooked. The greens are similar to lettuce or spinach. The leaves and flowers are dried for tea. The flower can be eaten fresh in salads or as garnish.

Author: Lady's thumb is also used as a medicinal treatment against the poison ivy rash and bug stings.

73
LAMBS QUARTERS

*L*ambs quarters is also known as white goosefoot and scientifically known as *Chenopodium album*. If you have ever weeded a garden, you probably know lambs quarters, if not by name then by annoyance. Lambs quarters is a very common weed, but it has started to revive its reputation due to its nutritious value of fiber, protein, and vitamins.

IDENTIFICATION OF THE PLANT

Lambs quarters can grow up to three feet. When it's younger it is more erect, but as it gets taller, it can droop slightly. The leaves are watery and green with a dusty white cast, much paler on the underside. The shape of them on the younger plant is an equal sided, rounded triangle with very scalloped edges. Newer, smaller leaves growing from the top, full sized, can be up to four inches long. As the plant gets taller, the leaves become longer and more narrow. They are toothed along the margin. As the plant gets older and branches, it looks more weedy.

The top part of the plant branches off in a few about three inch branches to create a narrow, sparse spike. The little branches can start up to over a foot from the top of the plant. The flowers are very small, round, green, and cluster in small, round florets/inflorescence. There clusters of flowers line the three inch branches. It does not look like a flower, it looks very weedy.

Where to gather it

This plant is a weed, so it's very common in most places, especially over ground areas. It is best to avoid plants in areas that can be contaminated. Best to harvest the greens in the spring. The seeds can be harvested in the fall.

How to gather it

You can pick the whole plant's leaves and stems when the plant is young in the spring. As it gets older, essentially before it flowers, you can harvest the younger growth off the top of the plant. To harvest seeds, cut the top of the plant off with the flower spike gently. Shake into a bag to gather the seeds and throw the top away.

How to cook with it

Edible: The young leaves and stems can be cooked like any other leafy green. The seeds can be boiled or ground into flour for baking.

WILD SPINACH COOKED GREENS

Time: 18-20 minutes
Serving Size: 4 servings
Prep Time: 10 minutes
Cook Time: 8-10 minutes
Ingredients:

- 1 bunch lambs quarters (like spinach, when cooked it cooks down to what seems a 100th of its size, if you think you have enough you probably don't)
- 3 tbsps cooking oil, preferably olive oil or butter
- optional: foraged field garlic, garlic mustard, wild leeks, or wild onion for taste.

Instructions:

1. Wash the greens like any other lettuce and pick out any wilting or undesirable pieces.
2. Chop the plant up into edible size, this will also help the cooking process.

3. If you are not cooking the greens and are making a salad instead, it's a good idea to try the leaves pretty well after washing, especially if you are setting it aside for a time because fresh plants like this can become less crisp fairly quickly from the water.
4. In a pan, heat up the oil and throw in your spices, make sure garlic or onion is nice and soft.
5. Greens cook down fairly quickly, so it might be easier to add them a handful at a time. Stirring as you add more can prevent stress from trying to cook and stir a heaping pile.
6. Once all the greens are added, cook them all down for a few minutes, making sure they are stirred gently.

Author: I have a bias towards weeds as foragable food because I love a redemption arc. As we know, weeds are only named so because they are perceived to be so. That being said, it is not my favorite when I see it make an appearance in my own gardens. Weeds are always my go to when it comes to foraging because there is no guilt on how much I take. I know I am doing the surrounding plants a favor and that there is no short supply for the local wildlife as well.

74
LILAC

The lilac is a name for the genus of plants named *Syringa*, but the common lilac is the most common, especially in the North east. The lilac is scientifically named *S. vulgaris*. While it is common in weedy, overgrown, or abandoned areas, it is not considered a weed. It can be a small tree or shrub.

IDENTIFICATION OF THE PLANT

The lilac is typically a bush, but the bush can range from anywhere between 3 to 20 feet tall. They often appear in small groups, becoming quite large. The bark is gray and smooth on the younger growth and becomes aged looking as it matures. The leaves are yellow green, basic oval point shape and up to five inches long. They are simple, growing in opposite pairs.

The flowers are in floret spikes that are fairly dense, sometimes more triangular shaped or more narrow. They can be anywhere between 3 inches to 10 inches long. The individual flowers are small with four petals. The shape is trumpet-like with a prominent narrow tube and the four petals open up flat. They are often a light purple, but can also be dark purple, pink, or white. They have a winged seed that is small.

Where to gather it

As noted above, it is common in weedy, overgrown, or abandoned areas like the sides of roads. Blooms in late spring.

How to gather it

Harvest the roses by bringing clippers strong enough to cut through the woody stems. Bring a basket that is big enough to carry the large florets. Be careful of bees and shake the florets gently beforehand to remove bugs. Since this is a flower that blooms in the spring, many bugs use it as a food source, you may want to leave them outside for an hour in the cool shade to let many of them escape before bringing them inside.

How to cook with it

Edible: The flowers are edible raw but are not prefered that way, although maybe lightly sprinkled in a salad. The flavor is very floral. This being said, there are many things you can do with lilac flowers. Most of the options are infusing the flowers in something else, like sugar, honey, or water.

Sugared Lilac Flowers

If you want to make more than this recipe, it's a good idea to have multiple small jars instead of one big one. It is really important to shake the jars everyday for at least a week or the water will clump the sugar.

Time: about 1 week
Prep Time: 20 minutes
Cook Time: 0 minutes
Ingredients:

- 1 cup white sugar
- ½ cup lilac flowers

Instructions:

1. Start to remove the small blooms from the stem and any hard part of the leaf. Note: this can take a while.
2. Submerge flowers in cool water to wash them. Let them dry completely before continuing.
3. In a clean jar, add a tbsp of sugar and the tbsp of lilac flowers.
4. Cover the flowers with a thin layer of sugar and repeat.
5. Put a lid on the jar.

6. Every day for a week, shake the jar to agitate the sugar and the blossoms.

Once the flowers are dry, you can strain the flowers or leave them in the sugar. The sugar will be infused with lilac and can be used in cooking.

Author: Lilacs are probably best known for their scent. Even wild rose bushes can smell too sweet for some people, but the lilac can be brought in the house for fragrance when it blooms as well.

75
LOTUS

The lotus flower is scientifically known as *Nelumbo lutea*. This is the only lotus native to America. They are not the same as a lily pad. The lily will sit in the water and the lotus will have a stem that pushes the plant above the waterline. Water lilies are poisonous.

IDENTIFICATION OF THE PLANT

The lotus is an aquatic plant that has two main parts above water. The leaf is the first part. They are round and can be over a foot in length. The stem pushes the above water, sometimes a foot out of the water. The pads are connected to the stem from the button in the center. This can create a cupping shape of the leaf, they are slightly wavy as well.

The flower sticks above water, typically higher than the leaf. The flowers seem disconnected completely from the pad. The flower is about seven inches wide and white to yellow, usually a pale yellow. Its flowers are a shallow cup shape, only curling up at the ends usually. The center is about an inch wide and tall, like a cylinder. It is surrounded by a thick ring of stamen.

Where to gather it

Grows in ponds and other slow or still water. The underwater stem gets about six feet tall, so it has to reach the bottom of water. Blooms late spring early summer. Roots are harvested in the fall. It prefers rich soil. Harvest seed after flower is done.

How to gather it

Harvesting all parts of this plant can be difficult since it is an aquatic plant. Finding plants that are located in shallow areas that can be waded through with rubber boots is best. The solid should be soft, so you might be able to pull the root up by the stem. Tug gently and see if it can be done without breaking the stem. Alternatively, use a small boat to reach plants in deeper water.

How to cook with it

Edible: Yes, all of it can be eaten.

The most popular part to eat is the root and large seed, but everything can be eaten. The leaves are preferred when they are young. The seed is eaten cooked or raw, and the root is cooked like a potato.

The greens are used like spinach. Seeds are eaten like nuts or starch.

Roasted Lotus Root

Time: 45-50 minutes
Serving Size: 4 servings
Prep Time: 5 minutes
Cook Time: 40-45 minutes
Ingredients:

- 4 cups Lotus root
- ¼ cup olive oil
- 4 tbsps honey
- garlic, pepper, and salt for taste

Instructions:

1. Preheat the oven to 400 °F.
2. Clean and chop root into 1 inch pieces.
3. Lay on the tray evenly and sprinkle oil, honey, and spices evenly.
4. Roast for 30 minutes and flip it, while checking for tenderness.
5. Cook for another 10-15 minutes.

76
MAPLE

Maple is a name for a genus of trees that go by the scientific name *Acer*. The maple is a national symbol of Canada. The sugar maple, *A. saccharum*, is most popular because of the maple syrup that it produces. It is commonly referred to as a sugarbush when there is an area of a forest that is being tapped for its sap.

IDENTIFICATION OF THE PLANT

The tree can grow up to 100 feet. It has a bark that is deeply grooved, rough textured, and dark gray.

Where to gather it

The sugar maple is a common tree, but it prefers areas that are not highly elevated. The trees can be tapped in the late winter to prepare for when the liquids start flowing come the warmer weather in fall. They grow in opposite pairs.

The leaves can range from a yellow green to dark and bright red to orange and yellow in the fall. The leaves are about eight inches long with five main lobes and are notched. The seed is known for its spinning through the air. It has two connected seeds and a pair of papery wings.

How to gather it

The tree is drilled into with a shallow hole. A metal tap is inserted to direct flow and a bucket is hung to collect the liquid. Collect buckets regularly until there is enough. Seeds can be plucked off three while still green.

How to cook with it

Edible: The sap is made into maple syrup. The seeds can be boiled, then roasted.

Maple Syrup

Serving Size: 4 servings
Ingredients:

- 3 gallons sap yields 12 cups

Instructions:

1. Boil outside only.
2. In a wide pan, add water and sap.
3. Add more sap as water dissolves.
4. When all has been added, bring to 4 degrees above boiling point.
5. Filter and add to jars.

77
MAYAPPLE

The mayapple is a family (one above genus) of flowers scientifically called *Podophyllum*. They are also called mandrakes or ground lemons. The edible species is called just mandrake or may apple, and it is scientifically called *P. peltatum*.

Identification of the Plant
The plant is only about a foot and a half tall. It usually grows in patches and can creep. The leaves are compound looking but are actually just deeply lobed. They attach to the plant from below in the middle, creating a circular fan. There are five lobes and a few large serrations, reaching up to 14 inches across. For the two leaves, the plant only slightly branches.

The flower is solitary in between the two branches. It is about two inches wide, cup shaped, and facing out, not up. The stamen in the center is short but prominent. The fruit looks like a miniature lemon, being only the size of a large grape. On the inside it is orange with four pairs of tear dropped hollow holes in a ring around the center that is softened when ripe.

Where to gather it
You can find this plant in wooded areas, meadows, or banks as long as it's rich and moist. Harvest ripe fruit in fall.

How to gather it

The plant should only be eaten when completely ripe. The fruit should be just about to fall to the ground.

How to cook with it

Edible: Only the ripe fruit can be eaten, otherwise it'll be poisonous. It can be eaten raw, but it is not for everyone. Can be made into jams and other preserves or used like lemon in juices.

Author: The root is used for treating parasites, among other things.

78
MELILOT, SWEET CLOVER

*S*weet clover is known scientifically as *Melilotus albus*, although other common names include honey clover.

This clover can be compared to other common clovers, the red clover and the wood sorrel. There is a white and yellow sweet clover, not to be confused with white clover. White clover more closely resembles the red clover in flower, the sweet white clover being a long spike, not a global foret.

Warning: If this plant is improperly dried, it will create a mold that can cause internal bleeding and **death**. Yellow sweet clover is often avoided.

IDENTIFICATION OF THE PLANT

This plant can grow up to 7 feet tall, with semi-erect, smooth stems, and sparse branches that are only 1-2 feet long. The leaves are typical of a clover, a compound of three, but unlike the other clovers in this book, the leaves are much more elongated and narrow, so it is not as noticeable as a clover.

The flower is a narrow spike at the top that is up to five inches long. The flowers are white, spaced out but not sparse, and often opened at the base, only budding at the top. The individual flowers are small and non-distinct, tubular shaped.

Where to gather it

This plant can be bunched in with other common weedy plants. It grows in abandoned areas.

How to gather it

Harvest shoots by cutting the young, tender plant before it matures.

How to cook with it

Edible: The flowers and young leaves are dried fresh for their vanilla flavor.

Author: This plant might be a great choice for people who are really stepping away from grocery stores and want to find good alternatives. In this case, vanilla. Since inpoper storage can be deadly, I do not recommend this plant be used unless you are experienced in foraging and can be confident in your skills to properly dry it.

79
MINT

Mint is a genus of plants that are known by the scientific name *Lamiaceae*. There are many common usable plants in this genus like peppermint, spearmint, catnip, and more. There are, however, members of this genus that are not edible like creeping charlie and more.

Mint is also invasive, if you are thinking about planting members of the mint family be sure to cut them back when you see that they are taking over your garden and the local environment.

Mint is probably best known for its cooling sensation and has many uses.

IDENTIFICATION OF THE PLANT

The mint family are able to be identified by their square stems. Peppermint, spearmint, and catnip all tend to stay under a foot tall, but can become bushy looking. All mint families have leaves that are opposite pair patterns. Peppermint tends to have darker leaves and a red stem. Spearmint tends to be yellow green and more herbaceous. Catnip is somewhere in between with a more bluish green color. Leaves on all of these are mighty wrinkled with scalloped edges. They are narrow, elongated heart shapes.

Catnip flowers with an elongated purple trumpet shaped flower that is on a small spiked floret. Spearmint is similar but the smaller spike is much more dense with much smaller individual flowers. The peppermint flower is almost identical to the spearmint flower.

If you are unsure whether a plant is mint, give it a smell. If it smells minty, give it a taste.

Where to gather it

The plant is invasive, but they like well drained soil that is well watered. They are common in abandoned areas.

How to gather it

Harvest the leaves any time of year that they are out. Since the plant is so invasive, you don't need to worry about giving it time to establish.

How to cook with it

Edible: Mint is a pretty diverse plant when it comes to cooking, being used in sweet and savory dishes. Most people use the fresh or dried leaves but the flowers are edible too. Mint is often used to settle stomachs and clear sinuses as well.

A list of ways to use mint:

- Mint tea
- Mint jelly (used on meats)
- Mint ice cream
- Mint candy
- Organic toothpaste
- Mint drinks
- Mint pea soup
- Aromatherapy
- Mint, caper, and lemon sauce
- Mint in salad
- Mint with chocolate
- And more

80
MUGWORT

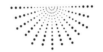

Mugwort is a common name for a few plants in the genus *Artemisia*. Most people are referring to *A. vulgaris* when they refer to mugwort though, which is also called wild wormwood, St. John's plant, and more. This, of course, can be confusing since this plant can be confused with *A. absinthium*, which is commonly called wormwood. Wormwood has a silvery color and is more ornamental. Its name might also be confused with St. John's wort, which is again different.

IDENTIFICATION OF THE PLANT

This plant grows up to two and a half feet tall. The stem is red, hardy, and branching. The leaves are up to eight inches long. They are deeply lobed looking, like individual narrow leaves with lobes on a compound stem.

The flowers are narrow spike florets that are only a few inches in length made up of small white to pinkish purple flowers. Their petals look stringy.

Where to gather it

The plant can be invasive and is found in other weedy areas. It flowers in July.

How to gather it

Harvest shoots by cutting the young, tender plant before the plant flowers.

How to cook with it

Edible: The leaves are eaten raw or cooked, sometimes used as tea. It is more commonly used as a bitter spice. It was traditionally used for flavoring in beer.

81
MULBERRY

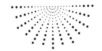

The mulberry refers most commonly to three mulberries: the white mulberry, scientifically known as *Morus alba* and used for the cultivation of silkworms, which are used to create silk, the red mulberry, known as *Morus ruba*, and the black as *Morus nigra*. They are not sold in stores because of the green stem they are attached to.

IDENTIFICATION OF THE PLANT

The mulberry can take form as a small tree or shrub, but can grow up to 60 feet on occasion. On the white and red mulberry, the young twigs are green and smooth, the other plant is brown and woody. The leaves on the young shoots are up to 12 inches long and deeply lobes into about three. The lobes are not always symmetrical. On older growth and the black mulberries, the leaves are only about five inches long and simple. Both have small serrated edges.

The flower is not noticeable, being small, sparse string-like petals on a green base. The berry of the mulberry looks similar to a blackberry, but the tiny sacs are less uniform and plump. They can be around the same shape or much more elongated to an inch and a half. The berries start off as white or green (wild blueberries typically have a variation of the three), then to red (red mulberries might be red or dark), and then parts of it get dark purple to black (black mulberries always black).

The black mulberry has hair on the bottom of its leaves.

Where to gather it

The white mulberry is invasive and found in thickets and other overgrown areas. The red and black mulberry prefers very moist places like flood lands and the like. All berries are ripe in the early summer.

How to gather it

With a ladder, you can pick the berries or lay a tarp and shake the bush to release the berries.

How to cook with it

Edible: Yes, the berries are eaten.

Do not eat unripe fruit or shoots. It can cause hallucinations. The red and black berries are preferred because they are sweeter. They are used similarly to other berries, see brambles. Spring leaves can be boiled.

Author: Although mulberries are similar to other berries, they don't grow on brambles and have slightly different nutritional information. Mulberries stain, so avoid white clothing and table clothes.

MUSTARD

Wild mustard is also known as field mustard or scientifically as *Sinapis arvensis*. Field mustard is scientifically known as *Brassica rapa*. Despite the scientific name, they are related. Other species of mustard such as *B. nigra* are also edible. This is also the same family that regular store mustard is made from as well. Be careful when handling this plant as it can cause rash and irritation. It is best to use gloves when handling this plant raw.

Identification of the plant

Wild mustard and other mustard varieties grow up to two feet high and are erect. Its stem is green with white hairs. As it gets older and taller it branches more, looking strange. The young leaves are long, oval, slightly tapered to the end, and slightly wrinkled in texture. The edges are slightly jagged or scalloped. Up the plant the leaves get smaller, up to one inch, and smooth.

The mustard plant has a yellow flower with four petals that looks like a buttercup but is part of a small round cluster of other flowers. The fruit is hard to notice, being an inch or so long and slightly wider than the stem, kind of like a hairy bean, with small black seeds inside.

Where to gather it

Wild mustard is invasive in many places. It grows everywhere in the world. It flowers from early summer to fall.

How to gather it

The leaves can be harvested by cutting them with gloves on. The seed pods can be gathered in the summer through to the fall when they appear.

How to cook with it

Edible: Yes, seeds, roots, and leaves are edible.

The seeds of wild mustard can be dried or fresh and used as a spice. The leaves can be cooked into leafy greens, like spinach but bolder in flavor.

Mustard

Time: 24 hours
Serving Size: 4 servings
Prep Time: 24 hours
Cook Time: 0 minutes
Ingredients:

- ½ cup mustard seed
- ½ cup water
- ¼ cup white vinegar
- pinch of salt

Instructions:

1. Remove seeds from seed pod.
2. In a mortar and pestle, gently crush.
3. In a jar, put the crush seed.
4. The next step is a chemical reaction when the water is added. The vinegar stops this reaction. The chemical reaction is instant, so add the vinegar right away for stronger flavor or wait for a more mild flavor.
5. Add salt and whatever other spices you like.
6. Let sit to thicken overnight.

Author: Did you know that mustard helps digest meat? This is the most amazing mustard recipe I've ever found! Try it once and you'll stick to it. It's very easy to preserve for longer periods of time in the fridge.

NASTURTIUM

Nasturtium is a genus of flower scientifically named *Tropaeolum*.

IDENTIFICATION OF THE PLANT

Nasturtium is a vining herbaceous plant that likes to climb. Its leaves are circular on long stems, slightly scalloped, and a pale blue-green color. The leaves resemble lily pads. The flowers have five petals that form a shallow trumpet shaped and delicate petals that range from yellow to red, sometimes multiple.

Where to gather it

While nasturtium does not grow wild in the northern part of the US, it is a common flower found in flower gardens and is a surprisingly great addition to your plate. It can be planted in poor quality soil and partial shade.

How to gather it

Once the plant has established itself in early summer, the leaves and flowers can be picked. Picking the flowers regularly encourages more growth.

How to cook with it

Edible: The leaves and flower have a strong peppery flavor that is unexpected with a flower. They are used fresh when used to cook with. Think of them like a garnish you can add at the last minute so as to not overcook it. Seeds can be pickled and used instead of capers.

See Yarrow for recipe.

84
NETTLES

*N*ettle is a genus of flower called *Urtica*. Stinging nettle or *U. dioica* is a plant that can cause **severe skin reaction**, but when handled carefully and cooked right is actually edible. Its relatives are wood, edward, and slender nettle, or otherwise known as *Laportea canadensis, U. gracilis,* and *U. urens*, that look like the stinging nettle, but they are also edible.

Also see henbit and deadnettles for more on nettles.

IDENTIFICATION OF THE PLANT

Stinging nettle can get up to four feet tall and erect. Its stem is lined with hairs, those are the nettles. Leaves are covered in the hair as well. They are opposite in pattern. The shape of the leaves are narrow and triangular with jagged edges. They also have a wrinkled texture.

The flowers are semi drooping spikes about four inches long. There are many of them. The individual flowers are whitish green and tiny. The shape is not distinguishable.

Where to gather it

The plant can be found in many areas because it is invasive. However, it prefers places with fertile soil. Harvest it in the spring.

How to gather it

Harvest young leaves by wearing gloves and other protective gear. Be careful not to let it touch your skin. Cut the leaves and follow the steps below to make it edible.

How to cook with it
Edible: Yes, the cooked leaves are edible.

STINGING NETTLE PREP

Time: 10 minutes
Prep Time: 2 minutes
Cook Time: 8 minutes
Ingredients:

- 4 cups stinging nettle
- 1 tbsp vinegar
- 1 tbsp butter
- pinch of salt

Instructions:

1. With gloves on, wash the nettle.
2. In a pot, add water and nettles and bring to a boil.
3. The boiling destroys the stinging chemical.
4. Remove leaves.
5. Add butter, salt, and vinegar for taste or use the cooked nettle in a different recipe.
6. Water can also be used as a drink or soup.

Author: Some may wonder why go to the trouble of risking a rash with this plant, and the answer is that it is high in nutrients. It also is used in herbal medicine to treat many things, mainly urinary tract infections.

85
OAK

The oak is a genus of trees scientifically called *Quercus*. The most edible oak in the Northeast include white oak (*Q. alba*), chestnut oak (*Q. prinus*), and Northern red oak (*Q. rubra*).

IDENTIFICATION OF THE PLANT

The white oak gets up to 100 feet tall. Its bark is furrowed and a light gray. The leaves are alternate, about nine inches long, and lobed up to 10 times. The chestnut oak is about 70 feet tall with darker red brown. The leaves are very similar with a more prominent middle point. The red oak is about 65 feet tall, leaves similar.

The fruit is the **acorn**, which is pretty similar for each tree and fairly recognizable to most. It is a cherry sized nut with a textured top that has a stem like a barret.

Where to gather it

The oak is a fairly common tree. The white oak is found in sandy forests, chestnut oak is found in moist forests, and the northern red oak is found in hilly areas. Gather acorns in autumn.

How to gather it

Harvest the nuts off the ground when they fall from the tree. They should be brown and intact. Make sure there are no blemishes or holes.

How to cook with it

Edible: Some acorns can be eaten raw. The nut of the Northern red oak must be cooked, since it can be poisonous. They can be used as a nut or ground into flour.

Northern Red Oak Acorns

The nut can be ground into flour and used best in baking heavy foods like muffins or dense bread, they can be candied or eaten as is. When roasted, it can be ground and used to make a coffee blend.

Time: 17 minutes
Prep Time: 2 minutes
Cook Time: 15 minutes
Instructions:

1. In a pot, bring water and acorns to a boil.
2. The acorns can be whole or chopped, but remove the caps.
3. Boil until the water is brown, then dump the water and refill.
4. Bring new water to a boil, repeat until water remains clear.
5. Once done, dry acorns in the oven or in the sun until completely dried.

OSTRICH FERN/ FIDDLEHEADS

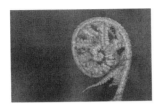

The ostrich fern, also known as *Matteuccia struthiopteris*, is the only species in the genus. Other ferns are used as fiddleheads as well, but not all of them. Ostrich fern as well as bracken (*Pteridium*) are found in the Northeast and are edible.

IDENTIFICATION OF THE PLANT

Fiddleheads are the young stalks of ferns. They are recognizable by the short green stem that curls up into a spiral at the stop which will eventually unravel into a fern. An identifying characteristic is a brown paper that protects the young fern that eventually falls away.

If you are identifying a grown fern for reference for next year, they have opposite pairs with no spacing. The leaves are scalloped and 2-3 inches each, narrow, and end at a point. The leaves come out of stems that come from a centralized spot in the ground, this is unlike some ferns that have a stem and branch. They can create a feathery bushy look. They get their name because they resemble ostrick tails.

Where to gather it

The plant can be found in damp soil areas, especially around water. They prefer fertile soil. They are harvested in the spring.

How to gather it

Harvest the plants that are up to eight inches by cutting them at the base.

How to cook with it

Edible: Yes, the young curled plant can be eaten raw, but people usually prefer them cooked.

Sauteed Fiddleheads

Time: 22 minutes
Serving Size: 4 servings
Prep Time: 2 minutes
Cook Time: 20 minutes
Ingredients:

- 3 cups fiddleheads
- 3 tbsps butter or olive oil
- 1 pinch of salt, garlic, and pepper for taste

Instructions:

1. Bring water and salt to a boil and add fiddleheads.
2. Cook for about 10 minutes or until tender.
3. In a pan, heat butter and spices to a sizzling heat, then add drained fiddleheads.
4. Cook until there is a bit of browning.

Author: Fiddleheads are considered a delicacy, and they are often fairly hard to get. The season is short, but timing it right is worth trying. Once I picked a plant that looked almost the same as an ostrich fern, and the first bite I took was seriously the most disgusting thing ever.

87
DAISIES

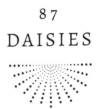

Daisy is a common name for a type of flower. As a family of flowers, one branch above a genus, it is a very large group. Under the family, there are multiple genus, and under the genus, multiple species. Some of the popular plants in this group are feverfew (*Tanacetum parthenium*), chamomile (*Matricaria recutita*), and the oxeye daisy. The flowers listed are just some of the flowers in this family that look like the common daisy that we know. There are many more varieties in this family that look completely different. Because this is a big family, it's important to identify closely.

In this chapter, we are going to focus on the three plants listed above.

IDENTIFICATION OF THE PLANT

All three of these flowers are well known for their golden yellow center and fan of white petals all the way around the edge. The oxeye daisy bloom is quite a bit larger than the other two. The petals on feverfew tend to be short and rounder than chamomiles as well.

The body of the oxeye daisy is spindly with only a few long stems. The other two are more like small shrubs, but feverfew tends to be a little harder and erect, while chamomile is more herbaceous and can end up almost creeping across the ground.

The leaves of chamomile are thin, like feathers or dill. Feverfew is about an inch long and deeply lobed. Oxeye daisies have small narrow leaves on the stem, but at the base have long three or four inch leaves that are rounded at the end, slightly reverse scalloped on the edges.

Where to gather it

All of the flowers are planted as flowers in the garden but are also seen as a weed in some places. They can grow in overgrown or weedy areas. They like well-drained soil. The oxeye daisy flowers from late spring to fall. Feverfew flowers a little later, in early summer, but goes a little longer into fall. Chamomile blooms in spring and summer but only if it has full sun.

Feverfew smells citrusy.

How to gather it

The blooms can be cut off throughout the season, this might even encourage more growth.

How to cook with it

Edible: The oxeye daisy unopened blooms are edible and usually picked. The head is edible but not preferred. The leaves can be eaten raw or cooked. Root can be eaten raw.

The feverfew flower and leaves are used fresh in cooking as a citrusy/bitter spice or dried as tea.

The chamomile is used as a tea. Leaves can be eaten but taste bitter.

Daisy Salad

Time: 10 minutes
Serving Size: 3 servings
Prep Time: 10 minutes
Cook Time: 0 minutes
Ingredients:

- 1 oxeye daisy root
- ¼ cup chamomile heads
- 2 cups oxeye daisy flower
- 2 tbsps chamomile infused oil
- 4 tbsps apple cider vinegar
- ½ tbsp honey
- 4 tbsps raspberries

Instructions:

1. Clean all of the plants well.
2. Chop root and leaves to bite size.
3. In a bowl, add oil, vinegar, honey, and 2 tbsps raspberries.
4. Mix together, crushing the berries as you go.
5. In a salad bowl, add the root, flowers, and leaves, then toss.
6. Drizzle dressing on top.
7. Serve as a side salad.

Author: The daisy family is similar to the rose, in that they are known for their beauty and useful in other ways too. Chamomile and feverfew are used for health purposes like calming, sleeping, headaches, infection, and so on. It is a great idea to get familiar with this plant and find ways to implement it in your life.

88
PARSNIP

The wild parsnip is a species scientifically called *Pastinaca sativa*. **Warning:** Wild parsnip can cause severe skin irritation, severe blistering, and burns. Use with caution.

IDENTIFICATION OF THE PLANT

The wild parsnip grows about two feet tall. The stem is herbaceous but thick. The branches come out in opposite rows. Many branches end in florets. The lower leaves have three lobes. They are compound, up to a foot long. The leaves on the floret are opposite rows of pairs. The leaves near the base are longer and have more points than the leaves at the top of the leaflet.

The flower is a round and flat topped floret. It consists of a few branches that end in a hollow circle of tiny yellow flowers. The circle doesn't touch, making it look delicate looking. The flowers are about eight inches across at the largest. Seeds replace flowers.

The root is long and carrot-like but white.

Where to gather it

The plant is a common weed that can be found in abandoned spaces. As such, it is very common in fields and can be harvested all year round, although it's best in the fall or winter.

How to gather it

Harvest the plant wearing complete protective gear. Pull out roots from the ground. Put the plant foliage inside a garbage bag and leave it in the sun for a week to dry it out. Be sure to dispose of it properly.

How to cook with it

Edible: The roots are considered very tasty even though the foliage can be so damaging. The recipe below is how to prepare and cook this member of the carrot family.

CARROT AND PARSNIP PUREE

Time: 30 minutes
Serving Size: 4 servings
Prep Time: 5 minutes
Cook Time: 25 minutes
Ingredients:

- 2 cups parsnip
- 2 cups carrot
- 2 tbsps of butter or olive oil
- a pinch of salt, pepper, dill, nutmeg, or cinnamon.

Instructions:

1. Bring water and salt to boil.
2. Wash, peel, and chop the roots.
3. Add to the pot and cook until they are soft (less than 20 minutes).
4. In a blender, add the strained roots and everything else.
5. Blend until smooth.
6. Serve like mashed potatoes.

Author: Roasting is super simple and brings out all the deeper flavors of the veggies you're roasting. But as delicious as roasted carrots or broccoli can be, roasted parsnips really take the cake! Honestly. These yummy root veggies are naturally sweet and earthy, and they really show off their flavors after roasting.

89
PAWPAW

The pawpaw plant is scientifically called the *Asimina triloba*.

IDENTIFICATION OF THE PLANT

The pawpaw plant is a shrub or small tree that grows up to 40 feet. The bark is smooth and dark. The leaves are up to 12 inches long. They alternate on reddish stems. They have parallel veining. The leaves are narrow at the base, begin to widen up the plant, and then end in a point.

The flower is dark red/burgundy. The shape is a trumpet/rosette. There are three smaller pointed petals in the center and, in their alternating spaces behind them, are larger, more rounded petals. The petals also have deep vertical veining causing seams. The center is large, yellow with a slightly raised point. They can slightly droop from the branches. The fruits are peanut-shaped and green. They grow to about four inches tall.

Where to gather it

The plant is found in patches of well-draining fertile soil. A good place to look is in valleys. The fruit is ready to pick in the fall.

How to gather it

Harvest the fruit when they are soft. Give them a twist off the plant.

You may need a ladder to reach. When the fruit is ready to pick, they turn a black color. You can also pick when green and then store.

How to cook with it

Edible: Yes, the fruit can be eaten raw or used in cooking in both sweet and savory dishes. Can be used like squash or bananas. Avoid seeds and skin.

Pawpaw bread

Time: 1 hour, 5 minutes
Serving Size: 8 servings
Prep Time: 5 minutes
Cook Time: 1 hour
Ingredients:

- 1 ½ cups pawpaw
- 1 cup sugar
- ⅓ cup butter
- 2 eggs
- 1 ½ cups flour
- 1 tsp baking soda
- pinch of salt
- ⅓ cup water

Instructions:

1. Preheat the oven to 350 °F.
2. In a bowl, combine sugar and butter. When smooth, beat in eggs.
3. Add the rest of the ingredients and mix.
4. Pour into a bread pan.
5. Bake for 1 hour.
6. Check to see if cooked with a toothpick, add more time if needed.
7. Let cool and slice.

90
PEACH

The peach is a common fruit that is scientifically named *Prunus persica*. This means that the peach is actually just one species, but it doesn't mean that there are no further variations of the plant, just that they are all related under the species. For example, nectarines are actually a variant of the peach. These variations are all thought to be probably edible, but usually not as pleasant. If you find the peaches from your tree are having these issues, it might be a variant like the ornamental peach tree that is, as the name implies, used for ornamental purposes. If your peach tastes good and juicy, then you are good to go.

IDENTIFICATION OF THE PLANT

The peach tree is about 20 feet tall, but the branches stretch out wide. The bark is dark and smooth, sometimes slightly peeling. The branches often start lower on the trunk and end up thick like two trunks. The leaves reach up to six inches long. They are narrow at the base, wide, and have a prominent, elongated point. They taper in a bit between the base and widest width, giving it a slightly peanut shape.

The flower of the peach tree grows in small clusters of 1-4 out of the branch. They put on a great show in the spring. The flowers are pink. They are about 1-2 inches big. Some of them have a cup shape with a single row of petals, while some are more rosette-like with multiple rows, but still open slightly in the middle. The fruit is five inches wide. The skin of a peach is thin and soft. The color of the peach is a yellowy orange, sometimes with darker purple tone or yellow tone patches. The skin often has a velvety feel but also can be smoother. The flesh is orangey-yellow, fleshy, juicy, and sometimes a bit stringy. The wrinkly pit is in the middle.

Where to gather it

The tree is often planted, although it might be found spreading in areas with warmer climates. They like sandy soil and full sun. The fruit is ready from early summer to late summer.

How to gather it

Harvest the peaches by twisting them off of the tree. Test to see if the peaches are ripe by feeling their softness or giving them a taste test. If picked too soon, they might not get sweet. If picked too late, they will go bad very quickly. If you are picking blooms, don't take too many as these will become the fruit. Leaves can be picked when the plant is fruiting.

How to cook with it

Edible: The fruits can be eaten raw or cooked into many dishes. They can be preserved in syrup. The blooms can also be eaten, usually only used for decoration because they are mild. The leaves can be eaten but must be boiled. They are used in sweet dishes or tea.

Peach Cobbler

Time: 1 hour
Prep Time: 15 minutes
Cook Time: 45 minutes
Ingredients:

- 4 cups (about 7) peach
- ½ cup butter
- 1 1/4 cup all-purpose flour
- ½ cups sugar (brown recommended)
- 1 tbsp baking powder
- pinch of salt
- 1/4 cup buttermilk
- 1-2 tbsps lemon juice
- 1 tsp Vanilla extract
- ground cinnamon or nutmeg

- ice cream

Instructions:

1. Clean and chop peaches into ½ inch pieces.
2. Combine flour, half the sugar, baking powder, and salt.
3. Mix in milk and pour the batter in a buttered pan.
4. In a clean bowl, add sugar, peaches, lemon, spices, and extract.
5. In a pot, bring to a boil.
6. Pour over batter. Don't stir.
7. Bake at 350 °F for about 4o minutes.
8. Serve hot or cold with ice cream.

91
PEAR VS PRICKLY PEAR

Pear is a common name for fruit that grows from trees, the prickly pear is a cactus. It might be shocking to consider the possibility that there are cacti in the northeast, but the Eastern prickly pear grows native to New England. The eastern prickly pear is scientifically called *Opuntia humifusa* and the pear tree is part of the genus *Pyrus*.

Appearance is not really an issue when it comes to the difference between the prickly pear and the pear, but the name can be confusing.

There are pear trees that are considered poisonous and invasive; take, for example, the species *P. calleryana*.

IDENTIFICATION OF THE PLANT

Pears are small trees that grow up to 60 feet but often can be shorter. The leaves are 1-2 inches long, basic oval point shaped, smooth, darker green, and thick in texture.

The flowers are up to two inches wide and star shaped. The petals are round and spaced. The stamens are prominent and tipped with darker ends. The fruit is pear shaped (obviously) but can be more round, with short stems. They are usually yellow to pale green in color.

The **prickly pear** is a cactus that is short, about 1-2 feet tall. It is composed of sections that are oval-shaped disks that stack vertically onto each other. They are green with widely distributed thorns.

They bloom in spring. The flowers are yellow and cup shaped that are 4-5 inches wide. The fruit grows in 4-5 inch egg shaped red fruit that grows out of the top of the disks. The fruit is yellow to red.

Where to gather it

Harvesting the pears is done in late summer to fall. Prickly pears are ready late summer, but they can be harvested all year.

How to gather it

Harvest pears by twisting them off the tree when the pear is ripe. You can tell they are ripe and sweet when they are turning slightly yellow. You can pick them before ripening for longer storage, but they won't be as sweet.

Prickly pears are cacti and so you need to be careful and use gloves. Only take ⅓ of a prickly pear. The new growth grows in oval shapes on the main plant. Harvest mid-morning by twisting them off the main plant.

How to cook with it

Edible: Pears can be eaten raw and cooked in sweet and savory dishes. It can be dried and preserved as well.

Eastern prickly pear can be peeled and eaten fresh. They can be made into sweet syrups and jams, sometimes used for flavoring meats as well. Peel with gloves on or sear the skin off.

Prickly Pear Lemonade

Time: 30 minutes
Prep Time: 5 minutes
Cook Time: 25 minutes
Ingredients:

- 1/2 cup prickly pear
- 1 cup sugar
- 1 cup water for syrup
- 1 cup cold water

Instructions:

1. Skin, clean, and chop the prickly pears.
2. Bring water and sugar to a boil.
3. In a blender, add prickly pear and puree.

4. Boil the simple syrup until it's reduced by half.
5. Take off heat and let cool.
6. Add to puree and mix.
7. In a glass, add cold water and mix in prickly pear syrup. Start with 1 tsp and add to desired strength.
8. Optional: add lemon.

Pear Meat Sauce
Time: 25-35 minutes
Prep Time: 5 minutes
Cook Time: 20-30 minutes
Ingredients:

- 2 tbsps butter
- 1/3 cup onion
- 2 tbsps ginger
- ½ pear
- 1 1/2 cups broth
- 3 tbsps vinegar
- 2 tbsps honey
- pinch of rosemary and ground black pepper

Instructions:

1. In a pan, add butter and onion and soften.
2. Add the pears until softened.
3. Add broth, vinegar, rosemary, and honey/sugar.
4. Reduce until thickened. If it takes too long, add a pinch of cornstarch.

PEPPERGRASS

*P*eppergrass, also known as virginia pepperweed, is scientifically known as *Lepidium virginicum*. It is invasive.

IDENTIFICATION OF THE PLANT

When it is young, it is a tuft of leaves growing out of a centralized point in the ground and folding outwards from it. It grows about a foot tall and looks bushy sometimes with multiple stems that are more densely packed. The leaves are about an inch long but are very narrow. The edges are serrated but get smooth when higher on the stem. In general, it is a weedy looking plant.

The feathers are a small florret on the top of the stem. They are spike shaped, but rounded out on top. It's more dense at the top and spaces out after an inch or so. The flowers are small and white with four petals in a star shaped pattern. It turns into a flat green seed.

Where to gather it

The plant can be found in weedy areas like places that have been abandoned. It prefers dry sunny areas.

How to gather it

Harvest leaves when they are young in the spring or early summer. The seeds can be removed from the stalk when they are green.

How to cook with it

Edible: The leaves can be eaten raw or cooked like spinach. The seeds can be dried or fresh and used for their peppery taste.

93
PINEAPPLE WEED

*P*ineapple weed might also be called wild chamomile or *Matricaria discoidea*. The plant is used medicinally to aid in digestion and infection, among other things.

The plant looks similar to chamomile and even smells similar. While they are different plants, they are part of the same genus and used similarly. The petals are almost completely unnoticeable; it might be not recognized as part of the daisy family.

IDENTIFICATION OF THE PLANT

This plant can grow about half a foot tall. The plant grows in bushy sections. The stems are yellow-green, smooth, and herbaceous. The leaves grow in opposite pairs. They grow up to four inches at the base and get smaller up the plant. The leaves are dark green and deeply lobed into thin points.

The flowers are at the end of a branch with a cupping bracket. The petals are white but are so short that they are sometimes completely unnoticeable. The head of the plant is where it gets its name. It is a pointed dome shape that is yellow with tiny sections that make it look like a pineapple skin. It can get about half an inch tall.

Where to gather it

The plant can be found in woodland areas especially near banks, but they also like well drained soil. Gather shoots in the spring. Berries are ripe very late in the season, even into the later parts of fall.

How to gather it

Harvest shoots by cutting the young, tender plant before it matures.

How to cook with it

Edible: The greens can be eaten as leafy greens, cooked, or raw. The flower and the rest of the plant is used to make tea. The tea can be used similarly to chamomile tea for calming and to aid with sleep. Since this plant can aid with sleeping, it is best used at night, not as a morning pick me up.

Drying Flowers

Instructions:

1. After you have picked the plants, clean them thoroughly.
2. Dry then completely with a towel.
3. It is best to avoid drying in the oven at the risk of cooking them and reducing their properties:
4. Option one is hanging and drying them in a bundle.
5. Option two is cutting the heads off and putting them in a mesh or fabric bag and hanging that in a place to dry.
6. Option three is laying them out evenly on a tray in the sun in the summer until dry.

94
PLANTAIN

*P*lantain, also known as broadleaf plantain or scientifically as *Plantago major*, should not be confused with the large banana-like fruit. Plantain is a common weed that grows in most gardens.

IDENTIFICATION OF THE PLANT

The plant is typically very small, only reaching a few inches tall; it blends into most grass lawns. The plant consists of a cluster of leaves that form a circle around a centralized spot on the ground. The leaves are round, sometimes more heart-shaped, sometimes leaning more narrow and pointed. The leaves can get fairly long, being about 12 inches. The leaf is textured with a wrinkle, sometimes more or less prominent. The flower is a stalk that stands erect a few inches. The floret is narrow, only slightly thicker than the stem. The individual flowers are indistinguishable. They are green and go a rusty brown.

Because it is part of many lawns, the constant mowing might keep the plant small. When young, its leaves are more yellow green, watery, and less textured. More noticeable on the young leaves are multiple faint parallel margins.

Where to gather it

The plant can be found almost everywhere, more specifically in places with grass. It likes well watered areas. They do really well in spring but can also be found through summer.

How to gather it

Harvest shoots by cutting the young, tender plant before it matures.

How to cook with it

Edible: The young leaves and seeds can be eaten raw. The older leaves should be cooked like spinach.

Author: The leaves and seeds can be dried and used for medicinal uses. The plantain is great to use on stings and other skin irritants.

95
POKEWEED

Pokeweed is also called inkberry among other common names. It is scientifically known as *Phytolacca americana*. It can look like a number of plants from the *Fallopia* genus. However, they can be differentiated by the fact that pokeberries have berries, but since they are poisonous and the plant is harvested in the summer, this can be an issue. Pokeweeds leaves tend to be more narrow and its stems are paler. Looking at the previous year's growth, the pokeweed tends to fall, whiten, and decay where the buckweeds tend to stay standing. When they are being harvested, this can be important when distinguishing them from one another.

The pokeweed has been used in medicinal medicine, but it has not been proven to work.

Identification of the Plant

The pokeweed can grow up to eight feet tall. It is a herbaceous plant with elongated oval-point leaves that alternate. The stem is a dark pinky red or green. It can look tree-like because of the thick stem and the way it branches at the top.

The flower grows on spike clusters about five inches long. The stem is white, and the flowers are on steam that stick out straight from the main stem. They are small and star shaped with a round, raised, green center.

The berries grow on long, straight, drooping clusters about a foot long. They are narrow with pink stems and brackets. The fruits are green that ripen to a red, then black. The cluster branches the berries straight out on the stems. As such, they don't droop like grapes. The berry dimples in the middle of the bottom and seems to run from it to the bracket top. They are about the size of blueberries and slightly more flat.

The young plant looks very different at the end of the season. When young, it looks more herbaceous and green. When mature, it is hardier and pink.

Where to gather it

The plant can be found in open weedy areas. Common in abandoned areas or edges of forests.

How to gather it

Harvest shoots by cutting the young, tender plant before it matures. It is not recommended to touch it with bare hands.

How to cook with it

Edible: Yes, the young leaves and stems are edible, but the mature plant, roots, leaves, stem, and berries are poisonous. They are a traditional food for the south.

Poke Sallet

Time: 1 hour, 10 minutes
Serving Size: 4 servings
Prep Time: 5 minutes
Cook Time: 1 hour, 5 minutes
Ingredients:

- 4 cups pokeweed leaves
- 1 onion
- 2 tsps garlic
- 1 cup cooked rice

Instructions:

1. Wear gloves, then clean and chop pokeweed.
2. In a pot, bring to a boil, boil for 5 minutes, then drain the water.
3. Fill the pot up and boil for 30 minutes.
4. If it's not clear, repeat one more time.
5. Strain.

6. In a pan, add oil, onion, garlic, and other spices like ginger, pepper, and salt.
7. Add rice and fry it so it starts to brown.
8. Add pokeweed.
9. Serve with soy sauce.

PURPLE DEAD NETTLE

*P*urple dead nettle is called red dead nettle, also known as *Lamium purpureum*. It has a look-alike, the henbit, which is also used for eating. As discussed in that chapter, the name dead nettle can be alarming. Nettles are actually the dangerous part, but the 'dead' descriptor means that the nettle is dead, not deadly. As such, it will not sting you.

Dead nettles are safe to handle, but they can look similar to the nettles. It is important to identify with complete confidence that the plant you are working with is the deadnettle before you touch it. The worst thing to not know is that they often grow together. The stinging nettle leaves tend to be a rounder and a bluer green. The large serrations on the edge are longer.

Identification of the plant

The purple dead nettle grows up to half a foot tall. The leaves and stem have fine hairs (the dead nettles). The leaves turn green at the bottom and get to a purple on the top. The green leaves are wrinkled with a red tinge on the edges. They are teardrop shaped with short serrations on the edges.

Flowers are a magenta pink. They grow right out of the stem. They are long, tubular, and open at the end to a non-symmetrical formation.

Two petals open out away from the plant, one petal on the other side is pointed up and over, like a hood. They tend to be less than the ones on the henbit, and are also smaller and more narrow.

Where to gather it

The plant can be found in many areas because it is invasive. However, it prefers places with fertile soil. Harvest it in the spring.

How to gather it

Harvest shoots by cutting the young, tender plant before it matures. Be aware of how early the plant's flowers need to be harvested very early in the year.

How to cook with it

Edible: Yes, the young plant is edible.

The leaves can be eaten raw or cooked, similar to stinging nettle.

Author: The first time I went out with my kids to forage for some purple dead nettle they thought I'd trick them into getting stung because they know what happens when they touch stinging nettles which look really similar to these.

This plant is used topically for healing wounds.

QUICKWEED

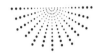

Quickweed is a herbaceous plant that is also called potato weed or *Galinsoga parviflora*. This plant is called many different names across the world.

The plant is applied to the skin to stop the stinging nettle rash.

IDENTIFICATION OF THE PLANT

It grows up to half a foot tall. It is weedy looking and almost looks like it is crawling. Its stem is semi erect. The leaves are opposite pairs, 1-2 inches long, basic pointed oval shape on bigger leaves and more narrow on smaller ones. The stem and underside of the leaves are covered in long white hairs.

It branches slightly, and they are topped with a few flowers. The flowers are similar to a daisy, but are much smaller, about ½ inch wide. The petals are small, short, and round. There are only five petals and they don't touch. The center is yellow, slightly domed, and has a honeycomb pattern.

Where to gather it

The plant grows in weedy areas like overgrown places or meadows. The plant blooms all summer.

How to gather it

Harvesting plants by cutting the young leaves, flowers, and stems.
How to cook with it
Edible: The leaves can be used fresh or dried as a spice. It can also be used as a leafy green, including the stem and flower.

A*jiaco*

Time: 43 minutes
Serving Size: 4 servings
Prep Time: 8 minutes
Cook Time: 35 minutes
Ingredients:

- 1 tbsp oil
- 1 chicken breast
- 1 onions
- 2 garlic cloves
- 4 cups broth
- pinch of salt and pepper
- 1 cup cilantro
- 1 green onion
- 1 tbsp Quickweed
- 1 pound mixed potatoes
- 1 ear of corn
- 1 cup cooked white rice
- ¼ cup heavy cream
- ¼ cup pickled juniper

Instructions:

1. Put oil, onion, garlic, and chicken in a pan and brown.
2. Add broth, green onion, spices, and quickweed, then bring to a boil.
3. Reduce to a simmer and cook for 20 minutes.
4. Take out chicken when cooked.
5. Add chopped potatoes and corn to broth.
6. Shred chicken.
7. When potatoes are cooked, add the chicken back in.
8. Add rice, cream, and juniper to serving bowls.

9. Pour soup on top.

Author: When I was helping out at a mountain hut, we'd serve this salad called "foraged greens." Only 1 in 100 people wouldn't like it because of the furry leaves. Everyone else was always super stoked about it.

RAMPS/WILD LEEK

*R*amps or wild leeks are known scientifically as *Allium tricoccum*. They are under consideration in Canada and some states in the US because they are a threatened species.

IDENTIFICATION OF THE PLANT

The leeks usually grow in patches. They appear above grown as a crown base (leaves that go from a centralized spot in the ground). The leaves are long, rounded blades. They are a little less than a foot long and an inch or so wide. When pulled from the ground, you will notice a red stem that ends in a white bulb. They also grow a stem that is about a foot tall with a floret at the top. The floret is a sparse global shape. The individual flowers are small, white, and cup shaped.

Noticeably smells like onion/garlic.

Where to gather it

Ramps like wet areas, like lowlands, more specifically wooded areas that flood in the spring. Available in the very early spring.

How to gather it

Gather the leaves in your hand and grasp the base at the ground firmly. Carefully pull the leek out of the ground, keeping the bulb intact.

How to cook with it

Edible: Yes, all of it can be eaten.

The leaves and the bulb are used in cooking for their oniony taste. Leeks are commonly used in potato leek soup.

Potato Leek Soup

Time: 30 minutes
Serving Size: 4 servings
Prep Time: 5 minutes
Cook Time: 25 minutes
Ingredients:

- 4 cups Ramps
- 4 cups red potatoes
- 4 cups broth
- 1 cup heavy cream
- salt and pepper to taste
- optional topping: bacon and sour cream
- flour for thickening

Instructions:

1. Clean and chop whole leeks and potatoes.
2. In a pan, cook bacon and use grease (if opting out, use butter).
3. Add leeks and potatoes, so leeks are soft.
4. Mix in a tbsp of flour.
5. Add broth, bring to a boil, and reduce to simmer.
6. Cook until potatoes are soft.
7. Add cream. Don't let it boil.
8. Remove from heat, and strain some, all, or none of the vegetable to blend into a puree, based on preference.
9. Serve hot or cold, top with bacon and sour cream.

Author: Leeks are considered a delicacy, but it is important to only take what is needed. If there aren't many leeks in the areas, leave them so that they can repopulate.

99
RED CLOVER

*R*ed clover is scientifically known as *Trifolium pratense*. There are a few common clovers that we see, the others being <u>wood sorrel</u> and <u>sweet clover</u>. There is a white and yellow sweet clover, not to be confused with white clover. While clover more closely resembles the red clover in flower, sweet white clover being a long spike not global foret.

IDENTIFICATION OF THE PLANT

The young plant is only about an inch tall, with three round leaves and a slightly white splat of white in the middle of each green leaf.

As the plant matures, it grows a flower stalk. The three pattern leaflet alternates up the stem. The floret is global, being about half an inch. The individual flowers are small and narrow, but long tubes that jut out from a center looks spikey. They are white and tinged with a purple/pink at the ends.

Where to gather it

The red clover is familiar to most people. Most people know the small three leaf clover that makes its way into almost every lawn. It likes moist, shady areas. Blooms mid spring to early summer.

How to gather it

Most lawns are trimmed, which means that the flower does not get a chance to grow, so any grassy, overgrown areas are a good place to look. Pluck flowers when in bloom or leaves anytime.

How to cook with it

Edible: The flowers and leaves can be dried or used fresh. They are diverse and can be used in salads, soups, and tea. Root can be eaten raw or cooked, although cooked is not prefered.

100
ROSE

The rose is a genus of many flowers with a large diversity, the genus is scientifically known as *Rosa*. To keep it simple, we will be talking about wild roses. These roses are quite different from the ornamental roses that we typically know. Wild roses are also diverse, they are not a separate genus but a group of roses in a subcategory. *R. acicularis* is commonly referred to as the wildrose but so is *R. canina*, or the dog rose, or even *R. palustris*, the swamp rose, and so on.

The diversity of wild roses should not overwhelm the forager though. They are all fairly similar looking and can be used in the same way, there can be more preference for one than the others. If you are using roses from a flower shop, remember that like produce, there can be things sprayed on it that you are not aware of. Many flower shops and farms use pesticides, dyes, and other preservatives. If you are going to reuse flowers that were given to you, ask where they are from and see if the florist is able to tell you if it is organic or safe to use in food.

IDENTIFICATION OF THE PLANT

The wild rose is typically grown as a shrub, some getting to almost 10 feet tall, with some even staying shorter, only reaching 2 or 3 feet. These shrubs can also be thick, lush with foliage, or be more spindly with sparse foliage. The leaves tend to be an inch or so long. They are round but come to a subtle tip. They are typically more watery and a medium bluish green. The edges are slightly serrated. The stem is smooth and green when young, but becomes more woody as it gets older, covered in short thorns.

The flower ranges from magenta pink to a white at about five inches wide. They typically have five that are in full bloom, splaying out completely into a star shape. The petals are very delicate. The center is about a half inch wide, pale to golden yellow, and has a few rings of short stigma.

Rosehips are round, sometimes more flattened into a disk, or elongated like an olive (about the same size). They are an orangy red and get transparent and wrinkly over the winter. They are filled with seeds and a little fluff. Like a blueberry, it has a crown, but on the bottom. This crown is about five long (up to an inch) and narrow.

Where to gather it

Wild roses can vary depending on their preference of landscape. Some prefer coastlines, others lowlands or even sandy, well drained places. This means that no matter where you are, you will probably have luck in finding a wild rose. The flower blooms in early summer. The rosehip starts to form in late summer, so it is best to harvest in fall, after the first frost is possible. They should be reddish orange and firm, but a skin should have formed.

How to gather it

Wild roses bloom in the early summer, and it is usually for a short period of a week or so. Since they are not dense like ornamental roses, the petals fall off and fall apart really easily. If you can, harvest *only* the petals, leaving the center and bracket. This will allow the rosehip to form as well, so that you can harvest both the flower petals and the fruit from the same flower. Of course, be careful because roses have thorns.

How to cook with it

Edible: Yes, the petals and the fruit.

The rose is a super diverse flower, and it has a lot of potential in the kitchen. Its petals can be made into rose tea, rose water, distilled rose water, a garnish, and so on. The rosehips are also super useful, typically made into a jam.

Dried Rosehips

Time: 24 hours

Prep Time: 24 hours
Cook Time: 0 minutes
Ingredients:

- 1 cup rosehips

Instructions:

1. Preheat the oven or preferably a dehydrator to as low as possible, about 110 °F.
2. Wash the rosehip and dry them well.
3. Cut off the crown and other pieces attached.
4. Lay them out evenly on a tray, try not to overcrowd them.
5. Put them in the oven and let them dry.
6. This might take a while, sometimes over 24 hours. Choose a time when this can be done safely.
7. When they are completely dried, they should look like raisins. For best use, they can now be stored for a year. You can store them whole or grind them.
8. Use for spice, teas, and more. They can be used fresh, but this way they can be stored for longer for use until next year.

Author: The rose is such an exciting flower to learn about when to foraging. It is so well known for its beauty, it is often forgotten when it comes to usefulness. It is used for beauty, fragrance, medicinal use, and food. They are full of antioxidants and vitamins. More than a pretty face.

101
SASSAFRAS

Sassafras is a genus of trees, but it is very small. In the Americas, the *S. albumin* is the scientific name that can also be called the silk, white, and red sassafras. There is some debate about the use of sassafras because it has been linked to cancer causing chemicals. The FDA has banned the use of this plant, more specifically the root and bark. Sassafras is also used as a drug that gives people a euphoric feeling. This plant should be used at your own risk, although many people claim use in moderation is probably safe.

IDENTIFICATION OF THE PLANT

The white sassafras grows up to 70 feet tall. The bark of the tree is an ashy brown with deep grooves. The trunk tends not to be as thick as some other trees. The leaves are distinct with three lobes. The middle lobe is slightly longer and rounded. The side lobes are more narrow, sometimes giving the leaf an arrow look (pointing at the base). The edges are smooth. The leaf is a little thicker and slightly glossy. Leaves are alternate.

The flowers are yellow. They branch off in small clusters at the end of branches. The petals are paler with more of a green hint to them. They fold back into a star shape but with six narrow, pointed petals. The stamen are more noticeable, being long with large stigma at the end. The fruit is a small black berry on a bright red bracket and stem.

The sapling might have the lobed leaves or they might have simple shaped leaves. Sometimes two lobes are a morph of the two.

Where to gather it

The plant can be found in woodland areas, especially near the edges of forests or in fields. It likes well-draining sandy soil. Gather shoots in the spring. Harvest root in the fall. Leaves and twigs in spring.

How to gather it

Harvest by finding full grown sassafras trees. In this area, there should be smaller trees (saplings) that you can pull for the root.

How to cook with it

Edible: Yes.

Twigs and leaves are edible raw or cooked. They can be dried and used as a spice. The roots are known for making root beer.

HOMEMADE ROOT BEER

Time: 53 minutes
Serving Size: 10 servings
Prep Time: 8 minutes
Cook Time: 45 minutes
Ingredients:

- 1 cup roots
- 4 cups water
- 2 cloves
- 1/2 tsp fennel
- 4 allspice berries
- 1 small stick cinnamon
- 1/4 cup molasses
- 1 cup sugar
- 2 quarts soda water

Instructions:

1. Clean and cut the roots into pieces.
2. In a pot, bring water, roots, and spices to a boil.
3. Turn down heat and simmer for half an hour.

4. Add molasses and simmer for 5 minutes.
5. Strain.
6. Add back in the pot and add sugar.
7. Simmer for 5 minutes.
8. Let cool.
9. Add carbonated water 1:2.

102
SHEPHERD'S PURSE

Shepherd's purse is a herbaceous flowering plant that goes by the scientific name *Capsella bursa-pastoris*. It is used in many Asian cuisines. It is also used as a medicine to treat a multitude of things like infection and health problems like circulation. This plant should not be consumed while pregnant.

IDENTIFICATION OF THE PLANT
The plant grows to about a foot tall. It grows a crown base of leaves that are only about 3-4 inches long. Some of the leaves might be more smooth on the edges, while some are more sharply lobed. The plant then grows a stem with blade-like leaves that are about one inch long. The plant may branch a little.

The top of the stem is the flower, the floret is more dense at the top and becomes less dense as it moves down the stem. The individual flower is very tiny star-shaped with four petals. The flowers turn into triangular shaped, flat seed pods.

Where to gather it
The plant can be found in places where the soil is soft but with a higher moisture content than sand. It also likes full sun.

How to gather it

Harvest the roots in the fall. Harvest the leaves while they still look fresh and green.

How to cook with it

Edible: The leaves are best when fresh. The plant is used for its peppery flavor. The root can be dried and ground to use instead of ginger.

SHEPHERD'S PURSE DUMPLINGS

Time: 25 minutes
Prep Time: 15 minutes
Cook Time: 10 minutes
Ingredients:

- 1 cup Shepards purse
- 1 cup minced meat
- 1 onion
- 2 tsps soy sauce
- 1 tsp vinegar
- dumpling wrappers

Instructions:

1. Clean and chop the shepherd's purse.
2. Add it to a bowl with the meat, chopped onion, soy sauce, vinegar, and spices.
3. Mix.
4. Take a tsp of the mix and add it to the center of the dumpling wrapper. Fold it in half and pinch the edges closed (adding water can help make it stick).
5. Once the dumplings are made, boil a pot of water.
6. Add the dumplings and cook for 10 minutes.
7. Serve them, freeze them, or add some oil in a pan, heat and fry the dumplings until golden brown
8. Serve with rice vinegar or soy sauce.

SILVERBERRY AND AUTUMN OLIVE

The silverberry and the autumn olive are similar, although the silverberry is more rare. The autumn olive also goes by the scientific name *Elaeagnus umbellata* and many more common names. It has become invasive in the US.

IDENTIFICATION OF THE PLANT

The autumn olive is a short tree or shrub that grows up to 10 feet tall. The branches are covered in longer thorns. The shrub is denser looking and has leaves that are two inches long, very thick, and semi-glossy that grow in an alternate pattern. They have smooth edges, and the bottom of them are paler than the cool toned green top.

The small flowers grow in small clusters in uniform rows off the branches. The petals are white and star-shaped with four petals and a tubular center. The petals are long, narrow, and end at a point. The berries grow in small clusters that droop. They are a little smaller than a marble and transparent red. When young, they are yellow.

Where to gather it

The plant can be found in disturbed areas and are commonly found on the side of the road. It's best not to harvest from near roads, but think of some similar areas you can reach.

How to gather it

Harvest the berries when they go completely red in the fall.
How to cook with it
Edible: Yes, the berries are edible.

Autumn Olive Jelly

Time: 30 minutes
Prep Time: 5 minutes
Cook Time: 25 minutes
Ingredients:

- 2 cups Autumn olive
- 2 cups water
- 1 cup sugar
- 2 tsps lemon

Instructions:

1. Bring water and fruit to a boil.
2. Cook for 10 minutes.
3. Strain with a large hole strainer and squeeze as much juice as possible out of flesh, seeds, and other impurities.
4. Add sugar and lemon to the juice in a clean pot.
5. Bring to a light boil, reduce heat slightly, and keep a steady light boil for about 10 minutes.
6. Add jelly to jars, seal the lids, and label.

104
SOLOMON'S SEAL

*S*olomon's Seal is a genus of plants known as *Polygonatum*. Great Solomon's seal, or *P. biflorum*, is native to eastern US. This plant has many look-alikes, see chapter 39 on false Solomon's seal.

IDENTIFICATION OF THE PLANT

Soloman's seal has a single stem that is semi-erect, slightly drooping, and stands 3-4 feet tall usually. The leaves alternate in two parallel rows. The leaves are simple with parallel veins. Their leaves are a few inches long and slightly elongated to a point.

The flowers droop in small clusters on short stems. The flowers are white, bell shaped, but elongated, not round, and slightly scalloped. The berries replace the flowers, ebing small dark round and drooping in small clusters. The root is a long rhizome.

Where to gather it

It prefers shaded areas with well draining soil. Typically flowers in May. I would recommend harvesting young shoots in March or April.

How to gather it

Harvest shoots by cutting the young, tender plant before it matures. Harvest roots whenever.

How to cook with it

Edible: The young shoots can be cooked like asparagus. Root is used as starch.

Soloman's Seal Root

Time: 45 minutes
Serving Size: 4 servings
Prep Time: 5 minutes
Cook Time: 40 minutes
Ingredients:

- 2 cups solomon's seal root
- 2 tbsps butter
- 3 pots water
- 4 wild leeks
- pinch of salt and pepper for taste

Instructions:

1. Clean and chop the roots into 1 inch pieces.
2. Bring water to a boil with the roots.
3. Strain the water out of the pot once boiled.
4. Refill with water and boil again.
5. Repeat steps 3 and 4 one more time.
6. Strain water one more time.
7. In a pan, heat butter and chopped leeks.
8. Add roots, salt, and pepper, and cook on medium high for 5 minutes.

105
SOW THISTLE

Sow thistle is a name for a group of flowers. However, in this chapter we are talking about common sow thistle or *Sonchus oleraceus*. It might also be called milk thistle or soft thistle, among other things. It is part of the same family of dandelions, but they are different.

IDENTIFICATION OF THE PLANT

The Sow thistle, with string like petals that are a dark yellow, looks very similar to the dandelion. The main difference is that the sow thistle branches and has multiple flowerheads. Before they bloom, they make a teardrop bud.

The leaves come from a center point at the base of the flower's stem. These leaves are up to five inches long, narrow with irregular reverse scalloped pattern, and a jagged edge. The sow thistles leaf end is round. The leaves are lined with tiny pickles. The whole plant can look a little more hardy than the herbaceous dandelion.

Where to gather it

The sow thistle is a weed and likes disturbed areas like the side of the road. Often found in lawns or near fences. They like moist soil.

How to gather it

Harvest stems and leaves by cutting the young, tender plant before it matures.

How to cook with it

Edible: The young leaves and stems can be eaten, but mature plants could be poisonous. They are used similar to spinach, raw or cooked. It is a good food to forage because it is high in antioxidants and other minerals.

106
STAGHORN SUMAC

The staghorn sumac is scientifically known as *Rhus typhina*. See chapter 41 for fragrant sumac. Poisonous look alike is poison sumac that is part of the poison ivy family. Poison sumac is typically short, does not grow red fruit, with short leaves that don't put on bright red show in fall like the staghorn.

IDENTIFICATION OF THE PLANT

Staghorn sumac is a shrub that grows to almost 20 feet tall. It has a light brown/gray stem that is covered in a soft orange fuzz. The leaves are compound with leaflets reaching 20 inches. Individual leaves are narrow, five inches long, and smooth edged. The leaves are not dense foliage and the bottom few feet of trunk/ stem is easily accessible. It is bright orange red in fall.

Flowers are noticeable as they are green and small. They form the shape of a spike wherever the fruit appears. Fruit is bright red, small, fuzzy balls that grow in triangles spike up to one foot long.

Where to gather it

Staghorn sumac can be a little invasive. They like infertile soil with good drainage like sand. The fruit is ready mid to late summer and stays on the shrub throughout the winter.

How to gather it

Rub the berry in between your fingers and taste the juice. It should taste tart. Best harvested when dry. Trim with cutters underneath the spike.

How to cook with it

Edible: The berries are often dried and ground to be used as spice in savory dishes. Adds a tart flavor. Also used to make tart drinks.

STAGHORN SUMAC LEMONADE

Time: 2 hours, 30 minutes
Prep Time: 2 hours
Cook Time: 30 minutes
Ingredients:

- 1 liter sparkling water
- 2 cups water
- 2 cups sugar
- 5 tbsps sumac

Instructions:

1. In a pot, bring water and sugar to a boil.
2. Turn down the heat until sugar is dissolved and water has reduced by about half.
3. Let cool until warm.
4. Add 5 tbsps fresh sumac, cover and set in a sunny window for a few hours.
5. In a glass or jug, add sparkling water, some syrup. Taste and add more if needed.
6. Don't over stir the carbonation.
7. Can be served with ice and garnished with a lemon slice.

Author: Sumac berries are so strange that it can be hard to believe that they are edible. Sumac can be one of the more exciting foraging plants for beginners because it is strange enough and fairly easy to identify.

107
THISTLE

Thistle is a common name for a group of plants that have thistles. *Cirsium edule*, edible thistle, is the plant that will be discussed in this chapter.

The burrs that this plant creates is similar to many plants that have burrs, including the burdock. Handling these plants can be dangerous because of the many look-alikes, as well as the sharp burrs.

IDENTIFICATION OF THE PLANT

When the plant is young, it is just a crown base, which is a centralized spot in the ground where the leaves fan out from. When they are at this stage, the leaves tend to be less lobed and jagged, but still reach up to six inches long.

It can grow seven feet tall with a red, hardy spine keeping it erect. It starts to branch and the leaves, including its point, can get bigger and more narrow. The stem is erect, herbaceous, and covered in thorns. The leaves are also lined in thorns.

Known for their burrs, which contain their tiny purple/pink flowers at the top with long, white stamen. The burrs are green and brown when dried. They are covered in what looks like one inch thorns but have a small hook on the end for clinging on to passersby.

Where to gather it

This is a common weed that is found in ditches and abandoned places.

How to gather it

Harvest stems and leaves by cutting the young, tender plant before it matures. Harvest the root in the fall. Make sure to wear gloves and cut off all spokes before consuming.

How to cook with it

Edible: Yes, all of it can be eaten.

THISTLE SOUP

Time: 35 minutes
Serving Size: 4 servings
Prep Time: 5 minutes
Cook Time: 30 minutes
Ingredients:

- 1 cup potato
- 4 cups broth
- 1 onion
- 2 cloves garlic
- 1 cup thistle root
- 1 pinch salt for taste

Instructions:

1. Clean and chop the onion, root, and potatoes.
2. In a pan, heat butter.
3. Add onions and garlic.
4. Add ⅓ cup broth, potatoes, and the root. Cover until soft.
5. Transfer to pot.
6. Add broth, bring to boil, and reduce to simmer.
7. Cook until potatoes and root are soft.
8. Add cream. Don't let it boil.
9. Remove from heat and strain some, all, or none of the vegetable to blend into a puree based on your preference.

VIOLET

The term 'violet' is a genus of flowers known by their latin name *viola*. There are a lot of violets that grow in the Northeast. One of the more common violets is the *V. sororia*, or the common blue violet. These flowers have been used medicinally, mostly due to their vitamin A and C content.

Identification of the plant

These common blue violets don't get more than a few inches off the ground. The leaves are heart-shaped. The base of the leaf curls out hiding the stem connecting in the middle, creating a cupping effect. They are serrated on the edges and textured like wrinkles in shape.

The flowers are star shaped with oval shaped petals. The petals are typically a purple to blue color. The veining on the petals shows up a little darker. The center of the flower has a white and dark purple pattern and a white hairy looking stamen.

Where to gather it

The plant can be found in areas where the soil retains more water, but not wetlands. They like shade.

How to gather it

Harvest shoots the blooms in the spring. The flowers are so small that to get a usable haul you need to find a patch with a decent amount of violets.

How to cook with it

Edible: It can be used in salads, as a garnish, or infused in vinegar.

Violet Syrup

Time: 20 minutes
Prep Time: 10 minutes
Cook Time: 10 minutes
Ingredients:

- 1 cup Violet blooms
- 1 cup water
- 1 cup sugar

Instructions:

1. Clean the flowers.
2. Bring water and sugar to a boil.
3. Boil the simple syrup until reduced by half.
4. Take off heat and add the violets (not when boiling).
5. Strain out the violets after 5-7 minutes.
6. You can seal this jar or store it in the fridge.
7. Mix with vinegar to make salad vinaigrette.
8. Mix with lemon and water to make juice.

109
WATERCRESS

Watercress is known by its scientific name *Nasturtium officinale*. It is related to the nasturtium, but unlike the regular garden flower, this plant is aquatic. There are two look-alikes that you should look out for when foraging for the watercress: fools watercress and lesser water parsnip. Fool's watercress smells like carrots, while watercress does not. The difference between the lesser water parsnip is more important though because it is poisonous. Lesser water parsnip does grow a flower, but the other way to tell between the two is the rings on its stem.

IDENTIFICATION OF THE PLANT

Watercress can be identified best when it's in water. The plant is simple, a thin herbaceous stem, and round, cupping, smooth, almost succulent-like leaves. The edges of the leaves are slightly scalloped. They might be in the water completely or reaching a few inches above the water.

The flower of the watercress is a small florret with a tiny star shape, four petal flowers. The center buds of the flower clusters are usually not budding.

Where to gather it
The plant can be found in shallow running water.

How to gather it

Harvest shoots by taking scissors and cutting a patch of watercress. Can be used from spring to fall. Make sure to wear your rubber boots and have someone with you when foraging near water.

How to cook with it

Edible: The leaves, stems, and flowers are used. Everything can be eaten raw or cooked. Has a peppery flavor.

WATERCRESS SALMON

Time: 25 minutes
Serving Size: 2 servings
Prep Time: 5 minutes
Cook Time: 20 minutes
Ingredients:

- 1 cup watercress
- 2 salmon filets
- 1 tbsp butter
- 1 tsp honey for taste
- 1 pinch salt, pepper, dill, and lemon

Instructions:

1. In a pan on medium high, heat up butter and spices.
2. When hot, use tongs to add salmon to the pan.
3. When one side is cooked, flip the salmon.
4. Add the watercress and brush the honey on the salmon.
5. Cover with a lid.
6. Turn down the heat, and when the watercress has cooked down it should be done.
7. Serve with a slice of lemon.

WILD BEAN

The wild bean, also called wild kidney bean or *Phaseolus polystachios*, are the only members of its genus. The wild bean can not be eaten raw like the kidney bean.

IDENTIFICATION OF THE PLANT

If the plant is crawling on the ground, it might be hard to notice because of the thin stem and understated leaves. The vine grows up to 1o feet. The leaves are opposite on the stem. The leaves are actually leaflets of three basic shaped leaves, but they can overlap and look like one lobed leaf.

The pea flower is unusual as it is not symmetrical. The upper side of the small hanging flowers are two short, cupped petals that are a lighter pink and create a hood. The bottom two petals do not touch, jutting out opposite angles. They are longer and more narrow, as well as darker pink in color. The center is a purplish tongue that sticks out slightly with a pearly looking stigma at the end.

The beans are like green bean pods, long and thin, but wild beans tend to be a little thicker and shorter. They hang off of the stem by itself or in rows. The beans get a dark green to brown color and patchy. They get harder and thicker as they dry.

Where to gather it

The plant can be found in dry areas with sand. They like the edges of forests and thickets. This is a vine that likes to climb, not as much as crawl. It is harvested in the summer.

How to gather it

Harvest shoots and the seed pods when they are green. They should be firm, but don't let them age too long to the point the seeds are bulging out of the pod. You can let the bean dry in the pod and treat it like a dried kidney bean.

How to cook with it

Edible: Yes, the bean is edible.

Unlike green beans, this bean must be cooked to make it edible.

WILD BEAN AND RICE

Serving Size: 4 servings

Ingredients:

- 1 cup dried wild beans
- 2 cups water
- 1 tbsp butter
- spices: garlic, onion, cumin, chili powder, salt, and black pepper
- 3 cups cooked rice

Instructions:

1. Fill a bowl or a pot with cold water and add the beans.
2. Let it soak overnight. The other option is to boil the beans, change the water, and cook until they are soft.
3. Drain the water and add in the rice and spices with the butter. Optional: add some tomato sauce.

WILD CARROT, QUEEN ANNE'S LACE

Wild carrot is known scientifically as *Daucus carota*. This plant can look similar to poison hemlock. Poison hemlock has no hairs on its stem and a purple hue. The flower also tends to be small clusters of flowers that create the floret, instead of one large plate. Hogweed also looks like queen anne's lace and is poisonous. Hogweed is much bigger and has a smooth stem.

IDENTIFICATION OF THE PLANT

The wild carrot grows up to three feet tall. The stem is herbaceous but thick. The branches come out in opposite rows. The lower leaves have three lobes. They are compound, up to a foot long. The leaves on the floret are opposite rows of pairs. The leaves near the base are longer and have more points than the leaves at the top of the leaflet.

The flower is a round and flat topped floret. It consists of a few branches that end in a hollow circle of tiny white flowers. The inner flowers are smaller, the pattern making it look like lace. The flowers are about eight inches across at the most.

Where to gather it

This is a common weed and is found in ditches and abandoned places.

How to gather it

Harvest roots in the late summer to early fall by tugging the plant.

The flowers can be cut off when they are in full bloom or until fruit appears.

How to cook with it

Edible: The flower, root, and fruit are all eaten for their carrot flavor. They are used in all dishes where carrots are used.

PICKLED JUNIPER BERRIES

Time: 10-15 minutes
Prep Time: 5 minutes
Cook Time: 5-10 minutes
Ingredients:

- 1 cup Queen Anne's lace root
- 1 cup pickling vinegar
- 1 tbsp salt
- 1 cup water
- 1 tbsp sugar
- spices of choice: garlic, onion, and pepper

Instructions:

1. Wash queen anne's lace, chop it and other produce.
2. In a pot, boil water, vinegar, salt and sugar until the sugar is dissolved.
3. While the brine is heating, add a mixture of spices and the chopped onion, root, and flower in sterilized jars (heat proof). Leave room at the top, but the pieces should be fully submerged.
4. Pour hot brine over the pieces in the jars.
5. Seal, label, and store in the fridge. Wait at least a week to pickle.

112
WILD GINGER

Wild ginger is also known as Canadian wild ginger and *Asarum canadense*. This plant has been used for medicinal purposes, mostly relieving common cold problems. This plant should not be used like ginger because it has been linked to cancer causing chemicals. That being said, that is strictly the root and not the rest of the plant.

IDENTIFICATION OF THE PLANT

Wild ginger grows in small little clusters of stems. It is about a few inches tall at the most. It might go unnoticed if it is a lone plant, but also, if clustered in a big group, it might look more like a vine or ground cover. The stems are herbaceous and green.

The leaves are the most identifiable part of the plant. It is heart shaped, but the leaf faces up and the middle of the heart bumps are quite deep, looking more like a dimple. The leaves are slightly wrinkled, with smooth edges and a medium cool green to its color. Leaves are covered in fine hair. Only one leaf per stem.

The flower is a dark burgundy red. It has three petals that are trumpet-like in shape, but the petals are very long, curling out like strings. The flower is slightly hairy.

Where to gather it

The plant can be found in woodland areas especially near banks, but it likes shady places without much sun. It likes lots of rich soil.

How to gather it

With a shovel, dig up the wild ginger when it is ready. Like most roots, it is best harvested in the late fall or (although less preferred) in the early spring.

How to cook with it

Edible: Yes, the root is used fresh or dried. Avoid eating too much of the root. Cook the root in water because the toxin is not water soluble. This tea is what is used for medicinal purposes.

Wild Ginger Ice Cream

Time: 10 minutes
Prep Time: 10 minutes
Cook Time: 0 minutes
Ingredients:

- 2 cups heavy whipping cream
- 2 cups half and half
- 1 cup white sugar
- 2 tsps vanilla extract
- 2 tbsps wild ginger
- optional: other warming spices like nutmeg and cinnamon

Instructions:

1. Combine all of the ingredients and stir until the sugar is completely dissolved.
2. In an ice cream maker, add the mixture.
3. Turn on the ice cream maker, making sure to occasionally stir the sides.
4. Depending on your ice cream maker, don't let it get too cold because it will end up hard and not creamy.
5. Once your ice cream is done, serve or freeze in a sealed container.
6. Optional: use one of the many fruits in this book to make a syrup to go on top.

113
WILD LETTUCE

Wild lettuce is interesting because, while its latin name is *Lactuca virosa*, it is also known by many other names, such as bitter lettuce, opium lettuce, poison lettuce, and more. This plant has a latex-like sap that is used in medicine, usually used to help people sleep. It also has been used to ease pain. Because of the medicinal qualities of this plant, it is also a good idea to not over consume it. If you are allergic to latex plants like this and other plants with a latex sap, this can be dangerous to you. Wild lettuce has some look-alikes like the thistle and the dandelion, but they are also edible.

IDENTIFICATION OF THE PLANT

This plant is called prickly and tall lettuce for a reason. It can grow four feet tall with a red, hardy spine keeping it erect. The leaves are covered in prickles, especially near the margins. When the plant is young, it is just a crown base, which is a centralized spot in the ground where the leaves fan out from. When they are at this stage, the leaves tend to be less lobed and jagged, but still grow up to six inches and rounded at the ends. As the stem grows in, the leaves end up looking almost torn. They are lobed, inverse scalloped, and jagged.

The flower is very similar to the dandelion. This flower instead has a prominent local bracket, and the leafy tube-like sepals hold the flower almost closed. When it opens more, there are less petals than a dandelion that are slightly wider, and the shape of the flower is more flat. When it goes to seed, it seeds like a dandelion too, but the global pod is less dense and the fluffy ends of the seed are more brown.

Where to gather it

The wild lettuce is a weed and likes disturbed areas like the side of the road. It's best not to harvest from near roads, but think of similar areas. It blooms all summer.

How to gather it

Harvest leaves by the young, tender plant before it matures. Even regular lettuce is better when it is young and crisp. Pick the plant as it is blooming when using it for medicinal purposes.

How to cook with it

Edible: Of course wild lettuce can be eaten like regular lettuce. It is also boiled, particularly as a tea.

Wild Lettuce Tincture

Time: 72 hours, 20 minutes
Prep Time: 72 hours, 20 minutes
Cook Time: 0 minutes
Ingredients:

- 1 cup wild lettuce stems and leaves
- 2 cups 40% alcohol

Instructions:

1. Wear gloves because the plant is prickly.
2. Clean and chop the plant.
3. Dry completely.
4. In a blender, add the plant and puree.
5. In a jar, add the puree and the alcohol.
6. Let soak for 3 days, shaking once a day. Keep in a cool, dark place.
7. After 3 days, use cheesecloth to strain out the plant material. Be careful not to get too much on your skin.
8. Add stained liquid to a dropper bottle.
9. Use for sleep and pain.

114
WOOD SORREL

Wood sorrel is a genus of flowers called *Oxalis*. One of the most common of the wood sorrels is *O. strictica*, or yellow woodsorrel, but most, if not all, wood sorrels are considered edible. They are also a part of the group of clovers that people find in their lawns. Also see the chapter on red clovers and the chapter on sweet clovers.

IDENTIFICATION OF THE PLANT

The plant is a common three leaf clover. When it is young or groomed by a lawn mower, it can stay as a one inch tall clover. This clover is a solid yellow green and lobed at the end to look like a heart. It can grow to a small patch of clovers on some spindly stems, even then staying only a few inches tall. The flower is on a spindly stem itself. It is star shaped, but the petals curl back a bit. They are bright yellow and about the size of a buttercup. The pod is green, rice shaped, with vertical grooves and slightly hair, at about half an inch long. The leaves curl up at night.

Where to gather it

Since most clovers are considered a weed in gardens, the clover is pretty common in most lawns. It blooms late spring to early fall.

How to gather it

Harvest any time it is out.

How to cook with it

Edible: Yes, all of it can be eaten, but it should only be consumed in small amounts. The leaves and flowers can be eaten raw or cooked, like leafy greens. Typically used in salads. It can also be made into teas. The fruit is tart and crisp.

Wood Sorrel Soup

Time: 20-25 minutes
Serving Size: 4 servings
Prep Time: 5 minutes
Cook Time: 15-20 minutes
Ingredients:

- 3 tbsps butter
- 1/2 cup onions
- 4 to 6 cups wood sorrel, packed
- 4 cups vegetable stock
- 1/2 cup cream
- pinch of salt

Instructions:

1. Melt butter in a pot and add chopped onions.
2. Cook until golden.
3. On medium heat, add sorrel and salt until cooked down.
4. Take off heat and add to a blender and puree.
5. Pour back in the pot and add cream. Cook on low heat for 5 minutes, but do not boil.
6. Serve cool or warm.

Author: Since the berries can aid in digestion, although they might not be the best snack, they can be helpful to have around when in need. This plant should be considered once a forager has a little bit more experience and can feel confident in identifying a plant early in the season that has many look-alikes.

115
YARROW

Yarrow is also known as sweet alyssum or scientifically known as *Lobularia maritima*.

IDENTIFICATION OF THE PLANT

Yarrow can be grown as a garden flower, although it can also be foraged for. The plant is bushy looking, having multiple stems in a dense cluster. They usually only grow a foot or two tall. The stems are thin, but dense/hard. The stem has vertical grooves. The flowers of the plant are compound. The individual leaves are very narrow like a herbaceous needle, similar to dill, they are short, and dark green. The leaflet is about six inches long, with a main margin and two rows on either side of dense flowers. It looks like a feather.

The flowers are dense firm florets. The flowers are five petal star shaped. The petals are round. The center has small craters. The shape of the floret is a roundish cluster, the face is flat, and 3-4 inches across on average. The flower is usually white or off white, but can be pink or yellow as well.

Where to gather it

Yarrow might be found blooming from the late spring through the summer. It likes direct sun, is not picky with soil, and can be found in weedy areas.

How to gather it

Use scissors because the stem is hard. Clip flowers and leaves as needed.

How to cook with it:

Edible: Yes, the flowers and leaves can be dried for spices or used fresh. Don't overcook. I'd recommended cooking it with beets and parsley flavors.

Author: Yarrow is really common in medicinal medicine; it is used in topical treatments to help healing and prevent infection.

116
WILD POTATO VINE

The wild potato vine, or *Ipomoea pandurata*, is also known as wild sweet potato and wild rhubarb. This seems like very different things to be compared to.

IDENTIFICATION OF THE PLANT

The wild potato vine can grow up to 30 feet long. The leaves of this plant are up to six inches long and alternate. The leaves are heart-shaped and smooth edged. Often they are tinged with bug holes.

The flower is white and trumpet-shaped. They are about two inches wide and fan out. The center tube is touched with purple. The roots might be small like a potato, but they are often large, growing up to a foot long and more carrot or yam-like in shape.

Where to gather it

The plant can be found in many places like forests, fields, and even rock areas. Since it is a vine, it likes to climb or crawl.

How to gather it

In the fall dig the plant up to get to the root, but it might be easier to take notice of it earlier in the year when it is flowering.

How to cook with it

Edible: Yes, the roots can be eaten when cooked. They are similar to a sweet potato.

Author: Like many of the root vegetables in this book, those who are foraging for a larger amount of their food intake should really take note of these kinds of plants. Many people think that low calories or low starch is a good thing, but it can be hard to find food with enough calories to sustain a healthy lifestyle. High starch foods like this one can make foraged meals heartier.

Leave a 1-Click Review!

Customer reviews

 5 out of 5

3 global ratings

5 star	██████████	100%
4 star		0%
3 star		0%
2 star		0%
1 star		0%

⌄ How are ratings calculated?

Review this product

Share your thoughts with other customers

Write a customer review

AFTERWORD

This book introduces the reader to over 100 wild edible herbs, which can certainly feel like an endless amount of information. Foraging is one of those things that you can't just master by reading a book. Learning is mostly done in the field. Some people might start identifying every plant that they pick up. While it can feel endless, it is important to remember that these are the most common plants you can forage for in this area. While there are a lot of plants that are edible, you don't need to know or memorize them all. Take your time and figure out what plants work for you.

Every single plant includes a recipe for the reader. This is a good way to introduce yourself to the plant, and then it's your turn to figure out what you are going to do with it. Food has endless possibilities and, as you learn about the plant in its habitat and get to know food on a more intimate level than the sterile grocery store, your kitchen will become a place that is full of inspiration. The amazing thing about so many of these plants is that you probably already know them. Since so many are common, it means accessibility for everyone for foraging food. These plants are probably already in your backyard.

I tried to begin each chapter with a hint of an experience on the plant so that the foraging community can be shared even through this book. Whether this insight was about taste, safety, or identification, I wanted people to be able to feel more connected with the plants and feel like they already had one up to go out and look for in the forest. The dynamic relationship then becomes a whole picture—the location, the plant, the exterior knowledge, how to interact with the plant, and how to use the plant. The outdoors and your kitchen become connected too. The grocery store and your kitchen are not separate from the outdoors, they are the same.

Foraging for food is more than a single purpose. You can save money, improve your health, prevent yourself from any illnesses, spend time in nature, and have fun cooking these extraordinary recipe ideas all at the same time. It is hard to bring all of these things into a situation, but you can enrich your life by taking a step outside to see what you can use. As you focus on the idea of foraging for more, you will notice a difference in how you eat too. You can appreciate the sophisticated taste that comes from the variation in leafy greens. You can taste the heightened sweetness from a fresh peach. This appreciation changes what your plate looks like, and eating better food becomes a gift. These plants are also known for their different capabilities in healing. All of this can be done without having to buy into any scheme.

Food from your backyard is healthier; you know where it comes from. You can make your food become your medicine and observe yourself rising and shining. Why would you still buy vegetables and herbs if you can use the wild woods as your free supermarket? You can have more control over what goes in your body. Much of the food that we eat from the store has a list of ingredients it doesn't need. Some food gets picked before it is ripe so that by the time it hits stores it isn't rotten, but this means that the plant doesn't have time to grow the way it needs to in order to be the same tasty, healthy food.

Let's spread this knowledge together. A review can help others to gain the same insights that you just got. What feels better than helping others rise? If you enjoyed the content of this book, please take 2 minutes to leave a review on this. We also have an active Facebook group and would love to have you.

https://www.facebook.com/groups/northeasthomestead

Let's help humanity rise together!

NORTHEAST MEDICINAL PLANTS FORAGING FROM YOUR BACKYARD HOMESTEAD NATIVE HERBALIST'S GUIDE TO IDENTIFYING WILD HERBS FOR HEALTH AND WELLNESS

NORTHEAST MEDICINAL PLANTS:
FORAGING FROM YOUR BACKYARD HOMESTEAD

NATIVE HERBALIST'S GUIDE TO IDENTIFYING WILD HERBS FOR HEALTH AND WELLNESS

J. B. MAXWELL

"The person who takes medicine must recover twice, once from the disease and once from the medicine."
–William Osler

INTRODUCTION

Did you know that nowadays, many people heal their bodies successfully by using herbal medicine?

Did you know that the famous herbalist Maria Treben purports to have cured many cancer patients by using herbs only?

In this book, we'll explore the various conditions that can be remedied by using medicinal plants. We will explore how this can improve your overall health and well-being holistically, but in a natural rather than a synthetic way. For some, medicinal plants may provide the long-term answers to pain or illness that you haven't been able to get from medical doctors. Not only that, but it's less expensive and can be less destructive to your body than traditional medicine.

If you're sick of being an experimental toy for Western Medicine, then taking natural healing into your own hands might be the answer. This can lead to a healthier family. It can also lead to the resolution of symptoms that recur and never seem to vanish. As a result, you could be living a healthier and happier life.

By being your doctor in the process of holistic healing, you'll find that you come to know your body better. You'll see what taking various herbs and plants does to your body, and by observing this, you'll end up more conscious of your bodily functions in general. As a result, it will be easier to make the right decisions for your health.

ABOUT THE AUTHOR

I am a family man who has taught himself how to be an expert in the field of medicinal plants. I grew up in a small farm town with no red lights in Maryland. Currently, I live in Pennsylvania with my beautiful wife and loving son. I love my family, our outdoor lifestyle, hiking, nature, gardening, and teaching others my knowledge of herbs. This knowledge extends to foraging wild herbs and plants, not just using them. Being outdoors makes me feel at peace.

I've always loved the idea of growing my own healthy, clean, organic food on a large enough scale that I can provide for my whole family without having to rely completely on grocery store produce as well as provide some for the neighbors. There's something about home-grown food's flavor that is unrivaled by its store-bought counterpart. On top of that, it's inexpensive and saves us a whole lot of money.

One of the things I enjoy about growing my food is that I have direct control over what is grown. I can ensure the plants are cared for properly while growing, which in turn makes high quality a certainty. This hands-on approach allows me to feed my family food with a high amount of nutrients, allowing for complete holistic health. I have been practicing homesteading principles for a little over eight years now on two properties, one being three-quarters of an acre and the other being an acre.

My knowledge, in turn, covers a large range of topics. This spans from the sphere of Western medicine to Chinese Eastern Medicine and Ayurvedic practices. I've traveled through the East where I gained this knowledge first-hand. Gaining this ancient wisdom gave me great comfort, and I am thankful for it.

Knowing this has allowed me to create a life that's off-grid with my family, and we are healthy and happy. I would love to share this knowledge so that others feel safe and empowered to do the same.

I love exploring forests and mountains with the knowledge that I'm safe and protected, whatever happens. This has led to a long-term journey of steady knowledge expansion about our natural environment. Because of my firsthand wilderness survival experience built up over more than a decade, I've reached a firm certainty of what I'm talking about. I've helped many people with herbal medicines and ancient practices that I've picked up along the way from shamans and practitioners of natural medicine.

I've studied and experimented with so much over the last 15 years.

During this period, I have helped many people in America improve their lifestyles and get back into contact with Mother Nature. The result has been an improvement in their overall mental and physical health. I've gotten to the point where I have a deep passion to share all the knowledge and experience I've built up over the years.

My goal is to help you achieve a healthier lifestyle by helping you create a natural home apothecary. This is my passion because I know how much freedom, joy, and health improvement can be created thereby.

In only one book you'll learn about the most powerful plants you can use to optimize your health and promote your well-being. These plants have been selected carefully to cover the healing properties needed for the most common ailments. Even if you do not know herbal medicine and medicinal plants yet, this is a detailed guide for any kind of person.

WILDCRAFTING BASICS

In this chapter, you'll be introduced to foraging. This will help you understand the importance and benefits of foraging to people's health. Wildcrafting can be a sustainable way of getting the herbs you need to stay vital in your everyday life if you practice it well. By following the right safety guidelines and adhering to ethical foraging standards, you'll find it to be a fulfilling addition to your life.

WHY WILDCRAFT MEDICINE FOR YOURSELF AND YOUR FAMILY?

One of the reasons wildcrafting is so important is that, with an added understanding of how much wild spaces can provide for you, you realize that you have tools at your disposal almost everywhere around you. These tools are nature's provisions for improving unwanted health conditions or for daily maintenance of general well-being. This will make you less dependent on other people when it comes to staying healthy, as you won't need to rely on pharmaceutical companies' doctors for all your conditions anymore.

The plants that you find in nature can help to propagate using proper wildcrafting techniques. Even when tubers are harvested, resulting in the whole plant being removed from the earth, you can still contribute to a healthier ecosystem. By removing the plant when it's seeding, you can plant the seeds in the earth you've just softened by removing the tuber. This causes the plant to maintain and often increase its numbers.

Besides the benefits the ecosystem receives from your responsible wildcrafting, there are many benefits that you'll receive too. The main one is that plants that grow in the wild often have more nutrients than those grown in agribusiness. You, therefore, benefit from increased vitamins and other nutrients in your diet.

You can help propagate the plants you find by using proper wildcrafting techniques. Even when tubers are harvested, resulting in the whole plant being removed from the earth, you can still contribute to a healthier ecosystem. By removing the plant when it's seeding, you can plant the seeds in the earth you've just softened by removing the tuber. This causes the plant to maintain and often increase its numbers.

In addition to the benefits the ecosystem receives from your responsible wildcrafting, there are many benefits that you'll receive too. The main one is that plants that grow in the wild often have more nutrients than those grown in agribusiness. You, therefore, benefit from increased amounts of vitamins, minerals, and fatty acids available in wild varieties of plants.

The mental effects of wildcrafting shouldn't be discounted either. By getting out in the open, breathing in the fresh air, and observing your environment, you'll find your mind becomes calmer. The hubbub you experience daily isn't hanging around with you out in the open, leaving you free to slow your mind down and notice the world around you.

ETHICAL FORAGING

There are many principles to take into account to ensure that your foraging is ethical and non-destructive. One of the most important is to ensure that you don't harvest a plant when there's only one clump of that plant in the foraging area, especially if it's a sparse clump. Ensuring that you only harvest when it's clear that the plant won't be eradicated from the site is the epitome of ethical foraging.

The takeaway with this principle is that when you're making use of wild spaces, only take what you need for your personal use. This way the space will be maintained and not made barren. Don't commodify the herb.

This goes hand in hand with the mindset that you're maintaining a relationship with the environment. There's a give and take, with you contributing to the propagation of plants by spreading their seeds and harvesting responsibly while the environment is contributing the materials you need for medicine, food, and various other needs. By finding time to go out foraging, you'll become more grounded, and you'll realize the true value of the land. Once you realize the value it holds, it will be very easy for you to respect the land and take steps, such as knowing the life cycles of the plants you'll be harvesting, to safeguard its natural resources.

Not altering the landscape of the wild space is an essential principle of ethical foraging. Keeping yourself from chopping down tree branches or driving off the road when possible will go a long way toward preserving the landscape. This can be difficult when you're trying to get to spaces that are untouched by pollution and chemical sprays. But, more often than not, you'll find that you can get to a truly wild spot while easily being conscientious about not damaging it.

A way you can make the environment better than before is to take a trash bag with you. This way you can pick up garbage you see lying around. In addition to helping keep the environment clean from others' trash, there's also a responsibility to pick up after yourself. If you've used something, keep it with you so that you can chuck it in the trash back home. You can go the extra mile by making it as if you've never been in space. This entails filling up holes you create and cleaning up any substances leftover from fires you make.

One of the more important points when it comes to ethical foraging is to ensure that you aren't breaking any laws. The law that would most directly affect you is trespassing. To avoid getting drawn into paying hefty fines for trespassing, ensure either that the area is for use by the general public or that you have permission from the private landowner to use their property.

SUSTAINABLE FORAGING TIPS

One way of avoiding sustainability issues is to harvest those plants that are considered to be weeds in the area. They may be considered weeds because they come from another area and pose a threat to local species. They also may be considered weeds because of an overabundance that threatens other species in the area. Harvesting these types of plants won't cause damage to the environment. Further, by keeping yourself aware of the at-risk species in your area, you'll be able to harvest other species that aren't listed. As a general rule of thumb, it's best to make use of the commonest wild plants in your area first.

Being aware of cultivation techniques can also be of use in ensuring sustainable foraging. In this way, you'll know how to sow the seeds of the plants you harvest. You'll also be aware of their life cycles so you can get them at the end of the cycle and facilitate their propagation. This is particularly useful to know for plants that are indigenous to the area you live in. Knowing this will enable you to cultivate the plants that belong in your region, thus preserving the natural landscape in question.

TOOLS

Tools improve safety and increase effectiveness while foraging. When using tools, you reduce unnecessary damage to plants while harvesting them. Below, I've delineated the best additions to any wildcrafter's toolkit. You can acquire most of these at a low cost, whether online or at a hiking store.

Pruning Shears

You use these to cut branches. They are extremely useful on most foraging trips. When choosing a pair of pruning shears, it's best to take a pair with non-slip handles or stippled handles. This prevents them from slipping when they're covered with plant juices. A sap groove on the front is a bonus because it lessens the amount of buildup while using your shears. As for what the shears are made from, I suggest a metal frame with a lightweight handle. This reduces the problem of snapping, chipping, and breakage that you may encounter with polymer shears. You'll also reduce unnecessary weight from a solid metal pair.

Knife

A knife is perfect for cutting off sections from tougher plants. There are curved-blade knives that are specifically designed for wildcrafting. They allow you to cut branches and twigs off in one motion. The best wildcrafting knives have rust-resistant blades and have non-slip handles. The rust-resistant blade is necessitated by the moisture present in plants you harvest. The non-slip handle is necessitated by the slippery oils and liquids that are exuded by plants that have been cut.

Scissors

Scissors are the best item to use when you're cutting off fine parts of a plant, such as leaves, flowers, or seed clusters. They can be used without causing any damage to the rest of the plant. I find that using a pair of kitchen scissors works quite fine because they tend to be rust-resistant, and they tend to be rather strong.

Foraging Bag

A bag is a necessity when it comes to foraging. A plastic bag is a no-no because it wilts your harvest. A paper bag is better because it provides more breathability. Some foragers even suggest keeping a bunch of paper bags in a small zipped plastic bag. This allows you to store a variety of plants that you've harvested. The weight of the paper bags is minimal, making any hiking you may do less tiring. The zipped plastic bag is useful for keeping your paper bags together and prevents them from getting wet before you've put them to use.

A step up from this is a canvas bag as it combines breathability, durability, and sustainability. A basket will also do the trick because it's sturdy and breathable. Your plants will thus remain fresh. The crème de la crème for holding your harvest is a bamboo bag. The bamboo fabric combines durability and breathability with easy carriage. This makes it perfect for harvesting trips.

Vegetable Brush

Vegetable brushes are a valuable addition to your toolkit because they allow you to clean dirt from plants that you've harvested. Dirt is an inevitable part of foraging, but much of it can be eliminated with a quick brush before placing it in your harvesting bag or basket. Not only does carrying a brush cut down on cleaning time at home, but the cost is also extremely low.

Shovel

Shovels make your wildcrafting adventures much easier. They allow you to get to roots and tubers with minimal effort. The best shovels for this purpose are ones that are small enough to fit in your backpack. They should preferably be rust-resistant and have sharpened edges. A heat-treated steel variety is great because it's strong. Polymer versions are often too soft, especially when dealing with hard, rocky soil.

Soil knife

Soil knives tend to be wide, with a sharp, smooth edge on one side and a serrated edge on the other. They are used for digging into hard-packed soil and can be great for cutting thick roots as well. Please go for a rust-resistant one because you'll find that roots often contain a lot of moisture and that soil can be rather wet a few inches down.

Magnifying Glass

When you're trying to identify a plant, sometimes you want to look at fine details. Occasionally your eyes won't be able to make out all the finer details, especially when you get a bit older. To get around this, you could use the zoom on your camera or phone, but this can have its shortcomings in terms of visual quality. A magnifying glass is much more effective for this purpose. You'll be able to zoom right in there without any reduction in visual quality. You can even get magnifying glasses that come in multiple strengths, allowing you to go to the most minute detail possible. With a trusty set of magnifying glasses, you'll be able to identify plants and any infections on them with ease.

Gloves

Gloves have the sole purpose of protecting your hands from sharp rocks and thorns as well as irritating hairs on the stems of plants. In the process of wearing them, they may become coated with sap or oils that contain poisonous or irritating substances. To prevent this from affecting your body, use care when handling gloves. Also, wash or replace your gloves occasionally. The best gloves also provide some level of breathability, allowing your hands to work without becoming hot and sweaty.

Guidebook

These are essential items for using in the field as well as for studying at home. It's best to have a variety of guidebooks because some books may have different pictures, illustrations, or descriptions than others. This helps when you're in the field because you'll have more than one perspective to determine which plant you're handling. The result is a heightened level of certainty. When you're not in the field, I advise going through your guidebooks in your spare time. An increase in theoretical understanding of the plant will help you work more smoothly when you're foraging in the wild.

SAFETY

Foraging in the wild is not without its risks. To prevent yourself from ending up in a sticky situation, use the below safety tips.

Go With Someone Else

If there are two or more people, there is always another set of hands in emergencies. Slipping on a rock and getting a concussion isn't something you plan for, but if it happens, it's far better to have someone there to contact emergency services. Foraging is one activity where the adage "too many cooks spoil the broth" doesn't apply.

Have a Mentor

Mentors give you the advantage of built-up experience. They can guide you when you have questions about what you've harvested, such as whether it's safe to eat. A mentor will sometimes be willing to come on foresting expeditions with you, thus providing a masterclass in wildcrafting. Take the advice of those with a lot of experience and use it to make yourself as skilled as possible in herb gathering.

Avoid Unhealthy Plants

Don't harvest unhealthy-looking plants. They might have infections, which isn't something you want to include in your dietary or medicinal stocks. Using a magnifying glass will occasionally be necessary for determining if something is wrong with the plant. But when you have determined that something is wrong, don't get yourself into trouble by including it with your edibles.

Avoid Spoiled Stock

Wild plants generally have a short shelf-life. Only harvesting what you need safeguards your health and protects the sustainability of the wild at the same time. To put it simply, why use old, ineffective herbs when it's so easy to get your hands on fresher ones?

Keep Potential Allergies in Mind

Concerning only taking the quantities you need, harvest even smaller amounts when it is your first time taking that particular plant with you. You may be allergic to the plant and not know it. Take the small amount to test it for an allergic reaction. You can harvest more once you've confirmed you don't have an allergy.

Be Mindful of Pollution and Pesticides

Some areas are not optimal for harvesting. These are generally areas that are close to sources of pollution, such as highways or smoggy city centers. It's also recommended that you avoid areas that are prone to being sprayed with pesticides. While some pesticides are plant-based and not full of synthetic chemicals, most aren't. Then again, even some plant-based pesticides can be harmful when used incorrectly, so altogether avoiding areas sprayed with pesticides is best. You could be putting yourself at risk of worse health by consuming herbs that have been sprayed with strong, harmful pesticides. Also realize that even if you wash plants that have been sprayed with potent pesticides, there may still be chemicals absorbed into the plant that you won't be able to wash out.

10 BENEFITS OF FORAGING WITH HERBAL MEDICINE

1. The plants are not harvested en masse. The result is a higher degree of sustainability because you aren't purchasing your herbs from someone who harvesting them for commercial purposes.
2. Plants obtained in the wild normally have a stronger medicinal effect. Without as many contaminants farmed into them and without genetic modification, the herb remains naturally complete.
3. The herbs are fresher. When you purchase from a herbal retailer, they may already have stored the herb for a while. When you harvest it yourself, you have it from the moment it's been harvested, thus ensuring freshness.
4. You'll be saving money because you won't have to buy from a herbal store or online supplier. All you'll have to spend on is your transportation costs to reach your harvesting location and the initial costs of setting up your wildcrafting kit.
5. When you have taken the steps necessary to correctly identify a plant, you have certainty that you have the correct variety of it, especially if you've verified it with your mentor. The same can't always be said with purchased herbs. When herbs are

purchased, you might occasionally find that the wrong variety has been identified. Foraging for the herb yourself, therefore, avoids this risk.

6. Having your own harvested herbs allows you the freedom to incorporate them into your daily life. When you purchase herbs, this could lead you to use them sparsely. Part of the reason this occurs is that you can't generally buy herbs in large quantities in herbal shops. You normally purchase a handful or so at a time, with pricing becoming unreasonable at larger quantities. Not only will you have access to larger quantities when you need them while in the wild, but you'll also find that you have almost no hesitancy to use your stocks for general use. You know that you can just go harvest more when your stocks run low.

7. Self-empowerment is a by-product of foraging. By gaining the confidence to gather your medicinal and food provisions, you realize that you can become truly self-sufficient. This removes multiple barriers you might have encountered to taking higher levels of control of your life.

8. By foraging for your provisions, you have a direct say in what you use for your health maintenance and improvement purposes. When you purchase things from the pharmacy, they are regulated by the government, namely the Food and Drug Administration. While the FDA is there to safeguard the community, the products they approve can be far-removed from nature. The level of complexity these health products pose to someone that doesn't have lots of training on chemicals can be frustrating. This is all circumvented in general when you use herbal medicines that are closely connected to nature. You may have to resort to medical drugs on occasion, but these instances will be few and far between when you're able to resort to nature's provisions for general illness.

9. You will have a more complete say in what goes into your body. There are little to no additives in wild herbs, resulting in pure additions to your diet. The same can't be said when purchasing things from your grocer. Even if your grocer can provide good quality foodstuffs, you can't always obtain sourcing information. Further, you'll find that often, the commercial needs of farmers result in pesticides and GMOs (genetically

modified organisms) being used without your direct knowledge. This isn't the case with wild foodstuffs.
10. You will understand your responsibility to the world you live in. The correct term for this is 'stewardship,' and it refers to having a care-taking attitude toward nature and its inhabitants. By foraging, you build a relationship with Mother Nature, thereby increasing your level of understanding of the environment. The result is a heightened level of care toward the world in most things you do daily. This result often occurs unconsciously, being based on the goodwill you build up while foraging.

PLANT IDENTIFICATION

The main point of this chapter is to understand how to identify a wild herb.

RECOGNIZING A PLANT

To effectively recognize a plant, you should be able to determine the types of leaves it has, the type of branches it has, and the type of flowers it has.

Leaf Shapes and Arrangements

The purpose of the leaves of a plant is to help it get the things it needs out of the air, to help it gather energy from the light, and to help protect the plant. Leaves have multiple shapes and arrangements. These vary from species to species, regulating how sunlight is harnessed by the plant.

First, you should understand what the parts of a leaf are. The image below should serve as a reference point. The petiole is the sticklike structure connecting the base of the leaf to the stem of the plant. The midrib is the single, thick, straight, vein-like line stretching from the petiole to the tip of the leaf. The midrib divides the leaf in two. The veins stretch out from the midrib, supplying the leaf with water and nutrients. The leaf's margins are the outside edge of the leaf that gives it its shape. The part of the leaf between the petiole and the midrib is known as the base, whereas the part of the leaf furthest from the base is known as its tip. The final part to note is the blade. This is the part of the leaf that fills in the leaf between the veins and the margin.

[Note: some leaves don't have a petiole. In this case, you would say that the leaf is sessile]

When it comes to classifying leaves, there are two main types. One is a simple leaf and the other is a compound leaf. A simple leaf is one leaf that isn't made up of smaller leaflets, whereas a compound leaf is made up of more than one leaflet coming from the same central vein (midrib).

Compound leaves are further divided into three sub-categories. The first is a palmate leaf. This is where there is more than one projection spread from a nexus, almost like how your fingers spread out from your palm. The other two types of compound leaves are a pinnate and a bi-pinnate leaf. A pinnate leaf is made up of multiple leaflets spreading out from a common stem. A bi-pinnate leaf is where smaller stems spring out of the common leaf stem, with each smaller stem sporting leaflets spreading out of it. When you look at a fern, you can see that there is a larger stem for each leaf. The larger stem then has smaller stems coming out of it. The leaflets of the fern then spread out from each smaller stem.

Arrangement

There are four main arrangements of leaves, namely opposite, alternate, rosette, and whorled. An opposite arrangement is where leaves come out on opposite sides of a stem, such as on an olive tree. An example of an alternate arrangement is a willow tree. With this type of arrangement, you'll notice that leaves grow on the sides across from each other, but none of them are directly opposite one another.

While not limited to one type of plant, rosette arrangements are commonly found in succulents such as aloe plants. In this arrangement, all the leaves of a plant come from one central stem. This is especially common on plants that don't grow very high. A whorl is also an arrangement of leaves from a central point, but rather than all the leaves of the plant coming from one central stem, there are many branches and twigs that each create a central point from which leaves spread. An example of this is a lemonwood tree.

The main purpose of all these arrangements is to optimize how sunlight falls on a given plant.

Shape

The shape of a leaf can help you identify a plant more accurately. The most basic distinction is whether a leaf has lobes or not. There are five other more precise shape classifications that I use when identifying a plant. They are linear, elliptical, ovate, truncate, and lanceolate.

A linear leaf shape is long and slim, like most grass leaves. Elliptical leaves are shaped like an oval, such as the leaves found on an American hornbeam tree. An ovate leaf is also in the shape of an oval. The difference between an ovate and an elliptical leaf is that the elliptic leaf remains the same width, but an ovate leaf is broader at the bottom and more narrow at the top. In other words, an ovate leaf is egg-like in shape. A further difference is that an elliptical leaf doesn't have lobes, whereas an ovate leaf could have lobes like an eggplant leaf does.

A lanceolate leaf can also be confused with elliptical and ovate leaves as it is also oval/egg-shaped. The difference is that a lanceolate leaf is broadest at the base, narrows at the midpoint, and then narrows to a fine tip. Lanceolate leaf types are much longer than they are wide, normally at least three times longer than their width. A willow tree leaf is an example of this.

The final shape I commonly use, a truncate leaf, is exactly what its name suggests. It seems to be truncated at the tip or the base, giving a flat appearance on one end. An example of this is a leaf on a tulip tree. The leaf has a few lobes along the side margins, but it seems to be flat at the base.

Margins

The margins of a leaf can vary a lot. That said, there are four main categories we use for speedy identification. There is a margin that is smooth the whole way around. Then there is a margin that is serrated the whole way around. The third is a lobed leaf, which has indentations; but the indents go less than halfway to the midrib. Finally, there is a parted leaf margin. This type of margin indents more than halfway to the midrib of the leaf.

Venation

Venation refers to the pattern or arrangement of the veins that can be seen on the surface of the leaf. There is parallel venation, in which veins normally occur parallel to each other in lines from the base of the leaf to the tip of the leaf. You also get dichotomous venation, in which the veins form a pattern that looks almost like a 'Y'. Palmate venation is when all the main veins come out from a central point on the leaf. And then there is pinnate venation, in which the veins are arranged coming out of the midrib.

Texture

Leaves of different species and subspecies have all sorts of textures on their margins that distinguish them from one another. This makes it much easier to identify a plant. Some of the most common leaf textures include wavy leaves, smooth leaves, toothed leaves, lobed leaves, and incised leaves. Both the textures and the degree to which these textures are present are distinguishing factors. For example, you can have a leaf with toothed margins where the toothing is fine, and another species where the toothing is ragged.

Other Factors

There are a few other distinguishing characteristics not mentioned yet. These include whether the leaves have thorns, hairs, or resin glands on them or not. The thickness of the leaf can also help in identifying the plant. The surface of the leaf, whether it be waxy, shiny, or dull, can also be used. The stiffness or limpness of the leaf also plays a role in identifying it.

Conifer Leaves

Conifers have slightly different types of leaves from other trees and plants, i.e. needles. These needles appear in multiple arrangements, depending on the species. These include clustered, bundled, single, linear, scale-like, and awl-shaped. Clustered, bundled, linear, and single should be self-explanatory. Scale-like refers to needles that are small and overlapping in nature. Awl-shaped needles are thin, linear, and taper to a sharp point.

Branching Patterns

There are multiple branching patterns you can use to identify plants, but the two most common types are opposite and alternate. Opposite branching patterns are where branches come out of a stem on opposite sides from each other and at the same point, sort of how ribs come out of your spine. Alternate branching patterns are where branches come out of a stem on opposing sides, but not at the same point.

One of the most useful things about using branching patterns to identify plants is that the branching pattern won't change from season to season. Even in winter, when many trees and shrubs have no leaves, you can still use their branching patterns for identification purposes.

Color and Number of Flower Petals

You may not always realize you're looking at a flower all the time because some of them look drab, very small, or like leaves. That said, you'll find that every plant has a flower of some sort. These may come out at different times of the year from plant to plant, depending on their life cycle, so expecting all flowers to bloom during the spring isn't going to provide you with the most accurate image of the plants you're foraging for.

The main characteristics you'll take into consideration when identifying a plant by its flowers include color, number of petals, size, petal stiffness, and petal/flower shape. Most field guides will give you a good description of the flowers of a plant, so it won't be difficult to determine if the plant you're looking at falls under the description in question.

There are often distinctive colors to the roots of a plant, its stem, and its leaves. Sometimes there are even distinctive colors for the same plant from season to season.

AGRIMONY

LATIN NAME

Agrimonia

DESCRIPTION

When they are young, agrimony plants have a basal rosette. As they grow older, their branches develop in an alternate arrangement. The leaves grow on petioles, and there are stipules at the base of the petiole. (Stipules are small leaf-like attachments at the base of the petiole). The leaf itself is a blade leaf. It's pinnate, with three to six pairs of leaflets on each leaf. It culminates in a terminal leaflet. There are small leaflets between each pair of larger leaflets. The leaf has a thin base that widens at the midpoint and then tapers to a point at the top. The margins are serrated, but the serration is large, rather than fine. The bottoms of the leaflets are hairy and have a gray tinge.

The flowers grow on sticks, creating structures called inflorescences. There are usually many flowers on each inflorescence, and they have an aromatic fragrance. The flower has five yellow petals that usually have a rounded tip. The sepals (the tougher petals that enclose the flower while it's still budding) also have five lobes, and they have small hooked spines underneath. There are between 10 and 12 stamens (the pollen-bearing structures in the middle of the flower), and two pistils (the parts in the middle of the flower that catch pollen in order to reproduce).

The fruit is small and has a green color that transitions to reddish color, then finally dulls to a brownish color. It also has many burr-like hairs that can cling onto your clothing. These burrs also go from green to red to a dull brown. In terms of size, the fruit doesn't grow much larger than a few millimeters. The shape of each fruit is bell-like at the base, ending in a small mass of burrs coming out the mid-points, and culminating in a rounded bud tip.

HABITAT

You can find agrimony on forest margins, in coppices, on banks of earth, in pastures, and in dryish meadows.

They should be in direct sunlight optimally, but they can also stand partial shade.

They prefer alkaline soil rich in calcium, growing particularly well in wettish, marshy conditions. You can also find them in dry soil; however, they normally don't flower in dryer soil.

SEASON TO GATHER THE PLANT

In the middle of summer, you'll find that it's best to harvest. If it's in bloom, this is an especially good time to gather some agrimony.

PARTS OF THE PLANT TO USE AS MEDICINE

The leaves are very useful for home remedies, so these can be harvested. But due to the prevalence of the plant and the number of ways in which you can use it, you can harvest the whole plant and hang it up to dry. This will allow you to use the entire plant for various reasons.

BENEFITS AND PROPERTIES

Agrimony has a host of benefits that you should be aware of. It can help cleanse the body. It can also help cleanse the mouth, cleanse mouth sores, clean out wounds, and clear up the skin. Due to its astringent qualities (helping to contract skin cells), it's not only effective for clearing up the skin, but is also effective as a lotion and as an ointment that heals skin irritations and sores. In the process of healing the wound, it will also help ease the pain you may feel in the wounded area, and it can help stanch any bleeding. As for your body's organs, agrimony can boost your kidneys and your liver and can ease stomach problems.

MEDICINE PREPARATION

Lotions and other skin applications: The easiest way to use agrimony for skin application purposes is simply to crush the parts of the plant you've selected so that the juice comes out. Once you have enough juice (about one tablespoon for every tablespoon of cream base), mix it in with a natural cream base, a natural fat, or a natural oil until it's mixed in smoothly.

Tea: made by adding a teaspoon of dried agrimony (any part of the plant that's been dried and crushed or cut up) to a cup of boiling water. You can steep for a few minutes, at which point it will be ready to consume.

Mouth gargle: made the same way as the tea, but you leave it to cool down afterward. I prefer to leave the agrimony in the water so that it gets stronger as I leave it overnight. Then a thorough swirl around the mouth will give the desired effect.

USING THE HERB

Lotions and skin applications: Apply directly to the affected area if the purpose of the application is to heal. You can also apply it to an open wound, so long as the other ingredients are safe for open wound application.

Tea: You should be able to drink this tea daily. Just note that it can have a constipating effect.

Mouth gargle: I prefer to let it get extra strong before using it. It has a more satisfying clean.

SIDE EFFECTS AND WARNINGS

Constipation is the most common side effect. Allergic reactions can also result from using this herb. Other side effects that can result from long-term use are nausea and vomiting. These reactions are due to the tannin content found in this herb.

FUN TIPS AND FACTS

Leaves of agrimony can be used as a source of yellow pigment.

AUTHOR'S PERSONAL STORY

I've helped many people cure digestive issues with agrimony. It helps even with IBS!

120
ALDER

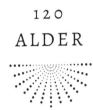

LATIN NAME

Alnus

DESCRIPTION

There is a large variety of alder species, with a vast difference in the sizes of alder trees, depending on the species. The dwarf species grows up to 15 feet tall, whereas some of the larger species grow up to 100 feet high. Most of the species, however, grow between 20 and 50 feet high. The tree is often used for wood. The wood is rather light, and the bark is quite thin. On top of the thin bark, you'll often find patches of lichen and moss.

The bark tends to be gray–sometimes lighter in hue, and sometimes darker. The bark itself also has unique coloration. There are two layers of bark on the tree. The outer layer is silvery gray, and the inner is brown. Once you've cut to the inner bark, it'll turn an orange color.

The leaves are arranged alternately on their twigs. Alder leaves have a serrated edge and are pointed at both the base and the tip. There's a slightly hairy texture underneath. Alder leaves are deciduous. Their leaves are green in the spring and summer, then in fall, the leaves go yellow, orange, red, and rust-colored. In some cases, the leaves are even purple. There is a distinctive, pleasant smell to this tree–similar to the scent of a cottonwood tree.

The flowers on alder grow on catkins (a type of inflorescence). The flowers are yellow at first then, after a while, they transition to a dark red color. The female flowers, on the other hand, develop on green growths, developing small red petals. Interestingly, most alder species first grow their flowers before they grow their leaves. The catkins give the tree a reddish hue in early spring.

Alder fruit comes in the form of half-inch wide cones. These start off green, then turn brown. Between the scales of the cones, you'll find small winged nuts.

HABITAT

These are very hardy trees. They can grow in areas that aren't fertile and that have recently gone through disasters such as fires or landslides or the clearing of land. Soil that isn't very fertile will increase in fertility when alder trees are growing in the area. This is because these trees can work symbiotically with bacteria, resulting in increases in nutrients present in the soil. Further, they can take the nitrogen from the air and transfer it to the soil.

Although they can grow in very rough areas, their ideal habitat is in areas with moist soil. They can often be found next to rivers and streams and in wetlands.

SEASON TO GATHER THE PLANT

Leaf buds should be harvested in February or March. Mature leaves, on the other hand, can be harvested from any time between the start of spring and the end of summer. The catkins can be harvested from when they appear until they become brown and hard in the winter months. As for the bark, this is best harvested from spring to fall.

PARTS OF THE PLANT TO USE AS MEDICINE

You can make use of the leaves, leaf buds, catkins (both mature and immature), and the bark. The bark is used more than the other parts of the tree because it's effective for medicinal purposes. I like using leaf buds and green catkins rather than mature leaves and mature catkins. They're just easier to work with and make a nice, fresh addition to your medicinal stocks.

BENEFITS AND PROPERTIES

Topical application is useful for the skin and for wounds. In terms of the skin, you'll be able to reduce acne breakouts, treat boils, and make your skin tauter. You can also eradicate inflammation and get rid of scabies.

For wounds, apply it either as a pulp, in a compress, as a wash, or in an ointment. The wash can be used to clean out a wound by getting rid of bacteria. Washes are also good for controlling bleeding and reducing swelling.

Sore muscles can be soothed greatly by applying alder creams or rubs. Rub it in quite thoroughly to soothe the muscles,

Your digestive tract will benefit greatly from using alder. Intestines will be stimulated, constipation will be alleviated, liver function will increase, and you'll produce more bile. The result will be more effective processing of food, such as better digestion of fats and better elimination of waste products.

Note that alder is said to have anti-carcinogenic attributes.

MEDICINE PREPARATION

Aperitif: Prepare the aperitif by getting some wine or fortified wine (white, pink, or red will do). Mix your alder (preferably fresh alder) with any other herbs you want to use. Don't worry if you crush it a bit–this will release some of the juices. Then pour over the wine (and ice if you prefer it cold). Leave it to infuse into the wine for a few minutes, at which point you should be able to sip and enjoy.

Poultice: Crushing the leaves or buds is all that's required to make an effective poultice.

Tea: Place the alder that you've harvested in a cup or mug–you won't require more than a teaspoon. Pour boiling water over it and leave it to soak for a few minutes. You can then strain and drink.

USING THE HERB

Aperitif: Use this before a meal as the purpose of an aperitif is to stimulate the digestive system.

Poultice: Once crushed, apply it directly to the irritated area.

Tea: Tea can be used for drinking, which is the usual reason for taking it. You can also use it for a mouthwash or a gargle to kill bacteria. It can also be used externally. For this purpose, you simply soak a cloth in the tea once it's cooled down a bit, then drape the cloth over any part of the body that you would like to soothe.

SIDE EFFECTS AND WARNINGS

Allergies are the most common side effect. This is especially so with alder because of the amount of pollen given off by the catkins blowing through the air.

A laxative effect is also a common side effect. When you've had a large amount of alder, you'll get a similar bowel reaction as when you take a mild laxative. Diarrhea is an indication that you should cut back on alder.

When you use bark from a tree within the first year of its growth, you could experience vomiting. The immature bark doesn't have the same properties as the older bark.

Other potential side effects you may notice are heart problems, bloody urine, an irritated stomach, weakening muscles, blood problems, and low potassium. Alder buckthorn in particular can have the side effect of cramps in your body.

FUN TIPS AND FACTS

The improvement in soil quality that alder brings about is due to the relationship it has with its symbiotic bacteria. The bacteria stimulate the roots so that they transfer nitrogen from the air into the earth. The tree then produces some natural sugars, which the bacteria consume.

AUTHOR'S PERSONAL STORY

When my wisdom teeth were growing, I was in really bad pain. Within 24 hours, gargling with alder alleviated my pain.

121
BEECH

LATIN NAME

Fagus

DESCRIPTION

The bark is gray with cracks or fissures arranged horizontally on the tree. They tend to be tall, normally between 40 and 60 feet in height. They also have large, dense crowns.

This tree is characterized by an alternate leaf arrangement. The leaves themselves are simple, not complex. They have an ovate shape, but with a pointed tip and have margins that are characterized by fine teeth. The leaves are shiny yet have fine hair when they're still young. The leaves are rather large, with a width of approximately four inches, and a length between two and six inches. Venation is pinnate, with the veins coming out of the midrib coming to distinctive points, thereby accentuating the toothed effect on its margins.

Their male flowers are found on catkins, and their female flowers grow in pairs on stalks above the male catkins. The flowers, in general, have a yellow-green appearance and are small clusters of a bunch of fuzzy pollen-carrying filaments. They weigh down the stem holding the cluster.

A beech tree produces beechnuts, which have three sides. They're brown and found in a cupule with a spined surface.

HABITAT

Fertile soil with good drainage is ideal for this tree. They do well in direct sun and in shade. You'll find them mainly in temperate areas, which includes most of the East US.

SEASON TO GATHER THE PLANT

You can harvest from this tree between spring and autumn. Leaf sprouts normally appear in April and May, and the fruit normally appears in fall. Sometimes you can find shoots that haven't sprouted yet in February already.

PARTS OF THE PLANT TO USE AS MEDICINE

The bark, buds, leaves, and flowers can all be used medicinally.

BENEFITS AND PROPERTIES

Beech can be advantageous for your skin as it can help with, open pores, and skin issues. Piles can also be handled effectively by using beech products. It is an astringent, so it makes for good creams. Your digestive tract can be stimulated by using beech, improving your nutrient absorption. Furthermore, it improves kidney functioning, which makes waste elimination operate optimally.

You can also use it orally. When used in this manner, it can have an antiseptic influence and alleviate toothache.

MEDICINE PREPARATION

Tar: You can collect tar by heating the wood or roots. The liquid that drips out is tar.

Decoction: Simply mash up the leaves, buds, or flowers. The seeds are also particularly useful for this purpose. Boil them up in some water and strain out the mashed bits.

Poultice: Mash up the plant material to create a soft mush.

Tea: The leaves are best for making tea. Pour boiling water over them and leave them to soak for a few minutes.

USING THE HERB

Tar: Tar is wonderful for skincare, particularly as an antiseptic. You simply rub it onto any affected area of your skin.

Decoction: Use the decoction for internal use, especially for improving the functioning of your kidneys.

Poultice: Apply it directly to your skin. You can also place it on your head, forehead, or temples to ease headaches.

Tea: The tea is great for intestinal and digestive troubles.

SIDE EFFECTS AND WARNINGS

The nuts should be eaten in moderation because they are poisonous in large doses and can cause problems, especially in your stomach. This effect is largely avoided by cooking the nuts before eating them, as this eliminates a lot of the poisonous substance found in the raw nut.

FUN TIPS AND FACTS

Beech is associated with femininity and is often considered the queen of British trees, where oak is the king. In Celtic mythology, Fagus was the god of beech trees. Beech was believed to have medicinal properties. One of these was relieving swelling by boiling its leaves to make a poultice.

AUTHOR'S PERSONAL STORY

I had a patient who was losing hair. I told him to get some fresh beech and to create an extract to put on his scalp. He wouldn't believe it, but within a few months, he had his hair back.

122
BIRCH

LATIN NAME

etula

DESCRIPTION

These are rather large species of trees. They generally grow between 40 and 70 feet high with a canopy between 30 and 60 feet wide. Dwarf birch, on the other hand, is generally shorter than 30 feet high, with most being much smaller than that.

The bark is papery and easily peels off from the inner cork layer. The outer layer can be likened to paper. In addition to its distinctive peeling nature, it can also be recognized by its horizontal diamond-shaped marks. You can even remove the outer bark without damaging the cork at all, but some training and knowledge of how to do this are required first.

Birch has an alternate leaf pattern. The leaves on a birch tree are egg-shaped and have pointed tips. Some birch species have more of a wedge shape to their leaves. The margins are serrated, and in a few of the species, the teeth are quite conspicuous. Their surface is glossy in appearance. In terms of size, they're between two and three inches long. When looking at the tree from a distance, you'll see that the leaves are denser close to the top and that they often aren't present on the lower parts of the tree.

Birch trees also have catkins. These have small, yellow flowers. Male catkins are just over an inch long, and female catkins are about half an inch long. You'll find the catkins in solitary and clustered arrangements at the end of a peduncle, but clusters of three catkins tend to be the most common. They start flowering in spring during the same season when birch leaves bud. As the seasons wear on, these catkins transition from yellow, through red, to a reddish-brown color.

Small winged nuts can be found in the hanging catkins after they've flowered.

HABITAT

Birch trees prefer moist soil to dry or wet soil. The soil should preferably be sandy and contain a large amount of decomposed plant matter for extra nutrition. They do, however, grow throughout the US, so you may find them in different habitats that aren't described here.

SEASON TO GATHER THE PLANT

It's best to forage birch during the spring months. At this stage, the birch will be full of shoots, and the bark will be flowing with nutrient-rich sap. During this season, there will also be many young and supple twigs. You can also harvest birch leaves, flowers, and bark in summer and up into early fall on occasion. As for the fruit, this is most easily available at the end of summer when the cones aren't too hard yet.

PARTS OF THE PLANT TO USE AS MEDICINE

You will be able to use the leaves, twigs, catkins, and bark of the tree medicinally. The sap in the tree can also be tapped and used medicinally. Fungi growing on the tree can also often be used for medicinal purposes. Although not part of the tree, these fungi are commonly found on a birch tree. Remember to identify the fungi before use to make sure they are safe.

BENEFITS AND PROPERTIES

If you have issues with your skin, birch is the right tree for you to be foraging. The bark of a birch tree contains a large amount of a chemical called betulin, which is fantastic for skin healing and maintaining healthy skin.

Pain is something that can be alleviated quite well by the tree as well. This includes joint pain, pain from injuries such as breaking a bone, and pain in your muscles. This is mainly due to a chemical found in birch that's similar to aspirin.

Your internal organs and systems can benefit from ingesting birch. Things such as bladder infections, bladder stones, and kidney stones are commonly remedied when using birch.

MEDICINE PREPARATION

Tea (made with twigs): The tea you can make from birch isn't only good at healing and maintaining your health, it's also tasty. Pour some water that's close to boiling over birch twigs for the best tea, and leave it to brew for a few minutes. Younger twigs that are more pliable are best as the older, more brittle twigs have fewer nutrients.

Flour: You can use the dried and crushed inner bark in the flour you use for your everyday baking. To do this, crush the bark until it's extra fine because it's unpleasant to have to chew on tough, barky grains. It doesn't rise very well, so it's better to use with unleavened baked goods. The flavor is slightly bitter, but this can be satisfying in some types of cookies and bread. I mix it in with other flours I use, such as coconut flour, to create a blend.

Oil: Cover birch leaves, bark, catkins, or twigs with a carrier oil of your choosing in a mason jar. Place the mason jar in a pot of water, making sure it doesn't fall over. At this point, put on the stove and put on very low heat (too hot for your hand to be comfortable, but not so hot that the jar would burst or so hot that the water boils). Keep the pot filled with water and on the stove for the entire day, and repeat the same process for the next two days as well. At this point, birch should be thoroughly infused into the oil. You can also use a process where you don't use the stove (which is the process I use because I don't like wasting gas unnecessarily). I place the birch pieces in a jar of carrier oil and put them outside in the sun during the day. I repeat this process for about five days, at which point it's ready to be strained and used.

Washes: simply soak birch pieces, whether it be leaves, bark, twigs, or flowers, in some water for a few hours. You can then use it to cleanse your skin. When injured, you can use this as a soak for a cloth which you then drape over the injured area. And when it comes to your hands and feet, you can use it as a soak to relieve any pain they may be going through. It's a great soak for your feet because it doesn't only relieve pain, but it can also be used to assist with killing foot infections and fungi.

USING THE HERB

Tea: The tea is rich in vitamin C and has a flavor similar to peppermint tea. I find that it's unnecessary to add anything to it to adjust the flavor, so I tend to not use honey or other herbs and spices in this type of tea. That said, it can be rather pleasant to add catkins to your tea for a fuller flavor.

Flour: I sift the bark through a fine strainer after grinding it because extremely fine bark is the easiest to work with.

Oil: Use the oil for any number of skin conditions—such as acne, eczema, or dry skin—and pain relief in massages. The oil is also particularly useful for making herbal creams and ointments. It makes for particularly soothing skincare.

Washes: Pouring the water you've infused as a wash into your bath water can also be beneficial. When you have sore muscles, you can do this to make a relaxing body soak.

SIDE EFFECTS AND WARNINGS

The pollen given off by birch trees is a very common allergen. For this reason, if you go foraging for birch in the spring, and you know you're allergic to its pollen, take some antihistamine when you go. This way, you can harvest without being affected by all the pollen in the air.

FUN TIPS AND FACTS

Birch trees symbolized renewal, purification, and beginnings in Celtic mythology.

AUTHOR'S PERSONAL STORY

Whenever I stand in front of a birch tree, I feel so much purity. As I told you in my other book, the first time I ever drank birch sap, I was fascinated by the immediate feeling of purification that flowed into my veins.

123
BLACKBERRY

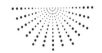

LATIN NAME

ubus

DESCRIPTION

A blackberry bush can grow to a height of a few feet, but it spreads out well. It can grow to a 20-foot-long mass, and in some areas, it forms a large thicket with more than one blueberry bush amassed into one. Their roots grow quite deep for a bramble bush–approximately three feet deep. This, in combination with their prickles, makes blackberries very sturdy in the ground.

Blackberries come in the form of bushes with a lot of prickles. From afar, they may just look like a messy mass of prickly branches and leaves. And in the winter, they may just appear to be a dried, prickly mass of branches. The stem and branches of the blackberry are woody and covered in prickles. They are rather long, with some being as long as 20 feet. They tend to arch up and have a green, red, or purple color. The prickles along the stems can vary in size, some being rather large, and others appearing as small hairs.

Blackberry bushes have alternate leaf patterns. Each leaf is made up of three to five leaflets that are one to three inches long each. This terminal leaflet (the one forming the end of the stem holding a cluster of leaflets) has a three-lobed shape. A few of the species don't have a three-lobed terminal leaf, but rather one lobe. The margins of these leaflets are normally deeply toothed, although some blackberry species have a finer toothed pattern on the margins. As for the design of each leaf, you'll notice that there are prickly hairs on the veins and on the stems to which the leaflets are attached.

At the base of the stems that support these leaves, you'll find a pair of stipules (small leaflike structures). The leaves are normally a darker green on the top and a lighter green below. The lower side of the leaf can get so light that it has a white-green appearance.

HABITAT

They are found in all types of settings, but the most common is in a forest or wooded area, or in areas where the ground has been cleared, such as in a landslide. That said, they can be found almost anywhere once they've been exposed to that area.

SEASON TO GATHER THE PLANT

The flowers can be harvested as soon as they start appearing. They generally bloom from April to May, and transition to fruiting at the end of May. The fruit is best harvested when they are ripe, which will be when they've gained their dark purple-black color. This is usually from July to August. The leaves can be harvested in spring and summer, but it's best to get them before they're dark and mature. When harvesting the leaves, using gloves is best because you can prick your fingers if you don't use them.

PARTS OF THE PLANT TO USE AS MEDICINE

The fruit, the flowers, and the leaves can be used medicinally.

BENEFITS AND PROPERTIES

Blackberry has some stellar benefits when it comes to keeping your blood in good condition. If you have anemia, this will help because blackberries help to absorb iron. It can also regulate a menstrual cycle better, reducing the amount of bleeding you experience. Your digestive and excretory systems will also benefit. If you have trouble with diabetes, blackberry leaves can assist with lowering your blood sugar. Diarrhea can be handled by taking blackberries. Likewise, if you have dysentery or cholera, blackberry leaves will help too.

Your oral health can also be improved by blackberries. Open sores in your mouth can make eating and speaking less pleasant to do. Blackberry juice can help with this. Other oral issues that can be improved with the juice include a sore throat and inflammation in your gums.

If you're feeling under the weather, blackberry can provide you with a solution. Blackberry leaves can strengthen your immunity. This, in turn, can assist with breaking fevers and getting over colds.

A final consideration is that blackberry has been linked with some people having successfully overcome cancer.

MEDICINE PREPARATION

Tea: for blackberry tea, you'll need about a teaspoon of dried blackberry leaf pieces. You throw about a cup of boiling water on this and leave it to soak for five minutes. After five minutes (or longer if you prefer a stronger brew), it'll be ready to drink.

Decoction: a decoction will require a handful of dried blueberry leaves, flowers, or fruit. Put this in a small pot and bring it to a simmer on the stove. After half an hour of simmering, the decoction will be ready for use.

Tincture: the tincture will require that you fill a sealable jar with fresh blackberry leaves or berries and cover it with vodka or brandy. You seal off the jar and leave it somewhere (not in direct sun) to soak for four to six weeks, giving it a shake every few days. After this, strain out the leaves and refrigerate the tincture. It will remain good to use for more than a year.

Poultice: thoroughly mix in a tablespoon of infusion or decoction, or a teaspoon of tincture, with three tablespoons of coconut oil.

USING THE HERB

Tea: you can have tea up to three times a day.

Decoction: the decoction is ideal for mouth infections, mouth sores, and a sore throat. Simply gargle it or use it as a mouthwash, and you'll start feeling the benefits. It's also good for drinking, especially if you want to handle a runny stomach.

Tincture: taking a teaspoon at a time will give you a strong enough dose. It's especially effective for coughs and a sore throat.

Poultice: the poultice is great for remedying scaly skin.

SIDE EFFECTS AND WARNINGS

If your stomach tends to be sensitive, avoid drinking a blackberry product. It contains tannins, which can result in nausea on occasion. This is especially the case when using blackberry fruit rather than leaves or flowers.

FUN TIPS AND FACTS

Just like its sister fruit, the raspberry, the blackberry enjoyed pride of place in Greek mythology. It was said that it sprang from the bloodshed by Titans in their wars against the gods.

AUTHOR'S PERSONAL STORY

I've always loved going into my grandparents' garden and eating a handful of blackberries with sweat on my body, sun in my face, and wind blowing through my hair. Such a refreshing and nourishing fruit!

124
BLACK CHERRY

LATIN NAME

Prunus serotina

DESCRIPTION

The black cherry tree grows to a moderate height of 20 to 30 feet. The bark is gray, brown, or black, and it has a scaly texture. The bark turns up at the edges. Under the bark, there is a greenish layer that later changes to a creamy color with a green undertone. The branches growing out are green when younger and red-brown when older. The inner branch of the tree gives off an almond smell.

Leaves on this plant grow in an alternate arrangement. They're simple leaves that grow between two and six inches long. Their shape is lanceolate or ovate, and their tips are pointed. The margins of these leaves are finely toothed, with the teeth curving inward towards the tip. The leaves are green and shiny, and the lower surface is paler than the upper. In the fall, these leaves go yellow or orange. The leaves are on petioles, and they have glands at the base on either side of the petiole.

Flowers grow as white blossoms on a long inflorescence and smell sweet.

The fruit is a single drupe with a large pip inside. It's red when it's not ripe yet, and it's dark red or black, and it has a tart, bitter flavor when it's ripe.

HABITAT

Direct sunlight and chalky or limestone-rich soil is the ideal habitat for black cherries. It's normally found in wooded areas, especially on sloping or hilly wooded areas.

SEASON TO GATHER THE PLANT

April to June is when the flowers bloom if you wish to harvest the flowers. August to September is when it begins to seed, so this is the best time to gather the fruit.

PARTS OF THE PLANT TO USE AS MEDICINE

The fruit and the bark are both good for medicinal use.

BENEFITS AND PROPERTIES

Black cherry helps with muscle healing, especially after you've done heavy work or strenuous exercise. Further, it has a sedative effect, which can help with relaxing muscles. If you're having spasms in your muscles, you'll find black cherry can make it subside.

If you have trouble falling asleep, this can help you overcome your insomnia.

Issues related to the nasal area and the immune system can be overcome with black cherry. The benefits include reduction of coughing, drying out mucus, and soothing a sore throat. You can also use it to treat colds, fevers, and whooping cough.

Black cherry works wonders when used on the skin. It can firm out the skin, and it can dry out things oozing out of the skin, making it great for wound healing. Further, it reduces inflammation–though this isn't restricted to topical inflammation.

Black cherries are also beneficial to the digestive system. It has a stimulating effect on your gut, allowing your food to process better. When experiencing diarrhea, you can take it to slow down and stop the condition.

If you experience pain, this is one of the better herbal shrubs that you can use. It can be used to soothe pain both internally and topically. Gout is one example of a condition that can be alleviated by using it topically.

Lung issues can also be treated with this shrub. Bronchitis and asthma can both be treated with it.

Finally, you'll find that it can boost the heart overall. Your overall blood circulation can also be improved using it.

MEDICINE PREPARATION

Juice: Pit the black cherries and juice them. Add mint or other natural forms of flavor if the cherry juice is too sour or tart for your liking.

Tea: Dry and powder the bark. Add a teaspoon of this to a cup of boiling water and seep it for ten minutes. You can sweeten it or add natural flavor enhancers–such as pieces of fruit.

Tincture: You'll need an ounce of dried and ground bark, 16 ounces of vodka, and a large mason jar. Put the bark in the jar then add the vodka. Stir it together, seal the jar, and shake the jar. Leave it in a sunny place for a month to a month and a half. Shake it every few days. Strain out the bark and pour the tincture into dark glass bottles.

Ointment: for this, you'll need half a cup of the bark–dried out and crushed. Boil the bark in a saucepan filled with three cups of water for a few minutes. After this, bring it down to a simmer for approximately two hours. Remember to stir every fifteen minutes or so; otherwise, the bark might burn to the bottom of the pot. When the four hours are over, pour the remaining liquid through a fine strainer so that you don't get any annoying bark pieces in your ointment. Use about four tablespoons of the liquid and place it in a saucepan on very low heat. Place in two tablespoonfuls of beeswax, and two tablespoonfuls of coconut oil. Let these melt into the liquid, gently stirring it so that the ingredients combine. Pour it into containers of your choice and let it cool into a more solid form.

USING THE HERB

Juice: The juice won't last long, so consume it within a few days. You can have up to two tablespoons per day, preferably before bed. This will allow you to sleep better as it contains natural melatonin. Note: you can freeze it.

Tea: if you have a cough, take the tea three times a day.

Tincture: The tincture is great for improving digestion. You can have a half teaspoon daily, either directly or mixed in with water.

Ointment: This helps to tighten and firm up the skin.

SIDE EFFECTS AND WARNINGS

Allergic reactions can take place, especially when you're allergic to other fruits.

Don't use large quantities of black cherry as it can lead to toxicity in your body.

If you're on any type of medication, first consult with your healthcare provider before taking it. It produces interactions with several types of drugs.

Women who are pregnant or breastfeeding should avoid using this plant.

Ingesting the leaves can cause cyanide poisoning, so avoid using them.

FUN TIPS AND FACTS

American voodoo traditions have used cherries in love spells.

AUTHOR'S PERSONAL STORY

It's such an immune-boosting berry! It's rich in antioxidants and melatonin, which strengthen the immune system. I take it for illness prevention, and it always works! I haven't been sick in years because I bolster my health with herbal medicine.

125
BLUE VERVAIN

LATIN NAME

Verbena hastata

DESCRIPTION

If you take a look at what is going on underground, you'll find this plant produces rhizomes. The rhizomes allow the plant to spread through its direct area by sending out root systems horizontally that can then send up plant shoots. As a tip, if you want to grow blue vervain in your garden, you can dig up a rhizome in the wild to plant it at home.

The stem on this plant is hairy, and it has a square shape. It can also be either red or green in color. This plant grows between two and five feet tall.

The leaves are arranged, and they grow in pairs along the stems of the plant. The leaves are lanceolate with toothed margins, and they grow about six inches long and an inch wide. The flowers are purple-blue with lobed petals. They are clustered loosely along stems that are up to five inches long, and individual flowers are about a quarter-inch in diameter.

The fruit of this plant is a group of four red-brown, oblong nuts found inside the flower.

HABITAT

You'll find blue vervain in areas that have full or partial sun. They grow well in moist soil, so areas in which you'll find them include thickets, prairies, meadows, and along the sides of rivers.

SEASON TO GATHER THE PLANT

The flowers bloom in summer, making this the ideal time to harvest this plant.

PARTS OF THE PLANT TO USE AS MEDICINE

You can use the nut-like seeds of the plant as well as the roots, the leaves, and the flowers.

BENEFITS AND PROPERTIES

The topical application of this herb aids in treating cuts, sores, acne, and cramps.

A mental benefit you could experience by taking this plant is alleviation of depression.

Internal benefits include alleviation of cramps, as well as the remedying of ulcers, jaundice, headaches, fevers, and coughs.

There has also been some association between taking this herb and the reduction of tumors.

MEDICINE PREPARATION

Powder: Roast the seeds and ground them up.

Snuff: The flowers should be dried and crushed into a powder.

Essential oil: Use four handfuls of fresh blue vervain (cleaned well first). Put it in half a pot of boiling water and cover it with the pot's lid upside down (so that the evaporated oils condensate and drip back down into the pot). Simmer this until the water level has dropped to a quarter of the pot. Switch it off and let it cool. Place the pot in the refrigerator overnight and scoop off the filmy residue the following day. This filmy residue is the congealed essential oil. Put it in a dark glass bottle.

Infusion: Place a handful of fresh or dried blue vervain in a glass of water. Let it soak for four hours, then strain out the vervain. The liquid is now ready to drink.

Tincture: Fill a jar with cleaned, fresh vervain. Cover it with vodka and seal the jar. Put it in a dark, cool space for six weeks, shaking it every four days or so. Strain the tincture into a dark glass jar.

USING THE HERB

Powder: The powder can be mixed into flour. It can also be mixed into smoothies and juices.

Snuff: When experiencing a nosebleed, use the snuff to stem it.

Essential oil: This is powerful, so you should dilute it into water or oil. Don't use more than a few drops per application.

Infusion: Use it within a few days.

Tincture: It will last for years.

SIDE EFFECTS AND WARNINGS

It can exacerbate anemia, especially iron-deficiency anemia.

Interactions with drugs can occur when taking this herb, especially with hormone medication and blood pressure drugs.

If you have a large amount of blue vervain, you could experience diarrhea and vomiting.

FUN TIPS AND FACTS

In ancient Egyptian mythology, vervain was sacred to the goddess Isis. Whenever she cried, vervain grew where her tears hit the ground.

AUTHOR'S PERSONAL STORY

I had this patient once, an older woman. When she walked into my studio for the first time her breath was so heavy and fast, her voice was shaking, she seemed very confused and out of herself–she was suffering from anxiety!

From the moment I prescribed her blue vervain, she changed. On the next appointment, 1 month later, she seemed like another person; calmer, slower, more present, and focused.

126
BORAGE

LATIN NAME

orago officinalis

DESCRIPTION

Borage is a plant that grows up to 36 inches tall and 24 inches wide. Its stems are hairy and prickly.

Borage leaves are between a rectangle or oval in shape and arranged alternately. Their margins are wavy, and their veins are visible on the surface of the leaf. They grow between two and six inches long, and y find there are short, stiff hairs that get quite prickly when mature growing on the leaves and stems. These hairs give a silver shimmer to the plant. In the fall, the leaves go brown and yellow, while in the summer and spring they're bright green.

The flowers are blue, but on occasion, you can find borage with white blossoms. They grow as drooping clusters on red stalks and have a star-like shape. The five-pointed petals are slightly hairy, and a short purple-black column protrudes from the center.

Its seeds grow above ground, allowing the plant to self-seed.

HABITAT

Borage likes direct sunlight and can tolerate slightly dry soil. It commonly grows in disturbed soil and on cultivated land.

SEASON TO GATHER THE PLANT

Spring and summer is normally the right time to harvest. When it's flowering, harvesting the flowers will keep the plant from deteriorating as quickly.

PARTS OF THE PLANT TO USE AS MEDICINE

Its flowers and leaves, as well as the oil from its seeds, are used as medicine

BENEFITS AND PROPERTIES

Borage can help purify your blood and prevent heart disease and strokes. You can also use it to treat adrenal deficiency, manage diabetes, regulate urine flow, and alleviate premenstrual syndrome.

In addition to all this, borage can increase your lung function, prevent lung inflammation, help manage asthma, and mitigate acute respiratory distress syndrome. You can use it to get over colds and bronchitis thanks to the way it promotes perspiration, and it treats coughs and fevers.

Topically, this herb can treat skin conditions including eczema, rashes, and itching. It can also reduce pain and inflammation in joints that have rheumatoid arthritis, and it can be used to reduce gum inflammation.

There are multiple other baby-related benefits to using borage like increased breast milk production. Additionally, can help premature infants grow and become stronger, and it aids in nervous system development

You can use it to manage stress and depression, and it can help with symptoms of ADHD (attention deficit-hyperactivity disorder). It may help manage alcoholism as well.

It also has a sedative effect, which is great if you have trouble sleeping.

MEDICINE PREPARATION

Oil: Cold pressing the seeds gives the highest quality results.

Tea: Use a quarter teaspoon of chopped-up fresh leaves or flowers. Put this in a cup of boiling water and leave it to steep for 10 minutes. Strain and drink.

Tincture: Fill a jar with fresh flowers and cover them with vodka. Seal the jar and put it in a dark space for a month. Strain out the flowers and pour the tincture into a dark glass bottle.

Infusion: Use a cup of water and a quarter cup of fresh, bruised leaves. Put the leaves in the water and leave it to steep for about four hours. Strain out the leaves, and it should be ready to use.

Poultice: Mash up some fresh borage and mix it in with a tiny bit of water and flour. It should be thick and sticky (the measurements of the ingredients aren't so important). Put it in a cloth and wrap the cloth around the affected body part.

USING THE HERB

Oil: This is good for external use (by rubbing it onto affected parts of your skin), as well as internal use (such as taking a tablespoonful).

Tea: The tea is great for stress.

Tincture: This is perfect to use for internal benefits.

Infusion: The infusion can be drunk, or you can use it as a wash.

Poultice: Use this for inflammation, soreness, bug bites, or stings.

SIDE EFFECTS AND WARNINGS

It's best not to use the oil for long periods. There are potential side effects that haven't been fully studied yet.

People can also experience allergic reactions when using borage.

When using borage while breastfeeding or on your baby, you'll need to consult a healthcare expert first. Some types of borage contain pyrrolizidine alkaloids, which are poisonous to humans.

Pyrrolizidine alkaloids damage the liver, so avoid borage if you have liver issues and you're not sure if the plant you have is a variety that doesn't contain these alkaloids. Further, avoid it if you're on any sort of liver medication, as there could be interactions.

Don't use borage if you bleed or bruise easily. It can exacerbate these issues. You should also avoid it if you're on medication that slows blood clotting.

Individuals taking phenothiazines should also avoid borage. Phenothiazines are included in drugs that prevent nausea and in some psychiatric drugs.

FUN TIPS AND FACTS

Borage is sometimes referred to as the 'herb of gladness'. The Roman scholar Pliny the Elder believed that borage was the 'Nepenthe' in Homer's Odyssey, which induced absolute forgetfulness when infused in wine.

AUTHOR'S PERSONAL STORY

This plant combined with a couple of others and a lifestyle transformation helped my mother a lot with depression during her menopause.

127
BURDOCK

LATIN NAME

Arctium

DESCRIPTION

Burdock can grow rather large, reaching heights of 10 feet. It's a plant with a central stem that's fleshy and round and thinner stems coming out at various points.

The leaves are alternating, and there are large basal leaves, which can grow up to three feet wide, in the plant's first year. As it grows, large heart-shaped leaves with downy bottom surfaces grow from peduncles on the branches. The top surface of the leaves is green, and the bottom surface is whitish.

The plant has a combination of sweet (especially while flowering) and slightly bitter scents.

A tall flower stalk grows between three and six feet tall in the second year of growth, allowing a cluster of pinkish-purple tassel-like flowers that grow on top of spiked, circular seed pods. The flower heads are about an inch across. The spiky seed pod dries out when the flower dies and hooks onto animals or people that pass by. It can be quite irritating if it hooks onto your skin.

HABITAT

It likes soil that's rich in nitrogen, and it prefers full or partial sun. It grows well in disturbed areas.

SEASON TO GATHER THE PLANT

Between July and September is when to harvest the flower, and September to October is best for seed harvesting. The roots can be harvested in the fall without inflicting too much damage on the plant. The leaves can be harvested at any time. It's best to harvest from the plant during its second year (once the central flower stalk has shot up) because harvesting from it in the first year may prevent it from growing the stalk–it's a plant that lives for two years.

PARTS OF THE PLANT TO USE AS MEDICINE

The roots, seeds, leaves, and flowers can be used.

BENEFITS AND PROPERTIES

It's good at combating fungi, bacteria, blood impurities, toxicity, and fluid retention. It also assists with feeding the healthy bacteria in your body. You can use it to get over constipation, regulate urination better, lessen flatulence, and improve digestion.

Burdock is good for overall skin health. This herb can help with inflammation as well as itchy and scaly skin. In addition, it can help regulate the sebaceous glands that produce oil, which is great for acne.

You can also use burdock for increasing bile production, increasing perspiration (and thereby preventing overheating), and encouraging the flow of lymph in your body.

MEDICINE PREPARATION

Tincture: Use two-thirds of a jar of chopped burdock root and cover it with vodka. Close the jar and put it in a cool, dark place for three months. Shake the jar occasionally until the three months come to an end. Strain the tincture into a dark glass bottle, and it'll be ready to use.

Tea: Use a tablespoon of the chopped fresh root, or two tablespoons of chopped and aged dried root. Boil three cups of water in a pot and put in the burdock. Let it simmer for half an hour, then steep for another 20 minutes once the stove is off. Strain out any of the roots, then drink the tea.

Oil: You'll need to break the seed heads and take out the seeds. Dry them and crush them. Use a ratio of one part seed powder and three parts extra virgin olive oil, placing it in a jar. It'll be ready to use instantly. Cover the jar with a cloth as the mixture needs to breathe. Store it in a refrigerator.

USING THE HERB

Tincture: It's very potent, so you should only have a few drops per day.

Tea: You can drink the whole pot in a day. Just make sure that you space it out throughout the day because having too much of it in one go will cause you to urinate a lot.

Oil: Use this for external purposes.

SIDE EFFECTS AND WARNINGS

Burdock can cause allergic reactions, and you should avoid high doses to prevent toxicity. Further, be extra certain when you identify it because it looks similar to belladonna nightshade, which has strong toxic effects.

Avoid using this plant during pregnancy and while breastfeeding. Further, avoid it while trying to get pregnant.

Avoid it when dehydrated, as it increases urination. Also, avoid it if you're on water pills, as it may make the water pills too strong.

FUN TIPS AND FACTS

Burdock extract can enhance sexual functioning and can increase sexual desire, so it can be used as an aphrodisiac.

AUTHOR'S PERSONAL STORY

It's crazy the amount and size of pimples people get when taking this plant's tincture! It's such a deep detox for the body.

CATNIP

LATIN NAME

Nepeta cataria

DESCRIPTION

Catnip plants can vary slightly in size from species to species, but at full size, most species grow up to three feet tall. You'll find that the stems tend to be thick with a hairy surface.

The leaves on a catnip plant tend to be toothed and hairy. The leaves have the shape of a heart-like oval, and while the leaves are silvery green for most catnip species, in some cases, the leaves can be dark green. The plant has a definitive minty smell to it. The flavor, on the other hand, is either grassy or woody.

The flowers occur in clusters on the stem, with each flower on the cluster having small tubular openings. Flower color is the main difference between the various catnip species. They're mainly white, but some have a violet tinge, and others are completely violet.

HABITAT

They can do well in soil with low nutrition. Gravelly or sandy soil is best. Sunlight should be direct, ideally. It grows in a wide array of areas, ranging from riverbanks to dumping grounds.

SEASON TO GATHER THE PLANT

It grows all year long, meaning that you'll be able to gather a harvest of the leaves and twigs the whole year round. The best season to harvest, however, is when the flowers are in bloom from July to October.

PARTS OF THE PLANT TO USE AS MEDICINE

The flowers, roots, and leaves can be used.

BENEFITS AND PROPERTIES

Catnip tea has a relaxing effect thanks to the chemical nepetalactone present in the plant. This chemical has a sedative effect when ingested, helping you with anxiety and insomnia. This is different in cases when the root is used, under which circumstances, catnip acts as a stimulant.

Your gastrointestinal system may benefit the catnip tea's ability to ease indigestion, gas, and stomach discomforts. Water retention is also reduced by taking catnip tea because there is a diuretic quality to the catnip herb. Similarly, it can help expel the placenta after giving birth as well as stimulate the uterus in cases of delayed menstrual cycles.

Other conditions that could be alleviated by catnip tea are fevers, hives, coughs, and viruses. In other words, there is an immune-system-boosting effect brought about by consuming the tea. Arthritis sufferers, be aware that this tea can aid in soothing this condition too.

MEDICINE PREPARATION

Tea: Use a sprig of catnip and put it in a cup of boiling water. Leave it to steep for 10 minutes before removing the catnip. The tea will now be ready to drink.

Tincture: Use a jar full of chopped-up fresh catnip and vodka. Put the catnip into a jar and cover it with vodka. Close the jar and place it in a cool, dark place. Leave it there for three months, giving it a shake weekly and adding a bit of vodka if the level has dropped. When the three months have passed by, you can strain the catnip out and place the tincture in a jar.

Infused oil: Finely chop up fresh catnip (enough to cover the bottom of a casserole dish) and place it on the bottom of a casserole dish. Cover it with olive oil, forming a layer of oil above the plant matter. Place it in the oven for two hours at 200 degrees Fahrenheit. Let it cool, then strain the oil into a jar.

USING THE HERB

Tea: Catnip Tea has a very relaxing effect on the body and mind.

Tincture: The tincture is great for sleep.

Infused oil: Store the infused oil in your refrigerator. You can use it for food purposes, internal medicinal purposes, or topical medicinal purposes.

SIDE EFFECTS AND WARNINGS

In some, it will have the opposite reaction on their gastrointestinal tract, creating stomach upsets.

For women with heavy menstruation or with pelvic inflammatory disease, catnip should be avoided. As catnip stimulates the uterus, this could intensify these conditions. And on a related note, pregnant women should avoid catnip too. The stimulation of the uterus could result in premature labor.

Catnip can cause headaches, so cease using it if you get a headache after each use. Other light conditions that could be brought about by using catnip include an increased urge to urinate or an increase in sweat-the result of its diuretic nature. You may also note that you're a bit more sleepy due to the relaxing chemical found in the plant.

An important note is that you shouldn't use catnip near times you've been scheduled for surgery. There could be interference with your central nervous system, which would make your surgery riskier. And in the same vein, it could also interfere with anesthesia, which also increases the risk of surgery complications.

FUN TIPS AND FACTS

When a cat sniffs the leaves of the plant, it experiences a hallucinogenic 'high.' This can last for 10 minutes. If the cat swallows the catnip, it acts as a sedative, making the cat sleepy and calm.

AUTHOR'S PERSONAL STORY

I've been giving catnip to my cats a few times to see if the effects are only a myth or if they're real. I mixed it into their food, and—seriously—within five minutes of eating the meal I prepared for them with catnip, all three of my cats were asleep.

129
CHICKWEED

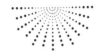

LATIN NAME

Stellaria

DESCRIPTION

Chickweed is normally found as a ground crawler. It forms dense thickets the closer it gets to full maturity, with the different plants pushing up against each other so that the mass is a few inches in height. Chickweed has a single row of hairs going up each stem. This is a great way of identifying the common variety of chickweed.

Chickweed has an opposite leafing arrangement. The leaves have an ovular shape, and they taper to a point. The leaves are quite small, and while common chickweed doesn't have hairy leaves, other varieties might.

The flowers are white. Beware the difference in coloration between scarlet pimpernel and chickweed. Scarlet pimpernel has red flowers, and it has reddish splotches under its leaves. Noting this difference is important because scarlet pimpernel is poisonous and looks rather similar to chickweed. Not only that, but it sometimes grows among chickweed. Chickweed flowers are small, with hairy sepals and a hairy flower stem. It looks like there are 10 petals, but there are only 5. It looks like this because there's a deep cleft in each petal that gives it a 'v' shape. The flowers will eventually be closed up by the sepals. The sepals have hairs growing on them, so this gives the capsule that forms a hairy look. The capsule allows several small, brown seeds to grow inside.

HABITAT

It prefers damp soil and full to partial sun. It often grows on agricultural land and disturbed land.

SEASON TO GATHER THE PLANT

The plant is best gathered in January and February. At this point, there should be thick and sustainable patches to harvest from. You may already find some patches in November and December, but at that point, the chickweed will most likely still be young, and the clumps will most likely be patchy. As a note, the plant tends to die off in the summer when the weather gets too hot and then returns in the fall when things cool down once again.

PARTS OF THE PLANT TO USE AS MEDICINE

You can use its stems, leaves, and flowers.

BENEFITS AND PROPERTIES

It's highly effective for topical use. Use it for diaper rash, burns, insect bites, wounds, psoriasis, rashes, joint pain, and eczema.

You can use it to handle conditions like rabies, asthma, respiratory illness, and peptic ulcers. It's an effective blood cleanser. It can be used to reduce menstrual pain as well.

Due to its high vitamin content (including vitamin C), it handles scurvy well.

MEDICINE PREPARATION

Tea: this can be made by steeping two to three tablespoons of chickweed in boiling water for a few minutes, then straining the solids out and drinking the liquid.

Infused oil: to make this, you simply soak the chickweed in a carrier oil–choosing one that you're not allergic to and that affects your skin well. Ensure the chickweed is covered completely (you can even shake it to ensure it's properly mixed in. Leave the chickweed to soak in it for a few weeks (two at a minimum), shaking it daily so that it infuses into the carrier oil. After a few weeks, you can strain out the chickweed bits and the oil will be ready for use.

Eating it fresh

Drying out chickweed is another effective way of using it. When dried, you can add it into your food or various herbal remedies, such as poultices. You can also use dried chickweed for making tea; you don't only need to use fresh chickweed.

Powder: the powder is mainly used in teas, but it can also be mixed into other remedies. I like mixing it into honey and using a teaspoon of the mixture when experiencing one of the conditions it alleviates, such as constipation.

USING THE HERB

Tea: you can use the tea to reduce inflammation. You can also use it as a diuretic. The diuretic property of chickweed tea has led some to use it effectively for weight loss. Other benefits you could experience from this type of tea are pain relief and a calming effect.

Infused oil: you can add the infused oil to your bath or apply it directly to your skin. This is beneficial both for your skin and for your mental health.

Eating it fresh: this is great for a daily health boost. The high amount of minerals in it makes it great for healthy salads.

SIDE EFFECTS AND WARNINGS

Some individuals develop a mild rash when applying it to their skin. This isn't a common side effect, but it is a possibility. Further, some may have allergies to it, so if you've found that you're having any indications of an allergic reaction to this weed, then discontinue its use, please.

Also, if you consume it to excess, you may experience some toxicity due to the nitrate salts and saponins present in the plant. Indications of toxicity include nausea, dizziness, weakness, and cyanosis, amongst others. This won't be a problem if you consume it in moderation, and in many cases, the excess needs to be quite extreme for toxicity to become a factor.

FUN TIPS AND FACTS

In European folklore and magic, chickweed was used to promote fidelity, attract love, and maintain relationships. Chickweed carried around was used to draw the attention of a loved one or ensure the fidelity of one's partner.

Whereas sailors used chickweed vinegar to prevent scurvy when fresh citrus wasn't available.

AUTHOR'S PERSONAL STORY

I've tried it on people with asthma and it did miracles! Within a short period, they'd have much fewer attacks. Nature is such a powerful medicine!

CHICORY

LATIN NAME

 ichorium intybus

DESCRIPTION

Specimens most commonly grow between two and five feet in height. A stem will grow out of the basal leaf rosette a while into the growing season. The lower part of this stem is hairy, whereas the higher parts of the stem have no hair and black coloration. It has a long taproot, which is often harvested as a coffee replacement. When cut, this root normally exudes a bitter, milky white liquid.

The basal leaves are arranged in a rosette. On the stalk, there are a few scattered small leaves. The rosette basal leaves have toothed margins and an oblong shape. They are rather flat and tend to be between three and six inches long. The smaller leaves growing from the stem have an oval shape, are lighter green, and have a shiny surface. These smaller leaves are only about an inch long.

The flowers are usually blue or purple, but there are some pink and white varieties. The flowers normally bloom between July and October. They will open in the early morning when in blooming season, and then close once the sun gets too intense. After closing, they'll lose color and wilt. The flower generally has up to 20 petals, all tapering to a frayed tip.

The plant produces about 3,000 seeds, which get scattered across the area so that the following year's plants may grow.

HABITAT

Chicory grows—for all intents and purposes—as a weed would. You'll find that it flourishes in open fields and enjoys growing in waste areas.

SEASON TO GATHER THE PLANT

Fall is usually the best time to gather this plant. This is because most of the time, the harvesting is being done largely to get the taproot. By waiting until the plant has seeded in the fall, there won't be any sustainability issues that result. Furthermore, harvesting the taproot in the hot summer might lead to a bitter-tasting root. You'll also need to take care to not damage the root while harvesting, as it's easier to use the root when there aren't dirt-filled nicks in it.

The stem, on the other hand, is best harvested in the spring when the plant is still young and the stem isn't too hard. If this is done, it's good to only harvest part of the stand so that the rest of the stand will be able to continue its life cycle as per usual.

Similarly, also harvest the leaves of the plant when it's still young so that you don't get the bitter taste associated with more mature leaves.

The advice is the opposite for flowers. It's best to harvest the flowers close to the end of summer when they're at full maturity.

PARTS OF THE PLANT TO USE AS MEDICINE

The whole plant is used. That said, the root is normally the main attraction. You can, however, also use the stem, the leaves, and the flowers for medicinal applications.

BENEFITS AND PROPERTIES

Chicory root contains beta-carotene, which is an antioxidant that converts into vitamin A inside of the body.

Benefits that have been associated with chicory include better urine production (i.e. it's a diuretic) and a mild laxative effect that alleviates constipation. Stimulation of bile production (thus easing gallbladder conditions) is also a common effect of using this herb. You can ease liver disorders, along with conditions such as stomach upsets and a loss of appetite, by using this herb. One of the most interesting benefits that have come to light is that it has been associated with improvements in people fighting cancer.

There are also major benefits when it comes to the gastrointestinal tract. Firstly, it helps boost the production of healthy gut bacteria, which in turn helps to reduce the number of unhealthy gut bacteria present in your system. Not only this, but it has also been noted that this herb can increase mineral absorption. It doesn't only help keep the body healthy, but it can also help get the body into shape. Chicory has been noted to help reduce hormones that cause you to feel hungry, thus helping with appetite regulation. Further, a reduction in blood sugar has also been seen to result from using this herb.

As for topical use, you'll find that swelling and inflammation of the skin are reduced.

MEDICINE PREPARATION

Root: The root isn't only used for medicinal purposes. The normal use is to create a dried powder that's used as a hot drink that has a flavor similar to coffee. This is achieved most easily by using a food dehydrator and placing it on the 'nuts' setting. The chopped-up root is then left to dehydrate, and then you can crush the dried root. You can also dry it out in the oven. To achieve this, simply place the chopped-up root pieces (about an inch long each) onto an oven tray, and leave them in the oven for five to seven hours at 170 degrees Fahrenheit.

Tonic: you can make a tonic from the dried plant by steeping its leaves, flowers, and pieces of the stem in vinegar or alcohol for a month. When the month is complete, you can strain out the solid bits and use the liquid as an effective tonic.

USING THE HERB

Root: The powdered root is a good caffeine-free alternative for coffee.

Tonic: The tonic lasts long. You'll only need a few drops at a time.

SIDE EFFECTS AND WARNINGS

Some will have an allergy to this herb. If you notice allergic reactions occurring, even if mild, it's better to look for alternative herbs to handle the condition you're trying to maintain or for food purposes.

As for the increase in bile production, while this is useful for some of us, it may be a problem if you have gallstones. Consult your medical practitioner if you have or are predisposed to gallstones, and you want to use this herb.

FUN TIPS AND FACTS

Since chicory opens its flowers only between five and eleven in the morning, Carl von Linné (1707–1778) included it in the Floral Clock which he had established in the Botanical Garden at Uppsala.

AUTHOR'S PERSONAL STORY

When I stopped drinking coffee because it was affecting my well-being, I replaced it with a cup of chicory 'coffee.' I love brewing my chicory coffee every morning and enjoying it with an audiobook. It prevents me from having any digestive issues all day long.

131
CLEAVERS

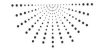

LATIN NAME

alium aparine

DESCRIPTION

The plant grows to approximately five feet in height. It is also rather large and bushy.

The leaves of this plant are arranged in whorls on the end of stems. Each whorl has eight leaflets, each of which is lanceolate. They have prickles on them that give your hand a sticky feeling when you come into contact with the leaf. The scent you get from the plant once you've cut it and left it to dry is that of freshly-mown hay.

The flowers are very small, and they're shaped like small stars and tend to be white or greenish. They bloom in spring and summer, growing in clusters of two to three flowers per flower head. The stem bearing the flower cluster will come out of the axis of the leaf.

The fruit takes the form of hooked burrs that grow in clusters (normally up to three in a cluster). They tend to hook onto people and animals as a form of dispersing for propagation.

HABITAT

Wet areas are generally its preferred location. They grow all over the world, and the Northeastern United States is no exception.

SEASON TO GATHER THE PLANT

I would suggest that you gather the plant in May and June as it's flowering. This is the best time, in my opinion, as the flowers are great for medicinal purposes.

PARTS OF THE PLANT TO USE AS MEDICINE

The leaves and flowers of cleavers are generally the best parts to use for herbal medicine.

BENEFITS AND PROPERTIES

There's a long list of benefits that you could get from using cleavers. This includes benefits from topical application. When applied topically, you can alleviate a range of skin conditions, such as eczema. It's also a great inflammation reducer. A further topical use that you could benefit from is wound care. Using it on wounds can help to speed the wound's recovery and can reduce inflammation around the wound.

There are benefits to the body's excretory system. It helps ease constipation and can increase urine output. It also increases sweat production, which goes hand in hand with its detoxification properties.

There is a special benefit for women. This herb helps stimulate the uterus, which can in turn lead to less intense menstrual cramps. Just don't use it while you're pregnant because you don't want to stimulate your uterus and accidentally cause premature labor.

There are also a few specific conditions that can be reduced by using cleavers. This includes tonsillitis, fevers, swollen lymph nodes, jaundice, and body spasms.

One of the most enjoyable benefits for me on a personal level is that it helps boost my energy levels. This is great for when you're starting to feel lethargic or burned out.

MEDICINE PREPARATION

Tea: The tea is best made by adding two to three teaspoons of the wet or dried herb to a cup of boiling water, and allowing it to steep for 10 to 15 minutes. Once steeped, strain it and enjoy.

Tinctures: Soak a handful of the fresh cleaver in alcohol (I normally use vodka) over a few nights. Strain out the plant mass. You can then take a small amount with an eyedropper under your tongue when needed.

Pulp: Apply the pulp directly to bug bites or wounds for instant relief.

Wash: Make a very strong cup of tea with either fresh or dried cleaver. Then strain out the pulp and apply the wash to skin that's not feeling well (e.g. itchy or inflamed).

USING THE HERB

Tea: The tea can be a good energy booster.

Tincture: The tincture can last for months, or sometimes even years. Just remember to keep it in a dark bottle.

Pulp: The pulp should only be used once, otherwise things could become unhygienic.

Wash: You can use it on wounds for a quick and relieving clean.

SIDE EFFECTS AND WARNINGS

The only real side effect I can mention here is an allergic reaction. Other than that, there are no known side effects of note.

FUN TIPS AND FACTS

It's possible to freeze cleaver juice for a few months. This way you'll be able to have a juice stock for poultices etc. even when the rest of your cleavers plant stock has dried out.

AUTHOR'S PERSONAL STORY

Since ancient times, this plant has been used as a diuretic.

When I help people detox, I add this plant sometimes, and after a month the person comes back to me and looks changed—slimmer, more energized, and overall healthier.

132
COMFREY

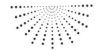

LATIN NAME

Symphytum officinale

DESCRIPTION

Comfrey grows between two and five feet high, and it reaches about two feet in width.

The roots are black in appearance, and when you break one open, you'll see that the inside is white and exudes juices.

The leaves have an alternate arrangement closer to the base of the plant and then transition to an opposite arrangement higher up on the plant. The leaves are larger closer to the base and get smaller higher up on the plant. The leaves closest to the base can be up to eight inches long. The leaves at the base also have a slightly different shape than those higher up on the plant. Lower down, the leaves have a broad base and taper to a tip, whereas higher up, the leaves tend to be broad along the whole margin (i.e. the leaves are oblong) and only narrow near the ends (base and tip). The leaves have a hairy texture above and below, but they are slightly more hairy on the underside. These stiff hairs give the leaves a rough texture. The veins on the leaves have a net arrangement, and the margins are smooth.

The flowers can vary quite a bit in color. The most common varieties are white, cream, and purple. But you can get other colors, and you can also get striped varieties with more than one color. The flowers grow in rather dense clusters. Individual flowers are small and have a bell shape to them. The various comfrey species can cross-pollinate with each other, which is one of the reasons there's such a diversity of color arrangements.

Its fruits are smooth on the surface and angle to a concave base. They are small and have a brown-black color.

HABITAT

Comfrey prefers to be in damp and shady spaces. This makes them most common near rivers and streams. You'll also be able to find them in woods and meadows.

SEASON TO GATHER THE PLANT

You can gather the plant multiple times a year because it's hardy and regrows even when you trim it within two inches of the ground. The first harvest is possible at the start of spring. After that, you'll be able to re-harvest the same plant approximately every month and a half. It's suggested that you only gather the leaves. You can gather the roots too, but the leaves aren't as strong, making them a better choice.

PARTS OF THE PLANT TO USE AS MEDICINE

The leaves and roots can both be used. It is, however, better to use the leaves as the roots contain a higher concentration of a chemical that can have toxic effects on the human body.

BENEFITS AND PROPERTIES

This herb can be used to improve ulcers, coughs, diarrhea, bloody urine, heavy menstruation, hemorrhoids, gum disease, and a sore throat. It's best to not overuse it for these internal applications. So if you use it for internal applications by drinking the tea, make the tea mild and don't use it often.

Topical application is where this herb shines. It works particularly well for reducing pain. This applies to pain in the joints, such as with arthritis and gout, as well as pain in the muscles. It's also effective at improving blood circulation, healing wounds (use on closed wounds, not open wounds), and repairing bruises.

MEDICINE PREPARATION

Tea: Make a tea with the herb by steeping it in warm or boiling water for a few minutes. Don't use much of the herb in one cup—I find that a teaspoon's worth of shredded leaves is sufficiently effective.

Ointment/cream/poultices/embrocations: I suggest drying out the leaves and then crushing them into a fine powder first. Once this is done, adding a small amount of the powder to a fatty substance (such as lanolin or coconut oil) and mixing it in evenly will do the trick. [Note: embrocation refers to a pain-relieving rub.]

USING THE HERB

Tea: Don't take a lot of tea. It can become toxic when used internally.

Ointment: This herb is especially effective for external applications. Pharmaceutical companies even use it as an ingredient in healing creams. I find that it's particularly effective when applied externally to painful parts of the skin and muscles. That said, only use it when needed as everyday use can cause toxicity.

SIDE EFFECTS AND WARNINGS

Comfrey contains pyrrolizidine alkaloids, which have a very strong effect on the human body. Negative effects that can result from these alkaloids include liver damage, cancer, and lung damage. The Food and Drug Administration has suggested that products containing comfrey that are used for oral consumption be taken off the market.

The root contains an especially high concentration of these chemicals, making it preferable to use the leaves (as they have a lower concentration).

You should also avoid using it on open sores or broken skin, as well as avoid using it for protracted periods.

FUN TIPS AND FACTS

If you plan on growing this herb in your homestead or garden, you'll see that the plants around it tend to do quite well. This is because comfrey encourages the presence of earthworms in the soil surrounding it.

The Ancient Greeks were already onto this use of the herb. 'Comfrey' comes from an Ancient Greek word meaning "to make grow together or bind."

AUTHOR'S PERSONAL STORY

There was this one gentleman who came to me for help recovering from bumps and bruises he got while playing football. I gave him a comfrey poultice to use on his bruises and sore muscles, and he never visited me again. When I bumped into him a few years later, he said that it helped so much that he's had a small container of comfrey poultice on standby for bumps and bruises ever since.

133
COMMON MALLOW

LATIN NAME

Malva sylvestris

DESCRIPTION

The plant can get up to about three feet tall. It is, however, a creeper. This means that it might not reach its full height, but rather, it spreads along the ground. The stem on this species of mallow has fine hairs on its surface. Common mallow stems branch in all directions, like any crawler.

The leaves of common mallow are alternate in their arrangement. They have palmate leaves that are approximately two and a half inches long and three inches wide. The leaves have a circular, kidney-like shape, with five or more shallow lobes. The leaves' margins are toothed, but not very deep, giving each tooth a rounded appearance. These leaves are attached to very long petioles (twice as long as the leaf itself). The leaves are a bright green color and have very fine hairs along their surface. Note that the leaves also have a deep indent at the base, thus they don't have a flat appearance.

The flowers are violet or whitish. The white flowers sometimes have light violet lines running along their length. There is a unique musky scent to the common mallow, and you'll find some perfumes that try to imitate this scent. Flowers on common mallow grow at the end of the peduncle, normally having between one and three flowers per peduncle. They are rather small—about three-quarters of an inch in width. There are five petals on each flower, with each petal having a small groove or notch at the tip. There are five calyxes below the petals, each shaped like an egg or oval at the tip. There is one female part (pistil) in each flower and a group of male parts (stamen) inside the flower.

The fruit of common mallow looks like a wheel with a tire on it. It is small and contains flat seeds, with the outer layer of seeds sometimes being hairy.

HABITAT

You can find them in sunny areas that are mildly moist to slightly dry. They enjoy areas that have been disturbed and flourish at establishing themselves in these areas. You'll find that they commonly occur in fields and open areas such as farm lots.

SEASON TO GATHER THE PLANT

The flowers generally bloom in the summer, although some bloom in the spring or autumn. You can harvest these flowers anytime you notice them in bloom.

As for the leaves, they are best gathered in spring when the leaves are still young. If you're planning on gathering leaves after the spring, stick to harvesting softer, younger-looking leaves.

The roots are best harvested over the fall period. This is because the plant is dormant during the fall.

PARTS OF THE PLANT TO USE AS MEDICINE

You can use the roots, the leaves, and the flowers. All three are practical when used medically.

BENEFITS AND PROPERTIES

The best benefits are those you'll get from topical application. This includes skin soothing, wound healing, and inflammation reduction. The benefits you may expect from internal use are diarrhea relief, bladder problem relief, and upset stomach relief. The mouth and respiratory tract can also benefit from the use of this plant. When using it for this purpose, you'll be able to treat conditions such as throat irritations, dry coughing, colds, and bronchitis.

MEDICINE PREPARATION

Tea: You can use the flowers, the roots, or the leaves for a good cup of mallow tea. Place three to four teaspoons of dried mallow into a cup of boiling water. After steeping it for 10 minutes, you can remove the dried mallow bits. For internal use, you would drink it at this point. For external use, you would soak a cloth in it and apply the cloth to an ailing area on your body surface, or you could splash some of the tea on directly.

Pulp: the best pulp is obtained by crushing fresh mallow bits together and applying them to the afflicted area of your body. You could also mix it in with natural fats and oils, but I tend to apply the pulp directly.

Cold infusion: a cold infusion just might be the most effective method of using mallow, both internally and externally. Take a decent amount of dried mallow (approximately 2 tablespoons) and steep it in a quart of water overnight. You will then be able to drink from it for internal benefits or soak a cloth in it and apply it to yourself for external use.

USING THE HERB

Tea: This tea can be used for both internal and external use.

Pulp: Placing the pulp in a rag and placing it over the afflicted area can also do the trick. In this case, you would be using it as a compress.

Cold fusion: This is the most effective preparation, so I suggest it. It's particularly effective when you're working through a cold and fever.

SIDE EFFECTS AND WARNINGS

The main side effects are nausea, diarrhea, and indigestion. That said, this is normally linked to an allergy, so if you experience any of these three while using it, you may find that you're allergic to the plant.

FUN TIPS AND FACTS

Mallow has been used by the Iroquois as a love medicine. It's eaten and then vomited up as a ritual act.

AUTHOR'S PERSONAL STORY

As a kid, I used to hike in the mountains a lot with my parents. Whenever I got cut, if mallow was around, my parents would put it directly on the wound, and it promoted my healing.

134
CRAMP BARK

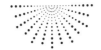

LATIN NAME

 *iburnum opulus*

DESCRIPTION

Cramp bark is a large (13 to 15-foot-tall) shrub. Its leaves are three-lobed and between two and four inches long and wide. They have a wrinkled surface with their venation impressed quite sharply. The margins are rough and jagged, and the leaves are green in budding and mature stages then transition to a purple color in the fall.

The flowers come in a flat-headed cluster, and each floret has five white petals. The flowers on the outer part of the head are larger (approximately half an inch in diameter), and the flowers in the center are smaller (about a fifth of an inch in diameter). Only the central flowers are fertile. The plant is a monocot, so there aren't separate male and female shrubs.

The fruit is a small, translucent red drupe with a diameter of approximately a third of an inch. The drupes grow in clusters that hang down. There is only one seed in each drupe.

The bark is brown and has a slightly cracked texture, and sometimes you'll find brown warts on its surface.

The shrub has a slightly bitter scent to it–especially the bark. The taste is also bitter, including the taste of the fruit.

HABITAT

Most cramp bark shrubs are found in nutrient-rich, moist soil and exposed to direct sun or partly in the shade. This means you'll mostly find them at the edge of forests, in woodlands, or in scrublands.

SEASON TO GATHER THE PLANT

The bark is best gathered in early spring or early fall before the leaves have started changing color to purple.

Flowers can be harvested in late spring and early summer.

Fruit is ready for harvesting in the fall.

PARTS OF THE PLANT TO USE AS MEDICINE

You can use the roots, bark, leaves, and flowers for medicine, but the bark and fruit are most commonly used.

BENEFITS AND PROPERTIES

Cramp bark is one of the most beneficial herbal medicines I know of. It handles and treats a host of conditions. It's known mostly for treating conditions related to muscle pain and muscle spasms. Rheumatism, heart palpitations, painful menstruation, bladder spasms, colic, and overly strained eyes can all be treated with cramp bark. One of the more common problems business people face is tension headaches, and these, too, can be alleviated with cramp bark.

Breathing conditions can be alleviated with it too. If you have asthma or difficulties breathing, I would suggest cramp bark.

You can reduce the effects of heart disease with it, as well as circulatory issues and high blood pressure. Just don't mix it with other blood pressure medication if you're already taking such.

A few other things that can be remedied using cramp bark include swollen glands and mumps, fluid retention, urinary conditions and kidney problems, irritable bowel syndrome, and some emotional issues.

Another condition that many people have issues with is difficulty sleeping. Cramp bark has a sedative effect, which means you can use it to finally get those elusive hours of sleep you've been needing. As this is one of the effects of this herb, avoid using it when you're tired and trying to stay awake (such as when taking exams after staying up to study).

MEDICINE PREPARATION

Decoction: Put a cup of water and two teaspoons of dried bark in a pot or pan. First, you'll need to bring the water to a boil. After this, you should bring it down to a simmer. Keep it simmering for 15 minutes or so, and then take it off the heat. Let it cool down, at which point it will be ready to use.

Tincture: You'll need a mason jar, a cup of water (preferably distilled), a cup and a half of very strong grain alcohol, and 4 ounces of dried cramp bark. Place all the ingredients in a mason jar, seal it, and shake it. Leave it to stand for a month to a month and a half, giving it a shake every few days. Once you've left it long enough, you can strain out the bark pieces and keep the tincture in a container that seals well.

USING THE HERB

Decoction: You can have up to three cups of decoction per day. The decoction is really helpful for painful menstrual cramps.

Tincture: You can have up to two teaspoons per day. The tincture is especially useful for muscle cramp relief of any kind (from your heart to your calves).

SIDE EFFECTS AND WARNINGS

There aren't many side effects with cramp bark. You may find that the berries can have a toxic effect if too many are eaten. But for medicinal purposes, I generally suggest using the bark rather than the berries because of its high degree of effectiveness.

You may also want to consult your doctor if you're on blood pressure medication, and you're planning on taking cramp bark. Some medications interact with cramp bark and can cause unintended side effects.

FUN TIPS AND FACTS

It has been used for millennia to treat cramps! In fact, the Meskwaki tribe of Wisconsin used it mainly to treat women's menstrual cramps.

It has also been used by Native American tribes to take the place of tobacco for smoking.

AUTHOR'S PERSONAL STORY

The plant name says what it treats: it helps for cramping muscles and it's a true elixir for that! I've used it many times over the years for cramp relief after a long day of work.

CRANBERRY

LATIN NAME

accinium macrocarpon

DESCRIPTION

Cranberries are bushes with thin, creeping stems. They reach between two to eight inches in height but stretch out for about seven feet in length and are green and brown.

Their leaves are arranged in an alternate pattern and are rather small (approximately half an inch long). The evergreen leaves have an oval shape and some have a slightly shiny surface.

They produce small pink flowers with four petals. You'll see the stamen protruding from the flower, and in some species, there will also be a purplish color in the center of the flower.

THE BERRIES THEMSELVES ARE WHITE WHEN THEY START GROWING, TURNING a bright red color as they mature. There are often spots on the berries. The average berry will be about the size of a raisin.

HABITAT

Cranberries love the wet, boggy ground. They are very finicky when it comes to where they grow. You'll find them in colder areas that are open and in direct sunlight. They have an acidic soil preference.

You're most likely to find them in Massachusetts, New Jersey, Oregon, Washington, and Wisconsin.

SEASON TO GATHER THE PLANT

You can harvest the leaves year-round since it's evergreen. The flowers should be available for harvesting in June and July, and the berries are normally ripe for picking during September and October.

PARTS OF THE PLANT TO USE AS MEDICINE

The leaves and berries are most useful for medicinal purposes. Generally, the other parts aren't used for medicine or food.

BENEFITS AND PROPERTIES

The most well-known benefit of cranberry consumption and taking cranberry medicines is that it combats urinary tract infections.

Your oral health can likewise be improved by taking cranberries. The plaque and bacteria that like to hang around in your mouth find it difficult to cling to your teeth and gums after consuming cranberries.

Heart-related problems can be reduced by taking cranberries. This includes cardiovascular disease and blood disorders.

If you have a sore stomach, then cranberries make a good solution. Cranberries can also assist with a bad appetite and in reducing your body mass index because it's a good blood sugar regulator.

Something that may give many people hope is that cranberries have been linked to cancer healing. There is far too little testing to indicate a definitive verdict, but thus far, the tests are promising.

MEDICINE PREPARATION

Fresh and dried berries: Probably the easiest and most direct way to get the benefits is to consume cranberry fruit directly. They're tasty to snack on and can also be used to make tasty salads. Fresh cranberry leaves can also make a nice addition to any salad.

Juice: I prefer to cold press the juice for a pure result. Diluting with water is a good idea because it can be quite strong.

Pulp: the fresh leaves make a great pulp. Simply crush them and apply them to the afflicted area.

USING THE HERB

Berries: Eating the berries is the best way to handle oral health issues using cranberries.

Juice: Juice is the best remedy when it comes to urinary tract infections.

Pulp: This will help with bruises, wounds, burns, and sprains.

SIDE EFFECTS AND WARNINGS

The side effects associated with cranberries are mainly runny stool or upset stomach. You could also find that you bleed more easily. Also, if you're predisposed to kidney stones, a high dose of cranberries can result in developing kidney stones.

Additionally, the drug warfarin can interact with and produce unintended side effects if you have large amounts of cranberries.

FUN TIPS AND FACTS

Cranberries are native to North America, soo if you like buying local food and goods, this is about as local as it gets.

AUTHOR'S PERSONAL STORY

As mentioned in the other book, I've helped many women with bladder infections. Homemade cranberry juice does pure magic to people who suffer from frequent bladder infections.

136
DANDELION

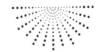

LATIN NAME

araxacum offinale

DESCRIPTION

These plants have a long and thick taproot topped by a cluster of floral leaves. The plant can reach a size of 25 inches high and 20 inches across.

These leaves are long and lobed. If snapped, the leaves produce a white, milky substance called latex.

Rising from the basal leaves are the flower stems. These are hollow and don't produce any branches. They are crowned by a bright yellow flower head made up of a large number of florets.

Eventually, this flower head is replaced by an ovary that grows a bunch of seeds. The seeds produce a white puffy ball, and if you blow on the ovary, several of the seeds will blow off.

If you smell it, the flower gives off a relatively sweet scent and the leaves have a bitter, citrusy scent.

HABITAT

The optimum habitat for a dandelion plant is a cool, shaded meadow. That said, they can also thrive in hot, direct sunlight. You may commonly find them in all sorts of pastures and disturbed areas too.

SEASON TO GATHER THE PLANT

The plant is most likely to be ready for harvesting in the fall and the spring.

PARTS OF THE PLANT TO USE AS MEDICINE

You can use the whole plant for medicinal purposes. This includes the flower, the stem, the leaves, and the root.

BENEFITS AND PROPERTIES

Dandelion is an especially good diuretic. Use of it will result in better regulation of urination.

It's commonly also used as an appetite stimulant, so if you haven't been able to stomach anything for a while, try out some dandelion as a solution. It's also good at increasing the effectiveness of your digestion, resulting in better metabolism of carbohydrates and reduction of fat absorption. Not only this, but your blood sugar regulation can also be improved using dandelion. This combination of benefits can help with weight loss.

Your immune system will benefit too. The plant is a good antiviral and antibacterial. Hepatitis B, specifically, has been shown to slow in its spread when one takes dandelion.

Some of the organs in your body that will especially benefit are your liver and gallbladder. This plant can be an effective means of detoxifying both.

There are skin benefits to using dandelions as well. In addition to its ability to reverse ultraviolet damage, it's an effective antioxidant, resulting in less cell damage from free radicals. Further, inflammation is effectively reduced by using this herb.

Cancer studies have found that dandelion can be of benefit in treating colon, liver, and pancreatic cancer. While more research needs to be done regarding this, there have been cases in which it has yielded results.

In terms of properties, dandelions are full of natural vitamins and minerals. You'll find that it's high in vitamins A, C, E, and K. It's also high in calcium, folate, iron, and potassium.

MEDICINE PREPARATION

Fresh salad: Add some fresh basil leaves along with dandelion stems and flowers to your salad.

Tea: You can use dry or fresh dandelion to make the tea. If you use the flowers or leaves, you need only steep it for a few minutes. If you're using dried root, put two tablespoons and a cup of water in a saucepan. Then bring it to a boil for three minutes before switching it off. Leave it to steep in the saucepan for another half hour, at which point the tea will be ready to drink.

Salve: You'll first need to make infused oil before getting started on the salve. Take about two cups full of fresh dandelion and put it in a jar. Cover it with a carrier oil of your choice (olive oil is quite good for this purpose). Leave it to soak for about two weeks, at which point you can strain out the dandelion pieces. At this point, heat the infused oil and melt in a few tablespoons of beeswax. After the beeswax, melt in a few tablespoons of shea butter. Stir until everything is incorporated quite well, and then leave it to cool off. At this point, you can place it in jars for your daily use.

USING THE HERB

Fresh salad: The flowers have a honey-like flavor, while the leaves have a slightly bitter but earthy flavor. Dandelion flowers and leaves can be consumed in the same quantity and frequency as any other salad leaves you might find in the supermarket. It's easy to incorporate into your daily salad routine.

Tea: Using the flowers gives a nice sweet flavor to the tea, while using the root gives you an earthy flavor similar to chicory. Adding a bit of honey to tea made from the root makes an extra tasty beverage.

Salve: The salve can be applied to any sun-damaged areas and any inflamed areas. It's great for dry hands too.

SIDE EFFECTS AND WARNINGS

The side effects include skin irritation and mouth sores if you're allergic to dandelion or latex.

Due to its acidic nature, it can increase stomach acid and contribute to heartburn.

If you have chronic gallbladder problems, consult your doctor before using it.

FUN TIPS AND FACTS

Many people see dandelion as weed and throw it in their compost! Instead of just being a nuisance, this plant grows in spring for people to detox their bodies from the heavy foods they've been eating throughout the colder seasons!

AUTHOR'S PERSONAL STORY

In my home, we eat fresh dandelion leaves, stems, and flowers every day for a month. Usually, we make a salad, and it's either the main dish with some hard-boiled eggs or a side dish.

137
ECHINACEA

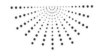

LATIN NAME

chinacea purpurea

DESCRIPTION

Echinacea is a hardy plant that comes in an upright, rounded shape. The stem is stiff and covered with hairs and usually has purple stripes running down its length. The plant grows to about three and a half feet at a maximum height and about two feet wide.

Simple leaves protrude from the branches, coming out in an alternating pattern. The leaves have a serrated margin, and their color can be various shades of green. The leaves have a lanceolate shape–going from a broader base to a tapering tip. Typically, they grow three to six inches long and one to three inches wide. The leaves gradually get smaller as they approach the top of the plant. At the bottom of the plant, the leaves have stalks, but as they get closer to the top of the plant, they become stalkless—note that the stalks are green or brown. Each leaf has between three and five clear veins. And as for the surface of the leaves, you'll find they can be either smooth or hairy.

Echinacea has a composite flower head, and the outer petals of this plant are usually pink, pink-purple, or purple. These petals range between 15 and 20 in number. Each petal grows from one and a half to three inches long and has an approximate width of a quarter inch. The tips of the petals typically have three notches. The center of the flower head consists of an orange-brown disc or cone with a mass of small yellow flowers on its surface.

The fruit of the plant consists of a cone with sharp spines. This cone is a seed head, and it has a purple or brown color.

HABITAT

You'll find these plants in soil that ranges from moist to slightly dry, usually easily draining soil. The plant prefers either direct sunlight or semi-shade. Echinacea can commonly be found in the East, Southeast, and Midwest.

SEASON TO GATHER THE PLANT

You should harvest echinacea in its second year for best results. It's not always possible to know how old the plant is in the wild, but you can generally tell by its size if it's fully matured or not. The flowers mainly bloom during the summer–which is the right season to harvest them. The seed cones appear in the fall, and you should usually wait until they've dried and gone brown before harvesting them. You can forage for the roots and the leaves at any time. That said, it's best to harvest the leaves in the summer, and you should ideally harvest the roots in the fall.

PARTS OF THE PLANT TO USE AS MEDICINE

The leaves and roots are the most used parts of this plant. You can also use flowers and stems, especially when preparing tea. You can use the seeds, but this isn't a common practice.

BENEFITS AND PROPERTIES

The benefits of using echinacea include improvement of skin conditions. It can help hydrate dry skin, and you can use it to assist with wrinkly skin. You can also use it to alleviate acne. Athlete's foot and inflammation can also be treated topically with echinacea

Echinacea is useful for tackling infections due to its antiviral properties. It can be used to remedy urinary tract infections, ear infections, cold sores, colds, and the flu. If you have nasal issues, echinacea can also help with that. Hay fever and sinusitis can both be relieved with echinacea.

Other conditions that can be alleviated or eradicated using this plant are pain, high blood sugar, anxiety, and wounds that won't heal.

MEDICINE PREPARATION

Juice: Wash the plant then simply squeeze the fresh plant matter so that the juice comes out. Add a teaspoon of the juice to a glass of water and drink it.

Tea: Dried and crushed leaves, roots, and flowers are best for the tea although you can also use the fresh versions if you want. Boil water and then let it cool down for a minute. Pour the hot water over the crushed echinacea and let it steep for 15 minutes. Strain it and drink.

Tincture: This requires vodka and two whole echinacea plants. Clean off the plants and place them in a jar. Cover the plants with vodka, then seal the jar. Leave it for one to three months in a cool place, shaking it every few days. You can then strain the liquid into a container for use.

Salve: you'll need three and a half ounces of carrier oil, half an ounce of beeswax, and one to four handfuls of dried leaves and flowers. You'll start by making infused oil. To do this, clean the echinacea plants and put them in a jar. Then cover the dried plant bits with the oil and seal off the jar. Leave this out of direct sunlight for a month to a month and a half. At this point, the oil should be strained into a pot. You then melt the beeswax into the infused oil and pour it into a container or containers so that it congeals. This is now ready for use.

USING THE HERB

Juice: The juice can also be used in skin pastes for wound care or skin conditions.

Tea: Tea can be taken daily for five days when you have a cold or flu to help get rid of the condition.

Tincture: Use about 5 drops of the tincture at a time. I prefer dropping it into a glass of water because it tastes very strong. The shelf life is very long—it lasts years.

Salve: Use this for skin conditions or wounds. The shelf life is between nine months and a year.

SIDE EFFECTS AND WARNINGS

Side effects that can commonly occur are feeling nauseous or dizzy, having a sore stomach, or having dry eyes. If you take it orally, such as with the tea, juice, or tincture, then you may experience a numb tongue for a while.

People who are allergic to this herb experience effects such as itchy skin, hives, nausea, shortness of breath, and pain in the stomach.

If you have an autoimmune disease, you should avoid this plant because it can affect your immune system. This is especially the case if you're on drugs that affect the immune system because you may experience an immune boost and drug interactions. Liver medication may also interact with echinacea, so consult your healthcare advisor before using it if you're on such medication.

FUN TIPS AND FACTS

This plant symbolizes strength and healing because of its properties.

AUTHOR'S PERSONAL STORY

A patient who would come to me and tell me that every autumn they get the flu stopped coming because echinacea helped them a lot with flu prevention by strengthening their immune system.

ELDER

LATIN NAME

Sambucus

DESCRIPTION

This is a large shrub (10 feet tall in some cases) with a short gray trunk that has smooth bark. The bark is soft, with corky bumps and furrows. When the shrub grows older, the bark becomes rougher and gets a brown-gray tinge. This older bark is marked by small fissures. The twigs are yellow-green and porous, and the pith inside the branches is white and soft.

The leaves of this shrub have an opposite arrangement. These leaves are pinnate, having between three and 11 dark green leaflets–although between five and nine is the most common number. The margins on these leaves are serrated. The leaf holding these leaflets has a total length between two and 12 inches.

The flowers are small, white, and have five petals and five stamens each. They form a clustered flower head that ranges between six and 12 inches in diameter. The flowers have a lovely floral, creamy scent.

The fruits (a type of berry) are very small—just over a tenth of an inch in diameter. They hang down in dark purple, drooping clusters.

HABITAT

Elder prefers direct sun and soil that ranges from moist to slightly dry. It grows well in the wild areas of the US—specifically to the east of the Rockies.

SEASON TO GATHER THE PLANT

If you do decide to harvest the leaves, it is best to harvest during April. This period before the flowers grow is best, but you can harvest the leaves until fall.

The flowers are best gathered in May and June. When gathering them, preserving the pollen by using a container or pot is ideal. The pollen has good qualities and adds to the flavor.

The berries should be harvested close to the end of summer. At this time they are soft, and their color is dark purple.

PARTS OF THE PLANT TO USE AS MEDICINE

The only parts you should use internally are the flowers and the berries. The rest can be toxic to your body. The leaves can be used but should only be used externally to alleviate bruises or pain. Please be cautious if you decide to use the leaves.

BENEFITS AND PROPERTIES

On a topical level, elder normally only works on mild skin conditions, joint pain, muscle pain, and inflammation. However, the plant is a winner when it comes to oral usage. It can be used for both mental and physical conditions.

In terms of mental conditions, it is effective at dealing with stress. I've used it for this purpose, and I know many other people that have used it for this purpose too. In terms of the brain itself, elder can be used to keep epilepsy in check, and it can assist in relieving headaches.

On a physical level, you can use it for immune-system-related issues and for boosting certain organs. Immune system issues that can be cured or alleviated using this plant are flu, fevers, and colds. Breathing difficulties due to infections can be improved with the elder herb as well. HIV and AIDS can also be more easily managed with this herb. In addition, using elder can help your heart and kidneys.

On another note, elderflowers can be used for alleviating allergies in many people. It's especially good for treating sinus issues due to allergies.

MEDICINE PREPARATION

Infusion: The infusion can be made hot or cold. A hot infusion is made by putting one to three tablespoons of the flowers (dried or fresh) into a cup of water. Bring this water to a boil then switch off the heat and let it steep for 15 minutes. The cold version is made by putting a few tablespoons of the flowers into a jar of water then leaving it to infuse overnight.

Berries: The berries should be cooked because, when raw, they can cause nausea. Throw them into any dish that could use a slightly sweet and tart flavor.

Cough syrup: You'll need a cup of fresh, dark elderberries, a cup and a half of raw honey, and four cups of distilled water. Mash the berries into the water in a saucepan. Bring the water to a brief boil then down to a simmer for 45 minutes. At this point, the mixture will have reduced. Switch it off and let it cool, adding the honey once it's finished cooling.

USING THE HERB

Infusion: The infusion can be diluted into a wash and used on the face. This is an effective agent for evening out your skin tone.

Berries: Due to their high vitamin content, adding the berries to your food is good for maintaining overall health and wellness.

Cough syrup: The cough syrup should last for about three weeks. It can be frozen too, in which case, it should last for several months. Just let the frozen cough syrup thaw when you want to use it.

SIDE EFFECTS AND WARNINGS

The plant contains a chemical that can be used to make cyanide. This chemical can induce nausea, diarrhea, and vomiting. The flowers and berries are particularly liable to induce these reactions.

If you're using medication for diabetes, then avoid using elder. It lowers blood sugar, and this may cause interactions and unintended side effects.

FUN TIPS AND FACTS

In some Christian mythology, people believed that burning elder wood would aggravate the Devil and bring death because it's a sacred plant.

AUTHOR'S PERSONAL STORY

I've used this lot with people who have had fevers. The tea makes people sweat a lot, and drinking it before bed with a spoon of honey would heal them overnight.

139
FEVERFEW

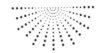

LATIN NAME

Tanacetum parthenium

DESCRIPTION

The stem of this plant is thin and circular and has a whitish fuzz closer to the top of the plant. The stem is usually a light green color, and the plant grows approximately two feet high.

The leaves are arranged alternately and are green or yellow-green. Their margins are bluntly toothed, with the teeth being rather large. In terms of size, the leaves range from one and a quarter inches long to six inches long, with the smaller ones closer to the top of the plant. The width of the leaves is between half an inch and two and a half inches. Feverfew leaves are pinnate, made up of three or five leaflets. The shape of the leaves is between an oval and a triangular oval. The leaflets making up the leaves are lanceolate or ovate. The upper part of each leaflet is smooth, but the lower part has a soft feel due to hair-like secretions from glands in the leaf. The leaves have petioles, with the ones close to the bottom being up to two inches long and the ones on the upper parts of the plant being very short to nonexistent.

The flowers on feverfew have white petals around a central disk of yellow florets. There are approximately 12 petals on a healthy flower, with each petal having a few teeth at the tip. The disk in the center sometimes looks quite puffed up with all the yellow florets in bloom. You'll find that the flowers give a relatively strong aromatic smell.

The fruit occurs in the form of achenes that are ribbed and brown. They are small and occur in clusters on the head where the flower once was.

HABITAT

Feverfew prefers disturbed landscapes. These and other wild areas such as fields are the most common locations for the plant. It prefers sunlight and well-draining soil.

SEASON TO GATHER THE PLANT

The flowers bloom during the summer, which is the best time to gather them. They can sometimes bloom until the start of fall. The leaves can be harvested the whole year round, but it's best to leave them during spring so the plant can sustain itself while growing flowers.

PARTS OF THE PLANT TO USE AS MEDICINE

The leaves are the main part used for medicinal purposes. You can, however, use the whole plant.

BENEFITS AND PROPERTIES

The main use of feverfew is as a pain remedy. This is especially so when it comes to headaches and migraines. Some properties of feverfew reduce the dilation of blood vessels in the brain, thus reducing pain in your head. Migraines won't be fully cured, but they can be managed and in many cases, their occurrence will be drastically reduced (if the migraines are chronic). Side effects of migraines, such as vomiting and nausea, should also be alleviated when using feverfew.

Inflammation is also effectively remedied using feverfew. Inflammation due to arthritis is particularly prone to relief using this herb. Inflammation in the colon (colitis) can be greatly eased by ingesting the herb as well. Insect bites and their related inflammation can be soothed by using it topically.

In addition, feverfew can ease menstrual symptoms. Additionally, if a period is delayed, you could use it to start your cycle, thereby making periods more regular. Further, when a woman is having strong contractions while giving birth, feverfew should help reduce the intensity of the sensations being experienced.

The digestive system can also benefit from taking feverfew. When your stomach is feeling funny, the tea can help.

MEDICINE PREPARATION

Leaf: Simply eat one or two fresh leaves.

Tea: Pour a cup of boiling water over a teaspoon of dried feverfew leaves. Let it steep for a few minutes, then strain and drink.

Compress: Pour a cup of boiling water over four teaspoons of dried leaves. Let it steep for 20 minutes or more. Soak a cloth in the liquid and apply it to the affected area.

USING THE HERB

Leaf: This is very effective for headaches. Don't eat more than one or two at a time because you could get sores in your mouth.

Tea: Use the tea when you have a headache. It's effective but won't leave you with mouth sores like eating the leaves directly might.

Compress: The compress is effective for recovering from bruises.

SIDE EFFECTS AND WARNINGS

Mouth ulcers are the most common side effect. This occurs when taking the fresh leaves orally.

Withdrawal symptoms can take place when you cease using it after a long period. Sleeping difficulties, sore muscles, anxiousness, and headaches are all symptoms you can expect when going through feverfew withdrawal.

Some have allergies to feverfew, so test it out before using it at full dosage levels.

During pregnancy, you shouldn't use feverfew. You can use it while going through labor, but cease using it when you begin breastfeeding.

Interactions can occur with blood pressure medication, especially if you're on blood thinners. Cytochrome P450 3A4, a type of protein used in many drugs to assist with metabolizing the drug in question, can also interact with feverfew. Due to the variety of drugs that contain this type of protein, it's important to consult your healthcare professional before planning on using feverfew.

FUN TIPS AND FACTS

In Medieval Europe, especially during the plague years, the feverfew flower was an essential part of cottage gardens. Local lore said that planting feverfew flowers by the house, especially near the door, would help protect those who were inside from the disease. Interestingly enough, there is some data to support that this may have worked.

AUTHOR'S PERSONAL STORY

As the name already says, feverfew helps people lower their fevers. I've tried this on a lot of patients, and it always works!

140
FIELD GARLIC

LATIN NAME

Allium vineale or *Allium ursinum*

DESCRIPTION

Field garlic, also called wild garlic, grows to approximately two feet tall, and the roots come in the form of bulbs clustered together, each looking like an onion.

The leaves are long and have a hollow tube shape. The leaves grow out in a bunch and resemble the leaves you'd find on chives. They give off a scent that smells like onion. Ensure that whatever you forage has a smell to it, otherwise, it might be a poisonous plant that looks similar.

The flowers are white and pink and are star-shaped. They grow in clusters at the end of stalks that shoot out directly from the root system.

The fruit is called a bulbil. It has an ovular shape and tapers to a tip. The color tends to be green or purple, and it has an oniony smell. These, just like the flowers, grow in clusters. When they're fully mature, they fall to the ground to establish a new wild garlic plant.

HABITAT

They're extremely common in open fields and woods, especially when there's moist soil–such as in a marsh. It loves to grow under trees that only sprout leaves in late spring.

SEASON TO GATHER THE PLANT

You can harvest this herb in the spring and the winter. The flowers bloom in late spring, making this the time to forage for flowers.

PARTS OF THE PLANT TO USE AS MEDICINE

You can use the whole plant for medicinal purposes.

BENEFITS AND PROPERTIES

The wild garlic plant is very healthy for your heart. It lowers blood cholesterol and blood pressure. It also improves blood flow and purifies the blood. People at risk for heart attacks and strokes may find that wild garlic is exactly the solution they've been looking for.

Your digestive system can also benefit from using this plant. It cleanses out the digestive system and improves digestive function. Part of the cause for this is that wild garlic improves bile production and urination, allowing you to break down food better and expel waste better. Cramps in the stomach and intestines can be reduced with wild garlic, and it can treat obesity and obesity-related issues.

Field garlic can also help clear up the skin.

Immune system function improves when you use wild garlic. This has the secondary effect of reducing the likelihood of getting colds, fevers, sore throat, and the flu.

MEDICINE PREPARATION

Tea: Chop up a tablespoonful of wild garlic. Pour over boiling water and let it steep for a few minutes. Strain, add anything you would like to use to adjust the flavor, and drink.

Macerated oil: Simply put a few handfuls of fresh or dry wild garlic (crushed or cut into small pieces) into a glass jar and cover it with your carrier oil of choice. Seal it tightly and place it in a sunny spot. Strain out the plant matter, and add new wild garlic to the oil once a week for three weeks. After this, it'll be ready for use.

In food: This plant is very easy to incorporate into everyday cooking. It ranges from a chive-like flavor for the leaves, to an onion-like flavor for the bulbs. It's generally chopped or mashed when added to fresh dishes and salads, or chopped up and cooked into hot dishes. It's particularly good for adding to homemade pesto.

USING THE HERB

Tea: You can have a cup of tea per day. It's effective for long-term health, especially for the heart and blood. You can use dried wild garlic for this, in which case you would also use about a tablespoonful of the plant.

Macerated oil: I like the oil because you can use the dried version of the plant for this purpose. I also like that you can use it for topical application.

In food: You can freeze wild garlic, allowing you to use it in a fresh state even when it's not available for foraging.

SIDE EFFECTS AND WARNINGS

Allergies are something you always need to watch out for when using wild plants, including wild garlic. Testing out a small amount before going the whole hog can prevent you from getting a full-on allergic reaction.

Having bad breath goes part and parcel with eating wild garlic, as it would with your average store-bought garlic. You might also feel a bit of a stomach upset on occasion. Heartburn and flatulence also occur when you have too much at a time–and it's easy to overindulge because it is a lovely addition to dishes for flavor.

Avoid wild garlic if you're on blood thinners. The blood-related benefits associated with wild garlic might interfere with your medication.

FUN TIPS AND FACTS

The plant's common name is 'bear garlic'. It comes from the belief that bears ate wild garlic to regain their strength after a long winter's slumber.

This can be said also about man; if we eat field garlic it strengthens our bodies.

AUTHOR'S PERSONAL STORY

My family and I have always cooked a lot with it when it's in season. Its taste is delicious and without realizing it, it boosted our bodies' strength and prevented us from catching several annual diseases. Oftentimes, when we're healthy and live a holistic life, we forget about being sick. Now and then, I take a conscious moment to be grateful for the herbs that constantly promote my health and well-being.

141
GARLIC MUSTARD

LATIN NAME

Alliaria petiolata

DESCRIPTION

It's a short plant, growing between one and three feet tall, and it has a green to pale gray color.

It has a white taproot, and under the base of the plant, the root has an s-shape.

There's a single, slightly hairy stem that grows from the base of the plant to the flower head. The stem is slender, and the leaves branch out from it.

Its leaves grow in an alternating pattern. They have rough, toothed margins. The leaves have a heart or triangular shape. The size of the leaves ranges between two and three inches long, and two and a half to three inches wide. The leaves have petioles that attach to the stem. There's a distinct garlic scent to the plant that can be quite strong. Note that in the first year, the plant has dark green leaves. These leaves are arranged in the pattern of a rosette and have a kidney shape. These rosette leaves also have large teeth.

The flowers form a clustered flower head called a raceme. The individual flowers in the head produce four white petals that are about a fifth of an inch long. These petals have a blunt or flat tip, and the overall shape of the individual flower is that of a cross or a plus.

The fruit is a silique, which is a slender seed pod that splits open to release its shiny black seeds. The silique grows erect and has four sides. Its coloration turns brown when it's close to releasing its seeds.

HABITAT

Garlic mustard often grows next to hedges and bushes. It generally prefers a colder environment, normally with well-draining soil in the form of loam or sandy soil.

SEASON TO GATHER THE PLANT

If you want to use the flowers, April to June is the optimum time for harvesting these. Otherwise, you can harvest the leaves any time from March to September. It's better to gather the plant before it's at full maturity. The flavor is mild and pleasant, tasting like both garlic and mustard. Note that it lives for two years then dies.

PARTS OF THE PLANT TO USE AS MEDICINE

You can use the leaves, the flowers, and the fruit.

BENEFITS AND PROPERTIES

Garlic mustard is very effective for tending to wounds, bruises, sores, and skin ulcers. It has an antiseptic effect that gives it the added benefit of warding off unwanted microorganisms around or in these. It can also be used topically to relieve muscular cramps, especially in the feet.

It's effective for warding off colds and related issues, such as head congestion and coughing. It can get your body to sweat, which helps get your body temperature back to where it should be when you have a fever or you're overheating. If you have bronchitis, try applying some to your chest.

You will find that it can assist with kidney stones.

As for babies, it can assist with colic. Just consult your baby's medical professional first.

MEDICINE PREPARATION

Fresh: Chop it up and use it in your homemade pesto or your homemade salads.

Poultice: Chop up fresh garlic mustard and mash it up to release any juices. Then add a bit of water so that it's not as thick. Add a bit of honey or soap for extra antibacterial protection and to help it stick to the sore or skin. It needs to be applied quite thick–about half an inch thick.

Oil: put about three handfuls of garlic mustard in a jar and add a carrier oil of your choice so that it covers the plant parts. Seal the jar and leave it in a sunny spot for two weeks, then strain it. You can now use it for topical or food purposes. I go the extra step of melting in a bit of coconut oil and beeswax to make it thick. This way it can be rubbed into the skin as an ointment for bruises and sores.

USING THE HERB

Fresh: It has a tasty flavor that can lend an extra edge to your food. Just don't use too much at once.

Poultice: The poultice is perfect for sores and related issues.

Oil: The oil can be made with fresh or dry garlic mustard, making it perfect for parts of the year when the plant isn't available. The oil will last you a few months.

SIDE EFFECTS AND WARNINGS

Don't take large quantities of garlic mustard because there are trace amounts of cyanide. In small quantities, this won't affect you, but in large quantities, it will.

FUN TIPS AND FACTS

Garlic mustard is invasive and can be harmful to local butterfly species. So don't hesitate to harvest it to your heart's content. There's no need to sustain its population unless you want to cultivate it.

AUTHOR'S PERSONAL STORY

I love using garlic mustard to cook the best blue cheese pasta! It's a treat that I sometimes enjoy, even though I mostly avoid gluten.

GERMAN CHAMOMILE

LATIN NAME

*M*atricaria recutita

DESCRIPTION

There is one basal stem, splitting into multiple light green stems that grow up to the flowers. There is often a light covering of hair along the stem. It's approximately three feet at maximum height but is generally closer to 20 inches high.

Leaves are normally delicate and look similar to fern leaves. They're bipinnate and arranged alternately. Crushing the leaves gives off a smell similar to that of apples.

The flowers have a raised and rounded yellow center. This is surrounded by white petals that span about an inch across. The base that connects the stalk to the flower is hollow.

The fruit of this plant consists of seeds that can be found on the central yellow part of the flower when it dries. The seeds are very small.

HABITAT

It grows well in temperate areas but can grow in slightly colder areas too. It prefers direct sun and soil that's not too nutritious.

SEASON TO GATHER THE PLANT

The flowers can be harvested from May to October. When you pluck a flower, normally another will start growing to replace the plucked one.

PARTS OF THE PLANT TO USE AS MEDICINE

The flowers are the best part to use for medicinal purposes, especially for topical use. The leaves and stems also are effective. Don't hesitate to use them as well.

BENEFITS AND PROPERTIES

German chamomile is great for oral issues. Use it when you have an abscess, gum inflammation, or a sore throat. Use it as a gargle for best results.

It works on eczema and psoriasis to reduce inflammation and scaly skin. Acne breakouts can be reduced too. When you get light burns on your skin, use it to soothe the skin while it's healing.

Internal benefits include relieving stomach ulcers and inflammatory bowel disease. It can also help you overcome a chest cold. Your stomach issues can be eased with the herb as well. When you have an upset tummy, indigestion, diarrhea, or cramps, this is the herb to use.

For mental health, German chamomile can reduce anxiety. Insomnia can be overcome with this herb as well, so drink a cup of its tea before bed if you have difficulty sleeping.

With children, it can be used to reduce the itching of diaper rash and chickenpox. In oral applications, it can also provide colic relief.

MEDICINE PREPARATION

Tea: Use two tablespoons of dried German chamomile. Pour over a cup of boiling water and let it steep for 10 minutes. Strain and drink.

Bath: Throw a few handfuls of dried German chamomile into your bath and soak in the bath.

Oil: Dry the flowers and crush them up. Then steam them, catching the steam on a pot lid turned upside down. After a few hours, switch off the stove and let it cool. The oily residue on the surface is what you're looking for. Remove it and put it in a dark glass bottle. The oil is removed most easily by placing the pot in the fridge for a few hours once it's cool enough. This allows the oil to congeal, making it easier to skim.

Ointment: Use about five drops of the oil and two tablespoons of coconut oil. Mix them together thoroughly, and apply to affected areas.

USING THE HERB

Tea: You can have up to three cups a day. You can also use it as a gargle

Bath: This helps with inflammation, scaly skin, burns, cuts, and body acne.

Oil: The oil can be added to water (about five drops per glass of water). This can then be drunk to reduce inflammation and viral or bacterial conditions.

Ointment: This is especially effective when applied to acne or acne-prone skin.

SIDE EFFECTS AND WARNINGS

It can cause an allergic reaction in some people.

Vomiting is a potential side effect, but almost always only if you've had a large amount in a short time.

It can cause sleepiness, which is great when you're trying to have a restful night but not so great when you need to drive on a long road or you need the energy to stay awake. Further, avoid it if you're on sleeping pills or sedatives because it could make these stronger than they already are.

German chamomile can also exacerbate asthma.

If you've had cancer linked to high estrogen levels, then avoid this herb, or consult your doctor/oncologist before using it.

If you're pregnant, don't use this herb. You could be putting yourself at risk of miscarriage.

If you're going to have surgery within two weeks, avoid German chamomile. It could cause extra bleeding. In a similar vein, avoid German chamomile if you're on blood pressure or blood-thinning medication.

Other medications that could interact with the plant are birth control, hormone regulators, diabetes medication, antifungals, cholesterol medication, or allergy medication. Ask your healthcare provider if you're on one of these and want to use German chamomile.

FUN TIPS AND FACTS

If you infuse chamomile for longer than 10 minutes in your hot water, it has the opposite effect. Instead of making you sleepy and ready for bed, it wakes you up.

AUTHOR'S PERSONAL STORY

My dad didn't know about German chamomile's potential to increase energy, and when I was a kid, he'd make me chamomile tea to make me tired in the evening. I'd always been a very energetic kid. To boost the effect, he'd soak it longer than the herbalist suggested. The funny story is that he then would get irritated because I just didn't get sleepy.

143
GOLDENROD

LATIN NAME

olidago spp.

DESCRIPTION

The stem of this plant is sturdy and grows between three and five feet tall. Most species are shorter (one to three feet) while others are taller (up to eight feet). The stems have tiny spikes on their surface.

The margins of the leaves are serrated, and the surface of the leaf is smooth. They are lanceolate, having a long tapering tip.

The flowers are small–a quarter of an inch in diameter. They grow in a cluster that's long and bound together closely. Their petals are yellow, except in one species called white goldenrod. To me, they look fuzzy.

HABITAT

Some goldenrod species prefer living in mountain and seaside climates. These species normally prefer partial shade to full shade. Most goldenrod, however, prefers direct sunlight and will grow in a variety of areas, such as pastures and fields.

SEASON TO GATHER THE PLANT

Late July to October is the best time to gather the plant. The earlier in this period, the better because the bitterness doesn't come through as much.

PARTS OF THE PLANT TO USE AS MEDICINE

You can use the leaves, the stem, and the flowers.

BENEFITS AND PROPERTIES

Goldenrod can remedy a number of issues including colds, the flu, and allergies.

You can also use goldenrod to treat urinary tract infections and related conditions. Additionally, it increases the flow of urination, allowing your body to expel waste better.

On the skin, this plant can help with eczema and swelling. Other topical benefits include the reduction of pain and muscle spasms. Joint pain is especially susceptible to goldenrod medicine.

A benefit specifically for men is that goldenrod can aid in preventing an enlarged prostate.

MEDICINE PREPARATION

Tea: You'll need about two teaspoons of dried goldenrod. Pour over a cup of water and let it steep for 15 minutes. Strain and drink.

Poultice: Use a handful of finely chopped fresh goldenrod and a cupful of coconut oil. Melt the coconut oil on low heat in a pot and mix in the goldenrod. Pour it into a container that you'll be able to close and let it cool until it's congealed. Apply a decent amount to any affected areas of your skin or muscles.

USING THE HERB

Tea: you can take the tea up to four times a day.

Poultice: keep the poultice refrigerated so that it lasts longer.

SIDE EFFECTS AND WARNINGS

It is possible to have an allergy to goldenrod, so of course, you shouldn't use it if you react poorly to it.

Goldenrod is also harmful if you have heart disease or kidney disease that causes fluid retention. Further, if you're on water pills, the herb may cause you to expel too much water since it has the same function as water pills.

Goldenrod can cause increases in sodium intake. For this reason, it's best to avoid the herb if you have blood pressure issues.

FUN TIPS AND FACTS

In mythology, the goldenrod is thought to indicate the source of a hidden spring (or hidden treasure). It's considered a sign of prosperity. If it starts growing near your home, it means that you could be on to a winning streak.

AUTHOR'S PERSONAL STORY

Clients who were dealing with .undereye bags for years came back after a month of taking goldenrod caps with no sign of bags. The ones who didn't believe in miracles now do!

144
HORSETAIL

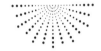

LATIN NAME

quisetum arvense

DESCRIPTION

The stem of this plant is jointed and hollow. It reaches about one to five feet tall with a few species growing taller. Horsetails also look a lot like rushes. The branches grow out of an underground rootstalk. The stalks are green, and they have gray or black horizontal stripes at their joints.

The leaves form a whorl coming out of the joints of the stem, almost like the spokes of a bicycle wheel. They look like green needles.

The fruit consists of cones that bear spores that have a peach color.

HABITAT

It loves moist areas such as marshes and wetlands, especially when the soil is rich. It can also be found in areas, such as on slopes.

SEASON TO GATHER THE PLANT

Springtime is the best time to harvest this plant. When the leaves turn bright green and turn upward or outward then you won't find a better time to harvest.

PARTS OF THE PLANT TO USE AS MEDICINE

All parts other than the roots are used.

BENEFITS AND PROPERTIES

Horsetail helps with conditions relating to the blood. If you need to reduce the ease with which you bleed, you can use this plant. If you have heavy menstruation, you can also use this herb.

Conditions relating to the joints such as gout and osteoarthritis can be treated with horsetail. The silica content in this herb is a contributing factor to this. The silica content can also contribute to stronger hair and nails, healthier teeth, improved cartilage and ligament health, strengthened lining in arteries and mucus membranes, and stronger bones.

This herb can treat skin injuries.. It can treat frostbite, thereby preventing loss of limbs. Wound care is also greatly enhanced by adding horsetail to your toolbox.

Further, horsetail can aid in weight loss. This is partly due to its ability to reduce blood sugar.

Finally, conditions relating to your urinary tract can be managed effectively when taking horsetail. Incontinence, bladder stones, kidney stones, and urinary tract infections are all remediable by taking this herb.

MEDICINE PREPARATION

Tea: Use a tablespoonful of finely chopped fresh horsetail or dried horsetail. Pour in a cup of boiling water and let it steep in 10 minutes. Strain and enjoy.

Infusion: Chop up a handful of horsetail finely and pour in two cups of hot water. Let it steep for some hours until it's very strong.

TINCTURE: YOU'LL WANT TO USE FRESH HORSETAIL. FINELY CHOP UP A FEW handfuls and put it in a mason jar. Pour in vodka until the jar is full. Seal it and place it out of the sun for six weeks, shaking it every few days. Strain it and pour it into a dark glass jar for use.

USING THE HERB

Tea: use it consistently for a few weeks to start seeing effects.

Infusion: the infusion can be drunk in smaller quantities–about half a cup per day. You can use it by pouring it directly onto wounds too, or soaking a cloth in it to use it as a compress. It's also great for rinsing out one's mouth or for washing hair. For the hair and nails, it's best to use it as a soak for about half an hour.

Tincture: Use a teaspoon of tincture in a glass of water. Take about one glass a day.

SIDE EFFECTS AND WARNINGS

Using this herb can cause lead to nutrient deficiencies, such as a lack of vitamin B1. Low potassium could be a side effect, specifically if the herb makes you urinate a lot. If you do urinate a lot while taking this herb, you should take a potassium supplement.

Horsetail can also lower your blood sugar. In someone with diabetes, this lowered blood sugar could reach dangerous levels. It's better not to take the herb if you have diabetes or if you're on diabetes medication.

CONSULT YOUR HEALTHCARE PROVIDER BEFORE TAKING HORSETAIL IF YOU'RE on water pills, lithium, or on medication for arrhythmia (a condition in which the heart doesn't beat normally).

Horsetail can make quitting nicotine products harder as it contains nicotine. If you're in the process of trying to get off cigarettes, put the horsetail on hold.

Toxicity is a possible side effect, but it's only likely if taken in large quantities.

FUN TIPS AND FACTS

Horsetail stems have been used as scouring brushes for hundreds of years. They've also been used to buff and shine metal and wooden objects.

AUTHOR'S PERSONAL STORY

I've helped a few recovering addicts detox and boost their kidney function with *equisetum* baths. It's a plant packed with minerals.

145
JAPANESE HONEYSUCKLE

LATIN NAME

Lonicera japonica

DESCRIPTION

This plant grows up to 16 feet long. It grows as a creeping or climbing vine with a downy stem. The color of the stem ranges from light brown to reddish-brown.

The leaves are arranged oppositely. They have an ovate shape and a smooth margin (except when they're young, in which case they can have serrated margins). A single leaf is normally between one and three inches long. It has a bright green color.

The flowers are white, yellow, and orange. They tend to start white and turn orange later in the season. They have a tubular shape, looking like there's one petal coming out the bottom of the tube and four attached petals coming out the top of the tube. It gives off a sweet scent, almost like honey and citrus.

Their fruit comes in the form of red or black berries. These are approximately a quarter inch in diameter, and they grow in pairs.

HABITAT

You can find these widespread as weeds, especially in hilly areas that abound with thickets or in the woods. You won't normally find them in very cold areas or very dry areas. In terms of light, it can grow in direct sun or full shade.

SEASON TO GATHER THE PLANT

Harvest the stems in the fall and winter.

The flowers should be harvested in the early morning before they've been opened. They normally flower during June and July.

PARTS OF THE PLANT TO USE AS MEDICINE

You can use the flowers and the leaves. The leaves should be boiled to prevent toxicity.

BENEFITS AND PROPERTIES

It's great at fighting bacteria, inflammation, and toxicity. This helps with conditions such as colds, fevers, and the flu, as well as pneumonia and other lung infections. Bacterial dysentery, enteritis, syphilitic skin disease, and mumps can also be treated with it.

Internal conditions such as hepatitis, difficulty urinating, blood pressure issues, and blood cholesterol levels can be improved with it.

External application can improve rashes (especially if infectious), inflammation, sores, pain, some skin tumors, muscle spasms, and rheumatoid arthritis.

It's also great for improving overall health.

MEDICINE PREPARATION

Tincture: Fill a mason jar with the flowers and cover them with strong brandy or vodka. Seal it off and put it in a dark place like a cupboard for a month and a half. Shake it every few days. When six weeks have elapsed, strain out the flowers and pour the tincture into a dark glass jar.

Extract: put some fresh or dried plant (about two tablespoons) into a jar of boiling water (about two cups). Leave it to soak for a few hours, at which point you can strain out the plant bits.

Bath: bathe with fresh or dried flowers scattered in a tub of hot water. Soak your body in it for half an hour.

USING THE HERB

Tincture: Take about two teaspoons a day max. You can take it directly or mixed in with a glass of water. Mixing it with water makes it less harsh.

Extract: This can be used internally by drinking it. You can use it externally by soaking a rag in it and applying it to your skin as a compress or using it as a wash on rashes, inflammation, and sores.

BATH: USE THIS METHOD WHEN YOU HAVE SORE MUSCLES OR MUSCLE spasms.

SIDE EFFECTS AND WARNINGS

Side effects of Japanese honeysuckle include rash, and diarrhea, both generally linked to honeysuckle allergies.

Avoid this plant when pregnant or breastfeeding unless you've consulted your healthcare provider, and they've given the green light on it.

Don't take it within two weeks of getting surgery because it could make it difficult for your blood to clot. In the same vein, don't take it when you're taking other medication that may thin out your blood, such as aspirin.

FUN TIPS AND FACTS

You can suck on the fresh flower, and it's sweet like honey!

AUTHOR'S PERSONAL STORY

Japanese honeysuckle flowers add a lovely flavor to herbal teas that otherwise taste unpleasant. In the past, I've kept some dried flowers aside in a jar and added them to teas for a bit of extra flavor.

146
LARCH

LATIN NAME

Larix

DESCRIPTION

Larch is a large type of coniferous tree, reaching between 50 and 80 feet in height. It has a sturdy stem, supporting branches that spread out wide, with a single tree reaching up to 50 feet wide. The stem can exude resin when injured.

The leaves consist of green needles that come out as a cluster from a bud. These needles go yellow in the fall then fall off during the colder months. The needles are short, reaching about an inch in total.

The fruit is a cone, with each cluster of leaves producing a single cone. These cones also fall off during fall, as the needles do. Cones are green, yellow, red, or purple, ripening to brown after the pollination season. These cones vary in size from species to species.

HABITAT

This tree generally prefers colder temperate areas or cold areas. They're most common in mountainous or hilly regions. A moisture-rich area is their ideal setup.

SEASON TO GATHER THE PLANT

April to May is when the tree buds. This is the best time to gather buds and needles. The inner bark should be harvested in spring when there is a lot of sap flowing through the tree. Just remember to strip vertically and not to remove too much bark, otherwise, the tree will be damaged permanently.

PARTS OF THE PLANT TO USE AS MEDICINE

The bark can be used as well as the resin. Shoots and needles can also be used.

BENEFITS AND PROPERTIES

It has a strong immune-system-boosting effect. This aids in conditions such as the flu, colds, and ear infections.

There is some evidence that it can prevent the growth of liver cancer cells.

Larch increases the number of healthy bacteria in the intestine. This can have a positive effect on one's digestive tract as well as overall health but doing such things as lowering cholesterol.

For brain health, there is evidence that larch can effectively prevent Alzheimer's disease.

Orally, it can be used to treat gum issues and to alleviate a sore throat, and topically, it can be used to heal cuts and bruises.

MEDICINE PREPARATION

Tea: Use a teaspoon of the inner bark (dried and crushed). Pour over a cup of boiling water and let it steep for 10 minutes. Strain out the bark with a fine strainer or a cloth, then drink.

Bath: Use a few handfuls of needles or buds and scatter them in a warm bath. Soak for half an hour.

Sap: You can tap a larch tree and obtain its sap. Do this by creating an inch-deep hole close to the base of the trunk and inserting a straw or tube. Drain the sap into a bottle or jar. Seal the hole afterward for the tree's health. Also, don't tap the same tree more than twice every few years.

USING THE HERB

Tea: This is effective for digestive issues. You can have up to three cups a day.

Bath: This bath will make your body feel stimulated and refreshed.

Sap: The sap doesn't last long (two days at the most), so use it fast. The sap works best for arthritis and inflammation.

SIDE EFFECTS AND WARNINGS

Larch can cause flatulence as well as bloating.

Further, its immune system boosting effect can cause undesirable consequences in patients with autoimmune diseases. The medications taken for this purpose may also interact with larch, causing them to be less effective or have negative reactions.

Individuals that have undergone organ transplants should avoid taking larch. It could cause the rejection of a new organ.

Pregnant and breastfeeding mothers should first consult their healthcare practitioner before taking larch.

FUN TIPS AND FACTS

In European folklore, Larch was thought to have protective powers against evil spirits. It was common to plant it on their property and in villages to protect society.

AUTHOR'S PERSONAL STORY

One of my family members has arthritis that has been giving her problems for years. I used larch sap and made it into a soak for her hands. After soaking her hands for half an hour, she said it was the first time her fingers had felt pain-free in years.

LEMON BALM

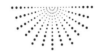

LATIN NAME

Melissa officinalis

DESCRIPTION

The plant comes in the form of a bush that typically grows between 20 and 30 inches high. The stems are thin, green, slightly hairy, and square.

The leaves have an opposite arrangement, and they have an ovular shape. Their margins have rounded teeth, and the veins on the surface of the leaf are rather pronounced. The surface of the leaves feels hairy, and they give off a lemon-like smell and taste similar to lemon.

Flowers grow right against the stem. They're small (half an inch), white, and tubular. There are three rounded petals at the bottom edge of the flower tube, and one at the top. The flower is also slightly hairy.

Lemon balm looks a lot like mint because it's a type of mint. The main distinguishing factor is the lemony scent and flavor.

HABITAT

Direct sun and fertile, well-drained soil are where this herb shines. It grows in thickets, next to ponds, on floodplains, and in disturbed sites.

SEASON TO GATHER THE PLANT

May to September is when you'll find they provide the best harvest. The flowers specifically are available from June to September.

PARTS OF THE PLANT TO USE AS MEDICINE

The flowers, leaves, and stems are generally used medicinally.

BENEFITS AND PROPERTIES

The main benefit that makes this herb sought after is that it's great for reducing stress and anxiety. This is especially true when it's taken daily. It's also good at making us function better cognitively.

Digestive issues can be managed with this herb too. Indigestion and nausea are common ailments it treats.

Pain can be alleviated well using it. This includes menstrual pain, toothaches, and headaches.

If you have sleep issues, this is a great herb to use. You can get over insomnia by taking it at night before you go to sleep.

Finally, you can use it to heal cold sores.

MEDICINE PREPARATION

Tea: Use half a teaspoon of dried and chopped-up lemon balm. Pour over a cup of boiling water and let it steep for five minutes. Strain, then drink.

Tincture: Chop up fresh lemon balm until you can fill up half a jar with it. Cover it with vodka until there's an inch of vodka above the plant material. Seal the jar and leave it out of direct sunlight for six weeks, shaking the jar occasionally. Strain it and pour the liquid into a dark glass container for storage and use.

Cream: Use a cup of lemon balm leaves (fresh or dried), a quarter cup of beeswax, four tablespoons of glycerine, and two-thirds of a cup of water. Melt the wax on low heat, then put in the water, glycerine, and leaves. Stir it and leave it on low heat for three hours. Strain out the leaves and put the cream into jars. Store it in the fridge.

USING THE HERB

Tea: You can take it up to four times a day.
    Tincture: Take up to a teaspoon per day.
    Cream: Apply it to affected parts of your skin up to three times a day.

SIDE EFFECTS AND WARNINGS

Pregnant and breastfeeding women may need to avoid it.

The main consideration is that it could interact with other medications and medicinal plants. Particular care should be taken if you're on sedatives, HIV medications, or thyroid medication.

FUN TIPS AND FACTS

Lemon balm is very enticing for bees. Even the ancient Greeks remarked that it was used as a food to draw bees.

AUTHOR'S PERSONAL STORY

I have a friend that had difficulties with sleeping. She'd tried sleeping pills but wanted to get off of pharmaceutical medication because it was causing her to feel odd on a mental level. I suggested lemon balm, and it was just the natural solution she needed.

148
LINDEN

LATIN NAME

ilia

DESCRIPTION

This is a type of tree with light wood. The bark on the trunk is light gray and there are ridges on it. The bark on the branches is also light gray but smooth.

The leaves are arranged alternately. They come in the shape of an ovular heart with serrated edges and are between four and eight inches long and two to five inches wide. The leaves are green in the spring and summer and yellow in the fall. There is a hairy texture at the bottom of the leaves when they're still small.

The flower is a creamy color, and it gives off a sweet and pleasant smell. It grows as a cyme, which is a cluster of flowers on which the terminal floret flowers first. Linden flowers have a fuzzy appearance.

The fruit of linden is a cluster of seeds that grow down from a peduncle. They are pea-sized and shaped but have a cream color. Each seed has a hard shell.

HABITAT

Lindens prefer a temperate climate, so you won't find them in extremely hot or cold areas.

SEASON TO GATHER THE PLANT

The flowers are gathered in spring. This is also the best time to harvest leaves and bark. Remember to harvest bark responsibly so as not to injure the tree irreparably.

PARTS OF THE PLANT TO USE AS MEDICINE

The flowers are the most valuable parts for medicinal use. The leaves and bark can also be used medicinally.

BENEFITS AND PROPERTIES

Use linden for conditions such as infections, colds, throat irritation, nasal congestion, and coughing for a speedy recovery.

You can also use it on the skin when you have itchy patches.

Linden can help your heart by reducing nervous palpitations, and it can lower your blood pressure.

Lastly, this tree makes medications that are great sedatives.

MEDICINE PREPARATION

Tea: Dry the flowers and cut or crush them up. Use a quarter teaspoon in a cup of boiling water. Let it steep for fifteen minutes, then strain and drink.

Wash: Make it the same way you would make the tea (but use a teaspoon instead of a quarter teaspoon of the dried flowers). Let it cool until it's lukewarm or cold before use so that you don't burn yourself.

USING THE HERB

Tea: Don't drink more than a cup a day. Use it before bed, ideally, as it is great as a sleep aid.

Wash: Wash any itchy skin with it. For intense itch relief, try soaking a cloth in the wash to make a compress.

SIDE EFFECTS AND WARNINGS

Heart damage can occur if you use the tea regularly, especially if you already have heart disease.

It's also suggested to avoid it if you're pregnant or breastfeeding.

Ironically, it can cause itching, even though it's normally a cure for itching.

Interactions with drugs such as water pills and lithium can occur as well.

FUN TIPS AND FACTS

Germanic mythology (pre-Christianity) considered linden trees to be holy. Dances and ceremonies occurred around the tree as well as community assemblies and judicial meetings. The tree was believed to aid in uncovering the truth.

AUTHOR'S PERSONAL STORY

I once had some itchy skin on my feet after wearing closed leather shoes for a few months. I used a linden wash daily for a week as I was getting concerned about my feet. The antifungal quality and the anti-itching quality sorted my feet out beautifully.

MINT

LATIN NAME

entha

DESCRIPTION

Many mint species have stolons, meaning underground stems that shoot out new stems.

Mint comes in a bush of many stems with leaves attached to them. The stems are normally bright or dark green, and they tend to be pliable. It grows as a bush that's normally 12 to 24 inches high.

The leaves have an opposite arrangement. They are dark green and hairy, with serrated margins (the teeth are rounded). The veins are normally darker than the leaf and very clear on the leaf's surface.

The flowers are lilac-colored, pink, or white. Depending on the species, the flowers grow on spikes or in whorls. There are normally four petals per floret.

HABITAT

Mint enjoys growing in temperate weather. Full or partial sun and moist soil are just right for this herb. It can grow in all sorts of locations, but next to streams and other bodies of water is most common.

SEASON TO GATHER THE PLANT

You can pick them throughout the year. The best time is just before they flower, but it's not necessary to limit yourself to this timeframe. Try harvesting in the morning before the moisture starts evaporating out of the plant.

PARTS OF THE PLANT TO USE AS MEDICINE

The leaves, stems, and flowers work for medicinal use.

BENEFITS AND PROPERTIES

Mint is commonly used to reduce indigestion, flatulence, and irritable bowel syndrome.

Mint can also improve respiratory function during illnesses like the common cold. This isn't necessarily due to physical changes caused by the mint, but normally more due to subjective perception of those using it. The mint makes you feel like your air passages are clearing up, even if they're not, giving slight relief.

Applying it topically to the nipples can relieve breastfeeding pain. In the same way, it can soothe itchy and irritated skin.

Additionally, mint can improve brain function. It can reduce anxiety, fatigue, and frustration, and it can increase alertness.

It also fights bad breath. There's a reason it's been used in toothpaste.

MEDICINE PREPARATION

Tea: Put a sprig of mint in a cup of boiling water and leave it to steep for 10 minutes. Take out the sprig and drink up.

Oil: Fill a jar with fresh mint and cover the mint with a carrier oil of your choosing. Seal the jar and put it in a spot out of the sun for three days. Strain out the leaves and fill the jar with new mint. Pour the oil back in and seal the jar again. Leave it to soak for another day, at which point you can strain it out again. Pour the oil into a container of your choosing. Store it in a cool and dry place.

Tincture: Fill a jar with fresh mint and cover it with vodka. Seal the jar and put it in a spot out of the sun for six weeks. Shake it daily. When the six weeks have elapsed, strain out the mint and pour the liquid into dark glass bottles for use and storage.

Mouthwash: Mix a teaspoon of tincture with a cup of water. Use it to rinse out your mouth.

USING THE HERB

Tea: Drinking the tea half an hour before a meal helps to keep the digestive system working well.

Oil: Simply rub it onto any affected areas, such as the nipples or dry skin.

Tincture: Mix a teaspoon with a glass of water, then take it orally.

Mouthwash: Use like any mouthwash to leave your breath smelling great.

SIDE EFFECTS AND WARNINGS

Allergic reactions and the triggering of asthma are the most common side effects.

FUN TIPS AND FACTS

Eating fresh mint leaves or putting a drop of its essential oil on your tongue opens your nose and senses like no other plant!

AUTHOR'S PERSONAL STORY

When facing exam stress as a teen, I drank mint tea a few times a day while studying. This helped me stay alert and focused while I was making sure I'd grasped the information I needed to.

MUGWORT

LATIN NAME

*A*rtemisia vulgaris

DESCRIPTION

The stem of this plant is stiff and purple, and it has hairs as well as grooves. The stem goes purplish-red when mugwort is in flower. It can reach up to six feet tall.

It's established in the ground with an eight-inch deep root with rhizomes and rootlets spreading out from it.

Mugwort has leaves that are light (almost white) on the bottom and dark green on the top. The margins are deeply lobed. The leaves can grow up to four inches long, and they're quite thin. The plant also gives off a smell similar to that of sage.

The flowers are small yellow or red wooly flowers. They are arranged as clusters on spikes at the top of the herb.

HABITAT

You can normally find mugwort in temperate areas. The most common areas are along rivers or streams. It's also common on disturbed sites.

SEASON TO GATHER THE PLANT

It's best to harvest the plant in spring before it flowers. But you can still harvest it into the summer when it's in flower.

PARTS OF THE PLANT TO USE AS MEDICINE

The root, stem, blossoms, and leaves can be used medicinally.

BENEFITS AND PROPERTIES

Mugwort is known to assist with stress reduction. It's also known to increase your energy.

Using mugwort can improve digestion as well as blood circulation and liver function. Your urinary tract should also function better, allowing for more regular urinary output.

You can also use the herb to reduce pain, including headaches and muscle aches.

If you have a problem with itching or eczema, this herb is the ideal solution. This is due in part to the antifungal and antibacterial qualities it possesses.

Mugwort can also be used to regulate the menstrual cycle and induce labor.

MEDICINE PREPARATION

Tincture: Fill a jar with dried mugwort and pour in some vodka until it reaches an inch above the mugwort. Close the jar and put it in a dark spot for a month, shaking it now and then for the best result. At the end of the month, strain the mugwort and pour the tincture into a dark glass bottle.

Tea: Use half a teaspoon of dried mugwort. Put it in a cup of water and let it steep for 10 minutes. Strain out the mugwort and drink your tea.

Oil: Fill a jar with dried mugwort and pour in carrier oil until it's level with the mugwort. Close the jar and put it somewhere out of the sun for four days. Shake it once a day, then strain the mugwort and pour the oil into a container.

USING THE HERB

Tincture: You can use up to a teaspoon per day. It's best to have a few drops (about 5) three times per day when using the tincture.

Tea: You should be able to drink it up to three times a day.

Oil: Apply it to your skin as a soothing agent or to sore muscles to reduce pain.

SIDE EFFECTS AND WARNINGS

Allergies to mugwort do occur, and the reaction can be quite strong in some people.

Pregnant women should watch out for this herb since can cause miscarriages. It's also smart to be cautious about using this herb while breastfeeding.

FUN TIPS AND FACTS

Mugwort has been used in alignment with acupuncture for three millennia. It's aged and bound together to form a burning herb called 'moxa.' This complements the acupuncture and is used for its healing power.

AUTHOR'S PERSONAL STORY

I have had several clients who had headaches that were resolved by rubbing mugwort oil into their temples three times a day.

151
MULBERRY

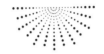

LATIN NAME

Morus alba

DESCRIPTION

Mulberries are trees that grow up to 40 feet high, though they're normally smaller. The trunk is short, and many branches stem out of it. There are normally pliable, thin twigs on the branches. The bark is orange-brown, and it has a knotted, fissured texture.

The leaves grow in an alternate arrangement. They grow up to about three inches long and have a toothed margin. They have a heart shape, but some of the leaves lower on the tree can have a lobed appearance or have incisions. The shape can vary, but in general, all the leaves have a downy bottom and a hairy top.

The flowers are catkins that are green, spiky, and small.

The fruit comes in the form of clustered drupes. They tend to be red but can be whitish or purple too. They're normally pink while ripening.

HABITAT

Mulberry trees like direct sunlight best as well as well-draining, nutritious, and mildly moist soil. They like temperate climates but can stand slightly hotter and colder climates.

SEASON TO GATHER THE PLANT

The fruit can be gathered from July to September.

PARTS OF THE PLANT TO USE AS MEDICINE

The fruit and the leaves are good for medicinal uses. Be careful if you decide to use the leaves, though, because a toxic reaction due to the composition of their latex could occur.

BENEFITS AND PROPERTIES

Mulberries have been linked to cancer risk reduction. This is because it helps prevent cells from breaking down due to oxidative stress.

Blood sugar spikes are preventable by taking mulberries. These berries don't prevent the blood sugar increase after a meal altogether, but they reduce the speed with which blood sugar levels rise.

Cholesterol reduction is possible by taking mulberries. The berries assist in breaking down fat and have even shown promise at reducing fatty liver in some experimental studies.

MEDICINE PREPARATION

Fruit: Eating the fresh fruit directly is the simplest form of medication.

Juice: Simply use enough mulberry fruit to fill your container and juice it up. You can also use frozen mulberries to make a smoothie.

Tea: you should use leaves that have been dried and crushed for this purpose. Use a teaspoon of the dried leaves per cup of boiling water. Allow it to steep for five minutes, then strain the leaves and drink the tea.

USING THE HERB

Fruit: Eating the fruit can prevent a blood sugar spike after a meal. The fruit can be frozen to preserve it.

Juice: One glass of mulberry juice is the recommended daily amount.

Tea: you can have this tea three times a day.

SIDE EFFECTS AND WARNINGS

Diarrhea, gas, bloating, or constipation are possible side effects.

Consult your healthcare provider if you want to take mulberries while pregnant or breastfeeding.

FUN TIPS AND FACTS

Mulberry leaves are the sole diet of silkworms. So, without mulberry trees, we wouldn't have silk in the world.

AUTHOR'S PERSONAL STORY

I suggested daily mulberry juice to a man who was having trouble staying awake after large meals due to a sugar spike and crash. The suggestion paid off when he no longer needed to take a nap in his car at work after eating lunch.

MULLEIN

LATIN NAME

Verbascum thapsus

DESCRIPTION

It's a tall plant, growing between five and 10 feet in height. The stem is winged, meaning it has a thin piece of soft green 'skin' running its length. The stem also has a wooly look to it.

There are basal leaves to the plant that grow to a diameter of about two feet. These are pale gray-green. They have an ovular shape and a downy surface texture. The leaves are large near the bottom of the plant and get smaller higher up the plant.

The flowers are yellow and come in the form of tall spikes. Individual florets have five petals with rounded tips that look almost like the round point of a shovel. Smaller flower spikes can grow out of the central flower spike.

The fruit is an oval capsule with a wooly texture, and it grows on the flower stalk. It's green when the plant flowers, and gradually turns brown.

HABITAT

The plant prefers meadows, woods, pastures, and disturbed areas of land. It likes dry, sandy soil, but it can stand mildly moist soil. Sunny areas are the best for this type of plant.

SEASON TO GATHER THE PLANT

The flowers can be harvested in the summer. The leaves are harvestable year-round and can already be harvested in the first year of growth–choose fresh, young leaves. If you want to harvest the root, it's best to gather in the first year of growth or before any signs of flowering occur during the second year.

PARTS OF THE PLANT TO USE AS MEDICINE

The flowers, leaves, and roots can all be used for this purpose.

BENEFITS AND PROPERTIES

Use the plant when you have an infection, whether it be a middle ear infection, a sinus infection, a urinary tract infection, or a different kind of infection.

Aches and cramps–such as earaches, menstrual cramps, migraines, or toothaches–can all be alleviated using common mullein.

You can use it to remedy a sore throat and coughing. Further, you can use it when you're trying to overcome bronchitis. IT can also aid in the management of asthma and other respiratory problems.

Mullein can also help with urinary control issues, including bed-wetting.

Topically, it is used for skin diseases, bruises, frostbite, arthritis, and rheumatism.

MEDICINE PREPARATION

Tea: Use a teaspoon of dried common mullein (flowers or leaves). Put it in a cup of boiled water and let it steep for 10 minutes. Strain out the plant pieces, then drink them.

Oil: You can make it with a cold or a hot procedure. The cold procedure requires you to use dried leaves or flowers (any amount) and cover it with a carrier oil (I suggest olive oil) until the oil's just above the dried plant bits. Steep it for a week, then strain the oil into a container for use. The hot procedure requires that you place leaves or flowers (dry or fresh) into a pot and cover it with a carrier oil. Heat the oil so that it's on low heat and leave it at that heat for three hours. You can take it off the heat after that and let it cool. After this, you can strain it into a container for use.

Smoking: It's best to dry it and crumble the leaf before smoking it.

USING THE HERB

Tea: You can drink up to four cups a day.

Oil: You can use it internally and externally.

Smoking: Its use is to increase lung health. The smoke it generates has a light quality when inhaled.

SIDE EFFECTS AND WARNINGS

If you're pregnant or breastfeeding, it's best to consult your healthcare provider before using it.

When handling it in the field or while preparing it for use, you may get a rash (due to the hairs on the surface). Not filtering out the hairs in your herbal preparations could also result in mouth irritation.

FUN TIPS AND FACTS

The seeds can make it easier to catch fish. They contain a small amount of a substance that makes fish inactive. Thus, if a fish eats it, you'll be able to get hold of it more easily.

AUTHOR'S PERSONAL STORY

There are a few parents I know who have used common mullein tea while getting their children to overcome bed-wetting. The normal procedure was to get their children to drink some of it an hour before bedtime, to allow the child to go to the bathroom, then put the child to bed.

153
OAK

LATIN NAME

 *uercus*

DESCRIPTION

There are hundreds of oak species. These trees generally grow quite large, growing between 60 and 80 feet (although they can grow as tall as 100 feet or as short as a shrub). Their bark is normally gray when young and becomes white-gray or black when older. Younger trees tend to have smooth bark, whereas older ones tend to have fissures.

The leaves have lobes on them (normally between five and 11). There are two main classifications of an oak tree when it comes to leaves–red and white. The red ones have pointy protrusions on their lobes, whereas the white ones have rounded lobes. A lobe protrudes quite far from the central vein, coming back close to the central vein before the next lobe protrusion starts. The leaves typically grow between five and nine inches long for both classifications. The arrangement of oak leaves is typically alternate. They normally have a green color during the spring and summer, then turn orange, red, and yellow in the fall before they fall off for the winter. Some species, however, are evergreen.

The flowers of an oak tree are normally found on soft, drooping, short stems. They are generally small and green, seemingly insignificant. You may not even realize you're looking at its flowers. However, some species may have flowers that vary widely from this description.

The fruit consists of acorns. Each fruit normally has a peduncle with a cup-shaped green or brown bit. This cup-shaped bit holds a nut that's covered in leathery skin.

HABITAT

Temperate climates are the preferred climate for this type of tree. These trees prefer sun and soil that's well-drained.

SEASON TO GATHER THE PLANT

The bark should be harvested during fall. Acorns should also be harvested during the fall. The leaves should be harvested while they're still green–preferably while they're still young.

PARTS OF THE PLANT TO USE AS MEDICINE

You can use the bark (especially the inner bark), the leaves, the acorns, and gallnuts. (Gallnuts are growths on the tree produced as a result of an infection caused by wasps.)

BENEFITS AND PROPERTIES

Oak is good for the skin because of the contraction it causes in the skin cells. Other skincare uses include reducing inflammation and dermatitis.

It's good for reducing inflammation in the oral region as well. Mouth diseases can be tackled effectively using it. Further, it can be used as a gargle to make a sore throat feel better.

Oak can help your digestive tract function better, and issues related to processing food can be alleviated. It can also regulate urination better, reduce or prevent diarrhea, and assist in breaking down or preventing kidney stones. If used as an enema, it can treat hemorrhoids.

The antibacterial properties of oak can assist in handling vaginal infections.

Lastly, it can help treat rheumatism.

MEDICINE PREPARATION

Tea: You'll need to crush bark into a powder. Add a teaspoon of the bark to a cup of boiling water. Stir it and let it steep for 15 minutes before straining it out. At this point, it should be ready to drink.

Enema: Prepare this in the same way you would the tea, but let it steep for 20 minutes rather than 15.

Snuff: grind inner oak bark until it's extremely fine. You can then snuff it.

USING THE HERB

Tea: The tea is very good at aiding intestinal functions. When cooled, it also makes a good mouthwash or gargle to help with swollen gums, mouth sores, and sore throat. Cooled tea can also be used as a wash to help the skin.

Enema: This is especially good for hemorrhoids.

Snuff: The snuff helps with nose bleeds.

SIDE EFFECTS AND WARNINGS

Intestinal issues could result from using oak bark longer than a few days at a time. It can also cause kidney and liver damage.

You should limit topical use to two weeks. Using it longer could expose you to unwanted side effects, such as eczema and skin irritation..

If you're pregnant or breastfeeding, you should consult your healthcare provider before using it.

Avoid using oak if you have nerve disorders, liver issues, kidney problems, a fever, extensive skin damage, or heart conditions.

FUN TIPS AND FACTS

Oak was representative of the most important god in ancient Greek mythology, ancient Roman mythology, Celtic mythology, Slavic mythology, and Teutonic mythology. The chief god in all these religions was linked to lightning, and ironically, the oak tree is a tree that has a high incidence of getting struck by lightning.

AUTHOR'S PERSONAL STORY

There was a man with hemorrhoids that were preventing him from sitting comfortably. He was embarrassed about it and asked me for advice. I told him how to do an oak enema, and after trying it out for a few days, it went away.

154
PINE

LATIN NAME

 inaceae

DESCRIPTION

This is a tree that can grow quite tall. There are 129 species, so there are many variations to the typical pine tree described here.

The typical pine tree has gray or red-brown bark.

It has needles that grow in clusters of two to five on twigs. They can be anywhere between an inch and 18 inches long.

Pines have seed-bearing cones that come in an egg shape. These cones hang, rather than grow upward (which can be a helpful fact when differentiating from other conifers). The cones release pollen or seeds when they're ripe then fall off.

HABITAT

Where pines grow can vary from deserts to rainforests to cold regions. Most, however, grow in cool, temperate regions. They prefer direct sun, sandy soil that's not too fertile, and soil that's not too wet.

SEASON TO GATHER THE PLANT

The pine is evergreen, so you can harvest it at any point of the year.

PARTS OF THE PLANT TO USE AS MEDICINE

The needles, the bark (especially the inner bark), and the resin of a pine tree can be used.

BENEFITS AND PROPERTIES

Pine can treat fevers, colds, bronchitis, and coughing as well as inflammation in the lungs.

It also helps regulate blood pressure.

It can relieve muscle and nerve pain as well.

When taken with vitamin C, it can improve memory and thinking ability.

MEDICINE PREPARATION

Tea: Take a few pine needles and put them in a cup of boiling water. Let them steep for five to 10 minutes, then remove them. Drink the tea. An alternative to using the needles is using pieces of the bark.

Steaming: Put a bunch of pine needles in a bowl of boiled water fresh from the stove. Put your face over the bowl and throw a towel over your head to prevent the steam from dispersing. Inhale for several minutes.

Bath: Break bark into small pieces and put it in your bathwater.

Wine infusion: Break bark into small pieces and put it in a container/jar with wine. Let the wine become infused with the bark for several hours to a day, then remove the bark. Drink the liquid.

Salve: Use two tablespoons of pitch, four teaspoons of olive oil, and one and a half tablespoons of beeswax. Melt them together on low heat before pouring them into a container. Let it cool and congeal, at which point you'll be able to use it.

USING THE HERB

Tea: The tea can be used as a preventative measure in seasonal changes so that you don't get colds. It can also be used as a wash when it's cooled.

Steaming: Do this to reduce phlegm.
Bath: Soaking in this can alleviate muscle aches.
Wine infusion: The Chinese traditionally use this for joint pain.
Salve: Use this for joint inflammation or insect bites.

SIDE EFFECTS AND WARNINGS

The bark can be toxic if you take larger quantities.

Pine should not be taken orally for long periods..

Allergies can occur even if pine allergy isn't detected in an allergy test.

If you have asthma, it may be a good idea to avoid pine.

Pregnant and breastfeeding women should avoid pine unless their healthcare provider says otherwise.

FUN TIPS AND FACTS

The ancient Romans associated pine with fertility, and they used it in fertility rituals. This is in part because of the phallic shape of a pine cone.

AUTHOR'S PERSONAL STORY

I steam with pine when I have congestion and phlegm. It clears it right up.

155
PLANTAIN

LATIN NAME

 lantago

DESCRIPTION

Plantains are low-growers with a basal leaf rosette and spikes with flowers. The leaves are either oval-shaped or lance-shaped and overlap loosely. Veins in the leaves run parallel to each other.

The flowers grow on spikes. They are small and have four transparent petals. The coloration of the spike from a distance is green, yellow, or brown. Note that the flowers don't cover the whole spike, only the upper half of the spike.

HABITAT

Plantain grows ideally where the soil is rocky, sandy, or compacted. It can grow in the shade or direct sunlight. You'll find them in disturbed areas, amongst others.

SEASON TO GATHER THE PLANT

You can gather them any time of the year. Younger leaves are the best.

PARTS OF THE PLANT TO USE AS MEDICINE

The leaves are used for medicinal purposes.

BENEFITS AND PROPERTIES

Plantain has several components that could reduce inflammation in the body. A bonus of this is that you could be protecting your liver health in the process.

It can boost the digestive system and regulate bowel movements. It also works effectively as a natural laxative.

In addition, plantain can help heal wounds, especially due to its antimicrobial characteristics.

It's also good for dealing with insect bites.

MEDICINE PREPARATION

Poultice: To make a good poultice, simply blend or mash some plantain leaves together until you've formed a paste. Apply it to the wound, injury, bite, etc. Once applied, cover it with a bandage.

Tea: Use two teaspoons of dried leaves or two tablespoons of fresh leaves. Put it in a cup of boiling water and stir, then let it steep for 10 minutes. Strain out the leaf bits, then drink up.

USING THE HERB

Poultice: This can only be used once. You'll need to use fresh leaves, not dried leaves.

Tea: You may find that you experience a laxative effect when drinking the tea, so don't have too much. If you do feel a laxative effect, drink water so you don't become dehydrated.

SIDE EFFECTS AND WARNINGS

Allergic reactions may occur. Some allergic reactions are quite strong.

Plantain supplements can have negative effects, such as digestive issues. This is especially the case if the supplements were made using plantain seeds.

FUN TIPS AND FACTS

Plantain can be put on mosquito bites to stop itching or on blisters as a protective barrier.

AUTHOR'S PERSONAL STORY

A family member once had an itchy bug bite. I whipped up a quick poultice and applied it. The poultice provided instant relief.

156
RASPBERRY

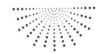

LATIN NAME

*ubus idaeus*

DESCRIPTION

Raspberries grow as bushes reaching up to six feet tall. The stem of a raspberry plant is called a cane. It's tall and stiff. Most are prickly, but some species have a smooth cane. In the first year of growth, the cane will be green, and in the second year, it'll be brown. Once it goes brown, it'll be ready to carry fruit then die.

The leaves are shaped like spades and have toothed margins. They have a silvery underside (that's slightly hairy) and a green top. Leaves are normally made up of three to five leaflets.

Flowers vary a lot from species to species, but they normally have five petals with rounded tips. These flowers are normally clustered. Their colors are mainly green or white.

The fruit of this plant is made up of a bunch of drupes. They're soft, with each drupe containing a seed. There are small hairs between the drupes. In terms of shape, a raspberry looks conical but with a blunted tip–and it usually hangs down. There are slight differences in size and color of the fruit from species to species (with the fruit being red, pinkish, purple, yellow, or black).

HABITAT

They are commonly found on river banks, in forest clearings, and in fields. It likes well-drained soil and direct sunlight.

SEASON TO GATHER THE PLANT

The fruit is ready for picking in late June and in July. The leaves can be picked whenever they're green–young leaves being the best.

PARTS OF THE PLANT TO USE AS MEDICINE

The leaves and the fruit are best for medicine.

BENEFITS AND PROPERTIES

Raspberries are good for your blood. They can lower blood pressure and blood sugar (contributing to diabetes management and weight loss). Furthermore, they can improve heart function, thereby combating heart disease. Cholesterol levels can be improved too, and they can reduce your risk of stroke

Eating raspberries is also good for the skin and bones.

MEDICINE PREPARATION

Tincture: Use dried raspberry leaves for this. Fill a mason jar with the leaves and cover it with vodka. Close the jar and put it in a cool space out of direct sunlight. Leave it there for six weeks. Give it a shake every few days to mix up everything in the jar. When the six weeks are up, strain the liquid into a dark glass bottle for use.

Tea: You can use dried or fresh raspberry leaves. Use a tablespoon of the leaf in a cup of boiling water and let it steep for 20 minutes. Remove the leaf pieces (by straining) and drink the tea.

Fresh berries: Simply clean the berries and eat them.

USING THE HERB

Tincture: You can use the same tincture for years without it expiring. Don't use more than a teaspoon per day.

Tea: It tastes similar to black tea, so you can use it as a replacement for your normal tea. As an added bonus, it doesn't contain caffeine.

Fresh berries: The berries are high in vitamins and have very low sugar levels, making them great for snacking.

SIDE EFFECTS AND WARNINGS

People on insulin should be cautious with raspberries due to their ability to lower blood sugar.

If you're on medication to prevent or slow blood clotting, you shouldn't consume raspberries.

Conditions that are sensitive to hormones, such as some cancers, can be exacerbated by raspberry consumption.

FUN TIPS AND FACTS

In the Christian religion, raspberries have often been used to represent kindness in art.

AUTHOR'S PERSONAL STORY

I once had a scare that I might become anemic after visiting a healthcare expert. After taking raspberries multiple times a week for a month, I went back to the expert. The potential crisis had been averted as my blood was carrying iron as it was supposed to.

157
RED CLOVER

LATIN NAME

Trifolium pratense

DESCRIPTION

Red clover grows between six and 24 inches tall. It has a green, hairy stem.

The leaves on this plant are compound, with three leaflets composing each leaf. The leaflets are between half an inch and two inches long. They're green, and there's a white 'v' shape on the top of the leaf (which is one of the plant's most easily identifiable characteristics). The overall compound leaves are arranged alternately.

The flowers grow on a head that's an inch long and an inch wide. The florets on the head are a half-inch across. They're pink or purple, but they go brown close to winter.

HABITAT

This type of plant likes direct sun and well-drained soil. It grows in pastures, fields, and meadows.

SEASON TO GATHER THE PLANT

It flowers from May to September, and the best time to harvest the flowers is in the latter part of this period, in August and September.

PARTS OF THE PLANT TO USE AS MEDICINE

The dried flower head is the main part of the plant used medicinally.

BENEFITS AND PROPERTIES

Red clover can help prevent heart disease.
 Additionally, it can lower the risk of prostate cancer.
 Red clover can improve skin and hair health as well. . In fact, there has been a noted connection between red clover and reduced hair loss.
 The herb can also reduce symptoms associated with menopause

MEDICINE PREPARATION

Tea: You need two teaspoons of dried flowers. Put it into a cup of hot water (not quite boiling) and let it steep for 15 minutes.

USING THE HERB

Tea: You can have up to three cups a day. You can also let the tea cool and apply it to your skin or hair as a wash.

SIDE EFFECTS AND WARNINGS

If you have hormone-related cancer, then avoid red clover.
 Pregnant and breastfeeding women should also avoid it unless their medical professional has advised them that it's okay to use.
 Red clover interacts with some drugs, including birth control, medication to reduce blood clotting and blood platelets, rheumatoid arthritis medication, and psoriasis medication. The last two types of medication could interact with red clover in such a way that it causes toxicity in your body.
 Avoid taking it within two weeks of surgery, as it could interfere with the medication that is required for the surgery.

FUN TIPS AND FACTS

In folk magic, red clover is used in a ritual bath to attract money and prosperity to the bather and is also used as a floor wash to chase out evil and unwanted ghosts. Four-leaf clovers are famous as a good luck charm believed to protect people from evil spirits, witches, disease, and the evil eye.

AUTHOR'S PERSONAL STORY

A friend of my grandmother's was starting to get concerned because her hair was starting to thin out. I suggested using a red clover wash for the first week of every month (using it to soak the hair for five minutes each of the days in the week). She tried it and her hair loss slowed down dramatically.

158
SAINT JOHN'S WORT

LATIN NAME

Hypericum perforatum

DESCRIPTION

St John's wort is a type of shrub that grows up to 31 inches high and has a stem that discharges a red liquid.

The leaves normally grow in pairs, and they have an ovular shape. They have glands visible on the surface that give off a foxy smell (i.e. a musky and earthy smell).

The flowers of this plant are bright yellow (petals, center, and reproductive organs), are small, and grow in clusters. Each flower has five petals.

The fruit is a soft red capsule that grows in clusters. There are three chambers in the flower that contain small black or brown seeds. It's covered in a sticky material that helps it stick to people and animals that pass by, allowing it to disperse. There are many species of the plant, and some have different types of fruit, such as a single, glossy red berry.

HABITAT

It grows next to hedges, in woods, and in wastelands. It likes rich and well-draining soil that's mildly moist and full sun or partial shade.

SEASON TO GATHER THE PLANT

June to September is the right time to gather Saint John's wort.

PARTS OF THE PLANT TO USE AS MEDICINE

The flowers of the plant are used for medicinal purposes.

BENEFITS AND PROPERTIES

Wounds, burns, and other skin damage is remedied using St John's wort. Muscle pain can also be managed with topical use.

It can also be used for its mental benefits. The plant can help manage ADHD, depression, insomnia, obsessive-compulsive disorder, and somatic symptom disorder. St. John's wort is particularly used to combat depression—specifically mild and moderate depression. It's known to liven your mood due to increases in impulses being sent in the brain.

St John's wort can also alleviate conditions related to menopause.

And internally, it can benefit your lungs and kidneys.

MEDICINE PREPARATION

Tea: You use the flowers (three teaspoons) to make the tea. Boil two cups of water in a saucepan and put in the fresh flowers. Let it steep for four minutes, then remove it from the heat, strain out the flowers, and serve it.

USING THE HERB

Tea: You can use it internally for a range of the conditions listed in the benefits section. It's good to take it before bedtime because it will assist with better sleep during the night. You can also use it externally, after it's cooled down, as a wash or as a compress.

SIDE EFFECTS AND WARNINGS

St. John's wort is known to interact with medications. These include birth control, depression medication, HIV medication, blood cholesterol medication, some cancer medication, heart medications, the blood thinner warfarin, and medication that prevents organ transplant rejection. There are other medications that it interacts with that aren't listed, so consult your healthcare practitioner if you're on regular medication and you want to take the herb.

It can also cause allergic reactions and sensitivity to sunlight.

It should be taken only with the approval of your medical professional if you're pregnant or breastfeeding.

FUN TIPS AND FACTS

Have you ever tried to soak this herb in oil and make an oil extract? You won't believe the color of the result–it's red and looks like blood!

In ancient medicine, herbalists used to pick it on the summer solstice because they believed that that was the day when the herb has the most healing properties.

AUTHOR'S PERSONAL STORY

There have been a few occasions when I wasn't able to fall asleep, so I drank the tea, spent a few minutes reading, then easily drifted off to sleep.

159
SASSAFRAS

LATIN NAME

assafras

DESCRIPTION

This is a tree that's small in stature, growing between 20 and 40 feet tall. The stem grows between one and two feet across. It has an extensive root system that gives rise to smaller trees. The bark has an aromatic scent and has a red-brown color. It's smooth in younger trees and fissured in older trees.

The leaves have an aromatic scent (almost citrusy), just like the bark. The shape can be triple-lobed (or in some cases, they have five or seven lobes), ovular, or mitten-shaped. They grow between three and seven inches long and up to four inches wide. The leaves have a yellow-green color, and they turn red, orange, purple, or yellow in the fall.

Their flowers grow in two-inch-long clusters at the end of the branches. Individual flowers span one to two inches and are yellow or green. They have six petals and come in the shape of a star.

The fruit of the sassafras tree comes in the form of black or dark blue drupes that grow in clusters. Each drupe contains a seed and grows in a red cup-like peduncle.

HABITAT

Forests, especially at their edges, are good areas to look for sassafras. It likes full to partial sun, and the best soil for this tree is well-drained and loamy.

SEASON TO GATHER THE PLANT

The flowers start growing in early spring, and the leaves are available from spring to late summer. However, the root should be harvested in the winter because all the nutrients will have receded to the roots at that point.

PARTS OF THE PLANT TO USE AS MEDICINE

The roots, the bark, and the leaves can be used.

BENEFITS AND PROPERTIES

It's good for your blood, providing a blood-purifying effect. It also improves blood circulation. You can use it to prevent heart attacks caused by overly viscous blood as it can lower coagulation of the blood.

Sassafras is good for keeping up your liver's health as well.

This tree can have a mild antiseptic effect as well as an immune system boosting effect. This aids in preventing infections, such as those in the stomach.

It can be an effective aphrodisiac. This is partly due to an increase in blood flow to the pelvic area.

Sassafras can also have an energy increasing effect.

This plant is good for treating bruising and swelling. Sassafras is also good for wound care and pain relief (including menstrual pain).

MEDICINE PREPARATION

Decoction: Chop up a piece of root into small pieces. Cut enough to cover the bottom of a small saucepan. Fill the saucepan with water (about three quarters of the way). Bring it to a boil then down to a simmer, letting it simmer until the water darkens. Strain out the root pieces.

Leaves: Wash up a few fresh leaves and rub them on open wounds.

Twigs: Use a fresh sassafras twig and rub it across your teeth and gums as a toothbrush.

USING THE HERB

Decoction: You can drink it as you would drink tea (sweetening and adding milk if you like)–not having more than one cup per day. For topical applications, you can add it to homemade soap to experience its skincare benefits daily. You can also use the decoction as a wash.

Leaves: This has been used by Native Americans to recover faster from wounds.

Twigs: the antiseptic effect this has is great for your oral health.

SIDE EFFECTS AND WARNINGS

Sassafras contains a chemical (safrole) that was labeled as mildly carcinogenic by the FDA in the 1970s. Since then, the same chemical has been linked to anti-cancer properties. Further study is needed to determine its effect.

Overconsumption of sassafras oil can be fatal due to the high quantities of safrole. Sassafras oil needs to be taken in microscopic amounts and should never be given to children.

Miscarriages may result from taking it while pregnant. It's also best not to take it while breastfeeding.

Hot flashes, vomiting, sweating, rashes, hallucinations, and high blood pressure can all be side effects of using this plant medicinally.

When taken in larger quantities, it can make you fall asleep by slowing down your central nervous system. It can also interact with sedative medication, making these medications too strong.

Avoid using it within two weeks of any surgery.

FUN TIPS AND FACTS

Sassafras became popular for its sweet-smelling wood and its healing qualities in the 16th Century. It was exported from the New World to the Old World, being a desirable form of wood at the time. On these journeys to the Old World, sassafras became known as a lucky tree because there were many safe voyages on which the tree was transported.

AUTHOR'S PERSONAL STORY

Once, while I was hiking, I slipped and cut myself on a sharp rock. After rinsing off the cut with water from my bottle, I spotted a clump of sassafras trees. I grabbed a few leaves and crushed them in my hands then rubbed them on my cut. I felt the pain gradually subside. Later, the cut healed much faster than I expected it would.

160
SHEPHERD'S PURSE

LATIN NAME

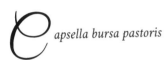

apsella bursa pastoris

DESCRIPTION

The plant grows to about 24 inches max. Most of this height comes from a central stalk that bears the flowers and seed pods.

There are large basal leaves (in a rosette arrangement), then there are smaller leaves on the stalk. The basal leaves die off when the plant flowers. As for their shape, the basal leaves have a long (four-inch), lobed appearance. The lobes on one side of a basal leaf normally correspond to the lobes on the other side–with some being shaped like a round simple leaf, and some having multiple lobes. These leaves are a bit hairy to the touch. The smaller leaves on the stalk are arranged alternately and are slightly toothed.

The flowers of the shepherd's purse are white and appear in a rounded cluster at the end of the central stalk. The individual flowers are very small–less than half an inch across.

The fruit consists of seed pods that have a heart shape or a triangular shape.

HABITAT

They grow in fields, wastelands, and cultivated areas.

SEASON TO GATHER THE PLANT

Collect the leaves in early spring, before the stalks appear. These leaves will be fresh and pleasant to use. The basal leaves are better to use than the smaller leaves on the stalk. The flowers can be collected from early spring until late fall.

PARTS OF THE PLANT TO USE AS MEDICINE

You can use the shoots, the leaves, the seeds, and the roots. The leaves can be eaten raw or cooked and can be used dry as medicine. The roots can be dried out and used in place of ginger.

BENEFITS AND PROPERTIES

Shepherd's purse can help with heart and blood conditions including (mild)heart failure, mild palpitations, and low blood pressure. Vomiting blood, nosebleeds, and bleeding injuries can also be mitigated.

This plant is also good for the excretory system, and it can treat bladder infections, blood in the urine, and diarrhea.

Menstrual issues can be managed with the herb. If you have cramps while menstruating, a menstrual cycle that lasts very long, or premenstrual syndrome, then you can take it as a remedy.

Headaches and skin burns can also be treated with shepherd's purse.

MEDICINE PREPARATION

Tincture: Fill a jar with fresh shepherd's purse plant matter (cleaned). Pour brandy or vodka in the jar until it's almost at the top. Close the bottle and shake it. Store it in a spot away from direct sunlight for three weeks, and it every few days. Strain the liquid into a dark glass jar once the three weeks are completed.

Food: Use the leaves and the sprouts in your everyday meals. They're good in both salads and cooked dishes.

USING THE HERB

Tincture: Take about 15 drops when needed.

Food: Eating shepherd's purse gives you some of the medicinal benefits of the plant while also feeding your body.

SIDE EFFECTS AND WARNINGS

Overconsumption can cause paralysis, difficulty breathing, and death.

In addition drowsiness, changes in thyroid function, changes in blood pressure, and heart palpitations can result from taking it in normal doses.

Using it while pregnant can result in miscarriage. Consult your healthcare provider if you want to use it while breastfeeding.

Avoid using it within two weeks of surgery because the lethargy it causes can make anesthesia operate contrary to how it should.

When you have chronic heart problems, you shouldn't use shepherd's purse. It won't assist with your heart health as it would in people without heart conditions. In fact, it could exacerbate any heart conditions you already have.

Shepherd's purse should not be taken by those with thyroid conditions.

This herb can cause those who are prone to kidney stones or have a history of kidney stones to develop more kidney stones.

It will often interact with sedative medication, so don't use it with sedatives.

FUN TIPS AND FACTS

The tincture has many uses, but it's one of the few medicinal plant remedies I know of that can assist with internal bleeding. It's a very good addition to your first aid kit.

AUTHOR'S PERSONAL STORY

I once used the roots (cleaned and finely chopped) in cookies that I was making for my wife while she was going through her menstrual cycle. It served the double purpose of fulfilling the cookie craving and easing the cramping.

161
SOLOMON'S SEAL

LATIN NAME

olygonatum biflorum

DESCRIPTION

The stem on this plant grows in an arch, reaching knee height. The stem doesn't grow branches, only leaves, and flowers, and it has rhizomes underground.

The leaves come in rows of two and are rather broad. They have an elliptical shape and are arranged alternately along the two rows. They grow between three and eight inches long. The margins are smooth, and the veins are parallel.

The flowers that grow out of the axils of the leaves are either green or white and droop down. They are egg-shaped and have a strong, sweet smell.

The plant produces dark blue berries the shape and size of marbles.

HABITAT

They like moist–but well-drained–soil, so they are commonly found on the banks of bodies of water or in moist forests.

SEASON TO GATHER THE PLANT

The flowers can be gathered in May and June.

PARTS OF THE PLANT TO USE AS MEDICINE

The berries, rhizomes, and leaves can be used.

BENEFITS AND PROPERTIES

The berries act as a laxative in large doses.

Topically, it can be used for a broad range of purposes. It keeps the skin taut, reduces skin redness, reduces swelling, aids in healing bruises, treats hemorrhoids, and helps treat boils.

It also assists with lung disorders and mitigates water retention.

MEDICINE PREPARATION

Tonic: You need fortified wine (enough to cover the other ingredients), Solomon's seal root (eight ounces), and ginger (two ounces). Bring it to a boil in a saucepan, then remove it from the heat as soon as it's started boiling. Let it steep while cooling. Put it in a jar and leave it in a cool, dry place for three weeks. Strain out the Solomon's seal and the ginger. Keep it refrigerated

Tea: Dry, chop and grind up some Solomon's seal root. Put half a teaspoon of this into hot water (just below boiling) and let it steep for 10 minutes. It should be ready to drink.

USING THE HERB

Tonic: This is good for stimulating your digestive tract before eating. Have one ounce before a meal, thrice daily.

Tea: This can also be used externally For this, you'll need to let it cool down, then you can apply it to your skin as a wash or compress. Drink three cups a day at the most.

SIDE EFFECTS AND WARNINGS

People with diabetes should beware of this herb. It could decrease blood sugar, requiring you to monitor your sugar levels. If you're on medication for your diabetes there may be drug interactions.

Pregnant and breastfeeding women shouldn't use it without approval from their healthcare provider.

When going for surgery, don't take it for two weeks prior. The drop in blood sugar that the herb can cause may make medication used in the surgery operate differently from how it's supposed to.

It can upset the stomach, causing diarrhea and vomiting if not used in moderation

FUN TIPS AND FACTS

King Solomon of the Bible is said to have placed his seal on this herb due to the high value he placed on it.

AUTHOR'S PERSONAL STORY

I once accidentally had too many of the berries and got some diarrhea while wildcrafting. Needless to say, the berries are great for cleansing your system.

STINGING NETTLE

LATIN NAME

Urtica

DESCRIPTION

Stinging nettle grows between two and five feet tall.

The leaves are arranged alternately. They have serrated margins and pointed tips, and their shape is a combination between lanceolate and a heart shape. The leaves of this plant have hairs that sting you, causing itchiness, rash, and pain. The itching comes from histamine and acetylcholine injected through the stinging hairs.

HABITAT

Full or partial sun and nitrogen-rich, nutritious soil is the best for stinging nettle. It's most commonly found near rivers.

SEASON TO GATHER THE PLANT

Don't harvest it after it's started blooming as it can cause kidney damage, whereas before this it can't. Early spring is a good time. Cover yourself while harvesting it because it hurts when it stings.

PARTS OF THE PLANT TO USE AS MEDICINE

The leaves are the main part of the plant used as medicine.

BENEFITS AND PROPERTIES

It's great for managing allergies and hay fever. This is because it contains antihistamine and anti-inflammatory chemicals.

Topical application can reduce pain in joints, tendons, and muscles and pain due to sprains. It can alleviate gout and arthritis as well. It's also good for pain and irritation from insect bites. Additionally, it helps with eczema.

Stinging nettle can help with urinary tract infections, other urinary conditions, and enlarged prostates.

MEDICINE PREPARATION

Tea: Put a handful of leaves in a cup of boiling water, then let it steep for 10 minutes. Afterward, remove the leaves, then drink the tea.

Infusion: The infusion is made the same way as the tea, with the added step of overnighting the steeping. Use this as a compress to affect the external benefits associated with stinging nettle.

USING THE HERB

Tea: Adding mint gives a nice flavor to the tea.

Infusion: Extra infusion that you don't want to drink can be thrown over your potted or garden plants. It's good for them.

SIDE EFFECTS AND WARNINGS

Using it medicinally can cause hives, a rash, diarrhea, sweating, a stomach upset, or fluid retention. However, these aren't commonly experienced.

Stinging nettle can alter the menstrual cycle and cause miscarriages.

It can also interfere with diabetes medication and cause reactions in diabetic patients by raising blood sugar.

Additionally, it is known to interact with medications and with other medicinal plants

Ask for your healthcare provider's guidance before using it if you have kidney or bladder issues.

FUN TIPS AND FACTS

Nettle can be used to make strong cloth. You'll need to learn the processes involved in making it to create your own, but the finish of this cloth is rather durable.

AUTHOR'S PERSONAL STORY

Once, while harvesting stinging nettle, I got pricked by the nettle and had a nasty red spot. Ironically, when I got home, I used a stinging nettle compress to alleviate the pain. So, it can be both the cause of pain and the solution to pain.

163
SUNFLOWER

LATIN NAME

Helianthus

DESCRIPTION

Sunflowers are plants that are used extensively in the food and natural medicine industries. There are many species, and there are large variations between some of the species. Characteristics that are common between most of the species include fast growth (up to a few inches a day in spring), a late summer blooming season.

It has a central stem that's upright and stiff. It's usually hairy.

The leaves are large and are hairy to the touch. The shape varies, with some species having heart-shaped leaves, some having oval leaves, and some having leaves that are shaped like spikes. Most have serrated margins.

The flowers have a big disk in the middle, with larger petals coming off the edges of the disk. The central disk is covered in many tiny florets. The tiny florets each have five petals, five stamens, and a large pistil. The flower changes direction through the course of the day to follow the sun.

The fruit of a sunflower is its seeds. Each of the florets on the central disk is replaced by a single seed. They're shorter than half an inch and covered with a thick husk. The husk is gray, black, and white-streaked vertically. The seed in the middle of the husk is a gray-tan color, and it's shaped like an oval with one pointy end.

HABITAT

Sunflowers grow in prairies and open areas. The climate can vary. Soil should be nutritious and too wet, and sunlight should be direct for long periods of the day.

SEASON TO GATHER THE PLANT

It should be harvested when the flower starts drying out. The base of the flower will be transitioning from green to yellow to brown. This is usually from September to October.

PARTS OF THE PLANT TO USE AS MEDICINE

The seeds are used medicinally.

BENEFITS AND PROPERTIES

Sunflower seeds are good for your heart. They protect against heart attacks, strokes, and high blood pressure by blocking an enzyme that constricts your blood vessels.

It contributes to lowering blood sugar, which can help with managing combat type two diabetes.

Sunflower seeds can also reduce inflammation.

MEDICINE PREPARATION

Oil: Blend the seeds until a paste is formed, adding a pinch of water. Place the paste in a pan at 300 degrees Fahrenheit. Keep it on, and stir it occasionally for 20 minutes. Place it in a fine strainer or cloth over a container for a few hours. The oil will drip out.

Seeds: eating the seeds directly contributes to a range of health benefits.

USING THE HERB

Oil: Heating the oil will reduce the efficacy, and Using shop-bought sunflower oil won't have the same benefits.

Seeds: simply eat an ounce a day to experience the benefits long-term. They can also be added to meals, salads, and baked goods.

SIDE EFFECTS AND WARNINGS

Some people may experience an allergic reaction to sunflower seeds and oil.

The seeds have trace amounts of cadmium, a heavy metal that can cause kidney damage. If you eat very large amounts for a long period, you could experience this side effect. That said, if you eat reasonable quantities, like an ounce per day, this won't be an issue.

There are many calories in sunflower seeds and oil, so overconsumption can lead to weight gain.

In addition, constipation is a common side effect of eating a lot of the seeds in one sitting.

FUN TIPS AND FACTS

Sunflowers don't just look like little suns. They also face the sun during the day, changing the direction of their flowers. Thus, they're appropriately named.

AUTHOR'S PERSONAL STORY

I have used natural sunflower oil on occasion to reduce inflammation in parts of my body. It worked like a charm.

164
TEASEL

LATIN NAME

ipsacus fullonum

DESCRIPTION

This plant is quite tall, growing up to six feet high. This is due to the hollow flower stems. These stems are prickly and green.

The leaves grow as a basal rosette at first. The basal leaves have a wrinkly surface, and the margins have rounded protrusions, like the lips of a clamshell. The bottoms of the basal leaves have spines along the midrib. Meanwhile, the leaves on the flower stalk are long, thin, and spiky, and they have a rainwater-holding cup at their base. These leaves have a white line running down the middle and a serrated margin. The leaves.

It grows a seed head that's spiky and shaped like an egg. This is situated at the top of the flowering stem and is about four inches tall. There are light purple or white flowers that grow in rings on this head.

HABITAT

They grow among clumps of trees and in pastures. Teasel can grow in most varieties of soil, so long as it's moist, and it likes the sun.

SEASON TO GATHER THE PLANT

The flowers are available to harvest from July to August. The seeds are ready to harvest from August to October. The root should be harvested in early fall.

PARTS OF THE PLANT TO USE AS MEDICINE

You can use the roots, flowers, and leaves.

BENEFITS AND PROPERTIES

Teasel is good for skincare and preventing skin diseases. It helps with acne, small wounds, warts, red skin, scaly skin, and itchy skin.

It can help with your excretory system, helping achieve more regular urination.

Teasel helps regulate liver health. Among the conditions it alleviates are liver obstructions and jaundice.

This herb can improve digestion. It can stimulate your appetite, strengthen your stomach, and ease stomach aches.

Two other benefits are that it can increase perspiration and it can alleviate arthritis.

MEDICINE PREPARATION

Tea: You can use the root or the leaves. Using the leaves requires about a teaspoon of dried leaf in a cup of boiling water. Steep the leaves for five minutes before straining. The root tea requires a teaspoon of dried and finely cut root per cup of water. Steep it for 10 to 15 minutes before using.

Infused oil: Fill a jar three quarters with dried or fresh teasel, whether it be the leaves, the flowers, or the roots. Cover it with the carrier oil of your choice to the top of the jar. Close the jar, shake it, then leave it in a cool, dark space for three days. Shake it every day. Strain it out after the third day.

Ointment: Use three quarters of a cup of infused oil, a third of a cup of aloe gel, and two thirds of a cup of water. Mix it well, then it'll be ready to use.

USING THE HERB

Tea: You can drink up to four cups of leaf tea or two cups of root tea per day. Other uses include topical use as a wash (especially good for acne) and as an eyewash.

Infused oil: Keep it stored in the refrigerator. You can rub it into your skin for external conditions. For internal use, you can take a spoon directly, or you can drizzle it over your food.

Ointment: The ointment is one of the best folk treatments you can use for warts.

SIDE EFFECTS AND WARNINGS

Pregnant and breastfeeding women should consult their medical practitioner if they plan on using teasel.

It interacts with drugs that are used for nerve conditions, eye conditions, and Alzheimer's.

FUN TIPS AND FACTS

A few drops of teasel tincture can sniff out Lyme disease bacterial cells where they hide burrowed in joints

AUTHOR'S PERSONAL STORY

I once used some leftover teasel tea to wash out the eyes of one of my nephews when they were red and swollen from rubbing. It calmed down the swelling in half an hour, and he was much happier than before.

165
VALERIAN

LATIN NAME

aleriana officinalis

DESCRIPTION

Valerian grows up to six feet tall, but normally only stands three feet tall. The plant's stems are hollow and straight.

The leaves have an opposite arrangement. They're pinnate, with six to 11 pairs of leaflets per leaf. The margins of these leaflets are toothed. The leaves have a slightly hairy bottom surface and an elongated oval shape, tapering to a pointed tip.

Flowers on this tree grow in clusters that are shaped almost like umbrellas. Florets are small (about a tenth of an inch) and are white, light purple, or pink.

The seeds are very small and have a tuft of hair.

HABITAT

It grows well in damp grasslands. It manages well in partial and direct sun and water-rich soil.

SEASON TO GATHER THE PLANT

The root can be harvested at any time of year, but it should be done after rain or when the soil is wet, and it should be done when the plant is at least two years old.

PARTS OF THE PLANT TO USE AS MEDICINE

The root is used for medicine.

BENEFITS AND PROPERTIES

Valerian is used mainly as a sedative and for mental health purposes. It assists with attention deficit hyperactivity disorder, anxiety disorders, and depression. It improves sleep quality, which in turn helps with getting over chronic fatigue syndrome.

Valerian is good for relaxing muscles, easing tremors, restlessness, convulsions, and epilepsy.

It can also alleviate premenstrual syndrome and postmenopausal hot flashes.

MEDICINE PREPARATION

Tincture: Fill a jar halfway with a few handfuls of the root. Cover it with vodka until the jar is full. Seal off the jar, give it a shake, then leave the jar in a cool spot out of direct sunlight for six weeks. After six weeks, strain the liquid into a dark glass bottle.

Tea: Half a teaspoon of dried root is enough. Place it in a cup of boiling water, stir, then leave it to steep for 15 minutes.

USING THE HERB

Tincture: You can have it in water or directly. I suggest a teaspoon per day when you're trying to get the benefits of the herb.

Tea: You can use the tea internally or externally. If used externally, you'll find it works well as a foot bath. You can leave it to steep for a longer period (such as four hours), then pour it into your bathwater. This works as a soak that relaxes muscle spasms.

SIDE EFFECTS AND WARNINGS

It can result in sedation, insomnia, and morning drowsiness.

Mental side effects include uneasiness and excitability in the short term and withdrawal syndrome over the long term.

Valerian can also cause heart issues and liver toxicity.

You may also get mild headaches, dizziness, itchiness, or an upset stomach when taking valerian.

It does interact with alcohol and certain drugs. These drugs include antidepressants, muscle relaxants, and sleeping medication.

FUN TIPS AND FACTS

The ancient Greeks hung bundles of valerian in their homes. They believed that it kept evil entities from entering, so they usually hung the bundles in their windows.

AUTHOR'S PERSONAL STORY

One of my family members used to spend her whole day standing in a shop in high heels. Her feet would be sore all the time. After she started using valerian tea as a foot soak, her feet became a lot less sore.

VIOLET

LATIN NAME

iola

DESCRIPTION

Violet is a low-growing plant. There's commonly a mass of medium-sized leaves growing out of the ground or out of a type of stem that grows horizontally on the ground.

The leaves are shaped like a pointed egg, and they come down at the base to form a bowl. The margins are slightly serrated.

The flowers have five petals, with one of the five functioning as a landing spot for insects that pollinate them. They're either white, purple, or blue. These flowers grow on soft stems that rise out of the ground or from the horizontal stem like the leaves do.

Their fruit is quite small and is either a capsule that explodes with seeds or a berry.

HABITAT

Temperate areas are this plant's preferred climate. It enjoys soil that's rich and well-drained, but moist. Slight shade is best.

SEASON TO GATHER THE PLANT

It flowers in late winter and early spring, so this is a good time to harvest.

PARTS OF THE PLANT TO USE AS MEDICINE

The entire plant can be used medicinally.

BENEFITS AND PROPERTIES

It's used for lung health, bronchitis, coughing, and nasal congestion.

It's also a natural pain medication, which means it can be used to ease headaches and other painful conditions.

This herb can treat your digestive system as well. It reduces inflammation in the intestinal tract, allowing food and drink to flow through better.

It's good for breast health when applied topically. Other topical application benefits include the reduction of swelling and easing skin irritation.

Furthermore, violet has a positive effect on the lymphatic system, letting lymph flow better through your body.

Your quality of sleep will improve while you're on it.

MEDICINE PREPARATION

Syrup: You'll need a cup of sugar, a cup of violet flowers, and a cup of boiled water. Break the petals off, as this is the part of the flower that you'll be using. Pour the cup of water over the petals and let it steep for 24 hours. Then put a pot on the stove, filled halfway with water, and rest a metal bowl on the pot (the bowl should not touch the bottom of the pot). Place the petal infusion in the metal bowl and slowly pour in the sugar, stirring constantly so that it dissolves into the infusion. After the sugar is dissolved into the infusion, strain the mixture into a jar. Let it cool, then it'll be ready for use.

Vinegar: You need a cup of violet flowers and a cup and a half of vinegar (preferably white or rice vinegar). Place the flowers into a jar, then heat the vinegar in a saucepan. Warm the vinegar on low heat, then add it to the jar.. Close the jar and store it in a cool, dry place for three days. After this, strain the flowers out, and the vinegar is ready.

Tea: Use two teaspoons of dried leaves per cup of boiling water. Let it steep for five minutes, then strain it.

Compress: Make it the same way as the tea, but let it steep for 20 minutes before soaking your cloth in the liquid.

Infused oil: You'll need a jar full of violet flowers and leaves, and a carrier oil. Pour the carrier oil into the jar so it covers the leaves and flowers, then close it off. Close the top with a cloth and rubber band. Put it in a cold, dark spot for a month, then strain out the violet leaves and flowers. You can now use it.

USING THE HERB

Syrup: The syrup is very effective for treating coughs.

Vinegar: Have a tablespoon or two of this when your immune system isn't doing well.

Tea: It tastes bitter and like grass, so you may want to adjust the flavor with other plants and herbs or a bit of honey.

Compress: Apply it directly to swollen or irritated skin.

Infused oil: Apply it to the skin or the hair. It benefits both. If used on the skin, it has a soothing quality.

SIDE EFFECTS AND WARNINGS

Pregnant and breastfeeding women should consult their healthcare provider before using it.

Use it in moderate, medicinal amounts. There could be unintended effects if it's used in large quantities.

Allergic reactions are possible.

FUN TIPS AND FACTS

Violets have been used in love potions over the centuries. This is because, in Roman mythology, Venus assaulted a group of girls who then turned into violets after Cupid said the girls were prettier than her.

AUTHOR'S PERSONAL STORY

I've helped someone get over internal inflammation that was preventing them from being able to eat comfortably by getting them to drink violet tea.

WILD SARSAPARILLA

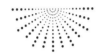

LATIN NAME

Aralia nudicaulis

DESCRIPTION

This plant grows between eight and 20 inches high. It's made up of thin, green stems that come out of the root system and the leaves and flowers attached to the stems

The leaves are alternately arranged compound leaves. The compound leaf splits into three stems that each hold five leaflets. The leaflets are in the shape of a pointed oval they are finely toothed. They're bronze during spring, green in summer, and red or yellow during fall.

Each flower stalk bears three flower clusters. Each cluster is made up of a group of small stalks bearing tiny white flowers. There are twenty to forty flowers in each cluster.

The flowers are replaced by quarter-inch berries that start green, transition to red, and finally turn dark purple. These have a sweet but spicy flavor.

HABITAT

You can find it next to trees, in bogs, and in woods. It grows in both well-drained and poorly-drained soil, and it prefers partial shade.

SEASON TO GATHER THE PLANT

Gather it at the end of fall when the leaves are starting to fade and the berries have ripened.

PARTS OF THE PLANT TO USE AS MEDICINE

The roots are used for medicinal purposes.

BENEFITS AND PROPERTIES

Internal benefits include protecting the liver from toxins, reducing fluid retention, and preventing kidney disease.

Topical uses include alleviating rheumatoid arthritis, reducing joint pain and swelling, and combatting skin disease.

MEDICINE PREPARATION

Tea: Put a teaspoon of dried and powdered root into a cup of boiling water. Let it steep for 20 minutes before straining and drinking.

Tincture: Fill a fifth of a jar of roots and the rest with vodka. Close the jar and store it in a spot out of the sun for six weeks. Strain the liquid into a dark glass container.

USING THE HERB

Tea: The maximum dosage is a cup per day. You can use it as a soak for sore joints as well.

Tincture: It has a shelf life of several years. You can take half a teaspoon directly, or mixed in with a glass of water.

SIDE EFFECTS AND WARNINGS

A runny nose and asthma-like symptoms can result from breathing in the root's dust.

Wild sarsaparilla can exacerbate kidney disease.

Pregnant and breastfeeding women should consult their medical professionals before use.

This plant can interact with heart medication and water pills.

FUN TIPS AND FACTS

A few Native American cultural groups have used the root as an energy-giving supplement while on journeys.

AUTHOR'S PERSONAL STORY

I've helped a girl lose weight by having her take the tincture so that her body would stop retaining water.

168
WILLOW

LATIN NAME

Salix

DESCRIPTION

Willow is a tree that grows many thin and flexible branches that arch out of the trunk and reaches between 30 and 70 feet tall.

Leaves growing on this tree are about a third of an inch wide and one to two inches long. They have finely toothed margins.

Its fruit comes in the form of catkins.

There are many species of willow, and they vary a lot in terms of looks. The above, however, are the descriptive characteristics that are true for most willows. The key identifying factor is the shorter trunk with arched, thin branches.

HABITAT

It prefers full sun and moist ground. It's found close to bodies of water.

SEASON TO GATHER THE PLANT

You can harvest from the willow the whole year long.

PARTS OF THE PLANT TO USE AS MEDICINE

The bark is the main part used for medicinal applications.

BENEFITS AND PROPERTIES

Internal benefits are prevention and recovery from the flu, fevers, and colds. Weight loss is also a possible internal benefit. Pain relief is the main use for willow bark.

Topical benefits revolve around pain reduction. This includes osteoarthritis pain, headaches, menstrual pain, rheumatoid arthritis, spinal pain, muscle pain, gout, and joint pain.

MEDICINE PREPARATION

Tea: Use two teaspoons of crushed bark and stir it into one cup of boiling water. Leave it to steep for 20 minutes, then strain out the bark.

Bark: Simply chew a piece of bark to get the internal benefits described above.

USING THE HERB

Tea: Drink it for internal use.. For external use, soak affected body parts in it or apply it as a compress.

Bark: This may not taste nice, but it's simple and fast pain relief.

SIDE EFFECTS AND WARNINGS

Side effects include allergic reactions, itchiness, rash, headaches, and stomach upsets.

Don't use it if you have a bleeding disorder or kidney disease. It can exacerbate these conditions.

Don't use it on children, as there are possible later brain and liver conditions that could result. More research is required for this.

Don't use it within two weeks of surgery as it could prevent blood clotting.

When pregnant, ask your pregnancy specialist if you can use it or not. While breastfeeding, don't take it because it could lead to damage to your child.

If you're sensitive to aspirin, this isn't the right medicinal plant for you.

It interacts with many medications, so consult your healthcare advisor if you're on medication, and you want to use this.

FUN TIPS AND FACTS

The willow tree can bounce back quickly. It can be cut down yet grow several feet in the following growing season. A piece of twig can be broken off and planted, with new growth occurring easily. These qualities earned it a connection with the concept of immortality in traditional Chinese cultures.

AUTHOR'S PERSONAL STORY

I've chewed on some willow bark after I fell and bruised myself while hiking. The pain faded very quickly after chewing for a few minutes.

169
WINTERGREEN

LATIN NAME

Gaultheria procumbens

DESCRIPTION

Wintergreen grows from a network of roots and underground branches that shoot out two to six inches from the ground.

The leaves are arranged alternately. They have an elliptical or oval shape and a length between one and two inches. They're glossy and bright green, and the margins of the leaves have widely-spaced fine teeth with a tiny spine on each tooth.

This plant grows white flowers that have a bell shape. These are waxy and small (about a quarter-inch long). Each flower has five petals.

The fruit is small and berry-like. They're a quarter of an inch in diameter and turn red when matured.

HABITAT

They normally prefer a temperate area. Acidic soil is the most common soil in which this plant flourishes, and it grows best in partial shade.

SEASON TO GATHER THE PLANT

The leaves can be harvested at any time.

PARTS OF THE PLANT TO USE AS MEDICINE

The leaves are used for medicinal purposes.

BENEFITS AND PROPERTIES

Internal uses include pain reduction, treating lung conditions, treating kidney problems, breaking fevers, and improving digestion.

Topical uses include pain reduction, improving skin health, reducing swelling, and killing germs.

MEDICINE PREPARATION

Oil: Put a few handfuls of wintergreen leaves in a saucepan of water. Bring it to a boil, then down to a simmer for three hours. The lid should be upside down on the saucepan the whole time, allowing condensed vapor to drip back into the pot. Let it cool, then place the saucepan in the refrigerator. Leave it there overnight, then scoop up the congealed essential oil (laying as a film on the surface of the water) the following day. Put this essential oil in a dark glass bottle.

USING THE HERB

Essential oil: Put a drop in a glass of water when taking it orally. Put three drops in your bathwater when using it as a soak. Put four drops into eight ounces of carrier oil when using it for topical application.

SIDE EFFECTS AND WARNINGS

The oil shouldn't be taken orally (without diluting it properly). It can cause diarrhea, headaches, stomach aches, ear ringing, nausea, and confusion. These conditions can rise to dangerous levels for children.

Internal side effects can cause intestinal inflammation and stomach inflammation.

The essential oil can irritate if applied directly to the skin.

It interacts with aspirin and Warfarin.

Don't use it if you're pregnant or breastfeeding unless your healthcare provider approves.

People can experience allergic reactions to wintergreen.

FUN TIPS AND FACTS

The scent of the essential oil makes it great for adding to natural cleaning products. You can make your entire house smell fresher by using it.

AUTHOR'S PERSONAL STORY

I've used wintergreen essential oil (breathing in the fumes from the bottle) to get over headaches.

YARROW

LATIN NAME

Achillea millefolium

DESCRIPTION

This is a plant that grows about one to three feet tall.

Its leaves are feathery and grow two to eight inches long. They're arranged in spirals along the stem and are bipinnate or tripinnate. The leaves in the middle and the lower parts of the stem are larger than the ones closer to the end of the stem.

Its flowers are white or pink, and they grow on a flower head. They have a pleasant sweet smell. The flower head has many small flowers (up to 40 sometimes) clustered closely together.

Be careful when identifying yarrow because there are similar plants that are very poisonous.

HABITAT

The plant is commonly found in clearings and meadows, and it likes slightly dry soil.

SEASON TO GATHER THE PLANT

Harvest the leaves in early spring and the flowers from June to August. The roots are best harvested during the fall months.

PARTS OF THE PLANT TO USE AS MEDICINE

The roots, leaves, and flowers can be used.

BENEFITS AND PROPERTIES

Topical uses include toothache relief, hair care, skin cleansing, stanching bleeding, reducing inflammation, and wound care.

There are digestive benefits in the form of stomach and intestinal discomfort relief and appetite stimulation by improving saliva production and stomach acid regulation.

Excretory tract functioning can improve when taking yarrow. It can handle diarrhea, dysentery, bloating, and flatulence.

Women, specifically, can benefit from using it by seeing a reduction in menstrual cramps and pelvic cramps.

Other internal uses include breaking fevers, treating colds, relieving hay fever, and promoting perspiration.

MEDICINE PREPARATION

Tea: Use a teaspoon of leaves or flowers. Put it in a cup of boiling water and let it steep for 20 minutes.

Tincture: Fill a third of a jar with flowers or leaves (fresh) and two thirds of the jar with vodka. Close the jar and put it in a cool, dry place for six weeks. Shake it every few days. Strain out the leaves/flowers.

Bath: Boil a gallon of water in a saucepan then put in a whole yarrow plant. Bring it down to a simmer, then let it simmer for half an hour. Pour this into your bath water, then have a soak.

USING THE HERB

Tea: Have up to two cups per day.
Tincture: Take about half a teaspoon per day.

Bath: You should remain in the bath for a long time so that you can soak up the yarrow.

SIDE EFFECTS AND WARNINGS

It can cause sleepiness, increased urination, and cause skin irritation.

Don't take it when pregnant or breastfeeding. If taken while pregnant, it can cause miscarriage.

If you have a bleeding disorder, you should avoid it.

When going to surgery, avoid using it during the two weeks prior.

Some experience allergic reactions.

It interacts with a range of medications, so consult your healthcare provider if you're on medication and would like to use yarrow.

FUN TIPS AND FACTS

In Greek mythology, the herb yarrow was considered so powerful it was believed to bestow immortality on those who bathed in its waters. According to legend, Achilles was one such hero, having been dipped in the Yarrow-laced water of the river Styx by his mother when he was a baby.

AUTHOR'S PERSONAL STORY

I gave a friend a yarrow leaf to chew when he had a toothache. This helped alleviate the discomfort until he managed to see the dentist later that day.

Leave a 1-Click Review!

Customer reviews

 5 out of 5

3 global ratings

5 star	██████████	100%
4 star		0%
3 star		0%
2 star		0%
1 star		0%

˅ How are ratings calculated?

Review this product

Share your thoughts with other customers

Write a customer review

AFTERWORD

This book describes the most powerful medicinal herbs from the Northeast. It's an in-depth guide into the world of wildcrafting and herbalism including fun stories, facts, and intricate myths about the plants and can be used by new to experienced herbalists.

Take your health into your own hands! Heal truly by getting in touch with nature, our true essence.

Why would you still waste hundreds of dollars yearly on expensive medicine that weakens your body? Go into nature and be your own pharmacist! It's free and in nature, that's where true healing occurs.

If you enjoyed the content of this book, please, take 2 minutes to leave a review. We also have an active Facebook group and we would love to have you so we can learn together.

https://www.facebook.com/groups/northeasthomestead

Let's help humanity rise together!

REFERENCES

A prescription for better health: Go alfresco. (2010, October 12). Harvard Health. https://www.health.harvard.edu/mind-and-mood/a-prescription-for-better-health-go-alfresco

Ananda. (2021, February 1). *28 best DIY raised bed garden ideas & designs.* A Piece of Rainbow. https://www.apieceofrainbow.com/20-diy-raised-bed-gardens/

April. (2016, June 2). *Getting into the permaculture zone.* Permaculture Visions. https://permaculturevisions.com/getting-permaculture-zone/

Autumn. (2017, March 6). *10 principles to live by for homesteading newbies.* A Traditional Life. https://atraditionallife.com/10-things-you-should-know-about-homesteading/

Berg Stack, L. (2017). *Soil and plant nutrition: A gardener's perspective.* Cooperative Extension: Garden & Yard; The University of Maine. https://extension.umaine.edu/gardening/manual/soils/soil-and-plant-nutrition/

BigRentz Inc. (2020, April 7). *How to build a life off the grid.* BigRentz. https://www.bigrentz.com/blog/off-grid-living

Bloom, J. (2016, August 2). *The basics of permaculture.* Mother Earth Living. https://content.motherearthliving.com/gardening/basics-of-permaculture-zmgz16sozolc/

Carlson, S. (2018, April 18). *What's the best type of soil for plants?*

Peterson Companies. https://blog.petersoncompanies.net/best-type-of-soil-for-plants

Cowan, S. (2019, March 26). *10 expert tips for raised garden beds and planters*. Eartheasy Guides & Articles. https://learn.eartheasy.com/articles/10-expert-tips-for-raised-garden-beds-and-planters/

Culver, B. (2021, May 19). *What is homesteading?* An off Grid Life. https://www.anoffgridlife.com/what-is-homesteading/

Faires, N. (2017). *10 excellent reasons to use raised beds in your garden*. Eartheasy Guides & Articles. https://learn.eartheasy.com/articles/10-excellent-reasons-to-use-raised-beds-in-your-garden/

Family Food Garden. (2018, December 10). *Design your homestead & backyard farm plans*. Family Food Garden. https://www.familyfoodgarden.com/homestead-backyard-farm/

Garden Heights Nursery. (2018, April 2). *What's the difference between perennial and annual plants?* Garden Heights Nursery. https://www.gardenheights.com/single-post/2018/03/30/whats-the-difference-between-perennial-and-annual-plants#:~:text=So%2C%20what%27s%20the%20difference%3F

Garman, J. (2017, January 20). *The basics of raising chickens*. Homesteaders of America. https://homesteadersofamerica.com/basics-raising-chickens/

Homesteading Family. (2020, September 6). *The first 7 things you must do on your new homestead property*. [Video] https://www.youtube.com/watch?v=sZ5wJc7v7Qs&ab_channel=HomesteadingFamily

Kellogg Garden Products. (2021). *Benefits of companion planting*. Kellogg Garden. https://www.kellogggarden.com/blog/gardening/benefits-of-companion-planting/

Lynn, T. (2020, March 18). *10 wonderful benefits of chickens*. Simple Living Country Gal. https://simplelivingcountrygal.com/benefits-of-chickens

Martin, S. (n.d.). *10 essential spring gardening tasks*. Proven Winners. https://www.provenwinners.com/learn/early-spring/10-essential-spring-gardening-tasks

Melanie. (2020, August 1). *How much does it cost to start beekeeping?* (Updated 2021). Beekeeping For Newbies. https://www.beekeepingfornewbies.com/starting-costs/

Milbrand, L. (2021, September 29). *A beginner's guide to indoor composting (without worms!)*. Real Simple. https://www.realsimple.com/home-organizing/green-living/indoor-composting

National Climate Assessment. (2021). *Northeast.* National Climate Assessment. https://nca2014.globalchange.gov/report/regions/northeast

Page, T. (2016, December 9). *Homestead goats: What you need to know to get started.* Common Sense Home. https://commonsensehome.com/homestead-goats/

Patterson, S. (n.d.). *Which soil is best for plant growth?* LoveToKnow. https://garden.lovetoknow.com/wiki/Which_Soil_Is_Best_for_Plant_Growth

RIMOL Greenhouse Systems. (2018, September 19). *How to achieve ideal environmental control in your greenhouse.* Rimol Greenhouses. https://www.rimolgreenhouses.com/blog/how-to-achieve-ideal-environmental-control-your-greenhouse

Sayner, A. (2021, July 20). *17 backyard homestead ideas for living independently.* GroCycle. https://grocycle.com/backyard-homestead-ideas/

Tilley, N. (2018, January 12). *What is a permaculture garden: The essence of permaculture gardening.* Gardening Know How. https://www.gardeningknowhow.com/special/organic/the-essence-of-permaculture-gardening.htm

Tropical Permaculture. (n.d.). *What is permaculture? How does permaculture work? Explanations, definitions, examples.* Tropical Permaculture. https://www.tropicalpermaculture.com/what-is-permaculture.html

US EPA. (2016, December). *Climate impacts in the Northeast.* Environmental Protection Agency. https://19january2017snapshot.epa.gov/climate-impacts/climate-impacts-northeast_.html

Vanderlinden, C. (2021, January 4). *10 tips for successful raised-bed gardening.* The Spruce. https://www.thespruce.com/tips-for-successful-raised-bed-gardening-2539792

Vanheems, B. (2019, January 11). *10 ways to boost yields in your vegetable garden.* GrowVeg. https://www.growveg.com/guides/10-ways-to-boost-yields-in-your-vegetable-garden/

Vinje, E. (2012, December 8). *Companion planting guide.* Planet Natural. https://www.planetnatural.com/companion-planting/

Watson, M. (2019, September 27). *What's in season? A monthly guide to the Northeast's fruits and veggies.* The Spruce Eats. https://www.thespruceeats.com/seasonal-fruits-and-vegetables-of-the-northeast-4165314

WeatherSpark. (2020). *Climate and average weather year round in North East.* Weatherspark. https://weatherspark.com/y/22771/Average-Weather-in-North-East-Maryland-United-States-Year-Round#:~:text=In%20North%20East%2C%20the%20summers

Winger, J. (2014, May 14). *Become a beekeeper: 8 steps to getting started with honeybees*. The Prairie Homestead. https://www.theprairiehomestead.com/2014/05/get-started-honeybees.html

All photos sourced from Unsplash. https://unsplash.com/

BIBLIOGRAPHY

5 tips for when you need help identifying a plant. (n.d.). Nature Mentor. Retrieved February 5, 2022, from https://nature-mentor.com/need-help-identifying-a-plant/

6 fantastic reasons for growing and using a comfrey plant. (2019, April 22). Preparedness Mama. https://preparednessmama.com/growing-and-using-comfrey/

10 fascinating and fun cranberries facts from That's It. (2015, November 3). That's It. https://www.thatsitfruit.com/blogs/default-blog/10-interesting-facts-about-cranberries

A guide to garden flower identification: What's in your garden? (n.d.). Plant Snap. Retrieved February 5, 2022, from https://www.plantsnap.com/blog/garden-flower-identification/

Acer negundo. (n.d.). Wild Flower. Retrieved February 22, 2022, from https://www.wildflower.org/plants/result.php?id_plant=acne2#:~:text=Leaf%3A%20Opposite%2C%20pinnately%20compound%2C

Acorn facts for kids. (n.d.). Kiddle. Retrieved March 2, 2022, from https://kids.kiddle.co/Acorn#:~:text=The%20acorn%20is%20the%20fruit

Adamant, A. (2018, May 12). *How to make burdock tincture.* Practical Self Reliance. https://practicalselfreliance.com/burdock-tincture/#:~:text=Chop%20the%20-root%20into%20chunks

Adamant, A. (2021, April 5). *15 ways to use borage.* Practical Self Reliance. https://practicalselfreliance.com/borage-uses/

Adriana. (2021, June 24). *Blackberry leaf tea: A herbal remedy for your health.* Backyard Garden Lover. https://www.backyardgardenlover.com/blackberry-leaf-tea/

Agarwal, S. (2021, October 19). *8 amazing mulberry benefits: Make the most of it while the season lasts.* NDTV Food. https://food.ndtv.com/food-drinks/8-amazing-mulberry-benefits-make-the-most-of-it-while-the-season-lasts-1685146

Agrimonia gryposepala (common agrimony, tall hairy agrimony). (n.d.). Native Plant Trust: Go Botany. Retrieved February 7, 2022, from https://gobotany.nativeplanttrust.org/species/agrimonia/gryposepala/

Agrimony health benefits and side effects. (n.d.). Medical Health Guide. Retrieved February 8, 2022, from http://www.medicalhealthguide.com/herb/agrimony.htm

Agrimony: Overview, uses, side effects, precautions, interactions, dosing and reviews. (n.d.). Web MD. Retrieved February 8, 2022, from https://www.webmd.com/vitamins/ai/ingredientmono-604/agrimony

Alcantara, S. T. (n.d.). *How to make burdock tea.* Live Strong. Retrieved March 2, 2022, from https://www.livestrong.com/article/52018-make-burdock-tea/

Alder. (n.d.). In Merriam Webster. Retrieved February 8, 2022, from https://www.merriam-webster.com/dictionary/alder

Alder buckthorn. (2021, June 11). RxList. https://www.rxlist.com/alder_buckthorn/supplements.htm

Alder tincture recipe. (2020, April 3). Cortes Currents. https://cortescurrents.ca/yulia-kochubievskys-alder-tincture-recipe/

Alder trees plants advantages and disadvantages, side effects and reviews. (n.d.). Review Guts. Retrieved February 8, 2022, from https://reviewguts.com/alder-trees-plants_2nd/

Alder trees: Leaves, bark, flowers, cones - Identification (pictures). (2021, April 19). Leafy Place. https://leafyplace.com/alder-trees/

American sarsaparilla (spikenard) – Aralia racemosa. (n.d.). Root Buyer. Retrieved March 4,

2022, from https://rootbuyer.com/wild-sarsaparilla-spikenard-aralia-racemosa/#:~:text=The%20rootstock%20is%20harvested%20in

American Survival Guide. (2018, March 22). *Foraging gear: The tools you need to collect, process and carry natural foods*. American Outdoor Guide. https://www.americanoutdoor.guide/how-to/foraging-gear-the-tools-you-need-to-collect-process-and-carry-natural-foods/

Ancient equisetum. (2015, May 21). In Defense of Plants. https://www.indefenseofplants.com/blog/2015/5/21/ancient-equisetum

Andrea. (2019, January 9). *Wild cherry bark & horehound tincture tea recipe*. Frugally Sustainable. https://frugallysustainable.com/cherry-bark-horehound-tincture/

Applebaum, G. (n.d.). *Moxa: The burning herb that heals*. Fabriq. Retrieved March 1, 2022, from http://www.fabriqspa.com/the-burning-herb-that-heals/

Baessler, L. (2021, April 6). *What is valerian: How to grow valerian plants in the garden*. Gardening Know-How. https://www.gardeningknowhow.com/edible/herbs/valerian/growing-valerian-herb-plants.htm

Baldridge, K. (2020, May 8). *How to make an elderberry tincture*. Traditional Cooking School. https://traditionalcookingschool.com/health-and-nutrition/make-your-own-elderberry-tincture/

Barth, B. (2018, July 18). *7 smokable plants you can grow that aren't marijuana*. Modern Farmer. https://modernfarmer.com/2018/07/7-smokable-plants-you-can-grow-that-arent-marijuana/#:~:text=Mullein%20(Verbascum%20thapsus)&text=Herbal%20Properties%3A%20Mullein%20has%20a

Beaulieu, D. (2021, August 11). *St. John's wort plant profile*. The Spruce. https://www.thespruce.com/st-johns-wort-plant-profile-4772327

Beech. (n.d.). In Merriam Webster. Retrieved February 8, 2022, from https://www.merriam-webster.com/dictionary/beech

Beech. (n.d.). Vild Mad. Retrieved February 11, 2022, from https://vildmad.dk/en/ingredients/beech

Beech - A guide to its food, medicine and other uses. (n.d.). Eat Weeds. Retrieved February 11, 2022, from https://www.eatweeds.co.uk/beech-fagus-sylvatica

Beech trees: Types, leaves, bark — Identification guide (pictures). (n.d.). Leafy Place. Retrieved February 8, 2022, from https://leafyplace.com/beech-trees/

Benefits of black cherries. (n.d.). Bremner Foods. Retrieved February 11, 2022, from https://www.bremnerfoods.com/health-benefits/benefits-of-black-cherries.html#:~:text=Health%20Benefits%20of%20Black%20Cherries&text=Black%20cherries%20are%20an%20excellent

Benefits of growing medicinal herbs. (2016, March 28). Joybilee Farm. https://joybileefarm.com/7-reasons-make-healing-homegrown/

Berries as symbols and in folklore. (n.d.). New York Berry News, 6(1). Cornell University's College of Agriculture and Life Sciences. Retrieved March 3, 2022, from chrome-extension://efaidnbmnnnibpcajpcglclefindmkaj/viewer.html?pdfurl=https%3A%2F%2Fcpb-us-e1.wpmucdn.com%2Fblogs.cornell.edu%2Fdist%2F0%2F7265%2Ffiles%2F2016%2F12%2Fberryfolklore-2ljzt0q.pdf&clen=100303&chunk=true

Birch. (n.d.). In Merriam Webster. Retrieved February 11, 2022, from https://www.merriam-webster.com/dictionary/birch

Birch fruits and seeds. (n.d.). Tree Guide. Retrieved February 11, 2022, from http://www.treeguide.com/birch-fruits-and-seeds

Birch Leaf. (n.d.). Mountain Rose Herbs. Retrieved February 11, 2022, from https://mountainroseherbs.com/birch-leaf

Birch perfume ingredient, birch fragrance and essential oils Betula, family betulaceae. (n.d.).

Gragrantica. Retrieved February 11, 2022, from https://www.fragrantica.com/notes/Birch-31.html
Birch tree allergen facts, symptoms, and treatment. (n.d.). Thermo Fisher. Retrieved February 11, 2022, from https://www.thermofisher.com/allergy/us/en/allergen-fact-sheets.html?allergen=birch-tree
Birch trees: Types, leaves, bark - Identification (with pictures). (n.d.). Leafy Place. Retrieved February 11, 2022, from https://leafyplace.com/birch-trees/
Birch: Uses, side effects, interactions, dosage, and warning. (n.d.). Web MD. Retrieved February 11, 2022, from https://www.webmd.com/vitamins/ai/ingredientmono-352/birch
Bjarnadottir, A. (2019, February 22). *Mulberries 101: Nutrition facts and health benefits.* Healthline. https://www.healthline.com/nutrition/foods/mulberries#bottom-line
Black cherry. (n.d.). In Merriam Webster. Retrieved February 11, 2022, from https://www.merriam-webster.com/dictionary/black%20cherry
Black cherry. (n.d.-a). Tree Guide. Retrieved February 11, 2022, from http://www.tree-guide.com/black-cherry
Black cherry. (n.d.-b). Natural Resource Stewardship. Retrieved February 11, 2022, from https://naturalresources.extension.iastate.edu/forestry/iowa_trees/trees/black_cherry.html
Blackberry. (n.d.). In Merriam Webster. Retrieved February 11, 2022, from https://www.merriam-webster.com/dictionary/blackberry
Blackberry. (2015, August 6). Kaiser Permanente. https://wa.kaiserpermanente.org/kbase/topic.jhtml?docId=hn-2045002#hn-2045002-side-effects
Blackberry | fruit. (2022). In Encyclopædia Britannica. https://www.britannica.com/plant/blackberry-fruit
Blankespoor, J. (2017, November 7). *Foraging for wild edibles and herbs: Sustainable and safe gathering practices.* Chestnut School of Herbal Medicine. https://chestnutherbs.com/foraging-for-wild-edibles-and-herbs-sustainable-and-safe-gathering-practices/
Blankespoor, J. (2021a, February 4). *The Medicine of Pine.* Chestnut School of Herbal Medicine. https://chestnutherbs.com/the-medicine-of-pine/#:~:text=Pine%20offers%20relief%20in%20sinus
Blankespoor, J. (2021b, April 13). *Violet's edible and medicinal uses.* Chestnut School of Herbal Medicine. https://chestnutherbs.com/violets-edible-and-medicinal-uses/#:~:text=Violet%20is%20cooling%20and%20moistening
Blue vervain. (n.d.). In Merriam Webster. Retrieved February 12, 2022, from https://www.merriam-webster.com/dictionary/blue%20vervain
Blue vervain: Pictures, flowers, leaves & identification | Verbena hastata. (n.d.). Edible Wild Food. Retrieved February 11, 2022, from https://www.ediblewildfood.com/blue-vervain.aspx
Borage. (n.d.). In Merriam Webster. Retrieved February 12, 2022, from https://www.merriam-webster.com/dictionary/borage
Borage leaves. (n.d.). Specialty Produce. Retrieved February 11, 2022, from https://specialtyproduce.com/produce/Borage_Leaves_11921.php
Borage: Uses, side effects and warnings, interactions, dosage, and warning. (n.d.). Web MD. Retrieved February 12, 2022, from https://www.webmd.com/vitamins/ai/ingredientmono-596/borage
Borago officinalis, borage: Identification, distribution, habitat. (n.d.). First Nature. Retrieved February 11, 2022, from https://www.first-nature.com/flowers/borago-officinalis.php#:~:text=Up%20to%2060cm%2C%20this
Bratianu, P. (n.d.). *The natural healing power of oak trees and acorns.* Off the Grid News. Retrieved March 2, 2022, from https://www.offthegridnews.com/alternative-health/the-natural-healing-power-of-oak-trees-and-acorns/

Brennan, D. (Ed.). (2020a, September 17). *Health Benefits of Mint Leaves*. Web MD. https://www.webmd.com/diet/health-benefits-mint-leaves#:~:text=When%20it%20-comes%20to%20medicinal

Brennan, D. (2020b, September 18). *Health benefits of raspberries*. Web MD. https://www.webmd.com/diet/health-benefits-raspberries#:~:text=They%20provide%20potassium%2C%20essential%20to

Brennan, D. (Ed.). (2020c, November 10). *Health benefits of mulberries*. Web MD. https://www.webmd.com/diet/health-benefits-mulberries#2-5

Buckner, H. (2020, March 20). *How to plant and grow plantain, a culinary and medicinal herb*. Gardener's Path. https://gardenerspath.com/plants/herbs/grow-plantain/#:~:text=All%20of%20these%20species%20grow

Burdock. (n.d.). In Merriam Webster. Retrieved February 12, 2022, from https://www.merriam-webster.com/dictionary/burdock

Burdock: Pictures, flowers, leaves & identification | Arctium lappa. (n.d.). Edible Wild Food. Retrieved February 12, 2022, from https://www.ediblewildfood.com/burdock.aspx

Can you juice soft summer fruits like cherries, berries, and peaches? (2017, July 19). Eujuicers. https://www.eujuicers.com/magazine/can-you-juice-soft-summer-fruits-like-cherries-berries-and-peaches

Carroll, J. (2021a, May 4). *Growing a larch tree: Larch tree types for garden settings*. Gardening Know-How. https://www.gardeningknowhow.com/ornamental/trees/larch/growing-a-larch-tree.htm#:~:text=Larch%20trees%20are%20large%20deciduous,flowers%20that%20eventually%20become%20cones.

Carroll, J. (2021b, May 10). *St. John's wort plant care: How to grow St. John's wort*. Gardening Know-How. https://www.gardeningknowhow.com/edible/herbs/st-johns-wort/st-johns-wort-plant-care.htm

Carryopsis, J. (n.d.). *Biology of dandelions*. Nature North. Retrieved February 16, 2022, from http://www.naturenorth.com/summer/dandelion/Dandelion2.html

Catnip. (n.d.). In Merriam Webster. Retrieved February 12, 2022, from https://www.merriam-webster.com/dictionary/catnip

Catnip oil extraction methods, process, techniques. (n.d.). Agri Farming. https://www.agrifarming.in/catnip-oil-extraction-methods-process-techniques

Catnip tea: Are there health benefits? (n.d.). Web MD. Retrieved March 2, 2022, from https://www.webmd.com/diet/catnip-tea-health-benefits#1

Catnip uses, benefits & side effects. (n.d.). Drugs. Retrieved February 12, 2022, from https://www.drugs.com/npc/catnip.html#:~:text=Medicinally%2C%20the%20plant%20has%20been

Chamomile: Matricaria recutita. (n.d.). Edible Wild Food. Retrieved February 24, 2022, from https://www.ediblewildfood.com/chamomile.aspx

Chappell, S. (2019, February 21). *A beginner's guide to making herbal salves and lotions*. Healthline. https://www.healthline.com/health/diy-herbal-salves#TOC_TITLE_HDR_1

Cherney, K. (2022, February 3). *Everything you need to know about borage oil*. Healthline. https://www.healthline.com/health/borage-oil#side-effects

Chickweed. (n.d.). In Merriam Webster. Retrieved February 12, 2022, from https://www.merriam-webster.com/dictionary/chickweed

Chicory. (n.d.). In Merriam Webster. Retrieved February 12, 2022, from https://www.merriam-webster.com/dictionary/chicory

Chicory - edible wild plant - how to find, identify, prepare, and other uses for survival. (2012, May 11). Wilderness Arena. https://www.wildernessarena.com/food-water-shelter/food-food-water-shelter/food-procurement/edible-wild-plants/chicory

Chicory: Health benefits, uses, side effects, dosage & interactions. (2021, November 6). Rx List. https://www.rxlist.com/chicory/supplements.htm

Choosing a location for raspberry plants. (n.d.). Stark Bro's. Retrieved March 3, 2022, from https://www.starkbros.com/growing-guide/how-to-grow/berry-plants/raspberry-plants/location

Christiansen, S. (2022a, January 10). *What is mugwort? Herb related to ragweed used in naturopathic and traditional Chinese medicine.* Verywell Health. https://www.verywellhealth.com/mugwort-benefits-side-effects-dosage-and-interactions-4767226

Christiansen, S. (2022b, February 5). *What Is Horsetail?* Very Well Health. https://www.verywellhealth.com/horsetail-4692253#:~:text=Traditionally%20horsetail%20has%20been%20used

Clark, P. (2013, May 21). *Blackberry sexuality. It's complicated.* The Washington Post. https://www.washingtonpost.com/wp-srv/special/metro/urban-jungle/pages/130521.html

Cleansing with cleavers. (2019, April 8). Botanica Health. https://www.botanicahealth.co.uk/cleansing-with-cleavers/

Cleavers. (n.d.). In Collins. Retrieved February 12, 2022, from https://www.collinsdictionary.com/dictionary/english/cleavers

Cleavers. (2015a, May 23). Peace Health. https://www.peacehealth.org/medical-topics/id/hn-2070002#:~:text=by%20Scientific%20Studies)-

Cleavers. (2015b, May 23). Kaiser Permanente. https://wa.kaiserpermanente.org/kbase/topic.jhtml?docId=hn-2070002#:~:text=by%20Scientific%20Studies)-

Climan, A. (2020, December 21). *What is cleavers (galium aparine)?* Very Well Health. https://www.verywellhealth.com/cleavers-health-benefits-5084341#toc-possible-side-effects

Colleen. (2018, February 2). *Wild violet flower infused vinegar.* Grow Forage Cook Ferment. https://www.growforagecookferment.com/wild-violet-flower-infused-vinegar/#:~:text=There%20are%20also%20some%20medicinal

Colleen. (2020a, March 26). *How to Make and Use Dandelion Salve.* Grow Forage Cook Ferment. https://www.growforagecookferment.com/how-to-make-dandelion-salve/

Colleen. (2020b, June 15). *Dandelion foraging: Identification, look-alikes, and uses.* Grow Forage Cook Ferment. https://www.growforagecookferment.com/foraging-for-dandelions/#:~:text=Identifying%20Dandelion

Colleen. (2020c, July 28). *Foraging plantain: Identification and uses.* Grow Forage Cook Ferment. https://www.growforagecookferment.com/plantain-natures-band-aid/#:~:text=Identifying%20Plantain

Comfrey information. (n.d.). Mount Sinai Health System. Retrieved February 12, 2022, from https://www.mountsinai.org/health-library/herb/comfrey#:~:text=Comfrey%20-roots%20and%20leaves%20contain

Comfrey: Uses, side effects, and more. (n.d.). Web MD. Retrieved February 12, 2022, from https://www.webmd.com/vitamins/ai/ingredientmono-295/comfrey

Common Agrimony, Agrimonia eupatoria - Flowers. (n.d.). Nature Gate. Retrieved February 7, 2022, from https://luontoportti.com/en/t/1025/common-agrimony

Common agrimony: Pictures, flowers, leaves & identification. (n.d.). Edible Wild Food. Retrieved February 2, 2022, from https://www.ediblewildfood.com/common-agrimony.aspx

Common chickweed. (2015, June 5). Michigan State University Integrated Pest Management; Michigan State University. https://www.canr.msu.edu/resources/common_chickweed

Common mallow (malva neglecta). (n.d.). Illinois Wildflowers. Retrieved February 12, 2022, from http://www.illinoiswildflowers.info/weeds/plants/cm_mallow.htm

Common mullein. (n.d.). Woodland Ways Bushcraft Blog. Retrieved March 2, 2022, from https://www.woodland-ways.co.uk/blog/hedgerow-medicines/common-mullein/#:~:text=Key%20Identification%20Features%3A%20Biennial%20up

Common name comfrey (Common comfrey, healing-herb, knit-back, knit-bone, backwort, bruise-wort, slippery-root, asses' ears). (n.d.). Friends of the Wild Flower Garden. https://www.friendsofthewildflowergarden.org/pages/plants/comfrey.html

Common teasel identification and control. (2022, January 7). King County. https://kingcounty.gov/services/environment/animals-and-plants/noxious-weeds/weed-identification/common-teasel.aspx#:~:text=Cutleaf%20teasel%20has%20irregularly%2Dcut

Common violet. (n.d.). St Olaf College. Retrieved March 4, 2022, from https://wp.stolaf.edu/naturallands/forest/ephemerals/commonviolet/#:~:text=Violets%20are%20flowers%20with%20five

Cramp Bark. (2021, June 11). Rx List. https://www.rxlist.com/cramp_bark/supplements.htm

Cramp bark. (n.d.). Monterey Bay Herb Co. Retrieved February 15, 2022, from https://www.herbco.com/c-253-cramp-bark.aspx

Cramp bark (viburnum opulus l.). (n.d.). Health Embassy. Retrieved February 15, 2022, from https://healthembassy.co.uk/en/bark/39-cramp-bark.html

Cranberry. (2020, May). National Center for Complementary and Integrative Health. https://www.nccih.nih.gov/health/cranberry

Cranberry. (2021). In Encyclopædia Britannica. https://www.britannica.com/plant/cranberry

Cronkleton, E. (2019, March 8). 10 benefits of lemon balm and how to use it. Healthline. https://www.healthline.com/health/lemon-balm-uses

Culturally and economically important nontimber forest products of northern Maine - Sustaining forests. (2010, May 24). United States Department of Agriculture: Forest Service - Northern Research Station. https://www.nrs.fs.fed.us/sustaining_forests/conserve_enhance/special_products/maine_ntfp/plants/raspberry/#:~:text=Habitat%3A%20Raspberries%20are%20often%20found

Cunha, J. P. (Ed.). (2021a, March 9). Valerian. Rx List. https://www.rxlist.com/consumer_valerian/drugs-condition.htm

Cunha, J. P. (2021b, August 24). Cranberry. Rx List. https://www.rxlist.com/consumer_cranberry/drugs-condition.htm#:~:text=Class%3A%20Urology%2C%20Herbals-

Dallmeier, L. (n.d.). How to make macerated oils. Formula Botanica. Retrieved February 24, 2022, from https://formulabotanica.com/how-to-make-macerated-oils/#:~:text=Macerating%20works%20best%20when%20done

Dandelion. (n.d.). Mount Sinai Health System. Retrieved February 16, 2022, from https://www.mountsinai.org/health-library/herb/dandelion#:~:text=The%20leaves%20are%20used%20to

Dandelions: Cheery signs of spring. (n.d.). Christian Science Monitor. Retrieved February 16, 2022, from https://www.csmonitor.com/The-Culture/The-Home-Forum/2008/0410/p19s01-hfes.html

Davidson, K. (2020, August 20). Red clover: Benefits, uses, and side effects. Healthline. https://www.healthline.com/nutrition/red-clover#benefits

Debret, C. (2021, July 20). 10 useful tools for foraging this summer. One Green Planet. https://www.onegreenplanet.org/lifestyle/useful-tools-for-foraging-this-summer/

Dellwo, A. (2020, June 14). What is Goldenrod? Very Well Health. https://www.verywellhealth.com/goldenrod-benefits-4586964

Dessinger, H. (n.d.). Plantain herb benefits, recipes & how to identify. Mommypotamus. Retrieved March 2, 2022, from https://mommypotamus.com/plantain/

Dipsacus fullonum. (n.d.). Plants for a Future. Retrieved March 4, 2022, from https://pfaf.org/user/Plant.aspx?LatinName=Dipsacus+fullonum#:~:text=Medicinal%20Uses&text=Teasel%20is%20little%20used%20in

Dodrill, T. (n.d.-a). *How to identify chicory*. New Life on a Homestead. Retrieved February 12, 2022, from https://www.newlifeonahomestead.com/how-to-identify-chicory/#:~:text=The%20basal%20leaves%20on%20the

Dodrill, T. (n.d.-b). *How to identify goldenrod (plus foraging tips)*. New Life on a Homestead. Retrieved February 24, 2022, from https://www.newlifeonahomestead.com/goldenrod/#:~:text=Goldenrod%20plant%20leaves%20have%20only

Douglas, J. (2021, May 6). *Ethical foraging–Responsibility and reciprocity*. Organic Growers School. https://organicgrowersschool.org/ethical-foraging-responsibility-and-reciprocity/#:~:text=Ethical%20foraging%20is%20an%20ongoing

Duiker, S. W., & Curran, W. C. (2007, October 30). *Management of red clover as a cover crop*. Penn State Extension. https://extension.psu.edu/management-of-red-clover-as-a-cover-crop#:~:text=Red%20clover%20does%20best%20on

Dyer, M. H. (2021, August 12). *Mullein herb plants – Tips on using mullein as herbal treatments*. Gardening Know-How. https://www.gardeningknowhow.com/ornamental/flowers/mullein/using-mullein-as-herbs.htm

Echinacea. (n.d.). In The Gale Encyclopedia of Diets: A Guide to Health and Nutrition. Cengage; Encyclopedia. Retrieved February 22, 2022, from https://www.encyclopedia.com/plants-and-animals/plants/plants/echinacea#:~:text=the%20United%20States.-

Echinacea information. (n.d.). Mount Sinai Health System. Retrieved February 22, 2022, from https://www.mountsinai.org/health-library/herb/echinacea

Echinacea purpurea (Eastern purple coneflower). (n.d.). Minnesota Wildflowers. Retrieved February 22, 2022, from https://www.minnesotawildflowers.info/flower/eastern-purple-coneflower#:~:text=Flowers%20are%20single%20on%20end

Echinacea purpurea - Purple cone flower - Medicinal perennial herbal / Flower - 100 seeds. (n.d.). Seeds for Africa. Retrieved February 22, 2022, from https://www.seedsforafrica.co.za/products/echinacea-purpurea-purple-cone-flower-medicinal-annual-flower-100-seeds#:~:text=It%20is%20native%20to%20eastern

Agrimony. (2019, August 14). Britannica. https://www.britannica.com/plant/agrimony

Elder tree remedies. (2015, May 14). Handmade Apothecary. https://www.handmadeapothecary.co.uk/blog/2015/5/12/elderflowerpower

Elderberry. (2020, September 21). Web MD. https://www.webmd.com/diet/elderberry-health-benefits#:~:text=The%20berries%20and%20flowers%20of

Elderberry cold and cough syrup recipe. (n.d.). Edible Wild Food. Retrieved February 22, 2022, from https://www.ediblewildfood.com/elderberry-cold-cough-syrup.aspx

Elderberry: Sambucus canadensis. (n.d.). Edible Wild Food. Retrieved February 22, 2022, from https://www.ediblewildfood.com/elderberry.aspx#:~:text=Elder%20is%20characterised%20by%20its

Elderflower. (2021, November 6). Rx List. https://www.rxlist.com/elderflower/supplements.htm

Elderflower tincture - Easy homemade recipe. (2021, June 3). Practical Frugality. https://www.practicalfrugality.com/elderflower-tincture-recipe/

Ellen. (2016, December 16). *Wild garlic (aka field garlic, aka allium vineale)*. Backyard Forager. https://backyardforager.com/wild-garlic-field-garlic-allium-vineale/#:~:text=Wild%20garlic%20flowers%20are%20edible

Ellis, N. (2021, April 5). *How to make sunflower oil in your homestead?* Farm & Animals. https://farmandanimals.com/how-to-make-sunflower-oil/

Erdemir, S. M. (2017, September 21). *Parts of a composite flower*. Garden Guides. https://www.gardenguides.com/123630-parts-composite-flower.html

Ripe for the Picking: Blackberry Harvesting Tips and Recipes. (2018, July 17). Espoma Organic. https://www.espoma.com/fruits-vegetables/ripe-for-the-picking-blackberry-harvesting-tips-and-recipes/

Everything mint. (n.d.). Lifestyle Home Garden. Retrieved February 28, 2022, from https://lifestyle.co.za/mint/#:~:text=Mint%20is%20a%20hardy%2C%20highly

Everything you need to know about everbearing mulberry trees. (2020, August 23). This Old House. https://www.thisoldhouse.com/gardening/21336910/everbearing-mulberry-trees

Facts about garlic mustard. (n.d.). Health Benefits Times. https://www.healthbenefitstimes.com/garlic-mustard/

False Solomon seal: Maianthemum racemosum. (n.d.). Edible Wild Food. Retrieved March 3, 2022, from https://www.ediblewildfood.com/false-solomon-seal.aspx#:~:text=Solomon

Feverfew. (2008, May 31). Wildflower Finder. https://wildflowerfinder.org.uk/Flowers/F/Feverfew/Feverfew.htm#:~:text=Distinguishing%20Feature%20%3A%20The%20few%20white

Feverfew (Tanacetum parthenium). (n.d.). Illinois Wildflowers. Retrieved February 23, 2022, from https://www.illinoiswildflowers.info/weeds/plants/feverfew.html#:~:text=Feverfew%20(Tanacetum%20parthenium)&text=Description%3A%20This%20perennial%20herbaceous%20plant

Feverfew growing guide. (n.d.). Grow Veg. Retrieved February 23, 2022, from https://www.growveg.co.za/plants/south-africa/how-to-grow-feverfew/

Fewell, A. K. (2020, September 2). *Medicinal uses of goldenrod & goldenrod tincture*. Amy K. Fewell: The Fewell Homestead. https://thefewellhomestead.com/medicinal-uses-of-goldenrod-goldenrod-tincture/

Fletcher, J. (2019, January 3). *Dandelion: Health benefits, research, and side effects*. Medical News Today. https://www.medicalnewstoday.com/articles/324083

Foraging and using birch: Bark, leaves, & sap. (2020, December 1). Grow Forage Cook Ferment. https://www.growforagecookferment.com/foraging-birch/

Ford, C. (2019, February 15). *Cramp bark*. Ford's Herbal & Doula Services. https://www.fordsherbaldoulaservices.com/fords-herb-diary/cramp-bark

Forest Health Staff. (n.d.). *Common mullein - Verbascum thapsus L*. USDA Forest Service. Retrieved March 2, 2022, from http://www.na.fs.fed.us/fhp/invasive_plants

Foster, J. (n.d.). *The easiest way to harvest echinacea seeds*. Grow It Build It. Retrieved February 22, 2022, from https://growitbuildit.com/harvest-echinacea-seeds-an-illustrated-guide/#:~:text=A%20couple%20of%20weeks%20after

Fragrant trees. (n.d.). Berkshire Natural Resources Council. Retrieved February 11, 2022, from https://www.bnrc.org/fragrant-trees/

Frey, M. (2021a, October 12). *The health benefits of echinacea: Can a tea made from purple cone flowers stave off colds and illnesses?* Very Well Fit. https://www.verywellfit.com/echinacea-tea-benefits-and-side-effects-4163612#toc-dosage-and-preparations

Frey, M. (2021b, October 18). *Comfrey tea benefits and side effects is comfrey root safe or healthy?* Very Well Fit. https://www.verywellfit.com/comfrey-tea-benefits-and-side-effects-4163901

Frey, M. (2021c, October 19). *The health benefits of linden: The flowers of this herb are said to have sedative powers*. Very Well Fit. https://www.verywellfit.com/linden-tea-benefits-and-side-effects-4163720

Garlic mustard. (n.d.). Ontario's Invading Species Awareness Program. Retrieved February 24, 2022, from http://www.invadingspecies.com/invaders/plants/garlic-mustard/#:~:text=How%20to%20Identify%20Garlic%20Mustard

Garlic Mustard – A foraging guide to its food, medicine and other uses. (n.d.). Eat Weeds. Retrieved February 24, 2022, from https://www.eatweeds.co.uk/garlic-mustard-alliaria-petiolata#:~:text=Garlic%20mustard%20has%20been%20used,feet%20to%20relieve%20the%20cramp.

Garlic mustard: A very nutritious invasive plant. (2019, January 27). Freak of Natural. https://freakofnatural.com/garlic-mustard/#:~:text=In%20traditional%20herbalism%20-garlic%20mustard

German chamomile Information. (n.d.). Mount Sinai Health System. Retrieved February 24, 2022, from https://www.mountsinai.org/health-library/herb/german-chamomile#:~:text=Animal%20studies%20have%20shown%20that

Gerow. (2019, October 15). *Stop and smell the blackberries (then, kill them): A mountain biker's guide to nature.* Singletracks Mountain Bike News. https://www.singletracks.com/mtb-trails/stop-and-smell-the-blackberries-a-mountain-bikers-guide-to-nature/

Ghoshal, M. (2020, March 13). *Mulling over mullein leaf.* Healthline. https://www.healthline.com/health/mullein-leaf#mullein-oil

Girvin, T. (2010, August 20). *The scent of birch tar.* Girvin. https://www.girvin.com/the-scent-of-birch-tar/

Goldenrod. (2021, June 11). Rx List. https://www.rxlist.com/goldenrod/supplements.htm

Goldenrod: Medicinal uses & benefits. (n.d.). Chestnut School of Herbal Medicine. Retrieved February 24, 2022, from https://chestnutherbs.com/medicinal-uses-and-benefits-of-goldenrod/

Gotter, A. (2018, September 18). *Catnip tea: Health benefits and uses.* Healthline. https://www.healthline.com/health/catnip-tea#side-effects-and-risks

Gotter, A. (2021, January 12). *What is burdock root?* Healthline. https://www.healthline.com/health/burdock-root

Grant, A. (2021, August 8). *Borage harvesting: How and when to harvest borage plants.* Gardening Know-How. https://www.gardeningknowhow.com/edible/herbs/borage/harvesting-borage-plants.htm

Grant, B. L. (2020, December 20). *Leaf identification–Learn about different leaf types in plants.* Gardening Know-How. https://www.gardeningknowhow.com/garden-how-to/info/different-leaf-types-in-plants.htm

Griffin, R. M. (2021, January 18). *Black cherry and your health.* Web MD. https://www.webmd.com/diet/supplement-guide-black-cherry#:~:text=Black%20cherry%20bark%20also%20seems

Growing & Foraging for Mullein (Plus Harvesting & Preserving tips!). (2021, June 10). Unruly Gardening. https://unrulygardening.com/growing-foraging-mullein/#:~:text=Summer%2C%20or%20whenever%20the%20plant

Growing Organic Mugwort from Seed to Harvest. (n.d.). Mary's Heirloom Seeds. Retrieved February 28, 2022, from https://www.marysheirloomseeds.com/blogs/news/78072001-growing-organic-mugwort-from-seed-to-harvest#:~:text=Harvest%20mugwort%20shortly%20before%20it

Haddock, B. (2012, May 11). *Cranberry - edible wild plant - how to find, identify, prepare, and other uses for survival.* Wilderness Arena. https://www.wildernessarena.com/food-water-shelter/food-food-water-shelter/food-procurement/edible-wild-plants/cranberry

Haines, A. (n.d.). *Why foraging?* Arthur Haines. http://www.arthurhaines.com/why-foraging#:~:text=It%20helps%20people%20become%20more

Hall, J. (2021, July 9). *How to find and prepare nutritious, edible mallows.* Den Garden. https://dengarden.com/gardening/malva#:~:text=Identifying%20Mallows

Hanrahan, C., & Frey, R. (2018). *Mugwort.* In Gale Encyclopedia of Alternative Medicine. Cengage; Encyclopedia. https://www.encyclopedia.com/medicine/drugs/pharmacology/mugwort#:~:text=Mugwort%20is%20a%20tall%20and

Harrington, J. (n.d.). *How to harvest echinacea for tea.* SF Gate. Retrieved February 22, 2022, from https://homeguides.sfgate.com/harvest-echinacea-tea-73456.html

Harris, J. (n.d.). *My homemade echinacea tincture.* Jillian Harris. Retrieved February 22, 2022, from https://jillianharris.com/

Harvesting birch bark. (n.d.). The Folk School Fairbanks. Retrieved February 11, 2022, from https://folk.school/classes/tutorials/harvesting-birch-bark/

Hatter, K. (2017, July 21). *How to identify camomile.* Garden Guides. https://www.gardenguides.com/13426932-how-to-identify-camomile.html

Health benefits of mullein tea. (n.d.). Web MD. Retrieved March 2, 2022, from https://www.webmd.com/diet/health-benefits-mullein-tea#1

Health benefits of smooth Solomon's seal. (2018, November 5). Health Benefits Times. https://www.healthbenefitstimes.com/smooth-solomons-seal/

Health benefits of valerian root. (n.d.). Web MD. Retrieved March 4, 2022, from https://www.webmd.com/diet/health-benefits-valerian-root#3

Heath, S. (2021, December 9). *How to grow a mullein plant.* The Spruce. https://www.thespruce.com/mullein-plant-growing-guide-5203326

Hegde, R. (2020, August 12). *How to make willow bark tea for pain relief.* Organic Facts. https://www.organicfacts.net/willow-bark-tea.html

Herb spotlight - Cramp bark. (n.d.). Sun God Medicinals. Retrieved February 15, 2022, from https://sungodmedicinals.com/pages/herb-spotlight-cramp-bark

Herb: Japanese Honeysuckle. (n.d.). Natural Medicinal Herbs. Retrieved February 24, 2022, from http://www.naturalmedicinalherbs.net/herbs/l/lonicera-japonica=japanese-honeysuckle.php#:~:text=Edible%20parts%20of%20Japanese%20Honeysuckle%3A&text=The%20parboiled%20leaves%20are%20used

Herbal, O. W. (2014, November 4). *Bark harvest & ethical wildcrafting.* Old Ways Herbal: Juliette Abigail Carr. https://oldwaysherbal.com/2014/11/04/ethical-wildcrafting/

Hodgson, D. (n.d.). *Cleavers ointment.* Woodland Ways. Retrieved February 12, 2022, from https://www.woodland-ways.co.uk/blog/hedgerow-medicines/cleavers-ointment/

Homemade blackberry tincture. (2021, August 31). Alco Reviews. https://alcoreviews.com/homemade-blackberry-tincture/

Honeysuckle. (2021, November 6). Rx List. https://www.rxlist.com/honeysuckle/supplements.htm

Horsetail. (2014, June 5). Britannica. https://www.britannica.com/plant/horsetail

Horsetail. (2021, June 11). Rx List. https://www.rxlist.com/horsetail/supplements.htm

How cranberries grow: Pollination. (n.d.). Massachusetts Cranberries. Retrieved February 16, 2022, from https://www.cranberries.org/how-cranberries-grow/pollination

How much cherry juice should you drink a day? Traverse Bay Farms. www.traversebayfarms.com/pages/cherries-recommended-dosage-of-cherry-juice. Accessed 16 Mar. 2022.

How to do a coffee enema. (2020, November 9). Pure Joy Planet. https://www.purejoyplanet.com/blog/how-to-do-a-coffee-enema

How to grow & use valerian. (2020, June 24). It's My Sustainable Life. https://www.itsmysustainablelife.com/how-to-grow-use-valerian/#:~:text=Ideally%2C%20valerian%20-root%20should%20not

How to grow big, tall sunflowers. (2019, June 1). Velcro Brand Blog. https://www.velcro.com/news-and-blog/2019/06/how-to-grow-big-tall-sunflowers/#:~:text=Sunflowers%20prefer%20a%20somewhat%20alkaline,before%20you%20do%20any%20planting!

How to harvest wild cherry bark and stop coughing so you can sleep. (n.d.). Joybilee Farm. Retrieved February 11, 2022, from https://joybileefarm.com/wild-cherry-bark-stop-coughing/

How to identify chickweed - Foraging for wild edible greens. (2017, December 15). Good Life Revival. https://thegoodliferevival.com/blog/chickweed#:~:text=Chickweed%20is%20easy%20to%20identify,each%20other%20along%20the%20stem.

How to identify elderflower. (2012, June 8). Stay & Roam. https://stayandroam.blog/how-to-identify-elderflower/#:~:text=the%20correct%20plant.-

How to make birch bark flour and bake with it. (2020, December 18). Tree Time. https://blog.treetime.ca/blog/how-to-make-and-bake-with-bark-flour/

How to make Dandelion Tea the perfect way each time!! (n.d.). Tea Swan. Retrieved February 16, 2022, from https://teaswan.com/blogs/news/how-to-make-dandelion-tea

How to make echinacea (purple coneflower) oil & salve. (n.d.). The Nerdy Farm Wife. Retrieved February 22, 2022, from https://thenerdyfarmwife.com/echinacea-purple-coneflower-oil-salve/

How to Make Homemade Echinacea Tea. (2022, October 2). Sencha Tea Bar. https://senchateabar.com/blogs/blog/how-to-make-echinacea-tea#:~:text=Echinacea%20tea%20can%20be%20made

Howland, G. (2018 6). *Red raspberry leaf tea recipes you'll actually want to drink*. Mama Natural. https://www.mamanatural.com/red-raspberry-leaf-tea-recipes/

Iannotti, M. (2021a, July 9). *How to grow borage*. The Spruce. https://www.thespruce.com/how-to-grow-borage-1402625#toc-harvesting-borage

Iannotti, M. (2021b, December 20). *How to grow and care for chamomile*. The Spruce. https://www.thespruce.com/how-to-grow-chamomile-1402627

Identify a mulberry - Find out what to look out for to hunt down a mulberry. (n.d.). Morus Londinium. Retrieved March 1, 2022, from https://www.moruslondinium.org/map/identify

Identifying burdock. (2014, October 20). The Druid's Garden. https://druidgarden.wordpress.com/tag/identifying-burdock/

International Culinary Center. (2018, November 28). *How to Safely Forage*. International Culinary Education. https://www.ice.edu/blog/how-to-safely-forage

J, C. (2018, December 21). *A refreshing, aromatic herbal aperitif*. The Inspired Home. https://theinspiredhome.com/articles/a-refreshing-aromatic-herbal-aperitif

Jaana. (n.d.). *Larch*. Herbal Picnic. Retrieved February 28, 2022, from https://herbalpicnic.blogspot.com/2015/04/larch.html

James. (2020a, April 29). *Burdock (arctium iappa) identification*. Totally Wild UK. https://totallywilduk.co.uk/2020/04/29/identify-burdock/#:~:text=Burdock%20will%20grow%20in%20pretty

James. (2020b, April 29). *Cleavers (gallium aparine) identification*. Totally Wild UK. https://totallywilduk.co.uk/2020/04/29/identify-cleavers/

James. (2020c, April 29). *Comfrey (symphytum officinale) identification*. Totally Wild UK. https://totallywilduk.co.uk/2020/04/29/identify-comfrey/

James. (2020d, April 29). *Yarrow (achillea millefolium) identification*. Totally Wild UK. https://totallywilduk.co.uk/2020/04/29/identify-yarrow/

James, T. (2016, January 19). *How to forage for wild catnip*. Adventure Cats. https://www.adventurecats.org/pawsome-reads/foraging-adventure-how-to-spot-wild-catnip/#:~:text=Catnip%20is%20grayish%2Dgreen%20and

Japanese honeysuckle (lonicera japonica). (n.d.). Invasive. Retrieved February 28, 2022, from https://www.invasive.org/alien/pubs/midatlantic/loja.htm#:~:text=It%20is%20a%20fast%2Dgrowing

Jeanroy, A. (2019, June 26). *How to make herbal infusions*. The Spruce Eats. https://www.thespruceeats.com/how-to-make-an-herbal-infusion-1762142

Joanna. (2014, July 9). *The benefits of raspberry leaf tincture & my raspberry leaf tincture recipe*. Joanna Steven. https://www.joannasteven.com/the-benefits-of-raspberry-leaf-tincture-my-raspberry-leaf-tincture-recipe/

Johnson, K. (2000, August). *Rubus ursinus*. Pdx.

http://web.pdx.edu/~maserj/ESR410/rubisursinus.html

Jones, L. (2017, October 11). *Homegrown blackberry leaf tea*. Windellama Organics. https://www.windellamaorganics.com/blog/2017/10/10/homegrown-blackberry-leaf-tea

Keeler, K. (n.d.). *Plant story: Common mullein and its folklore*. A Wandering Botanist. Retrieved March 2, 2022, from http://khkeeler.blogspot.com/2013/07/plant-story-common-mullein-and-its.html#:~:text=Historically%20mullein%20was%20considered%20a,to%20be%20their%20preferred%20torch.&text=Common%20mullein%20has%20yellow%20flowers,Mercury%20gave%20Odysseus%20common%20mullein.

Kendle. (2018, September 14). *How to make herbal infusions & decoctions for wellness support*. Mountain Rose Herbs. https://blog.mountainroseherbs.com/herbal-infusions-and-decoctions

Kirk, S., Belt, S., & Berg, N. A. (2011). *Plant fact sheet verbena hastata (L.) Plant symbol = VEHA2*. Natural Resources Conservation Service. National Plant Materials Center. https://www.nrcs.usda.gov/Internet/FSE_PLANTMATERIALS/publications/mdpmcfs10335.pdf

Krohn, E. (2016). Alder. *Wild Foods and Medicines*. http://wildfoodsandmedicines.com/alder/

Kubala, J. (2019, November 29). *Mulberry leaf: Uses, benefits, and precautions*. Healthline. https://www.healthline.com/nutrition/mulberry-leaf#benefits

Lang, A. (2020, June 8). *What is vervain? All you need to know*. Healthline. https://www.healthline.com/nutrition/vervain-verbena

Lapcevic, K. (2021, July 21). *Lemon balm tincture*. Homespun Seasonal Living. https://homespunseasonalliving.com/lemon-balm-tincture/

Larch. (n.d.-a). Muster Kiste. Retrieved February 24, 2022, from http://www.musterkiste.com/en/holz/pro/1016_Larch.html#:~:text=The%20larch%20is%20the%20heaviest

Larch. (n.d.-b). Gaia Herbs. Retrieved February 28, 2022, from https://www.gaiaherbs.com/blogs/herbs/larch

Larch. (n.d.-c). Medicinal Herb Info. Retrieved February 28, 2022, from http://medicinalherbinfo.org/000Herbs2016/1herbs/larch/

Larch. (n.d.-d). Alaska's Wilderness Medicines. Retrieved February 28, 2022, from http://www.ankn.uaf.edu/curriculum/Books/Viereck/vierecklarch.html

Larch. (n.d.-e). Dr. Hauschka. Retrieved February 28, 2022, from https://www.drhauschka.co.uk/medicinal-plant-glossary/larch/

Larch arabinogalactan: Uses, side effects, and more. (2019). Web MD. https://www.webmd.com/vitamins/ai/ingredientmono-974/larch-arabinogalactan

Lemm, E. (2021, July 23). *Wild garlic adds subtle flavor*. The Spruce Eats. https://www.thespruceeats.com/what-is-wild-garlic-435437

Lemon balm. (n.d.). Mount Sinai Health System. Retrieved February 28, 2022, from https://www.mountsinai.org/health-library/herb/lemon-balm#:~:text=Lemon%20balm%20(Melissa%20officinalis)%2C

Lemon balm (melissa officinalis). (n.d.). Illinois Wildflowers. Retrieved February 28, 2022, from https://www.illinoiswildflowers.info/weeds/plants/lemon_balm.html

Lemon balm – Identification, edibility, distribution, ecology. (2019, July 9). Galloway Wild Foods. https://gallowaywildfoods.com/lemon-balm-identification-edibility-distribution-ecology/#:~:text=Identification%20%E2%80%93%204%2F5%20%E2%80%93%20Lemon

Lemon balm cream. (2021, April 7). Herba Zest. https://www.herbazest.com/herbs/lemon-balm/lemon-balm-cream

Lemon balm production (Second). (2012). Department of Agriculture, Forestry and Fisheries | Directorate: Pant production. chrome-extension://efaidnbmnnnibpcajpcglclefindmkaj/viewer.html?pdfurl=https%3A%2F%2Fwww.dalrrd.gov.za%2FPortals%2F0%2FBrochures%2520and%2520Production%2520guidelines%2FProduction%2520Guidelines%2520Lemon%2520Balm.pdf&clen=1437819&chunk=true

Lime tree in culture. (n.d.). Wikipedia. Retrieved February 28, 2022, from https://en.wikipedia.org/wiki/Lime_tree_in_culture#:~:text=Germanic%20mythology

Linden. (n.d.). Drugs. Retrieved February 28, 2022, from https://www.drugs.com/npc/linden.html#:~:text=Linden%20has%20been%20used%20to

Linden. (2021, June 11). Rx List. https://www.rxlist.com/linden/supplements.htm

Linden trees: Types, leaves, flowers, bark – Identification (with pictures). (n.d.). Leafy Place. Retrieved February 28, 2022, from https://leafyplace.com/linden-trees/#:~:text=size%20and%20shape.-

Link, R. (2020, June 10). *What is plantain weed, and how do you use it?* Healthline. https://www.healthline.com/nutrition/plantain-weed#side-effects

Lisa, A. (2022, January 18). *How to extract oil from plants (plus the numerous benefits and uses).* The Practical Planter. https://thepracticalplanter.com/how-to-extract-oil-from-plants/

Lofgren, K. (2020, May 27). *What's the difference between English and German chamomile?* Gardener's Path. https://gardenerspath.com/plants/flowers/english-german-chamomile/#German-Chamomile

Longacre, C. (2020, September 12). *How to harvest sunflower seeds.* Almanac. https://www.almanac.com/harvesting-sunflower-seeds

Making birch bark oil. (2018, January 24). Plant Pioneers. https://www.plantpioneers.org/blog/2018/1/24/making-birch-bark-oil

Making catnip (nepeta cataria) tincture. (2014, September 2). Spiraea. https://spiraeaherbs.ca/making-catnip-nepeta-cataria-tincture/

Mallow. (2015, May 28). Peace Health. https://www.peacehealth.org/medical-topics/id/hn-3263004#hn-3263004-how-it-works

Mallow. (n.d.). E Medicine Health. Retrieved February 13, 2022, from https://www.emedicinehealth.com/mallow/vitamins-supplements.htm#UsesAndEffectiveness

Mallow - common (malva sylvestris) organically grown flower seeds. (n.d.). Floral Encounters. Retrieved February 13, 2022, from https://www.floralencounters.com/Seeds/seed_detail.jsp?grow=Mallow+-+Common&productid=1102

Mallow is medicine. (2018, September 29). Indigenous Goddess Gang. https://www.indigenousgoddessgang.com/self-care-medicine/2018/9/27/white-flowered-medicine

Mallow: Overview, uses, side effects, and more. (n.d.). Web MD. Retrieved February 12, 2022, from https://www.webmd.com/vitamins/ai/ingredientmono-192/mallow

Matricaria chamomilla (wild chamomile). (n.d.). Go Botany: Native Plant Trust. Retrieved February 24, 2022, from https://gobotany.nativeplanttrust.org/species/matricaria/chamomilla/

Matthews, C. (Ed.). (2022, January 12). *Wild garlic guide: Where to find, how to cook it and recipe ideas.* Countryfile. https://www.countryfile.com/how-to/food-recipes/wild-garlic-guide-where-to-find-how-to-cook-it-and-recipe-ideas/#:~:text=What%20are%20the%20health%20benefits,as%20heart%20attack%20or%20stroke.

May, D. (2011, September 6). *Nature notes: common mallow.* The Times. https://www.thetimes.co.uk/article/nature-notes-common-mallow-lmrrwlmh76x

McCulloch, M. (2018, November 22). *Are sunflower seeds good for you?* Nutrition, benefits and more. Healthline. https://www.healthline.com/nutrition/sunflower-seeds#eating-tips

McCulloch, M. (2019, April 4). *Goldenrod: Benefits, dosage, and precautions.* Healthline. https://www.healthline.com/nutrition/goldenrod#inflammation

McKenzie, R. (2019). *Solomon's seal.* Eclectic School of Herbal Medicine. https://www.eclecticschoolofherbalmedicine.com/solomons-seal/

McMinn, S. (n.d.). *How to steep sassafras roots.* Chickens in the Road. Retrieved March 3, 2022, from https://chickensintheroad.com/cooking/how-to-steep-sassafras-roots/#:~:text=The%20best%20time%20to%20dig

Medicinal uses of beech trees. (n.d.). What Tree Where. Retrieved February 11, 2022, from https://whattreewhere.com/tag/medicinal-uses-of-beech-trees/

Melissa officinalis L. (n.d.). A Vogel. Retrieved February 28, 2022, from https://www.avogel.com/plant-encyclopaedia/melissa_officinalis.php#:~:text=Lemon%20Balm%20is%20a%2050cm

Mentha spicata - Spearmint. (n.d.). Northwest Oregon Wetland Plants Project. Retrieved February 28, 2022, from http://web.pdx.edu/~maserj/ESR410/mentha.html#:~:text=Habitat

Meredith, L. (2021, September 14). *Violet flower syrup.* The Spruce Eats. https://www.thespruceeats.com/violet-flower-syrup-recipe-1327872

Merva, V. (2020, March 20). *How to make Violet oil and its uses.* Simply beyond Herbs. https://simplybeyondherbs.com/violet-oil-recipe/

Minifie, K. (2014, June 5). *What the heck is chickweed and why is it on my plate?* Epicurious. https://www.epicurious.com/archive/blogs/editor/2014/05/what-the-heck-is-chickweed-and-why-is-it-on-my-plate.html

Mint. (2021, July 5). Encyclopedia Britannica. https://www.britannica.com/plant/Mentha

Moline, P. (2015, June 26). *How to make your own herb tincture or peppermint oil.* Los Angeles Times. https://www.latimes.com/home/la-he-healing-garden-recipes-20150627-story.html

Monoecious. (n.d.). In Merriam Webster. Retrieved February 8, 2022, from https://www.merriam-webster.com/dictionary/monoecious

Mugwort. (n.d.). Sawmill Herb Farm. Retrieved February 28, 2022, from http://www.sawmillherbfarm.com/herb%20profile/mugwort/

Mugwort. (2021, June 11). Rx List. https://www.rxlist.com/mugwort/supplements.htm#SpecialPrecautionsWarnings

Mulberry tree facts that are absolutely compelling to read. (n.d.). Gardenerdy. Retrieved March 1, 2022, from https://gardenerdy.com/mulberry-tree-facts/

Nash, K. (2021, June 5). *Where do pine trees grow? (Best habitat for natural growth).* Tree Vitalize. https://www.treevitalize.net/where-do-pine-trees-grow/#:~:text=agriculture%2C%20or%20fire.-

Nielsen, L. (2021, January 5). *How to harvest mint and store it for later.* Epic Gardening. https://www.epicgardening.com/how-to-harvest-mint/#:~:text=When%20Should%20I%20Harvest%20Mint%20Leaves%3F

Nix, S. (2021a, May 7). *Identify the larch.* Treehugger. https://www.treehugger.com/identify-the-larch-1341861#:~:text=How%20to%20Identify%20Larches&text=Most%20common%20larches%20in%20North

Nix, S. (2021b, June 7). *How to identify a tree using leaf shape, margin, and venation.* Treehugger. https://www.treehugger.com/id-trees-using-leaf-shape-venation-1343511

Types of Oak trees with their bark and leaves – Identification guide (pictures). (n.d.). Leafy Place. Retrieved March 2, 2022, from https://leafyplace.com/oak-tree-types-bark-leaves/#:~:text=The%20bark%20of%20young%20oak

Oak. (2020, June 18). Herba Zest. https://www.herbazest.com/herbs/oak

Oak - A foraging guide to its food, medicine and other uses. (n.d.). Eat Weeds. Retrieved March 2,

2022, from https://www.eatweeds.co.uk/oak-quercus-robur#:~:text=sugars%20and%20tannins.-

Oak bark. (2021, June 11). Rx List. https://www.rxlist.com/oak_bark/supplements.htm#SpecialPrecautionsWarnings

Oak flowers. (n.d.). Backyard Nature. Retrieved March 2, 2022, from https://www.backyardnature.net/fl_bloak.htm

Oak mythology and folklore. (n.d.). Trees for Life. Retrieved March 2, 2022, from https://treesforlife.org.uk/into-the-forest/trees-plants-animals/trees/oak/oak-mythology-and-folklore/#:~:text=To%20the%20Greeks%2C%20Romans%2C%20Celts

Oak Tree. (n.d.). Tree Works: Qualified Tree Surgery. Retrieved March 2, 2022, from http://treeworksguernsey.co.uk/tree-identification/oak/

Oak tree facts. (n.d.). Soft Schools. Retrieved March 2, 2022, from https://www.softschools.com/facts/plants/oak_tree_facts/505/

Orr, E. (n.d.). *Stinging nettle: Where to find & how to identify.* Wild Edible. Retrieved March 3, 2022, from https://www.wildedible.com/wild-food-guide/stinging-nettle#:~:text=Nettles%20grow%202%20to%205

Parallel venation. (2021, June 17). Maximum Yield. https://www.maximumyield.com/definition/1733/parallel-venation

Parisian, K. (2020, December 17). *Infused oils benefits and warnings.* Parisian's Pure Indulgence. https://parisianspure.com/blogs/news/infused-oils-benefits-and-warnings

Pearson, K. (2017, December 13). *8 health benefits of mint.* Healthline. https://www.healthline.com/nutrition/mint-benefits#TOC_TITLE_HDR_10

Perforate St John's-wort. (n.d.). The Wildlife Trusts. Retrieved March 3, 2022, from https://www.wildlifetrusts.org/wildlife-explorer/wildflowers/perforate-st-johns-wort#:~:text=Perforate%20st%20John

Phillips, Q. (2019, September 4). *How to make valerian tea.* Everyday Health. https://www.everydayhealth.com/diet-nutrition/make-valerian-tea-how-prepare-brew-steep-this-herbal-tea/

Pietrangelo, A. (2018, June 7). *St. John's wort: The benefits and the dangers.* Healthline. https://www.healthline.com/health-news/is-st-johns-wort-safe-080615

Pillsbury, C. (2017, August 23). *Forage through borage seed oil.* Watson. https://blog.watson-inc.com/nutri-knowledge/forage-through-borage-seed-oil

Pine. (2021, June 11). Rx List. https://www.rxlist.com/pine/supplements.htm#UsesAndEffectiveness

Plantain. (2015, May 24). Kaiser Permanente. https://wa.kaiserpermanente.org/kbase/topic.jhtml?docId=hn-2148003

Poulson, B., Horowitz, D., & Trevino, H. M. (Eds.). (n.d.). *Feverfew.* University of Rochester Medical Center. Retrieved February 23, 2022, from https://www.urmc.rochester.edu/encyclopedia/content.aspx?contenttypeid=19&contentid=Feverfew#:~:text=Feverfew%20may%20reduce%20painful%20inflammation

Product information teaseltea. (n.d.). Teasel Shop. Retrieved March 4, 2022, from https://www.teaselshop.com/c-2283855/dosage-and-use/

Pruisis, E. (2021, August 9). *Discover varieties of alder trees and shrubs.* The Spruce. https://www.thespruce.com/alder-trees-and-shrubs-3269701

Raman, R. (2018, October 25). *Echinacea: Benefits, uses, side effects and dosage.* Healthline. https://www.healthline.com/nutrition/echinacea#:~:text=The%20bottom%20line-

Red Clover. (n.d.). Brandeis University. Retrieved March 3, 2022, from http://www.bio.brandeis.edu/fieldbio/EFG_DEB_SHU/species%20pages/Red%20Clover/Red%20-Clover.html#:~:text=Identifying%20Characteristics%3A%20The%20white%20V

Red clover. (n.d.-a). Bellarmine University. Retrieved March 3, 2022, from https://www.bellarmine.edu/faculty/drobinson/RedClover.asp

Red clover. (n.d.-b). Plant Life. Retrieved March 3, 2022, from https://www.plantlife.org.uk/uk/discover-wild-plants-nature/plant-fungi-species/red-clover#:~:text=Flowers%20May%20to%20September.

Red clover (trifolium pratense). (n.d.). Illinois Wildflowers. Retrieved March 3, 2022, from http://www.illinoiswildflowers.info/weeds/plants/red_clover.htm#:~:text=Habitats%20include%20fields%2C%20pastures%2C%20weedy

Red raspberry: Uses, side effects, & more. (n.d.). Web MD. Retrieved March 3, 2022, from https://www.webmd.com/vitamins/ai/ingredientmono-309/red-raspberry

Reeves, K. (2010). *Exotic species: St. Johnswort.* U.S. National Park Service. https://www.nps.gov/articles/st-johnswort.htm#:~:text=Flowers%20and%20Fruits&text=along%20the%20margins.-

Rose, S. (n.d.). *Herbal guide to feverfew.* Garden Therapy. Retrieved February 23, 2022, from https://gardentherapy.ca/herbal-guide-to-feverfew/

Rowland, B. (n.d.). *Cramp Bark.* Encyclopedia; Gale Encyclopedia of Alternative Medicine. Retrieved February 15, 2022, from https://www.encyclopedia.com/medicine/encyclopedias-almanacs-transcripts-and-maps/cramp-bark

Sacred tree profile: Cherry (prunus serotina)'s magic, mythology, medicine and meaning. (n.d.). Retrieved February 12, 2022, from https://druidgarden.wordpress.com/2019/06/23/sacred-tree-profile-cherry-prunus-serotinas-magic-mythology-medicine-and-meaning/

Sacred tree profile: Sassafras' medicine, magic, mythology and meaning. (n.d.). The Druid's Garden. Retrieved March 3, 2022, from https://druidgarden.wordpress.com/2017/08/20/sacred-tree-profile-sassafras-medicine-magic-mythology-and-meaning/

Sarsaparilla. (n.d.). Rx List. Retrieved March 4, 2022, from https://www.rxlist.com/sarsaparilla/supplements.htm

Sassafras. (n.d.). University of Kentucky. Retrieved March 3, 2022, from https://www.uky.edu/hort/Sassafras#:~:text=Introduction%3A%20Sassafras%20has%20exceptional%20features

Sassafras. (2021, June 11). Rx List. https://www.rxlist.com/sassafras/supplements.htm

Sassafras tree: Leaves, flowers, bark (pictures) - Identification guide. (n.d.). Leafy Place. Retrieved March 3, 2022, from https://leafyplace.com/sassafras-tree/#:~:text=Sassafras%20tree%20identification%20is%20by

Schonbeck, J., & Frey, R. (n.d.). *Oak.* In Gale Encyclopedia of Alternative Medicine. Encyclopedia. Retrieved March 2, 2022, from https://www.encyclopedia.com/plants-and-animals/plants/plants/oak#:~:text=oak%20%2F%20%C5%8Dk%2F%20%E2%80%A2%20n.

Scots pine mythology and folklore. (n.d.). Trees for Life. Retrieved March 2, 2022, from https://treesforlife.org.uk/into-the-forest/trees-plants-animals/trees/scots-pine/scots-pine-mythology-and-folklore/#:~:text=Pine%20was%20also%20a%20fertility

Scott, C. (n.d.). *Medicinal plant: Japanese honeysuckle.* George Mason University. Retrieved February 24, 2022, from http://mason.gmu.edu/~cscottm/plants.html

Sedgwick, I. (2019, February 16). *Violets are blue: The folklore of February's birth flower.* Icy Sedgwick. https://www.icysedgwick.com/violets-folklore/

Seed information: Common name: valerian | Scientific name: Valeriana officinalis. (n.d.). Herb Garden. Retrieved March 4, 2022, from https://www.herbgarden.co.za/mountainherb/seedinfo.php?id=74#:~:text=Seed%20Information&text=Valerian%20is%20native%20to%20Britain

Seladi-Schulman, J. (2020, June 3). *About wintergreen essential oil*. Healthline. https://www.healthline.com/health/wintergreen-oil#uses

Shepherd's purse. (2021, June 11). Rx List. https://www.rxlist.com/shepherds_purse/supplements.htm

Shepherd's purse – and the value of stories. (2020, June 25). Diego Bonetto. https://www.diegobonetto.com/blog/shepherd-purse-and-the-value-of-stories#:~:text=It%20is%20also%20a%20very

Shepherd's purse tincture. (2017, March 13). Women's Heritage. https://www.womensheritage.com/blog/2017/2/27/shepards-purse-tincture

Shepherds purse: Capsella bursa pastoris. (n.d.). Edible Wild Food. Retrieved March 3, 2022, from https://www.ediblewildfood.com/shepherds-purse.aspx#:~:text=Shepherd

Shore, T. (2018, December 14). *How to identify red raspberry bushes & leaves*. Home Guides. https://homeguides.sfgate.com/identify-red-raspberry-bushes-leaves-56436.html

Silver birch - A foraging guide to its food, medicine and other uses. (n.d.). Eat Weeds. Retrieved February 14, 2022, from https://www.eatweeds.co.uk/birch-betula-spp#Harvest_Time

Simone. (2015, May 19). *How to make blackberry leaf tincture*. Solar Ripe. http://solarripe.eu/2015/05/how-to-make-blackberry-leaf-tincture-may-2015/

Smith, E. (n.d.). *Plant profile: Violet*. Integrative Family Medicine of Asheville. Retrieved March 4, 2022, from https://www.integrativeasheville.org/plant-profile-violet/#:~:text=Violet%20is%20moist%20and%20cooling

Snyder, C. (2021, May 14). *What is an herbal tonic? Benefits, weight loss, and efficacy*. Healthline. https://www.healthline.com/nutrition/herbal-tonic

Solomon's seal. (2019, November 18). The Witchipedia. https://witchipedia.com/book-of-shadows/herblore/solomons-seal/

Solomon's seal. (2021, June 11). Rx List. https://www.rxlist.com/solomons_seal/supplements.htm

Spengler, T. (2018, August 23). *How to identify mint plants*. Garden Guides. https://www.gardenguides.com/78357-history-mint-plant.html

Spengler, T. (2020, February 11). *Scale leaf evergreen varieties: What is a scale leaf evergreen tree*. Gardening Know-How. https://www.gardeningknowhow.com/ornamental/trees/tgen/scale-leaf-evergreen-varieties.htm

St. John's Wort. (2020, October). National Center for Complementary and Integrative Health. https://www.nccih.nih.gov/health/st-johns-wort#:~:text=Currently%2C%20St.

Staughton, J. (2020a, July 13). *5 surprising benefits of agrimony tea*. Organic Facts. https://www.organicfacts.net/agrimony-tea.html

Staughton, J. (2020b, July 28). *10 surprising benefits of sassafras*. Organic Facts. https://www.organicfacts.net/health-benefits/other/sassafras.html

Staughton, J. (2020c, August 25). *6 incredible benefits of St John's wort tea*. Organic Facts. https://www.organicfacts.net/st-johns-wort-tea.html

Stein, J., Binion, D., & Acciavatti, R. (2001). *Field guide to native oak species of Eastern North America (FHTET-03-01)*. USDA Forest Service, Forest Health Technology Enterprise Team. chrome-extension://efaidnbmnnnibpcajpcglclefindmkaj/viewer.html?pdfurl= https%3A%2F%2Fwww.fs.fed.us%2Fforesthealth%2 Ftechnology%2Fpdfs%2Ffieldguide.pdf&clen= 10803156&chunk=true

Stewart, S. (n.d.). *Mullein tincture*. Just a Pinch Recipes. Retrieved March 2, 2022, from https://www.justapinch.com/recipes/non-edible/non-edible-other-non-edible/mullein-tincture.html

Stinging nettle. (n.d.). Mount Sinai Health System. Retrieved March 3, 2022, from https://www.mountsinai.org/health-library/herb/stinging-nettle#:~:text=Stinging%20nettle%20has%20been%20used

Stobart, A. (2019, April 22). *Making herbal poultices and compresses*. Medicinal Forest Garden Trust. https://medicinalforestgardentrust.org/making-herbal-poultices-and-compresses/#:~:text=Herb%20poultices&text=You%20will%20need%20to%20crush

Streit, L. (2019, November 14). *5 emerging benefits and uses of chicory root fiber*. Healthline. https://www.healthline.com/nutrition/chicory-root-fiber#_noHeaderPrefixedContent

Strobile. (n.d.). In Merriam Webster. Retrieved February 8, 2022, from https://www.merriam-webster.com/dictionary/strobile

Susannah. (2021, November 1). *Cleavers plant uses & 5 best cleavers herb benefits*. Healthy Green Savvy. https://www.healthygreensavvy.com/cleavers-plant-herb-benefits/

Sweet violet - Uses, side effects, and more. (n.d.). Web MD. Retrieved March 4, 2022, from https://www.webmd.com/vitamins/ai/ingredientmono-212/sweet-violet#

Tapping tree sap. (2011, March 26). Judy of the Woods. http://www.judyofthewoods.net/forage/tree_sap.html

Taylor, K. (2021, April 21). *How to dry echinacea flowers And roots*. Urban Garden Gal. https://www.urbangardengal.com/how-to-dry-echinacea-flowers-roots/#:~:text=Echinacea%20roots%20can%20be%20harvested

Tea time: Violet leaf tea. (2020, April 15). Awkward Botany. https://awkwardbotany.com/2020/04/15/tea-time-violet-leaf-tea/

Teazle. (2021, June 14). EMedicine Health. https://www.emedicinehealth.com/teazle/vitamins-supplements.htm

Teazle - Uses, side effects, and more. (n.d.). Web MD. Retrieved March 4, 2022, from https://www.webmd.com/vitamins/ai/ingredientmono-187/teazle

Tello, C. (2021, September 9). *What is sarsaparilla? A plant lost in time + tea recipe*. Self Decode. https://supplements.selfdecode.com/blog/sarsaparilla-plant-drink-how-to-make-tea/

Terry, S. (2017, September 21). *How to identify willow trees*. Garden Guides. https://www.gardenguides.com/109710-care-corkscrew-willow-tree.html

The benefits of wild cherry bark. (n.d.). Kaya Well. Retrieved February 11, 2022, from https://www.kayawell.com/Food/The-Benefits-of-Wild-Cherry-Bark-whooping-cough-diarrhea

The raspberries are ready for picking. (2019, July 9). The Martha Blog. https://www.themarthablog.com/2019/07/the-raspberries-are-ready-for-picking.html

Tikkanen, A. (n.d.). *Borage*. Encyclopedia Britannica. Retrieved February 12, 2022, from https://www.britannica.com/plant/borage

Tiller, B. (2019, January 24). *Field garlic: Allium vineale*. Mossy Oak. https://www.mossyoak.com/our-obsession/blogs/how-to/field-garlic-allium-vineale

Tilley, N. (2021, July 26). *Wild violets care – How to grow wild violet plants*. Gardening Know How. https://www.gardeningknowhow.com/ornamental/bulbs/violet/wild-violets-care.htm#:~:text=While%20they%20tolerate%20many%20soil

Tips to harvest sunflowers. (2020, May 2). Grainvest Group. https://grainvest.co.za/2020/05/02/tips-to-harvest-sunflowers/#:~:text=Harvest%20sunflowers%20when%20their%20petals

Tirrell, R. (1974, June 2). Herb, of folklore. *The New York Times*, 149. https://www.nytimes.com/1974/06/02/archives/herb-of-folklore.html#:~:text=COMFREY%2C%20a%20magical%20herb%20of

Tutorial: How to make a traditional tincture with roots. (2013, October 31). Minnesota Herbalist. https://minnesotaherbalist.com/2013/10/31/tutorial-how-to-make-a-traditional-tincture-with-roots/

Tyler, S. (2019, May 27). *Western larch - New uses for an ancient medicine.* Botanical Medicine. https://www.botanicalmedicine.org/western-larch-new-uses-for-ancient-medicine/

Types of pine trees with identification guide, chart and pictures. (n.d.). Leafy Place. Retrieved March 2, 2022, from https://leafyplace.com/types-of-pine-trees-identification-and-pictures/

Undlin, S. (2020, July 27). *Top mugwort uses (and where to find it).* Plantsnap. https://www.plantsnap.com/blog/top-mugwort-uses-and-where-to-find-it/#:~:text=Identifying%20Mugwort%20Out%20In%20The%20World&text=Its%20dark%20green%20leaves%20are

Valerian. (2015, May 12). Kaiser Permanente. https://wa.kaiserpermanente.org/kbase/topic.jhtml?docId=hn-2179004

Valerian: Valeriana officinalis. (n.d.-a). Edible Wild Food. Retrieved March 4, 2022, from https://www.ediblewildfood.com/valerian.aspx#:~:text=Valerian%20is%20a%20perennial%20plant

Valerian: Valeriana officinalis. (n.d.-b). Edible Wild Food. Retrieved March 4, 2022, from https://www.ediblewildfood.com/valerian.aspx

Verma, R., Gangrade, T., Ghulaxe, C., & Punasiya, R. (2014). *Rubus fruticosus (blackberry) use as an herbal medicine.* Pharmacognosy Reviews, 8(16), 101. https://doi.org/10.4103/0973-7847.134239

Viburnum opulus. (n.d.). Gardeners World. Retrieved February 15, 2022, from https://www.gardenersworld.com/plants/viburnum-opulus/

Viburnum opulus: Cramp bark. (n.d.). Gaia Herbs. Retrieved February 15, 2022, from https://www.gaiaherbs.com/blogs/herbs/cramp-bark

Ware, M. (2019, November 1). *What to know about cranberries.* Medical News Today. https://www.medicalnewstoday.com/articles/269142#:~:text=Many%20people%20consider%20cranberries%20to

Westover, J. (n.d.). *How to identify a purple coneflower when not in bloom.* SF Gate. Retrieved February 22, 2022, from https://homeguides.sfgate.com/identify-purple-coneflower-not-bloom-62343.html

What happens in your body if you drink larch tea. (2021, February 21). Newsy Today. https://newsy-today.com/what-happens-in-your-body-if-you-drink-larch-tea/

What is awl shaped? (n.d.). Movie Cultists. Retrieved February 13, 2022, from https://moviecultists.com/what-is-awl-shaped

White oak. (n.d.). Natural Resource Stewardship. Retrieved March 2, 2022, from https://naturalresources.extension.iastate.edu/forestry/iowa_trees/trees/white_oak.html#:~:text=White%20oak%20leaves%20are%20simple

Wild foraging: How to identify, harvest, store and use horsetail. (2016, May 2). The Daring Gourmet. https://www.daringgourmet.com/wild-foraging-how-to-identify-harvest-store-and-use-horsetail/#:~:text=What%20does%20horsetail%20look%20like,the%20nodes%E2%80%9D%20(Wikipedia).

Wild garlic or ramsons – A foraging guide to its food, medicine and other uses. (n.d.). Eat Weeds. Retrieved February 23, 2022, from https://www.eatweeds.co.uk/wild-garlic-allium-ursinum

Wild horse tail. (n.d.). Recipes from the Wild. Retrieved February 28, 2022, from https://recipesfromthewild.wordpress.com/wild-horse-tail/#:~:text=Creating%20a%20Tincture%3A&text=Within%20one%20to%20two%20hours

Wild sarsaparilla (aralia nudicaulis). (n.d.). MPG North. Retrieved March 4, 2022, from https://mpgnorth.com/field-guide/araliaceae/wild-sarsaparilla

Wild violet vinegar infusion. (n.d.). Grow a Good Life. Retrieved March 4, 2022, from https://growagoodlife.com/wild-violet-vinegar/

Wildflowers of the Adirondacks: Wild sarsaparilla (aralia nudicaulis). (n.d.). Wild Adirondacks. Retrieved March 4, 2022, from https://wildadirondacks.org/adirondack-wildflowers-wild-sarsaparilla-aralia-nudicaulis.html#:~:text=Identification%20of%20Wild%20Sarsaparilla

Wildflowers of the Adirondacks: Wintergreen (gaultheria procumbens). (n.d.). Wild Adirondacks. Retrieved March 4, 2022, from https://wildadirondacks.org/adirondack-wildflowers-wintergreen-gaultheria-procumbens.html#:~:text=Identification%20of%20Wintergreen

Wildlife friendly landscapes. (n.d.). NC State Extension. Retrieved February 24, 2022, from https://wildlifefriendlylandscapes.ces.ncsu.edu/#:~:text=Identification%3A%20Japanese%20Honeysuckle%20is%20an

Wilen, C A, et al. *Pesticides: Safe and Effective Use in the Home and Landscape.* University of California Agriculture and Natural Resources, 2019, ipm.ucanr.edu/PMG/PESTNOTES/pn74126.html. Accessed 14 Mar. 2022.

Willis, E. (n.d.). *Herb article - Catnip.* Rebecca's Herbal Apothecary. Retrieved March 2, 2022, from https://www.rebeccasherbs.com/pages/herb-article-br-catnip#:~:text=Preparations%20%26%20Applications&text=Catnip%20can%20be%20prepared%20as

Willow bark. (2021, June 11). Rx List. https://www.rxlist.com/willow_bark/supplements.htm

Willow tree mythology and folklore. (n.d.). Trees for Life. Retrieved March 4, 2022, from https://treesforlife.org.uk/into-the-forest/trees-plants-animals/trees/willow/willow-mythology-and-folklore/

Windling, T. (2016, May 12). *The folklore of nettles.* Myth & Moor. https://www.terriwindling.com/blog/2016/05/from-the-archives-picking-nettles.html

Wintergreen. (2021, June 11). Rx List. https://www.rxlist.com/wintergreen/supplements.htm

Wong, C. (2021a, January 9). *What you need to know about chickweed.* Very Well Health. https://www.verywellhealth.com/chickweed-what-should-i-know-about-it-89437

Wong, C. (2021b, March 3). *What is cramp bark (viburnum)?* Very Well Health. https://www.verywellhealth.com/the-benefits-of-viburnum-cramp-bark-88657

Wong, C. (2021c, November 9). *What is red clover?* Very Well Health. https://www.verywellhealth.com/the-benefits-of-red-clover-89577#:~:text=In%20herbal%20medicine%2C%20red%20clover

Wresting burdock seed and its medicinal uses. (2017, December 1). Northeast School of Botanical Medicine. https://7song.com/wresting-burdock-seed-and-its-medicinal-uses/

Yarrow. (2021, June 11). Rx List. https://www.rxlist.com/yarrow/supplements.htm

IMAGES

Chai, S. (2021). *Anonymous person with bag of plastic bottles* [Online image]. In Pexels. https://www.pexels.com/photo/anonymous-person-with-bag-of-plastic-bottles-7262933/

Cottonbro. (2020). *Leaves and twigs on a canvas bag* [Online image]. In Pexels. https://www.pexels.com/photo/leaves-and-twigs-on-a-canvas-bag-6033829/

Fotios, L. (2018). *Person digging on soil using garden shovel* [Online image]. In Pexels. https://www.pexels.com/photo/person-digging-on-soil-using-garden-shovel-1301856/

Hamra, J. (2018). *Person Holding Round Framed Mirror Near Tree at Daytime* [Online image]. In Pexels. https://www.pexels.com/photo/person-holding-round-framed-mirror-near-tree-at-daytime-979927/

Hatchett, M. (2019). *Folding knife* [Online image]. In Pexels. https://www.pexels.com/photo/folding-knife-2599276/

Jameson, L. (2021). *Man in blue t-shirt and brown shorts sitting on ground With green plants*

[Online image]. In Pexels. https://www.pexels.com/photo/man-in-blue-t-shirt-and-brown-shorts-sitting-on-ground-with-green-plants-9324354/

Jess Bailey Designs. (2017). *Close-up photography scissors* [Online image]. In Pexels. https://www.pexels.com/photo/close-up-photography-scissors-755991/

Kool, A. (2015). *El Capitan on a sunny afternoon* [Online image]. In Unsplash. https://unsplash.com/photos/ndN00KmbJ1c?modal=%7B%22tag%22%3A%22Login%22%2C%22value%22%3A%7B%22tag%22%3A%22Like%22%2C%22value%22%3A%7B%22photoId%22%3A%22ndN00KmbJ1c%22%2C%22userId%22%3A%22AjxdOkQCJr8%22%7D%7D%7D

Lewis, J. (2020). *Yellow leaf in close up photography* [Online image]. In Pexels. https://www.pexels.com/photo/yellow-leaf-in-close-up-photography-5497873/

Mazumder, A. (2018). *Person holding a green plant* [Online image]. In Pexels. https://www.pexels.com/photo/person-holding-a-green-plant-1072824/

Monstera. (2021). *Wooden brushes prepared for washing and cleaning* [Online image]. In Pexels. https://www.pexels.com/photo/wooden-brushes-prepared-for-washing-and-cleaning-6621326/

Patel, S. (2020). *Green leaves on tree branch* [Online image]. In Pexels. https://www.pexels.com/photo/green-leaves-on-tree-branch-4400283/

Pixabay. (2012). *Green Leaf Plant* [Online image]. In Pexels. https://www.pexels.com/photo/green-leaf-plant-86397/

Pixabay. (2016). *Green tree plant leaves* [Online image]. In Pexels. https://www.pexels.com/photo/green-tree-plant-leaves-40896/

Rodnikova, M. (2021). *Pruning shears and a flower wreath* [Online image]. In Pexels. https://www.pexels.com/photo/pruning-shears-and-a-flower-wreath-9797607/

Schwartz, K. (2021). *Green leaves of growing fern* [Online image]. In Pexels. https://www.pexels.com/photo/green-leaves-of-growing-fern-8117889/

Sunsetoned. (2020). *Crop woman reading book on grass* [Online image]. In Pexels. https://www.pexels.com/photo/crop-woman-reading-book-on-grass-5981113/

Tis, A. (2021). *Yellow maple leaf on yellow background* [Online image]. In Pexels. https://www.pexels.com/photo/yellow-maple-leaf-on-yellow-background-9563330/

Tran, V. (2019). *Photo of jar near cinnamon sticks* [Online image]. In Pexels. https://www.pexels.com/photo/photo-of-jar-near-cinnamon-sticks-3273989/

Webb, S. (2018). *Green leafed indoor plant* [Online image]. In Pexels. https://www.pexels.com/photo/green-leafed-indoor-plant-1048035/

BIBLIOGRAPHY

5 tips for when you need help identifying a plant. (n.d.). Nature Mentor. Retrieved February 5, 2022, from https://nature-mentor.com/need-help-identifying-a-plant/

6 fantastic reasons for growing and using a comfrey plant. (2019, April 22). Preparedness Mama. https://preparednessmama.com/growing-and-using-comfrey/

10 fascinating and fun cranberries facts from That's It. (2015, November 3). That's It. https://www.thatsitfruit.com/blogs/default-blog/10-interesting-facts-about-cranberries

A guide to garden flower identification: What's in your garden? (n.d.). Plant Snap. Retrieved February 5, 2022, from https://www.plantsnap.com/blog/garden-flower-identification/

Acer negundo. (n.d.). Wild Flower. Retrieved February 22, 2022, from https://www.wildflower.org/plants/result.php?id_plant=acne2#:~:text=Leaf%3A%20Opposite%2C%20pinnately%20compound%2C

Acorn facts for kids. (n.d.). Kiddle. Retrieved March 2, 2022, from https://kids.kiddle.co/Acorn#:~:text=The%20acorn%20is%20the%20fruit

Adamant, A. (2018, May 12). *How to make burdock tincture.* Practical Self Reliance. https://practicalselfreliance.com/burdock-tincture/#:~:text=Chop%20the%20root%20into%20chunks

Adamant, A. (2021, April 5). *15 ways to use borage.* Practical Self Reliance. https://practicalselfreliance.com/borage-uses/

Adriana. (2021, June 24). *Blackberry leaf tea: A herbal remedy for your health.* Backyard Garden Lover. https://www.backyardgardenlover.com/blackberry-leaf-tea/

Agarwal, S. (2021, October 19). *8 amazing mulberry benefits: Make the most of it while the season lasts.* NDTV Food. https://food.ndtv.com/food-drinks/8-amazing-mulberry-benefits-make-the-most-of-it-while-the-season-lasts-1685146

Agrimonia gryposepala (common agrimony, tall hairy agrimony). (n.d.). Native Plant Trust: Go Botany. Retrieved February 7, 2022, from https://gobotany.nativeplanttrust.org/species/agrimonia/gryposepala/

Agrimony health benefits and side effects. (n.d.). Medical Health Guide. Retrieved February 8, 2022, from http://www.medicalhealthguide.com/herb/agrimony.htm

Agrimony: Overview, uses, side effects, precautions, interactions, dosing and reviews. (n.d.). Web MD. Retrieved February 8, 2022, from https://www.webmd.com/vitamins/ai/ingredient-mono-604/agrimony

Alcantara, S. T. (n.d.). *How to make burdock tea.* Live Strong. Retrieved March 2, 2022, from https://www.livestrong.com/article/52018-make-burdock-tea/

Alder. (n.d.). In Merriam Webster. Retrieved February 8, 2022, from https://www.merriam-webster.com/dictionary/alder

Alder buckthorn. (2021, June 11). RxList. https://www.rxlist.com/alder_buckthorn/supplements.htm

Alder tincture recipe. (2020, April 3). Cortes Currents. https://cortescurrents.ca/yulia-kochubievskys-alder-tincture-recipe/

Alder trees plants advantages and disadvantages, side effects and reviews. (n.d.). Review Guts. Retrieved February 8, 2022, from https://reviewguts.com/alder-trees-plants_2nd/

Alder trees: Leaves, bark, flowers, cones - Identification (pictures). (2021, April 19). Leafy Place. https://leafyplace.com/alder-trees/

American sarsaparilla (spikenard) – Aralia racemosa. (n.d.). Root Buyer. Retrieved March 4,

2022, from https://rootbuyer.com/wild-sarsaparilla-spikenard-aralia-racemosa/#:~:text=The%20rootstock%20is%20harvested%20in

American Survival Guide. (2018, March 22). *Foraging gear: The tools you need to collect, process and carry natural foods*. American Outdoor Guide. https://www.americanoutdoor.guide/how-to/foraging-gear-the-tools-you-need-to-collect-process-and-carry-natural-foods/

Ancient equisetum. (2015, May 21). In Defense of Plants. https://www.indefenseofplants.com/blog/2015/5/21/ancient-equisetum

Andrea. (2019, January 9). *Wild cherry bark & horehound tincture tea recipe*. Frugally Sustainable. https://frugallysustainable.com/cherry-bark-horehound-tincture/

Applebaum, G. (n.d.). *Moxa: The burning herb that heals*. Fabriq. Retrieved March 1, 2022, from http://www.fabriqspa.com/the-burning-herb-that-heals/

Baessler, L. (2021, April 6). *What is valerian: How to grow valerian plants in the garden*. Gardening Know-How. https://www.gardeningknowhow.com/edible/herbs/valerian/growing-valerian-herb-plants.htm

Baldridge, K. (2020, May 8). *How to make an elderberry tincture*. Traditional Cooking School. https://traditionalcookingschool.com/health-and-nutrition/make-your-own-elderberry-tincture/

Barth, B. (2018, July 18). *7 smokable plants you can grow that aren't marijuana*. Modern Farmer. https://modernfarmer.com/2018/07/7-smokable-plants-you-can-grow-that-arent-marijuana/#:~:text=Mullein%20(Verbascum%20thapsus)&text=Herbal%20Properties%3A%20Mullein%20has%20a

Beaulieu, D. (2021, August 11). *St. John's wort plant profile*. The Spruce. https://www.thespruce.com/st-johns-wort-plant-profile-4772327

Beech. (n.d.). In Merriam Webster. Retrieved February 8, 2022, from https://www.merriam-webster.com/dictionary/beech

Beech. (n.d.). Vild Mad. Retrieved February 11, 2022, from https://vildmad.dk/en/ingredients/beech

Beech - A guide to its food, medicine and other uses. (n.d.). Eat Weeds. Retrieved February 11, 2022, from https://www.eatweeds.co.uk/beech-fagus-sylvatica

Beech trees: Types, leaves, bark — Identification guide (pictures). (n.d.). Leafy Place. Retrieved February 8, 2022, from https://leafyplace.com/beech-trees/

Benefits of black cherries. (n.d.). Bremner Foods. Retrieved February 11, 2022, from https://www.bremnerfoods.com/health-benefits/benefits-of-black-cherries.html#:~:text=Health%20Benefits%20of%20Black%20Cherries&text=Black%20cherries%20are%20an%20excellent

Benefits of growing medicinal herbs. (2016, March 28). Joybilee Farm. https://joybileefarm.com/7-reasons-make-healing-homegrown/

Berries as symbols and in folklore. (n.d.). New York Berry News, 6(1). Cornell University's College of Agriculture and Life Sciences. Retrieved March 3, 2022, from chrome-extension://efaidnbmnnnibpcajpcglclefindmkaj/viewer.html?pdfurl=https%3A%2F%2Fcpb-us-e1.wpmucdn.com%2Fblogs.cornell.edu%2Fdist%2F0%2F7265%2Ffiles%2F2016%2F12%2Fberryfolklore-2ljzt0q.pdf&clen=100303&chunk=true

Birch. (n.d.). In Merriam Webster. Retrieved February 11, 2022, from https://www.merriam-webster.com/dictionary/birch

Birch fruits and seeds. (n.d.). Tree Guide. Retrieved February 11, 2022, from http://www.tree-guide.com/birch-fruits-and-seeds

Birch Leaf. (n.d.). Mountain Rose Herbs. Retrieved February 11, 2022, from https://mountainroseherbs.com/birch-leaf

Birch perfume ingredient, birch fragrance and essential oils Betula, family betulaceae. (n.d.).

Gragrantica. Retrieved February 11, 2022, from https://www.fragrantica.com/notes/Birch-31.html

Birch tree allergen facts, symptoms, and treatment. (n.d.). Thermo Fisher. Retrieved February 11, 2022, from https://www.thermofisher.com/allergy/us/en/allergen-fact-sheets.html?allergen=birch-tree

Birch trees: Types, leaves, bark - Identification (with pictures). (n.d.). Leafy Place. Retrieved February 11, 2022, from https://leafyplace.com/birch-trees/

Birch: Uses, side effects, interactions, dosage, and warning. (n.d.). Web MD. Retrieved February 11, 2022, from https://www.webmd.com/vitamins/ai/ingredientmono-352/birch

Bjarnadottir, A. (2019, February 22). *Mulberries 101: Nutrition facts and health benefits.* Healthline. https://www.healthline.com/nutrition/foods/mulberries#bottom-line

Black cherry. (n.d.). In Merriam Webster. Retrieved February 11, 2022, from https://www.merriam-webster.com/dictionary/black%20cherry

Black cherry. (n.d.-a). Tree Guide. Retrieved February 11, 2022, from http://www.tree-guide.com/black-cherry

Black cherry. (n.d.-b). Natural Resource Stewardship. Retrieved February 11, 2022, from https://naturalresources.extension.iastate.edu/forestry/iowa_trees/trees/black_cherry.html

Blackberry. (n.d.). In Merriam Webster. Retrieved February 11, 2022, from https://www.merriam-webster.com/dictionary/blackberry

Blackberry. (2015, August 6). Kaiser Permanente. https://wa.kaiserpermanente.org/kbase/topic.jhtml?docId=hn-2045002#hn-2045002-side-effects

Blackberry | fruit. (2022). In Encyclopædia Britannica. https://www.britannica.com/plant/blackberry-fruit

Blankespoor, J. (2017, November 7). *Foraging for wild edibles and herbs: Sustainable and safe gathering practices.* Chestnut School of Herbal Medicine. https://chestnutherbs.com/foraging-for-wild-edibles-and-herbs-sustainable-and-safe-gathering-practices/

Blankespoor, J. (2021a, February 4). *The Medicine of Pine.* Chestnut School of Herbal Medicine. https://chestnutherbs.com/the-medicine-of-pine/#:~:text=Pine%20offers%20relief%20in%20sinus

Blankespoor, J. (2021b, April 13). *Violet's edible and medicinal uses.* Chestnut School of Herbal Medicine. https://chestnutherbs.com/violets-edible-and-medicinal-uses/#:~:text=Violet%20is%20cooling%20and%20moistening

Blue vervain. (n.d.). In Merriam Webster. Retrieved February 12, 2022, from https://www.merriam-webster.com/dictionary/blue%20vervain

Blue vervain: Pictures, flowers, leaves & identification | Verbena hastata. (n.d.). Edible Wild Food. Retrieved February 11, 2022, from https://www.ediblewildfood.com/blue-vervain.aspx

Borage. (n.d.). In Merriam Webster. Retrieved February 12, 2022, from https://www.merriam-webster.com/dictionary/borage

Borage leaves. (n.d.). Specialty Produce. Retrieved February 11, 2022, from https://specialtyproduce.com/produce/Borage_Leaves_11921.php

Borage: Uses, side effects and warnings, interactions, dosage, and warning. (n.d.). Web MD. Retrieved February 12, 2022, from https://www.webmd.com/vitamins/ai/ingredientmono-596/borage

Borago officinalis, borage: Identification, distribution, habitat. (n.d.). First Nature. Retrieved February 11, 2022, from https://www.first-nature.com/flowers/borago-officinalis.php#:~:text=Up%20to%2060cm%20tall%2C%20this

Bratianu, P. (n.d.). *The natural healing power of oak trees and acorns.* Off the Grid News. Retrieved March 2, 2022, from https://www.offthegridnews.com/alternative-health/the-natural-healing-power-of-oak-trees-and-acorns/

Brennan, D. (Ed.). (2020a, September 17). *Health Benefits of Mint Leaves*. Web MD. https://www.webmd.com/diet/health-benefits-mint-leaves#:~:text=When%20it%20comes%20to%20medicinal

Brennan, D. (2020b, September 18). *Health benefits of raspberries*. Web MD. https://www.webmd.com/diet/health-benefits-raspberries#:~:text=They%20provide%20potassium%2C%20essential%20to

Brennan, D. (Ed.). (2020c, November 10). *Health benefits of mulberries*. Web MD. https://www.webmd.com/diet/health-benefits-mulberries#2-5

Buckner, H. (2020, March 20). *How to plant and grow plantain, a culinary and medicinal herb*. Gardener's Path. https://gardenerspath.com/plants/herbs/grow-plantain/#:~:text=All%20of%20these%20species%20grow

Burdock. (n.d.). In Merriam Webster. Retrieved February 12, 2022, from https://www.merriam-webster.com/dictionary/burdock

Burdock: Pictures, flowers, leaves & identification | Arctium lappa. (n.d.). Edible Wild Food. Retrieved February 12, 2022, from https://www.ediblewildfood.com/burdock.aspx

Can you juice soft summer fruits like cherries, berries, and peaches? (2017, July 19). Eujuicers. https://www.eujuicers.com/magazine/can-you-juice-soft-summer-fruits-like-cherries-berries-and-peaches

Carroll, J. (2021a, May 4). *Growing a larch tree: Larch tree types for garden settings*. Gardening Know-How. https://www.gardeningknowhow.com/ornamental/trees/larch/growing-a-larch-tree.htm#:~:text=Larch%20trees%20are%20large%20deciduous,flowers%20that%20eventually%20become%20cones.

Carroll, J. (2021b, May 10). *St. John's wort plant care: How to grow St. John's wort*. Gardening Know-How. https://www.gardeningknowhow.com/edible/herbs/st-johns-wort/st-johns-wort-plant-care.htm

Carryopsis, J. (n.d.). *Biology of dandelions*. Nature North. Retrieved February 16, 2022, from http://www.naturenorth.com/summer/dandelion/Dandelion2.html

Catnip. (n.d.). In Merriam Webster. Retrieved February 12, 2022, from https://www.merriam-webster.com/dictionary/catnip

Catnip oil extraction methods, process, techniques. (n.d.). Agri Farming. https://www.agrifarming.in/catnip-oil-extraction-methods-process-techniques

Catnip tea: Are there health benefits? (n.d.). Web MD. Retrieved March 2, 2022, from https://www.webmd.com/diet/catnip-tea-health-benefits#1

Catnip uses, benefits & side effects. (n.d.). Drugs. Retrieved February 12, 2022, from https://www.drugs.com/npc/catnip.html#:~:text=Medicinally%2C%20the%20plant%20has%20been

Chamomile: Matricaria recutita. (n.d.). Edible Wild Food. Retrieved February 24, 2022, from https://www.ediblewildfood.com/chamomile.aspx

Chappell, S. (2019, February 21). *A beginner's guide to making herbal salves and lotions*. Healthline. https://www.healthline.com/health/diy-herbal-salves#TOC_TITLE_HDR_1

Cherney, K. (2022, February 3). *Everything you need to know about borage oil*. Healthline. https://www.healthline.com/health/borage-oil#side-effects

Chickweed. (n.d.). In Merriam Webster. Retrieved February 12, 2022, from https://www.merriam-webster.com/dictionary/chickweed

Chicory. (n.d.). In Merriam Webster. Retrieved February 12, 2022, from https://www.merriam-webster.com/dictionary/chicory

Chicory - edible wild plant - how to find, identify, prepare, and other uses for survival. (2012, May 11). Wilderness Arena. https://www.wildernessarena.com/food-water-shelter/food-food-water-shelter/food-procurement/edible-wild-plants/chicory

Chicory: Health benefits, uses, side effects, dosage & interactions. (2021, November 6). Rx List. https://www.rxlist.com/chicory/supplements.htm

Choosing a location for raspberry plants. (n.d.). Stark Bro's. Retrieved March 3, 2022, from https://www.starkbros.com/growing-guide/how-to-grow/berry-plants/raspberry-plants/location

Christiansen, S. (2022a, January 10). *What is mugwort? Herb related to ragweed used in naturopathic and traditional Chinese medicine.* Verywell Health. https://www.verywellhealth.com/mugwort-benefits-side-effects-dosage-and-interactions-4767226

Christiansen, S. (2022b, February 5). *What Is Horsetail?* Very Well Health. https://www.verywellhealth.com/horsetail-4692253#:~:text=Traditionally%20horsetail%20has%20been%20used

Clark, P. (2013, May 21). *Blackberry sexuality. It's complicated.* The Washington Post. https://www.washingtonpost.com/wp-srv/special/metro/urban-jungle/pages/130521.html

Cleansing with cleavers. (2019, April 8). Botanica Health. https://www.botanicahealth.co.uk/cleansing-with-cleavers/

Cleavers. (n.d.). In Collins. Retrieved February 12, 2022, from https://www.collinsdictionary.com/dictionary/english/cleavers

Cleavers. (2015a, May 23). Peace Health. https://www.peacehealth.org/medical-topics/id/hn-2070002#:~:text=by%20Scientific%20Studies)-

Cleavers. (2015b, May 23). Kaiser Permanente. https://wa.kaiserpermanente.org/kbase/topic.jhtml?docId=hn-2070002#:~:text=by%20Scientific%20Studies)-

Climan, A. (2020, December 21). *What is cleavers (galium aparine)?* Very Well Health. https://www.verywellhealth.com/cleavers-health-benefits-5084341#toc-possible-side-effects

Colleen. (2018, February 2). *Wild violet flower infused vinegar.* Grow Forage Cook Ferment. https://www.growforagecookferment.com/wild-violet-flower-infused-vinegar/#:~:text=There%20are%20also%20some%20medicinal

Colleen. (2020a, March 26). *How to Make and Use Dandelion Salve.* Grow Forage Cook Ferment. https://www.growforagecookferment.com/how-to-make-dandelion-salve/

Colleen. (2020b, June 15). *Dandelion foraging: Identification, look-alikes, and uses.* Grow Forage Cook Ferment. https://www.growforagecookferment.com/foraging-for-dandelions/#:~:text=Identifying%20Dandelion

Colleen. (2020c, July 28). *Foraging plantain: Identification and uses.* Grow Forage Cook Ferment. https://www.growforagecookferment.com/plantain-natures-bandaid/#:~:text=Identifying%20Plantain

Comfrey information. (n.d.). Mount Sinai Health System. Retrieved February 12, 2022, from https://www.mountsinai.org/health-library/herb/comfrey#:~:text=Comfrey%20roots%20and%20leaves%20contain

Comfrey: Uses, side effects, and more. (n.d.). Web MD. Retrieved February 12, 2022, from https://www.webmd.com/vitamins/ai/ingredientmono-295/comfrey

Common Agrimony, Agrimonia eupatoria - Flowers. (n.d.). Nature Gate. Retrieved February 7, 2022, from https://luontoportti.com/en/t/1025/common-agrimony

Common agrimony: Pictures, flowers, leaves & identification. (n.d.). Edible Wild Food. Retrieved February 2, 2022, from https://www.ediblewildfood.com/common-agrimony.aspx

Common chickweed. (2015, June 5). Michigan State University Integrated Pest Management; Michigan State University. https://www.canr.msu.edu/resources/common_chickweed

Common mallow (malva neglecta). (n.d.). Illinois Wildflowers. Retrieved February 12, 2022, from http://www.illinoiswildflowers.info/weeds/plants/cm_mallow.htm

Common mullein. (n.d.). Woodland Ways Bushcraft Blog. Retrieved March 2, 2022, from https://www.woodland-ways.co.uk/blog/hedgerow-medicines/common-mullein/#:~:text=Key%20Identification%20Features%3A%20Biennial%20up

Common name comfrey (Common comfrey, healing-herb, knit-back, knit-bone, backwort, bruise-wort, slippery-root, asses' ears). (n.d.). Friends of the Wild Flower Garden. https://www.friendsofthewildflowergarden.org/pages/plants/comfrey.html

Common teasel identification and control. (2022, January 7). King County. https://kingcounty.gov/services/environment/animals-and-plants/noxious-weeds/weed-identification/common-teasel.aspx#:~:text=Cutleaf%20teasel%20has%20irregularly%2Dcut

Common violet. (n.d.). St Olaf College. Retrieved March 4, 2022, from https://wp.stolaf.edu/naturallands/forest/ephemerals/commonviolet/#:~:text=Violets%20are%20flowers%20with%20five

Cramp Bark. (2021, June 11). Rx List. https://www.rxlist.com/cramp_bark/supplements.htm

Cramp bark. (n.d.). Monterey Bay Herb Co. Retrieved February 15, 2022, from https://www.herbco.com/c-253-cramp-bark.aspx

Cramp bark (viburnum opulus l.). (n.d.). Health Embassy. Retrieved February 15, 2022, from https://healthembassy.co.uk/en/bark/39-cramp-bark.html

Cranberry. (2020, May). National Center for Complementary and Integrative Health. https://www.nccih.nih.gov/health/cranberry

Cranberry. (2021). In Encyclopædia Britannica. https://www.britannica.com/plant/cranberry

Cronkleton, E. (2019, March 8). 10 benefits of lemon balm and how to use it. Healthline. https://www.healthline.com/health/lemon-balm-uses

Culturally and economically important nontimber forest products of northern Maine - Sustaining forests. (2010, May 24). United States Department of Agriculture: Forest Service - Northern Research Station. https://www.nrs.fs.fed.us/sustaining_forests/conserve_enhance/special_products/maine_ntfp/plants/raspberry/#:~:text=Habitat%3A%20Raspberries%20are%20often%20found

Cunha, J. P. (Ed.). (2021a, March 9). Valerian. Rx List. https://www.rxlist.com/consumer_valerian/drugs-condition.htm

Cunha, J. P. (2021b, August 24). Cranberry. Rx List. https://www.rxlist.com/consumer_cranberry/drugs-condition.htm#:~:text=Class%3A%20Urology%2C%20Herbals-

Dallmeier, L. (n.d.). How to make macerated oils. Formula Botanica. Retrieved February 24, 2022, from https://formulabotanica.com/how-to-make-macerated-oils/#:~:text=Macerating%20works%20best%20when%20done

Dandelion. (n.d.). Mount Sinai Health System. Retrieved February 16, 2022, from https://www.mountsinai.org/health-library/herb/dandelion#:~:text=The%20leaves%20are%20used%20to

Dandelions: Cheery signs of spring. (n.d.). Christian Science Monitor. Retrieved February 16, 2022, from https://www.csmonitor.com/The-Culture/The-Home-Forum/2008/0410/p19s01-hfes.html

Davidson, K. (2020, August 20). Red clover: Benefits, uses, and side effects. Healthline. https://www.healthline.com/nutrition/red-clover#benefits

Debret, C. (2021, July 20). 10 useful tools for foraging this summer. One Green Planet. https://www.onegreenplanet.org/lifestyle/useful-tools-for-foraging-this-summer/

Dellwo, A. (2020, June 14). What is Goldenrod? Very Well Health. https://www.verywellhealth.com/goldenrod-benefits-4586964

Dessinger, H. (n.d.). Plantain herb benefits, recipes & how to identify. Mommypotamus. Retrieved March 2, 2022, from https://mommypotamus.com/plantain/

Dipsacus fullonum. (n.d.). Plants for a Future. Retrieved March 4, 2022, from https://pfaf.org/user/Plant.aspx?LatinName=Dipsacus+fullonum#:~:text=Medicinal%20Uses&text=Teasel%20is%20little%20used%20in

Dodrill, T. (n.d.-a). *How to identify chicory*. New Life on a Homestead. Retrieved February 12, 2022, from https://www.newlifeonahomestead.com/how-to-identify-chicory/#:~:text=The%20basal%20leaves%20on%20the

Dodrill, T. (n.d.-b). *How to identify goldenrod (plus foraging tips)*. New Life on a Homestead. Retrieved February 24, 2022, from https://www.newlifeonahomestead.com/goldenrod/#:~:text=Goldenrod%20plant%20leaves%20have%20only

Douglas, J. (2021, May 6). *Ethical foraging–Responsibility and reciprocity*. Organic Growers School. https://organicgrowersschool.org/ethical-foraging-responsibility-and-reciprocity/#:~:text=Ethical%20foraging%20is%20an%20ongoing

Duiker, S. W., & Curran, W. C. (2007, October 30). *Management of red clover as a cover crop*. Penn State Extension. https://extension.psu.edu/management-of-red-clover-as-a-cover-crop#:~:text=Red%20clover%20does%20best%20on

Dyer, M. H. (2021, August 12). *Mullein herb plants – Tips on using mullein as herbal treatments*. Gardening Know-How. https://www.gardeningknowhow.com/ornamental/flowers/mullein/using-mullein-as-herbs.htm

Echinacea. (n.d.). In The Gale Encyclopedia of Diets: A Guide to Health and Nutrition. Cengage; Encyclopedia. Retrieved February 22, 2022, from https://www.encyclopedia.com/plants-and-animals/plants/plants/echinacea#:~:text=the%20United%20States.-

Echinacea information. (n.d.). Mount Sinai Health System. Retrieved February 22, 2022, from https://www.mountsinai.org/health-library/herb/echinacea

Echinacea purpurea (Eastern purple coneflower). (n.d.). Minnesota Wildflowers. Retrieved February 22, 2022, from https://www.minnesotawildflowers.info/flower/eastern-purple-coneflower#:~:text=Flowers%20are%20single%20on%20end

Echinacea purpurea - Purple cone flower - Medicinal perennial herbal / Flower - 100 seeds. (n.d.). Seeds for Africa. Retrieved February 22, 2022, from https://www.seedsforafrica.co.za/products/echinacea-purpurea-purple-cone-flower-medicinal-annual-flower-100-seeds#:~:text=It%20is%20native%20to%20eastern

Agrimony. (2019, August 14). Britannica. https://www.britannica.com/plant/agrimony

Elder tree remedies. (2015, May 14). Handmade Apothecary. https://www.handmadeapothecary.co.uk/blog/2015/5/12/elderflowerpower

Elderberry. (2020, September 21). Web MD. https://www.webmd.com/diet/elderberry-health-benefits#:~:text=The%20berries%20and%20flowers%20of

Elderberry cold and cough syrup recipe. (n.d.). Edible Wild Food. Retrieved February 22, 2022, from https://www.ediblewildfood.com/elderberry-cold-cough-syrup.aspx

Elderberry: Sambucus canadensis. (n.d.). Edible Wild Food. Retrieved February 22, 2022, from https://www.ediblewildfood.com/elderberry.aspx#:~:text=Elder%20is%20characterised%20by%20its

Elderflower. (2021, November 6). Rx List. https://www.rxlist.com/elderflower/supplements.htm

Elderflower tincture - Easy homemade recipe. (2021, June 3). Practical Frugality. https://www.practicalfrugality.com/elderflower-tincture-recipe/

Ellen. (2016, December 16). *Wild garlic (aka field garlic, aka allium vineale)*. Backyard Forager. https://backyardforager.com/wild-garlic-field-garlic-allium-vineale/#:~:text=Wild%20garlic%20flowers%20are%20edible

Ellis, N. (2021, April 5). *How to make sunflower oil in your homestead?* Farm & Animals. https://farmandanimals.com/how-to-make-sunflower-oil/

Erdemir, S. M. (2017, September 21). *Parts of a composite flower*. Garden Guides. https://www.gardenguides.com/123630-parts-composite-flower.html

Ripe for the Picking: Blackberry Harvesting Tips and Recipes. (2018, July 17). Espoma Organic. https://www.espoma.com/fruits-vegetables/ripe-for-the-picking-blackberry-harvesting-tips-and-recipes/

Everything mint. (n.d.). Lifestyle Home Garden. Retrieved February 28, 2022, from https://lifestyle.co.za/mint/#:~:text=Mint%20is%20a%20hardy%2C%20highly

Everything you need to know about everbearing mulberry trees. (2020, August 23). This Old House. https://www.thisoldhouse.com/gardening/21336910/everbearing-mulberry-trees

Facts about garlic mustard. (n.d.). Health Benefits Times. https://www.healthbenefitstimes.com/garlic-mustard/

False Solomon seal: Maianthemum racemosum. (n.d.). Edible Wild Food. Retrieved March 3, 2022, from https://www.ediblewildfood.com/false-solomon-seal.aspx#:~:text=Solomon

Feverfew. (2008, May 31). Wildflower Finder. https://wildflowerfinder.org.uk/Flowers/F/Feverfew/Feverfew.htm#:~:text=Distinguishing%20Feature%20%3A%20The%20few%20white

Feverfew (Tanacetum parthenium). (n.d.). Illinois Wildflowers. Retrieved February 23, 2022, from https://www.illinoiswildflowers.info/weeds/plants/feverfew.html#:~:text=Feverfew%20(Tanacetum%20parthenium)&text=Description%3A%20This%20perennial%20herbaceous%20plant

Feverfew growing guide. (n.d.). Grow Veg. Retrieved February 23, 2022, from https://www.growveg.co.za/plants/south-africa/how-to-grow-feverfew/

Fewell, A. K. (2020, September 2). *Medicinal uses of goldenrod & goldenrod tincture.* Amy K. Fewell: The Fewell Homestead. https://thefewellhomestead.com/medicinal-uses-of-goldenrod-goldenrod-tincture/

Fletcher, J. (2019, January 3). *Dandelion: Health benefits, research, and side effects.* Medical News Today. https://www.medicalnewstoday.com/articles/324083

Foraging and using birch: Bark, leaves, & sap. (2020, December 1). Grow Forage Cook Ferment. https://www.growforagecookferment.com/foraging-birch/

Ford, C. (2019, February 15). *Cramp bark.* Ford's Herbal & Doula Services. https://www.fordsherbaldoulaservices.com/fords-herb-diary/cramp-bark

Forest Health Staff. (n.d.). *Common mullein - Verbascum thapsus L.* USDA Forest Service. Retrieved March 2, 2022, from http://www.na.fs.fed.us/fhp/invasive_plants

Foster, J. (n.d.). *The easiest way to harvest echinacea seeds.* Grow It Build It. Retrieved February 22, 2022, from https://growitbuildit.com/harvest-echinacea-seeds-an-illustrated-guide/#:~:text=A%20couple%20of%20weeks%20after

Fragrant trees. (n.d.). Berkshire Natural Resources Council. Retrieved February 11, 2022, from https://www.bnrc.org/fragrant-trees/

Frey, M. (2021a, October 12). *The health benefits of echinacea: Can a tea made from purple cone flowers stave off colds and illnesses?* Very Well Fit. https://www.verywellfit.com/echinacea-tea-benefits-and-side-effects-4163612#toc-dosage-and-preparations

Frey, M. (2021b, October 18). *Comfrey tea benefits and side effects is comfrey root safe or healthy?* Very Well Fit. https://www.verywellfit.com/comfrey-tea-benefits-and-side-effects-4163901

Frey, M. (2021c, October 19). *The health benefits of linden: The flowers of this herb are said to have sedative powers.* Very Well Fit. https://www.verywellfit.com/linden-tea-benefits-and-side-effects-4163720

Garlic mustard. (n.d.). Ontario's Invading Species Awareness Program. Retrieved February 24, 2022, from http://www.invadingspecies.com/invaders/plants/garlic-mustard/#:~:text=How%20to%20Identify%20Garlic%20Mustard

Garlic Mustard – A foraging guide to its food, medicine and other uses. (n.d.). Eat Weeds. Retrieved February 24, 2022, from https://www.eatweeds.co.uk/garlic-mustard-alliaria-petiolata#:~:text=Garlic%20mustard%20has%20been%20used,feet%20to%20relieve%20the%20cramp.

Garlic mustard: A very nutritious invasive plant. (2019, January 27). Freak of Natural. https://freakofnatural.com/garlic-mustard/#:~:text=In%20traditional%20herbalism%20garlic%20mustard

German chamomile Information. (n.d.). Mount Sinai Health System. Retrieved February 24, 2022, from https://www.mountsinai.org/health-library/herb/german-chamomile#:~:text=Animal%20studies%20have%20shown%20that

Gerow. (2019, October 15). *Stop and smell the blackberries (then, kill them): A mountain biker's guide to nature.* Singletracks Mountain Bike News. https://www.singletracks.com/mtb-trails/stop-and-smell-the-blackberries-a-mountain-bikers-guide-to-nature/

Ghoshal, M. (2020, March 13). *Mulling over mullein leaf.* Healthline. https://www.healthline.com/health/mullein-leaf#mullein-oil

Girvin, T. (2010, August 20). *The scent of birch tar.* Girvin. https://www.girvin.com/the-scent-of-birch-tar/

Goldenrod. (2021, June 11). Rx List. https://www.rxlist.com/goldenrod/supplements.htm

Goldenrod: Medicinal uses & benefits. (n.d.). Chestnut School of Herbal Medicine. Retrieved February 24, 2022, from https://chestnutherbs.com/medicinal-uses-and-benefits-of-goldenrod/

Gotter, A. (2018, September 18). *Catnip tea: Health benefits and uses.* Healthline. https://www.healthline.com/health/catnip-tea#side-effects-and-risks

Gotter, A. (2021, January 12). *What is burdock root?* Healthline. https://www.healthline.com/health/burdock-root

Grant, A. (2021, August 8). *Borage harvesting: How and when to harvest borage plants.* Gardening Know-How. https://www.gardeningknowhow.com/edible/herbs/borage/harvesting-borage-plants.htm

Grant, B. L. (2020, December 20). *Leaf identification–Learn about different leaf types in plants.* Gardening Know-How. https://www.gardeningknowhow.com/garden-how-to/info/different-leaf-types-in-plants.htm

Griffin, R. M. (2021, January 18). *Black cherry and your health.* Web MD. https://www.webmd.com/diet/supplement-guide-black-cherry#:~:text=Black%20cherry%20bark%20also%20seems

Growing & Foraging for Mullein (Plus Harvesting & Preserving tips!). (2021, June 10). Unruly Gardening. https://unrulygardening.com/growing-foraging-mullein/#:~:text=Summer%2C%20or%20whenever%20the%20plant

Growing Organic Mugwort from Seed to Harvest. (n.d.). Mary's Heirloom Seeds. Retrieved February 28, 2022, from https://www.marysheirloomseeds.com/blogs/news/78072001-growing-organic-mugwort-from-seed-to-harvest#:~:text=Harvest%20mugwort%20shortly%20before%20it

Haddock, B. (2012, May 11). *Cranberry - edible wild plant - how to find, identify, prepare, and other uses for survival.* Wilderness Arena. https://www.wildernessarena.com/food-water-shelter/food-food-water-shelter/food-procurement/edible-wild-plants/cranberry

Haines, A. (n.d.). *Why foraging?* Arthur Haines. http://www.arthurhaines.com/why-foraging#:~:text=It%20helps%20people%20become%20more

Hall, J. (2021, July 9). *How to find and prepare nutritious, edible mallows.* Den Garden. https://dengarden.com/gardening/malva#:~:text=Identifying%20Mallows

Hanrahan, C., & Frey, R. (2018). *Mugwort.* In Gale Encyclopedia of Alternative Medicine. Cengage; Encyclopedia. https://www.encyclopedia.com/medicine/drugs/pharmacology/mugwort#:~:text=Mugwort%20is%20a%20tall%20and

Harrington, J. (n.d.). *How to harvest echinacea for tea.* SF Gate. Retrieved February 22, 2022, from https://homeguides.sfgate.com/harvest-echinacea-tea-73456.html

Harris, J. (n.d.). *My homemade echinacea tincture*. Jillian Harris. Retrieved February 22, 2022, from https://jillianharris.com/

Harvesting birch bark. (n.d.). The Folk School Fairbanks. Retrieved February 11, 2022, from https://folk.school/classes/tutorials/harvesting-birch-bark/

Hatter, K. (2017, July 21). *How to identify camomile.* Garden Guides. https://www.gardenguides.com/13426932-how-to-identify-camomile.html

Health benefits of mullein tea. (n.d.). Web MD. Retrieved March 2, 2022, from https://www.webmd.com/diet/health-benefits-mullein-tea#1

Health benefits of smooth Solomon's seal. (2018, November 5). Health Benefits Times. https://www.healthbenefitstimes.com/smooth-solomons-seal/

Health benefits of valerian root. (n.d.). Web MD. Retrieved March 4, 2022, from https://www.webmd.com/diet/health-benefits-valerian-root#3

Heath, S. (2021, December 9). *How to grow a mullein plant.* The Spruce. https://www.thespruce.com/mullein-plant-growing-guide-5203326

Hegde, R. (2020, August 12). *How to make willow bark tea for pain relief.* Organic Facts. https://www.organicfacts.net/willow-bark-tea.html

Herb spotlight - Cramp bark. (n.d.). Sun God Medicinals. Retrieved February 15, 2022, from https://sungodmedicinals.com/pages/herb-spotlight-cramp-bark

Herb: Japanese Honeysuckle. (n.d.). Natural Medicinal Herbs. Retrieved February 24, 2022, from http://www.naturalmedicinalherbs.net/herbs/l/lonicera-japonica=japanese-honeysuckle.php#:~:text=Edible%20parts%20of%20Japanese%20Honeysuckle%3A&text=The%20parboiled%20leaves%20are%20used

Herbal, O. W. (2014, November 4). *Bark harvest & ethical wildcrafting.* Old Ways Herbal: Juliette Abigail Carr. https://oldwaysherbal.com/2014/11/04/ethical-wildcrafting/

Hodgson, D. (n.d.). *Cleavers ointment.* Woodland Ways. Retrieved February 12, 2022, from https://www.woodland-ways.co.uk/blog/hedgerow-medicines/cleavers-ointment/

Homemade blackberry tincture. (2021, August 31). Alco Reviews. https://alcoreviews.com/homemade-blackberry-tincture/

Honeysuckle. (2021, November 6). Rx List. https://www.rxlist.com/honeysuckle/supplements.htm

Horsetail. (2014, June 5). Britannica. https://www.britannica.com/plant/horsetail

Horsetail. (2021, June 11). Rx List. https://www.rxlist.com/horsetail/supplements.htm

How cranberries grow: Pollination. (n.d.). Massachusetts Cranberries. Retrieved February 16, 2022, from https://www.cranberries.org/how-cranberries-grow/pollination

How much cherry juice should you drink a day? Traverse Bay Farms. www.traversebayfarms.com/pages/cherries-recommended-dosage-of-cherry-juice. Accessed 16 Mar. 2022.

How to do a coffee enema. (2020, November 9). Pure Joy Planet. https://www.purejoyplanet.com/blog/how-to-do-a-coffee-enema

How to grow & use valerian. (2020, June 24). It's My Sustainable Life. https://www.itsmysustainablelife.com/how-to-grow-use-valerian/#:~:text=Ideally%2C%20valerian%20root%20should%20not

How to grow big, tall sunflowers. (2019, June 1). Velcro Brand Blog. https://www.velcro.com/news-and-blog/2019/06/how-to-grow-big-tall-sunflowers/#:~:text=Sunflowers%20prefer%20a%20somewhat%20alkaline,before%20you%20do%20any%20planting!

How to harvest wild cherry bark and stop coughing so you can sleep. (n.d.). Joybilee Farm. Retrieved February 11, 2022, from https://joybileefarm.com/wild-cherry-bark-stop-coughing/

How to identify chickweed - Foraging for wild edible greens. (2017, December 15). Good Life Revival. https://thegoodliferevival.com/blog/chickweed#:~:text=Chickweed%20is%20easy%20to%20identify,each%20other%20along%20the%20stem.

How to identify elderflower. (2012, June 8). Stay & Roam. https://stayandroam.blog/how-to-identify-elderflower/#:~:text=the%20correct%20plant.-

How to make birch bark flour and bake with it. (2020, December 18). Tree Time. https://blog.treetime.ca/blog/how-to-make-and-bake-with-bark-flour/

How to make Dandelion Tea the perfect way each time!! (n.d.). Tea Swan. Retrieved February 16, 2022, from https://teaswan.com/blogs/news/how-to-make-dandelion-tea

How to make echinacea (purple coneflower) oil & salve. (n.d.). The Nerdy Farm Wife. Retrieved February 22, 2022, from https://thenerdyfarmwife.com/echinacea-purple-coneflower-oil-salve/

How to Make Homemade Echinacea Tea. (2022, October 2). Sencha Tea Bar. https://senchateabar.com/blogs/blog/how-to-make-echinacea-tea#:~:text=Echinacea%20tea%20can%20be%20made

Howland, G. (2018 6). *Red raspberry leaf tea recipes you'll actually want to drink.* Mama Natural. https://www.mamanatural.com/red-raspberry-leaf-tea-recipes/

Iannotti, M. (2021a, July 9). *How to grow borage.* The Spruce. https://www.thespruce.com/how-to-grow-borage-1402625#toc-harvesting-borage

Iannotti, M. (2021b, December 20). *How to grow and care for chamomile.* The Spruce. https://www.thespruce.com/how-to-grow-chamomile-1402627

Identify a mulberry - Find out what to look out for to hunt down a mulberry. (n.d.). Morus Londinium. Retrieved March 1, 2022, from https://www.moruslondinium.org/map/identify

Identifying burdock. (2014, October 20). The Druid's Garden. https://druidgarden.wordpress.com/tag/identifying-burdock/

International Culinary Center. (2018, November 28). *How to Safely Forage.* International Culinary Education. https://www.ice.edu/blog/how-to-safely-forage

J, C. (2018, December 21). *A refreshing, aromatic herbal aperitif.* The Inspired Home. https://theinspiredhome.com/articles/a-refreshing-aromatic-herbal-aperitif

Jaana. (n.d.). *Larch.* Herbal Picnic. Retrieved February 28, 2022, from https://herbalpicnic.blogspot.com/2015/04/larch.html

James. (2020a, April 29). *Burdock (arctium iappa) identification.* Totally Wild UK. https://totallywilduk.co.uk/2020/04/29/identify-burdock/#:~:text=Burdock%20will%20grow%20in%20pretty

James. (2020b, April 29). *Cleavers (gallium aparine) identification.* Totally Wild UK. https://totallywilduk.co.uk/2020/04/29/identify-cleavers/

James. (2020c, April 29). *Comfrey (symphytum officinale) identification.* Totally Wild UK. https://totallywilduk.co.uk/2020/04/29/identify-comfrey/

James. (2020d, April 29). *Yarrow (achillea millefolium) identification.* Totally Wild UK. https://totallywilduk.co.uk/2020/04/29/identify-yarrow/

James, T. (2016, January 19). *How to forage for wild catnip.* Adventure Cats. https://www.adventurecats.org/pawsome-reads/foraging-adventure-how-to-spot-wild-catnip/#:~:text=Catnip%20is%20grayish%2Dgreen%20and

Japanese honeysuckle (lonicera japonica). (n.d.). Invasive. Retrieved February 28, 2022, from https://www.invasive.org/alien/pubs/midatlantic/loja.htm#:~:text=It%20is%20a%20fast%2Dgrowing

Jeanroy, A. (2019, June 26). *How to make herbal infusions.* The Spruce Eats. https://www.thespruceeats.com/how-to-make-an-herbal-infusion-1762142

Joanna. (2014, July 9). *The benefits of raspberry leaf tincture & my raspberry leaf tincture recipe.* Joanna Steven. https://www.joannasteven.com/the-benefits-of-raspberry-leaf-tincture-my-raspberry-leaf-tincture-recipe/

Johnson, K. (2000, August). *Rubus ursinus.* Pdx.

http://web.pdx.edu/~maserj/ESR410/rubisursinus.html

Jones, L. (2017, October 11). *Homegrown blackberry leaf tea*. Windellama Organics. https://www.windellamaorganics.com/blog/2017/10/10/homegrown-blackberry-leaf-tea

Keeler, K. (n.d.). *Plant story: Common mullein and its folklore*. A Wandering Botanist. Retrieved March 2, 2022, from http://khkeeler.blogspot.com/2013/07/plant-story-common-mullein-and-its.html#:~:text=Historically%20mullein%20was%20considered%20a,to%20be%20their%20preferred%20torch.&text=Common%20mullein%20has%20yellow%20flowers,Mercury%20gave%20Odysseus%20common%20mullein.

Kendle. (2018, September 14). *How to make herbal infusions & decoctions for wellness support*. Mountain Rose Herbs. https://blog.mountainroseherbs.com/herbal-infusions-and-decoctions

Kirk, S., Belt, S., & Berg, N. A. (2011). *Plant fact sheet verbena hastata (L.) Plant symbol = VEHA2*. Natural Resources Conservation Service. National Plant Materials Center. https://www.nrcs.usda.gov/Internet/FSE_PLANTMATERIALS/publications/mdpmcfs10335.pdf

Krohn, E. (2016). Alder. *Wild Foods and Medicines*. http://wildfoodsandmedicines.com/alder/

Kubala, J. (2019, November 29). *Mulberry leaf: Uses, benefits, and precautions*. Healthline. https://www.healthline.com/nutrition/mulberry-leaf#benefits

Lang, A. (2020, June 8). *What is vervain? All you need to know*. Healthline. https://www.healthline.com/nutrition/vervain-verbena

Lapcevic, K. (2021, July 21). *Lemon balm tincture*. Homespun Seasonal Living. https://homespunseasonalliving.com/lemon-balm-tincture/

Larch. (n.d.-a). *Muster Kiste*. Retrieved February 24, 2022, from http://www.musterkiste.com/en/holz/pro/1016_Larch.html#:~:text=The%20larch%20is%20the%20heaviest

Larch. (n.d.-b). *Gaia Herbs*. Retrieved February 28, 2022, from https://www.gaiaherbs.com/blogs/herbs/larch

Larch. (n.d.-c). *Medicinal Herb Info*. Retrieved February 28, 2022, from http://medicinalherbinfo.org/000Herbs2016/1herbs/larch/

Larch. (n.d.-d). *Alaska's Wilderness Medicines*. Retrieved February 28, 2022, from http://www.ankn.uaf.edu/curriculum/Books/Viereck/vierecklarch.html

Larch. (n.d.-e). *Dr. Hauschka*. Retrieved February 28, 2022, from https://www.drhauschka.co.uk/medicinal-plant-glossary/larch/

Larch arabinogalactan: Uses, side effects, and more. (2019). Web MD. https://www.webmd.com/vitamins/ai/ingredientmono-974/larch-arabinogalactan

Lemm, E. (2021, July 23). *Wild garlic adds subtle flavor*. The Spruce Eats. https://www.thespruceeats.com/what-is-wild-garlic-435437

Lemon balm. (n.d.). Mount Sinai Health System. Retrieved February 28, 2022, from https://www.mountsinai.org/health-library/herb/lemon-balm#:~:text=Lemon%20balm%20(Melissa%20officinalis)%2C

Lemon balm (melissa officinalis). (n.d.). Illinois Wildflowers. Retrieved February 28, 2022, from https://www.illinoiswildflowers.info/weeds/plants/lemon_balm.html

Lemon balm – Identification, edibility, distribution, ecology. (2019, July 9). Galloway Wild Foods. https://gallowaywildfoods.com/lemon-balm-identification-edibility-distribution-ecology/#:~:text=Identification%20%E2%80%93%204%2F5%20%E2%80%93%20Lemon

Lemon balm cream. (2021, April 7). Herba Zest. https://www.herbazest.com/herbs/lemon-balm/lemon-balm-cream

Lemon balm production (Second). (2012). Department of Agriculture, Forestry and Fisheries | Directorate: Pant production. chrome-extension://efaidnbmnnnibpcajpcglclefindmkaj/viewer.html?pdfurl=https%3A%2F%2Fwww.dalrrd.gov.za%2FPortals%2F0%2FBrochures%2520and%2520Production%2520guidelines%2FProduction%2520Guidelines%2520Lemon%2520Balm.pdf&clen=1437819&chunk=true

Lime tree in culture. (n.d.). Wikipedia. Retrieved February 28, 2022, from https://en.wikipedia.org/wiki/Lime_tree_in_culture#:~:text=Germanic%20mythology

Linden. (n.d.). Drugs. Retrieved February 28, 2022, from https://www.drugs.com/npc/linden.html#:~:text=Linden%20has%20been%20used%20to

Linden. (2021, June 11). Rx List. https://www.rxlist.com/linden/supplements.htm

Linden trees: Types, leaves, flowers, bark – Identification (with pictures). (n.d.). Leafy Place. Retrieved February 28, 2022, from https://leafyplace.com/linden-trees/#:~:text=size%20and%20shape.-

Link, R. (2020, June 10). *What is plantain weed, and how do you use it?* Healthline. https://www.healthline.com/nutrition/plantain-weed#side-effects

Lisa, A. (2022, January 18). *How to extract oil from plants (plus the numerous benefits and uses)*. The Practical Planter. https://thepracticalplanter.com/how-to-extract-oil-from-plants/

Lofgren, K. (2020, May 27). *What's the difference between English and German chamomile?* Gardener's Path. https://gardenerspath.com/plants/flowers/english-german-chamomile/#German-Chamomile

Longacre, C. (2020, September 12). *How to harvest sunflower seeds*. Almanac. https://www.almanac.com/harvesting-sunflower-seeds

Making birch bark oil. (2018, January 24). Plant Pioneers. https://www.plantpioneers.org/blog/2018/1/24/making-birch-bark-oil

Making catnip (nepeta cataria) tincture. (2014, September 2). Spiraea. https://spiraeaherbs.ca/making-catnip-nepeta-cataria-tincture/

Mallow. (2015, May 28). Peace Health. https://www.peacehealth.org/medical-topics/id/hn-3263004#hn-3263004-how-it-works

Mallow. (n.d.). E Medicine Health. Retrieved February 13, 2022, from https://www.emedicinehealth.com/mallow/vitamins-supplements.htm#UsesAndEffectiveness

Mallow - common (malva sylvestris) organically grown flower seeds. (n.d.). Floral Encounters. Retrieved February 13, 2022, from https://www.floralencounters.com/Seeds/seed_detail.jsp?grow=Mallow+-+Common&productid=1102

Mallow is medicine. (2018, September 29). Indigenous Goddess Gang. https://www.indigenousgoddessgang.com/self-care-medicine/2018/9/27/white-flowered-medicine

Mallow: Overview, uses, side effects, and more. (n.d.). Web MD. Retrieved February 12, 2022, from https://www.webmd.com/vitamins/ai/ingredientmono-192/mallow

Matricaria chamomilla (wild chamomile). (n.d.). Go Botany: Native Plant Trust. Retrieved February 24, 2022, from https://gobotany.nativeplanttrust.org/species/matricaria/chamomilla/

Matthews, C. (Ed.). (2022, January 12). *Wild garlic guide: Where to find, how to cook it and recipe ideas*. Countryfile. https://www.countryfile.com/how-to/food-recipes/wild-garlic-guide-where-to-find-how-to-cook-it-and-recipe-ideas/#:~:text=What%20are%20the%20health%20benefits,as%20heart%20attack%20or%20stroke.

May, D. (2011, September 6). *Nature notes: common mallow*. The Times. https://www.thetimes.co.uk/article/nature-notes-common-mallow-lmrrwlmh76x

McCulloch, M. (2018, November 22). *Are sunflower seeds good for you? Nutrition, benefits and more*. Healthline. https://www.healthline.com/nutrition/sunflower-seeds#eating-tips

McCulloch, M. (2019, April 4). *Goldenrod: Benefits, dosage, and precautions.* Healthline. https://www.healthline.com/nutrition/goldenrod#inflammation

McKenzie, R. (2019). *Solomon's seal.* Eclectic School of Herbal Medicine. https://www.eclecticschoolofherbalmedicine.com/solomons-seal/

McMinn, S. (n.d.). *How to steep sassafras roots.* Chickens in the Road. Retrieved March 3, 2022, from https://chickensintheroad.com/cooking/how-to-steep-sassafras-roots/#:~:text=The%20best%20time%20to%20dig

Medicinal uses of beech trees. (n.d.). What Tree Where. Retrieved February 11, 2022, from https://whattreewhere.com/tag/medicinal-uses-of-beech-trees/

Melissa officinalis L. (n.d.). A Vogel. Retrieved February 28, 2022, from https://www.avogel.com/plant-encyclopaedia/melissa_officinalis.php#:~:text=Lemon%20Balm%20is%20a%2050cm

Mentha spicata - Spearmint. (n.d.). Northwest Oregon Wetland Plants Project. Retrieved February 28, 2022, from http://web.pdx.edu/~maserj/ESR410/mentha.html#:~:text=Habitat

Meredith, L. (2021, September 14). *Violet flower syrup.* The Spruce Eats. https://www.thespruceeats.com/violet-flower-syrup-recipe-1327872

Merva, V. (2020, March 20). *How to make Violet oil and its uses.* Simply beyond Herbs. https://simplybeyondherbs.com/violet-oil-recipe/

Minifie, K. (2014, June 5). *What the heck is chickweed and why is it on my plate?* Epicurious. https://www.epicurious.com/archive/blogs/editor/2014/05/what-the-heck-is-chickweed-and-why-is-it-on-my-plate.html

Mint. (2021, July 5). Encyclopedia Britannica. https://www.britannica.com/plant/Mentha

Moline, P. (2015, June 26). *How to make your own herb tincture or peppermint oil.* Los Angeles Times. https://www.latimes.com/home/la-he-healing-garden-recipes-20150627-story.html

Monoecious. (n.d.). In Merriam Webster. Retrieved February 8, 2022, from https://www.merriam-webster.com/dictionary/monoecious

Mugwort. (n.d.). Sawmill Herb Farm. Retrieved February 28, 2022, from http://www.sawmillherbfarm.com/herb%20profile/mugwort/

Mugwort. (2021, June 11). Rx List. https://www.rxlist.com/mugwort/supplements.htm#SpecialPrecautionsWarnings

Mulberry tree facts that are absolutely compelling to read. (n.d.). Gardenerdy. Retrieved March 1, 2022, from https://gardenerdy.com/mulberry-tree-facts/

Nash, K. (2021, June 5). *Where do pine trees grow? (Best habitat for natural growth).* Tree Vitalize. https://www.treevitalize.net/where-do-pine-trees-grow/#:~:text=agriculture%2C%20or%20fire.-

Nielsen, L. (2021, January 5). *How to harvest mint and store it for later.* Epic Gardening. https://www.epicgardening.com/how-to-harvest-mint/#:~:text=When%20Should%20I%20Harvest%20Mint%20Leaves%3F

Nix, S. (2021a, May 7). *Identify the larch.* Treehugger. https://www.treehugger.com/identify-the-larch-1341861#:~:text=How%20to%20Identify%20Larches&text=Most%20common%20larches%20in%20North

Nix, S. (2021b, June 7). *How to identify a tree using leaf shape, margin, and venation.* Treehugger. https://www.treehugger.com/id-trees-using-leaf-shape-venation-1343511

Types of Oak trees with their bark and leaves – Identification guide (pictures). (n.d.). Leafy Place. Retrieved March 2, 2022, from https://leafyplace.com/oak-tree-types-bark-leaves/#:~:text=The%20bark%20of%20young%20oak

Oak. (2020, June 18). Herba Zest. https://www.herbazest.com/herbs/oak

Oak - A foraging guide to its food, medicine and other uses. (n.d.). Eat Weeds. Retrieved March 2,

2022, from https://www.eatweeds.co.uk/oak-quercus-robur#:~:text=sugars%20and%20tannins.-

Oak bark. (2021, June 11). Rx List. https://www.rxlist.com/oak_bark/supplements.htm#SpecialPrecautionsWarnings

Oak flowers. (n.d.). Backyard Nature. Retrieved March 2, 2022, from https://www.backyardnature.net/fl_bloak.htm

Oak mythology and folklore. (n.d.). Trees for Life. Retrieved March 2, 2022, from https://treesforlife.org.uk/into-the-forest/trees-plants-animals/trees/oak/oak-mythology-and-folklore/#:~:text=To%20the%20Greeks%2C%20Romans%2C%20Celts

Oak Tree. (n.d.). Tree Works: Qualified Tree Surgery. Retrieved March 2, 2022, from http://treeworksguernsey.co.uk/tree-identification/oak/

Oak tree facts. (n.d.). Soft Schools. Retrieved March 2, 2022, from https://www.softschools.com/facts/plants/oak_tree_facts/505/

Orr, E. (n.d.). *Stinging nettle: Where to find & how to identify.* Wild Edible. Retrieved March 3, 2022, from https://www.wildedible.com/wild-food-guide/stinging-nettle#:~:text=Nettles%20grow%202%20to%205

Parallel venation. (2021, June 17). Maximum Yield. https://www.maximumyield.com/definition/1733/parallel-venation

Parisian, K. (2020, December 17). *Infused oils benefits and warnings.* Parisian's Pure Indulgence. https://parisianspure.com/blogs/news/infused-oils-benefits-and-warnings

Pearson, K. (2017, December 13). *8 health benefits of mint.* Healthline. https://www.healthline.com/nutrition/mint-benefits#TOC_TITLE_HDR_10

Perforate St John's-wort. (n.d.). The Wildlife Trusts. Retrieved March 3, 2022, from https://www.wildlifetrusts.org/wildlife-explorer/wildflowers/perforate-st-johns-wort#:~:text=Perforate%20st%20John

Phillips, Q. (2019, September 4). *How to make valerian tea.* Everyday Health. https://www.everydayhealth.com/diet-nutrition/make-valerian-tea-how-prepare-brew-steep-this-herbal-tea/

Pietrangelo, A. (2018, June 7). *St. John's wort: The benefits and the dangers.* Healthline. https://www.healthline.com/health-news/is-st-johns-wort-safe-080615

Pillsbury, C. (2017, August 23). *Forage through borage seed oil.* Watson. https://blog.watson-inc.com/nutri-knowledge/forage-through-borage-seed-oil

Pine. (2021, June 11). Rx List. https://www.rxlist.com/pine/supplements.htm#UsesAndEffectiveness

Plantain. (2015, May 24). Kaiser Permanente. https://wa.kaiserpermanente.org/kbase/topic.jhtml?docId=hn-2148003

Poulson, B., Horowitz, D., & Trevino, H. M. (Eds.). (n.d.). *Feverfew.* University of Rochester Medical Center. Retrieved February 23, 2022, from https://www.urmc.rochester.edu/encyclopedia/content.aspx?contenttypeid=19&contentid=Feverfew#:~:text=Feverfew%20may%20reduce%20painful%20inflammation

Product information teaseltea. (n.d.). Teasel Shop. Retrieved March 4, 2022, from https://www.teaselshop.com/c-2283855/dosage-and-use/

Pruisis, E. (2021, August 9). *Discover varieties of alder trees and shrubs.* The Spruce. https://www.thespruce.com/alder-trees-and-shrubs-3269701

Raman, R. (2018, October 25). *Echinacea: Benefits, uses, side effects and dosage.* Healthline. https://www.healthline.com/nutrition/echinacea#:~:text=The%20bottom%20line-

Red Clover. (n.d.). Brandeis University. Retrieved March 3, 2022, from http://www.bio.brandeis.edu/fieldbio/EFG_DEB_SHU/species%20pages/Red%20Clover/Red%20Clover.html#:~:text=Identifying%20Characteristics%3A%20The%20white%20V

Red clover. (n.d.-a). Bellarmine University. Retrieved March 3, 2022, from https://www.bellarmine.edu/faculty/drobinson/RedClover.asp

Red clover. (n.d.-b). Plant Life. Retrieved March 3, 2022, from https://www.plantlife.org.uk/uk/discover-wild-plants-nature/plant-fungi-species/red-clover#:~:text=Flowers%20May%20to%20September.

Red clover (trifolium pratense). (n.d.). Illinois Wildflowers. Retrieved March 3, 2022, from http://www.illinoiswildflowers.info/weeds/plants/red_clover.htm#:~:text=Habitats%20include%20fields%2C%20pastures%2C%20weedy

Red raspberry: Uses, side effects, & more. (n.d.). Web MD. Retrieved March 3, 2022, from https://www.webmd.com/vitamins/ai/ingredientmono-309/red-raspberry

Reeves, K. (2010). *Exotic species: St. Johnswort.* U.S. National Park Service. https://www.nps.gov/articles/st-johnswort.htm#:~:text=Flowers%20and%20Fruits&text=along%20the%20margins.-

Rose, S. (n.d.). *Herbal guide to feverfew.* Garden Therapy. Retrieved February 23, 2022, from https://gardentherapy.ca/herbal-guide-to-feverfew/

Rowland, B. (n.d.). *Cramp Bark.* Encyclopedia; Gale Encyclopedia of Alternative Medicine. Retrieved February 15, 2022, from https://www.encyclopedia.com/medicine/encyclopedias-almanacs-transcripts-and-maps/cramp-bark

Sacred tree profile: Cherry (prunus serotina)'s magic, mythology, medicine and meaning. (n.d.). Retrieved February 12, 2022, from https://druidgarden.wordpress.com/2019/06/23/sacred-tree-profile-cherry-prunus-serotinas-magic-mythology-medicine-and-meaning/

Sacred tree profile: Sassafras' medicine, magic, mythology and meaning. (n.d.). The Druid's Garden. Retrieved March 3, 2022, from https://druidgarden.wordpress.com/2017/08/20/sacred-tree-profile-sassafras-medicine-magic-mythology-and-meaning/

Sarsaparilla. (n.d.). Rx List. Retrieved March 4, 2022, from https://www.rxlist.com/sarsaparilla/supplements.htm

Sassafras. (n.d.). University of Kentucky. Retrieved March 3, 2022, from https://www.uky.edu/hort/Sassafras#:~:text=Introduction%3A%20Sassafras%20has%20exceptional%20features

Sassafras. (2021, June 11). Rx List. https://www.rxlist.com/sassafras/supplements.htm

Sassafras tree: Leaves, flowers, bark (pictures) - Identification guide. (n.d.). Leafy Place. Retrieved March 3, 2022, from https://leafyplace.com/sassafras-tree/#:~:text=Sassafras%20tree%20identification%20is%20by

Schonbeck, J., & Frey, R. (n.d.). Oak. In Gale Encyclopedia of Alternative Medicine. Encyclopedia. Retrieved March 2, 2022, from https://www.encyclopedia.com/plants-and-animals/plants/plants/oak#:~:text=oak%20%2F%20%C5%8Dk%2F%20%E2%80%A2%20n.

Scots pine mythology and folklore. (n.d.). Trees for Life. Retrieved March 2, 2022, from https://treesforlife.org.uk/into-the-forest/trees-plants-animals/trees/scots-pine/scots-pine-mythology-and-folklore/#:~:text=Pine%20was%20also%20a%20fertility

Scott, C. (n.d.). *Medicinal plant: Japanese honeysuckle.* George Mason University. Retrieved February 24, 2022, from http://mason.gmu.edu/~cscottm/plants.html

Sedgwick, I. (2019, February 16). *Violets are blue: The folklore of February's birth flower.* Icy Sedgwick. https://www.icysedgwick.com/violets-folklore/

Seed information: Common name: valerian | Scientific name: Valeriana officinalis. (n.d.). Herb Garden. Retrieved March 4, 2022, from https://www.herbgarden.co.za/mountainherb/seedinfo.php?id=74#:~:text=Seed%20Information&text=Valerian%20is%20native%20to%20Britain

Seladi-Schulman, J. (2020, June 3). *About wintergreen essential oil*. Healthline. https://www.healthline.com/health/wintergreen-oil#uses

Shepherd's purse. (2021, June 11). Rx List. https://www.rxlist.com/shepherds_purse/supplements.htm

Shepherd's purse – and the value of stories. (2020, June 25). Diego Bonetto. https://www.diegobonetto.com/blog/shepherd-purse-and-the-value-of-stories#:~:text=It%20is%20also%20a%20very

Shepherd's purse tincture. (2017, March 13). Women's Heritage. https://www.womensheritage.com/blog/2017/2/27/shepards-purse-tincture

Shepherds purse: Capsella bursa pastoris. (n.d.). Edible Wild Food. Retrieved March 3, 2022, from https://www.ediblewildfood.com/shepherds-purse.aspx#:~:text=Shepherd

Shore, T. (2018, December 14). *How to identify red raspberry bushes & leaves*. Home Guides. https://homeguides.sfgate.com/identify-red-raspberry-bushes-leaves-56436.html

Silver birch - A foraging guide to its food, medicine and other uses. (n.d.). Eat Weeds. Retrieved February 14, 2022, from https://www.eatweeds.co.uk/birch-betula-spp#Harvest_Time

Simone. (2015, May 19). *How to make blackberry leaf tincture*. Solar Ripe. http://solarripe.eu/2015/05/how-to-make-blackberry-leaf-tincture-may-2015/

Smith, E. (n.d.). *Plant profile: Violet*. Integrative Family Medicine of Asheville. Retrieved March 4, 2022, from https://www.integrativeasheville.org/plant-profile-violet/#:~:text=Violet%20is%20moist%20and%20cooling

Snyder, C. (2021, May 14). *What is an herbal tonic? Benefits, weight loss, and efficacy*. Healthline. https://www.healthline.com/nutrition/herbal-tonic

Solomon's seal. (2019, November 18). The Witchipedia. https://witchipedia.com/book-of-shadows/herblore/solomons-seal/

Solomon's seal. (2021, June 11). Rx List. https://www.rxlist.com/solomons_seal/supplements.htm

Spengler, T. (2018, August 23). *How to identify mint plants*. Garden Guides. https://www.gardenguides.com/78357-history-mint-plant.html

Spengler, T. (2020, February 11). *Scale leaf evergreen varieties: What is a scale leaf evergreen tree*. Gardening Know-How. https://www.gardeningknowhow.com/ornamental/trees/tgen/scale-leaf-evergreen-varieties.htm

St. John's Wort. (2020, October). National Center for Complementary and Integrative Health. https://www.nccih.nih.gov/health/st-johns-wort#:~:text=Currently%2C%20St.

Staughton, J. (2020a, July 13). *5 surprising benefits of agrimony tea*. Organic Facts. https://www.organicfacts.net/agrimony-tea.html

Staughton, J. (2020b, July 28). *10 surprising benefits of sassafras*. Organic Facts. https://www.organicfacts.net/health-benefits/other/sassafras.html

Staughton, J. (2020c, August 25). *6 incredible benefits of St John's wort tea*. Organic Facts. https://www.organicfacts.net/st-johns-wort-tea.html

Stein, J., Binion, D., & Acciavatti, R. (2001). *Field guide to native oak species of Eastern North America (FHTET-03-01)*. USDA Forest Service, Forest Health Technology Enterprise Team. chrome-extension://efaidnbmnnnibpcajpcglclefindmkaj/viewer.html?pdfurl=https%3A%2F%2Fwww.fs.fed.us%2Fforesthealth%2Ftechnology%2Fpdfs%2Ffieldguide.pdf&clen=10803156&chunk=true

Stewart, S. (n.d.). *Mullein tincture*. Just a Pinch Recipes. Retrieved March 2, 2022, from https://www.justapinch.com/recipes/non-edible/non-edible-other-non-edible/mullein-tincture.html

Stinging nettle. (n.d.). Mount Sinai Health System. Retrieved March 3, 2022, from https://www.mountsinai.org/health-library/herb/stinging-nettle#:~:text=Stinging%20nettle%20has%20been%20used

Stobart, A. (2019, April 22). *Making herbal poultices and compresses.* Medicinal Forest Garden Trust. https://medicinalforestgardentrust.org/making-herbal-poultices-and-compresses/#:~:text=Herb%20poultices&text=You%20will%20need%20to%20crush

Streit, L. (2019, November 14). *5 emerging benefits and uses of chicory root fiber.* Healthline. https://www.healthline.com/nutrition/chicory-root-fiber#_noHeaderPrefixedContent

Strobile. (n.d.). In Merriam Webster. Retrieved February 8, 2022, from https://www.merriam-webster.com/dictionary/strobile

Susannah. (2021, November 1). *Cleavers plant uses & 5 best cleavers herb benefits.* Healthy Green Savvy. https://www.healthygreensavvy.com/cleavers-plant-herb-benefits/

Sweet violet - Uses, side effects, and more. (n.d.). Web MD. Retrieved March 4, 2022, from https://www.webmd.com/vitamins/ai/ingredientmono-212/sweet-violet#

Tapping tree sap. (2011, March 26). Judy of the Woods. http://www.judyofthewoods.net/forage/tree_sap.html

Taylor, K. (2021, April 21). *How to dry echinacea flowers And roots.* Urban Garden Gal. https://www.urbangardengal.com/how-to-dry-echinacea-flowers-roots/#:~:text=Echinacea%20roots%20can%20be%20harvested

Tea time: Violet leaf tea. (2020, April 15). Awkward Botany. https://awkwardbotany.com/2020/04/15/tea-time-violet-leaf-tea/

Teazle. (2021, June 14). EMedicine Health. https://www.emedicinehealth.com/teazle/vitamins-supplements.htm

Teazle - Uses, side effects, and more. (n.d.). Web MD. Retrieved March 4, 2022, from https://www.webmd.com/vitamins/ai/ingredientmono-187/teazle

Tello, C. (2021, September 9). *What is sarsaparilla? A plant lost in time + tea recipe.* Self Decode. https://supplements.selfdecode.com/blog/sarsaparilla-plant-drink-how-to-make-tea/

Terry, S. (2017, September 21). *How to identify willow trees.* Garden Guides. https://www.gardenguides.com/109710-care-corkscrew-willow-tree.html

The benefits of wild cherry bark. (n.d.). Kaya Well. Retrieved February 11, 2022, from https://www.kayawell.com/Food/The-Benefits-of-Wild-Cherry-Bark-whooping-cough-diarrhea

The raspberries are ready for picking. (2019, July 9). The Martha Blog. https://www.themarthablog.com/2019/07/the-raspberries-are-ready-for-picking.html

Tikkanen, A. (n.d.). *Borage.* Encyclopedia Britannica. Retrieved February 12, 2022, from https://www.britannica.com/plant/borage

Tiller, B. (2019, January 24). *Field garlic: Allium vineale.* Mossy Oak. https://www.mossyoak.com/our-obsession/blogs/how-to/field-garlic-allium-vineale

Tilley, N. (2021, July 26). *Wild violets care – How to grow wild violet plants.* Gardening Know How. https://www.gardeningknowhow.com/ornamental/bulbs/violet/wild-violets-care.htm#:~:text=While%20they%20tolerate%20many%20soil

Tips to harvest sunflowers. (2020, May 2). Grainvest Group. https://grainvest.co.za/2020/05/02/tips-to-harvest-sunflowers/#:~:text=Harvest%20sunflowers%20when%20their%20petals

Tirrell, R. (1974, June 2). Herb, of folklore. *The New York Times,* 149. https://www.nytimes.com/1974/06/02/archives/herb-of-folklore.html#:~:text=COMFREY%2C%20a%20magical%20herb%20of

Tutorial: How to make a traditional tincture with roots. (2013, October 31). Minnesota Herbalist. https://minnesotaherbalist.com/2013/10/31/tutorial-how-to-make-a-traditional-tincture-with-roots/

Tyler, S. (2019, May 27). *Western larch - New uses for an ancient medicine*. Botanical Medicine. https://www.botanicalmedicine.org/western-larch-new-uses-for-ancient-medicine/

Types of pine trees with identification guide, chart and pictures. (n.d.). Leafy Place. Retrieved March 2, 2022, from https://leafyplace.com/types-of-pine-trees-identification-and-pictures/

Undlin, S. (2020, July 27). *Top mugwort uses (and where to find it)*. Plantsnap. https://www.plantsnap.com/blog/top-mugwort-uses-and-where-to-find-it/#:~:text=Identifying%20Mugwort%20Out%20In%20The%20World&text=Its%20dark%20green%20leaves%20are

Valerian. (2015, May 12). Kaiser Permanente. https://wa.kaiserpermanente.org/kbase/topic.jhtml?docId=hn-2179004

Valerian: Valeriana officinalis. (n.d.-a). Edible Wild Food. Retrieved March 4, 2022, from https://www.ediblewildfood.com/valerian.aspx#:~:text=Valerian%20is%20a%20perennial%20plant

Valerian: Valeriana officinalis. (n.d.-b). Edible Wild Food. Retrieved March 4, 2022, from https://www.ediblewildfood.com/valerian.aspx

Verma, R., Gangrade, T., Ghulaxe, C., & Punasiya, R. (2014). *Rubus fruticosus (blackberry) use as an herbal medicine*. Pharmacognosy Reviews, 8(16), 101. https://doi.org/10.4103/0973-7847.134239

Viburnum opulus. (n.d.). Gardeners World. Retrieved February 15, 2022, from https://www.gardenersworld.com/plants/viburnum-opulus/

Viburnum opulus: Cramp bark. (n.d.). Gaia Herbs. Retrieved February 15, 2022, from https://www.gaiaherbs.com/blogs/herbs/cramp-bark

Ware, M. (2019, November 1). *What to know about cranberries*. Medical News Today. https://www.medicalnewstoday.com/articles/269142#:~:text=Many%20people%20consider%20cranberries%20to

Westover, J. (n.d.). *How to identify a purple coneflower when not in bloom*. SF Gate. Retrieved February 22, 2022, from https://homeguides.sfgate.com/identify-purple-coneflower-not-bloom-62343.html

What happens in your body if you drink larch tea. (2021, February 21). Newsy Today. https://newsy-today.com/what-happens-in-your-body-if-you-drink-larch-tea/

What is awl shaped? (n.d.). Movie Cultists. Retrieved February 13, 2022, from https://moviecultists.com/what-is-awl-shaped

White oak. (n.d.). Natural Resource Stewardship. Retrieved March 2, 2022, from https://naturalresources.extension.iastate.edu/forestry/iowa_trees/trees/white_oak.html#:~:text=White%20oak%20leaves%20are%20simple

Wild foraging: How to identify, harvest, store and use horsetail. (2016, May 2). The Daring Gourmet. https://www.daringgourmet.com/wild-foraging-how-to-identify-harvest-store-and-use-horsetail/#:~:text=What%20does%20horsetail%20look%20like,the%20nodes%E2%80%9D%20(Wikipedia).

Wild garlic or ramsons – A foraging guide to its food, medicine and other uses. (n.d.). Eat Weeds. Retrieved February 23, 2022, from https://www.eatweeds.co.uk/wild-garlic-allium-ursinum

Wild horse tail. (n.d.). Recipes from the Wild. Retrieved February 28, 2022, from https://recipesfromthewild.wordpress.com/wild-horse-tail/#:~:text=Creating%20a%20Tincture%3A&text=Within%20one%20to%20two%20hours

Wild sarsaparilla (aralia nudicaulis). (n.d.). MPG North. Retrieved March 4, 2022, from https://mpgnorth.com/field-guide/araliaceae/wild-sarsaparilla

Wild violet vinegar infusion. (n.d.). Grow a Good Life. Retrieved March 4, 2022, from https://growagoodlife.com/wild-violet-vinegar/

BIBLIOGRAPHY

Wildflowers of the Adirondacks: Wild sarsaparilla (aralia nudicaulis). (n.d.). Wild Adirondacks. Retrieved March 4, 2022, from https://wildadirondacks.org/adirondack-wildflowers-wild-sarsaparilla-aralia-nudicaulis.html#:~:text=Identification%20of%20Wild%20Sarsaparilla

Wildflowers of the Adirondacks: Wintergreen (gaultheria procumbens). (n.d.). Wild Adirondacks. Retrieved March 4, 2022, from https://wildadirondacks.org/adirondack-wildflowers-wintergreen-gaultheria-procumbens.html#:~:text=Identification%20of%20Wintergreen

Wildlife friendly landscapes. (n.d.). NC State Extension. Retrieved February 24, 2022, from https://wildlifefriendlylandscapes.ces.ncsu.edu/#:~:text=Identification%3A%20Japanese%20Honeysuckle%20is%20an

Wilen, C A, et al. *Pesticides: Safe and Effective Use in the Home and Landscape*. University of California Agriculture and Natural Resources, 2019, ipm.ucanr.edu/PMG/PESTNOTES/pn74126.html. Accessed 14 Mar. 2022.

Willis, E. (n.d.). *Herb article - Catnip*. Rebecca's Herbal Apothecary. Retrieved March 2, 2022, from https://www.rebeccasherbs.com/pages/herb-article-br-catnip#:~:text=Preparations%20%26%20Applications&text=Catnip%20can%20be%20prepared%20as

Willow bark. (2021, June 11). Rx List. https://www.rxlist.com/willow_bark/supplements.htm

Willow tree mythology and folklore. (n.d.). Trees for Life. Retrieved March 4, 2022, from https://treesforlife.org.uk/into-the-forest/trees-plants-animals/trees/willow/willow-mythology-and-folklore/

Windling, T. (2016, May 12). *The folklore of nettles*. Myth & Moor. https://www.terriwindling.com/blog/2016/05/from-the-archives-picking-nettles.html

Wintergreen. (2021, June 11). Rx List. https://www.rxlist.com/wintergreen/supplements.htm

Wong, C. (2021a, January 9). *What you need to know about chickweed*. Very Well Health. https://www.verywellhealth.com/chickweed-what-should-i-know-about-it-89437

Wong, C. (2021b, March 3). *What is cramp bark (viburnum)?* Very Well Health. https://www.verywellhealth.com/the-benefits-of-viburnum-cramp-bark-88657

Wong, C. (2021c, November 9). *What is red clover?* Very Well Health. https://www.verywellhealth.com/the-benefits-of-red-clover-89577#:~:text=In%20herbal%20medicine%2C%20red%20clover

Wresting burdock seed and its medicinal uses. (2017, December 1). Northeast School of Botanical Medicine. https://7song.com/wresting-burdock-seed-and-its-medicinal-uses/

Yarrow. (2021, June 11). Rx List. https://www.rxlist.com/yarrow/supplements.htm

IMAGES

Chai, S. (2021). *Anonymous person with bag of plastic bottles* [Online image]. In Pexels. https://www.pexels.com/photo/anonymous-person-with-bag-of-plastic-bottles-7262933/

Cottonbro. (2020). *Leaves and twigs on a canvas bag* [Online image]. In Pexels. https://www.pexels.com/photo/leaves-and-twigs-on-a-canvas-bag-6033829/

Fotios, L. (2018). *Person digging on soil using garden shovel* [Online image]. In Pexels. https://www.pexels.com/photo/person-digging-on-soil-using-garden-shovel-1301856/

Hamra, J. (2018). *Person Holding Round Framed Mirror Near Tree at Daytime* [Online image]. In Pexels. https://www.pexels.com/photo/person-holding-round-framed-mirror-near-tree-at-daytime-979927/

Hatchett, M. (2019). *Folding knife* [Online image]. In Pexels. https://www.pexels.com/photo/folding-knife-2599276/

Jameson, L. (2021). *Man in blue t-shirt and brown shorts sitting on ground With green plants*

[Online image]. In Pexels. https://www.pexels.com/photo/man-in-blue-t-shirt-and-brown-shorts-sitting-on-ground-with-green-plants-9324354/

Jess Bailey Designs. (2017). *Close-up photography scissors* [Online image]. In Pexels. https://www.pexels.com/photo/close-up-photography-scissors-755991/

Kool, A. (2015). *El Capitan on a sunny afternoon* [Online image]. In Unsplash. https://unsplash.com/photos/ndN00KmbJ1c?modal=%7B%22tag%22%3A%22Login%22%2C%22value%22%3A%7B%22tag%22%3A%22Like%22%2C%22value%22%3A%7B%22photoId%22%3A%22ndN00KmbJ1c%22%2C%22userId%22%3A%22AjxdOkQCJr8%22%7D%7D%7D

Lewis, J. (2020). *Yellow leaf in close up photography* [Online image]. In Pexels. https://www.pexels.com/photo/yellow-leaf-in-close-up-photography-5497873/

Mazumder, A. (2018). *Person holding a green plant* [Online image]. In Pexels. https://www.pexels.com/photo/person-holding-a-green-plant-1072824/

Monstera. (2021). *Wooden brushes prepared for washing and cleaning* [Online image]. In Pexels. https://www.pexels.com/photo/wooden-brushes-prepared-for-washing-and-cleaning-6621326/

Patel, S. (2020). *Green leaves on tree branch* [Online image]. In Pexels. https://www.pexels.com/photo/green-leaves-on-tree-branch-4400283/

Pixabay. (2012). *Green Leaf Plant* [Online image]. In Pexels. https://www.pexels.com/photo/green-leaf-plant-86397/

Pixabay. (2016). *Green tree plant leaves* [Online image]. In Pexels. https://www.pexels.com/photo/green-tree-plant-leaves-40896/

Rodnikova, M. (2021). *Pruning shears and a flower wreath* [Online image]. In Pexels. https://www.pexels.com/photo/pruning-shears-and-a-flower-wreath-9797607/

Schwartz, K. (2021). *Green leaves of growing fern* [Online image]. In Pexels. https://www.pexels.com/photo/green-leaves-of-growing-fern-8117889/

Sunsetoned. (2020). *Crop woman reading book on grass* [Online image]. In Pexels. https://www.pexels.com/photo/crop-woman-reading-book-on-grass-5981113/

Tis, A. (2021). *Yellow maple leaf on yellow background* [Online image]. In Pexels. https://www.pexels.com/photo/yellow-maple-leaf-on-yellow-background-9563330/

Tran, V. (2019). *Photo of jar near cinnamon sticks* [Online image]. In Pexels. https://www.pexels.com/photo/photo-of-jar-near-cinnamon-sticks-3273989/

Webb, S. (2018). *Green leafed indoor plant* [Online image]. In Pexels. https://www.pexels.com/photo/green-leafed-indoor-plant-1048035/

Made in the USA
Columbia, SC
21 October 2024